ARK PAPERBACKS

S0-BCJ-373

THE NEED FOR ROOTS
PRELUDE TO A DECLARATION OF DUTIES
TOWARDS MANKIND

When she was in England in 1942, Simone Weil was commissioned by General de Gaulle, head of the Free French forces, to write a report on the duties and privileges of the French in a France at peace. She became concerned with the idea of 'uprootedness' (*déracinement*) and wrote this study of the need for security.

Simone Weil deals with the needs of the soul, discussing order, liberty, obedience, responsibility and many other subjects, finishing with the need for truth.

SIMONE WEIL

Born in Paris in 1909, Simone Weil was educated at the Lycée Henri IV and the Ecole Normale Supérieure, where she was one of the first women students. She became a teacher, but also worked on farms and at the Renault car factory, choosing hard manual labour in order to experience the life of the working class with whom she had a profound sympathy. In 1936 she joined the Republican forces in the Spanish Civil War, returning from the front when she was badly burned in an accident. In 1938 she had the first of several mystical experiences which were deeply to affect her thought, although she was never received into the Catholic church. In 1942 Simone Weil left France and joined the Free French forces in London. She died there of tuberculosis the following year, refusing to eat more than the rations of those suffering Nazi occupation in her native France.

Simone Weil's writings reflect her intellectual and spiritual concerns: the nature of oppression, the reasons for human exploitation and, in the last years of her life, the relationship of the human condition to the realm of the transcendent. Her major works, published posthumously, include *Waiting on God*, *Gravity and Grace*, *The Need for Roots* and her *Notebooks*.

ARK

SIMONE WEIL
THE NEED FOR ROOTS
PRELUDE TO A DECLARATION OF DUTIES
TOWARDS MANKIND
Preface by T.S.Eliot

ARK PAPERBACKS
London and New York

This translation first published in 1952
Reprinted in 1952
First published as a paperback in 1978
ARK edition 1987
ARK PAPERBACKS is an imprint of
Routledge & Kegan Paul Ltd
11 New Fetter Lane, London EC4P 4EE

Published in the USA by
Routledge & Kegan Paul Inc.
in association with Methuen Inc.
29 West 35th Street, New York, NY 10001

Printed in Great Britain by
Cox & Wyman Ltd, Reading, Berks

L'Enracinement
First French edition 1949
Translated from the French by A. F. Wills

ISBN 0-7448-0058-7

PREFACE

THE only kind of introduction which could merit permanent association with a book by Simone Weil would be—like that provided by M. Gustave Thibon to *Gravity and Grace**—an introduction by someone who knew her. The reader of her work finds himself confronted by a difficult, violent and complex personality; and the assistance of those who had the advantage of long discussions or correspondence with her, especially those who knew her under the peculiar conditions of the last five years of her life, will be of permanent value in the future. I lack these qualifications. My aims in writing this preface are, first, to affirm my belief in the importance of the author and of this particular book; second, to warn the reader against premature judgment and summary classification—to persuade him to hold in check his own prejudices and at the same time to be patient with those of Simone Weil. Once her work is known and accepted, such a preface as this should become superfluous.

All of Simone Weil's work is posthumous. *Gravity and Grace* —the selection from her voluminous notebooks made by M. Thibon, and the first volume to appear in France—is admirable in its contents, but somewhat deceptive in its form. The comparison with Pascal (a writer of whom Simone Weil sometimes spoke with asperity) may be pressed too far. The fragmentariness of the extracts elicits the profound insights and the startling originality, but suggests that hers was a mind of occasional flashes of inspiration. After reading *Waiting on God*† and the present volume I saw that I must try to

* *La Pésanteur et la Grâce.*   † *Attente de Dieu.*

v

understand the personality of the author; and that the reading and re-reading of all of her work was necessary for this slow process of understanding. In trying to understand her, we must not be distracted—as is only too likely to happen on a first reading—by considering how far, and at what points, we agree or disagree. We must simply expose ourselves to the personality of a woman of genius, of a kind of genius akin to that of the saints.

Perhaps 'genius' is not the right word. The only priest with whom she ever discussed her belief and her doubts has said: *je crois que son âme est incomparablement plus haute que son génie.* That is another way of indicating that our first experience of Simone Weil should not be expressible in terms of approval or dissent. I cannot conceive of anybody's agreeing with all of her views, or of not disagreeing violently with some of them. But agreement and rejection are secondary: what matters is to make contact with a great soul. Simone Weil was one who might have become a saint. Like some who have achieved this state, she had greater obstacles to overcome, as well as greater strength for overcoming them, than the rest of us. A potential saint can be a very difficult person: I suspect that Simone Weil could be at times insupportable. One is struck, here and there, by a contrast between an almost superhuman humility and what appears to be an almost outrageous arrogance. There is a significant sentence by the French priest whom I have already quoted. He reports that he does not remember 'ever having heard Simone Weil, in spite of her virtuous desire for objectivity, give way in the course of a discussion'. This comment throws light on much of her published work. I do not believe that she was ever animated by delight in her own forensic skill—a self-indulgence to which I suspect Pascal came dangerously near, in the *Letters*—the display of power in overcoming others in controversy. It was rather that all her thought was so intensely lived, that the abandonment of any opinion required modifications in her whole being: a process which could not take place painlessly, or in the course of a conversation.

And—especially in the young, and in those like Simone Weil in whom one detects no sense of humour—egotism and selflessness can resemble each other so closely that we may mistake the one for the other.

The statement that Simone Weil's 'soul was incomparably superior to her genius' will, however, be misunderstood if it gives the impression of depreciating her intellect. Certainly she could be unfair and intemperate; certainly she committed some astonishing aberrations and exaggerations. But those immoderate affirmations which tax the patience of the reader spring not from any flaw in her intellect but from excess of temperament. She came of a family with no lack of intellectual endowment—her brother is a distinguished mathematician; and as for her own mind, it was worthy of the soul which employed it. But the intellect, especially when bent upon such problems as those which harassed Simone Weil, can come to maturity only slowly; and we must not forget that Simone Weil died at the age of thirty-three. I think that in *The Need for Roots* especially, the maturity of her social and political thought is very remarkable. But she had a very great soul to grow up to; and we should not criticise her philosophy at thirty-three as if it were that of a person twenty or thirty years older.

In the work of such a writer we must expect to encounter paradox. Simone Weil was three things in the highest degree: French, Jewish and Christian. She was a patriot who would gladly have been sent back to France to suffer and die for her compatriots: she had to die—partly, it would seem, as the result of self-mortification, in refusing to take more food than the official rations of ordinary people in France—in 1943 in a sanatorium at Ashford, Kent. She was also a patriot who saw clearly, as this book shows, the faults and the spiritual weakness of contemporary France. She was a Christian with an intense devotion to Our Lord in the Sacrament of the Altar, yet she refused baptism, and much of her writing constitutes a formidable criticism of the Church. She was intensely Jewish, suffering torments in the affliction of the Jews in Germany; yet she castigated Israel* with all the severity of a Hebrew Prophet. Prophets, we are told, were stoned in Jerusalem: but Simone Weil is exposed to lapidation from several quarters. And in her political thinking she appears as a stern critic of both Right and Left; at the same time more truly a lover of order and hierarchy than most of those who call themselves Conservative, and more truly a lover of the people than most of those who call themselves Socialist.

As for her attitude towards the Church of Rome and her attitude towards Israel I wish, in the space of a preface, to make only one observation. The two attitudes are not only compatible but coherent, and should be considered as one. It was in fact her rejection of Israel that made her a very heterodox Christian. In her repudiation of all but a few parts of the Old Testament (and in what she accepted she discerned traces of Chaldaean or Egyptian influence) she falls into something very like the Marcionite heresy. In denying the divine mission of Israel she is also rejecting the foundation of the Christian Church. Hence the difficulties that caused her so much agony of spirit. I must affirm that there is no trace of the Protestant in her composition: for her, the Christian Church could only be the Church of Rome. In the Church there is much to which she is blind, or about which she is strangely silent: she seems to give no thought to the Blessed Virgin; and as for the Saints, she is concerned only with those who attract her interest through their writings—such as St. Thomas Aquinas (whom she dislikes, perhaps on insufficient acquaintance) and St. John of the Cross (whom she admires because of his profound knowledge of spiritual method).

In one respect she has, at first sight, something in common with those intellectuals of the present day (mostly with a vague liberal Protestant background) who can find their way towards the religious life only through the mysticism of the

* I use the term 'Israel' as she used it, and not, of course, with reference to the modern State.

East. Her enthusiasm for everything Greek (including the mysteries) was unbounded. For her, there was no revelation to Israel, but a good deal of revelation to the Chaldaeans, the Egyptians and the Hindus. Her attitude may appear to be dangerously close to that of those universalists who maintain that the ultimate and esoteric truth is one, that all religions show some traces of it, and that it is a matter of indifference to which one of the great religions we adhere. Yet she is saved from this error—and this is a matter for admiration and thankfulness—by her devotion to the person of Our Lord.

In her criticism of the Jewish and the Christian faiths, I think that we have to try to make for ourselves a threefold distinction, asking ourselves: how much is just? how much is serious objection that must be rebutted? and how much, in the way of error, can be extenuated on the ground of the immaturity of a superior and passionate personality? Our analyses may differ widely: but we must ask and answer these questions for ourselves.

I do not know how good a Greek scholar she was. I do not know how well read she was in the history of the civilisations of the Eastern Mediterranean. I do not know whether she could read the Upanishads in Sanskrit; or, if so, how great was her mastery of what is not only a very highly developed language but a way of thought the difficulties of which only become more formidable to a European student the more diligently he applies himself to it. But I do not think that she shows, in this field, the mind of an historian. In her adulation of Greece, and of the 'wisdom of the East', as in her disparagement of Rome and Israel, she seems to me almost wilful. In one quarter she sees only what she can admire; in another, she repudiates without discrimination. Because she dislikes the Roman Empire, she dislikes Virgil. Her admirations, when not motivated by her dislikes, seem to be at least intensified by them. One may sympathise with her horror at the brutalities of expanding or imperialistic peoples (as the Romans in Europe and the Spanish in America) in crushing local civilisations. But when, in order to enhance her denunciation of the Romans, she attempts to make out a case for the culture of the Druids, we do not feel that our meagre knowledge of that vanished society gives any ground for her conjectures. We can share her revulsion from the atrocities committed in the suppression of the Albigensian heresy, and yet speculate whether the peculiar civilisation of Provence had not come to the end of its productivity. Would the world be a better place to-day if there were half a dozen different cultures flourishing between the English Channel and the Mediterranean, instead of the one which we know as France? Simone Weil begins with an insight; but the logic of her emotions can lead her to make generalisations so large as to be meaningless. We may protest that we are so completely in the dark as to what the world would be like now if events had taken a different course, that such a question as that whether the latinisation of Western Europe by Roman conquest was a good or bad thing is unanswerable. Her flights of fancy of this kind must not, however, be taken as invalidating her fundamental concept of *rootedness*, and her warnings against the evils of an over-centralised society.

This book was written during the last year or so of Simone Weil's life, during her employment at French Headquarters in London; and it issues, I understand, from memoranda which she submitted in connexion with the policy to be pursued after the Liberation. The problems of the moment led her to much larger considerations; but even those pages in which she is concerned with the programme to be followed by the Free French during the war and immediately after the Liberation show such foresight and maturity of judgment that they are of permanent value. This is, I think, among those works of hers already published, the one which approximates most closely to the form in which she might herself have chosen to release it.

I have dwelt chiefly upon certain ideas which are to be met with in all her writings, with some emphasis upon her errors and exaggerations. I have taken this course in the belief that many readers, coming for the first time upon some assertion likely to arouse intellectual incredulity or emotional antagonism, might be deterred from improving their acquaintance with a great soul and a brilliant mind. Simone Weil needs patience from her readers, as she doubtless needed patience from the friends who most admired and appreciated her. But in spite of the violence of her affections and antipathies, in spite of such unjustified generalisations as I have instanced, I find in the present book especially a balanced judgment, a wisdom in avoiding extremes, astonishing in anyone so young. It may be that in her conversations with Gustave Thibon she profited more than she knew from her contact with that wise and well-balanced mind.

As a political thinker, as in everything else, Simone Weil is not to be classified. The paradoxicality of her sympathies is a contributing cause of the equilibrium. On the one hand she was a passionate champion of the common people and especially of the oppressed—those oppressed by the wickedness and selfishness of men and those oppressed by the anonymous forces of modern society. She had worked in the Renault factory, she had worked as a field labourer, in order to share the life of people of town and country. On the other hand, she was by nature a solitary and an individualist, with a profound horror of what she called the *collectivity*—the monster created by modern totalitarianism. What she cared about was human souls. Her study of human rights and human obligations exposes the falsity of some of the verbiage still current which was used during the war to serve as a moral stimulant. Not the least striking example of her shrewdness, balance and good sense is her examination of the principle of monarchy; and her short review of the political history of France is at once a condemnation of the French Revolution and a powerful argument against the possibility of a restoration of the kingship. She cannot be classified either as a reactionary or as a socialist.

This book belongs in that category of prolegomena to

politics which politicians seldom read, and which most of them would be unlikely to understand or to know how to apply. Such books do not influence the contemporary conduct of affairs: for the men and women already engaged in this career and committed to the jargon of the market-place, they always come too late. This is one of those books which ought to be studied by the young before their leisure has been lost and their capacity for thought destroyed in the life of the hustings and the legislative assembly; books the effect of which, we can only hope, will become apparent in the attitude of mind of another generation.

T. S. ELIOT

September 1951

CONTENTS

TRANSLATOR'S FOREWORD

THIS book, published in France in 1949 under the title of *L'Enracinement*, and now offered in an English translation, was written during the early months of 1943, in London. Towards the end of August of the same year, the author died at Ashford, Kent.

Shortly after her arrival in England, the previous November, Simone Weil had been asked by the Free French in London to write a report on the possibilities of bringing about the regeneration of France.

That report is this book, and in calling passionately upon her fellow-countrymen to set about recovering their spiritual roots before it is too late, and suggesting to them how this may be done, Simone Weil addresses herself to men of every nationality, but more particularly, of course, to those who share the spiritual heritage of the West.

Every effort has been made to give a faithful rendering of the French text, to preserve its substance, style, actuality and sense of urgency. Both the publishers and the translator felt that to tamper in any way, on any grounds, with the original would be to take away from its directness of approach. Footnotes have therefore been added where considered necessary to situate any remark or reference no longer applicable, or only partially so, or having particular reference to France.

It only remains for the translator to salute the spirit of the remarkable human being who lived and wrote the original.

Paris
December 1950

PART ONE

THE NEEDS OF THE SOUL

PART ONE

THE NEEDS OF THE SOUL

THE notion of obligations comes before that of rights, which is subordinate and relative to the former. A right is not effectual by itself, but only in relation to the obligation to which it corresponds, the effective exercise of a right springing not from the individual who possesses it, but from other men who consider themselves as being under a certain obligation towards him. Recognition of an obligation makes it effectual. An obligation which goes unrecognized by anybody loses none of the full force of its existence. A right which goes unrecognized by anybody is not worth very much.

It makes nonsense to say that men have, on the one hand, rights, and on the other hand, obligations. Such words only express differences in point of view. The actual relationship between the two is as between object and subject. A man, considered in isolation, only has duties, amongst which are certain duties towards himself. Other men, seen from his point of view, only have rights. He, in his turn, has rights, when seen from the point of view of other men, who recognize that they have obligations towards him. A man left alone in the universe would have no rights whatever, but he would have obligations.

The notion of rights, being of an objective order, is inseparable from the notions of existence and reality. This becomes apparent when the obligation descends to the realm of fact;

3

consequently, it always involves to a certain extent the taking into account of actual given states and particular situations. Rights are always found to be related to certain conditions. Obligations alone remain independent of conditions. They belong to a realm situated above all conditions, because it is situated above this world.

The men of 1789 did not recognize the existence of such a realm. All they recognized was the one on the human plane. That is why they started off with the idea of rights. But at the same time they wanted to postulate absolute principles. This contradiction caused them to tumble into a confusion of language and ideas which is largely responsible for the present political and social confusion. The realm of what is eternal, universal, unconditioned is other than the one conditioned by facts, and different ideas hold sway there, ones which are related to the most secret recesses of the human soul.

Obligations are only binding on human beings. There are no obligations for collectivities, as such. But they exist for all human beings who constitute, serve, command or represent a collectivity, in that part of their existence which is related to the collectivity as in that part which is independent of it.

All human beings are bound by identical obligations, although these are performed in different ways according to particular circumstances. No human being, whoever he may be, under whatever circumstances, can escape them without being guilty of crime; save where there are two genuine obligations which are in fact incompatible, and a man is forced to sacrifice one of them.

The imperfections of a social order can be measured by the number of situations of this kind it harbours within itself.

But even in such a case, a crime is committed if the obligation so sacrificed is not merely sacrificed in fact, but its existence denied into the bargain.

The object of any obligation, in the realm of human affairs, is always the human being as such. There exists an obligation towards every human being for the sole reason that he or she

4

is a human being, without any other condition requiring to be fulfilled, and even without any recognition of such obligation on the part of the individual concerned.

This obligation is not based upon any *de facto* situation, nor upon jurisprudence, customs, social structure, relative state of forces, historical heritage, or presumed historical orientation; for no *de facto* situation is able to create an obligation.

This obligation is not based upon any convention; for all conventions are liable to be modified according to the wishes of the contracting parties, whereas in this case no change in the mind and will of Man can modify anything whatsoever.

This obligation is an eternal one. It is coextensive with the eternal destiny of human beings. Only human beings have an eternal destiny. Human collectivities have not got one. Nor are there, in regard to the latter, any direct obligations of an eternal nature. Duty towards the human being as such—that alone is eternal.

This obligation is an unconditional one. If it is founded on something, that something, whatever it is, does not form part of our world. In our world, it is not founded on anything at all. It is the one and only obligation in connexion with human affairs that is not subject to any condition.

This obligation has no foundation, but only a verification in the common consent accorded by the universal conscience. It finds expression in some of the oldest written texts which have come down to us. It is recognized by everybody without exception in every single case where it is not attacked as a result of interest or passion. And it is in relation to it that we measure our progress.

The recognition of this obligation is expressed in a confused and imperfect form, that is, more or less imperfect according to the particular case, by what are called positive rights. To the extent to which positive rights are in contradiction with it, to that precise extent is their origin an illegitimate one.

Although this eternal obligation is coextensive with the eternal destiny of the human being, this destiny is not its direct

5

motive. A human being's eternal destiny cannot be the motive of any obligation, for it is not subordinate to external actions.

The fact that a human being possesses an eternal destiny imposes only one obligation: respect. The obligation is only performed if the respect is effectively expressed in a real, not a fictitious, way; and this can only be done through the medium of Man's earthly needs.

On this point, the human conscience has never varied. Thousands of years ago, the Egyptians believed that no soul could justify itself after death unless it could say: 'I have never let any one suffer from hunger.' All Christians know they are liable to hear Christ himself say to them one day: 'I was an hungered, and ye gave me no meat.' Every one looks on progress as being, in the first place, a transition to a state of human society in which people will not suffer from hunger. To no matter whom the question may be put in general terms, nobody is of the opinion that any man is innocent if, possessing food himself in abundance and finding some one on his doorstep three parts dead from hunger, he brushes past without giving him anything.

So it is an eternal obligation towards the human being not to let him suffer from hunger when one has the chance of coming to his assistance. This obligation being the most obvious of all, it can serve as a model on which to draw up the list of eternal duties towards each human being. In order to be absolutely correctly made out, this list ought to proceed from the example just given by way of analogy.

Consequently, the list of obligations towards the human being should correspond to the list of such human needs as are vital, analogous to hunger.

Among such needs, there are some which are physical, like hunger itself. They are fairly easy to enumerate. They are concerned with protection against violence, housing, clothing, heating, hygiene and medical attention in case of illness. There are others which have no connexion with the physical side of life, but are concerned with its moral side. Like the former, however, they are earthly, and are not directly related, so far as our intelligence is able to perceive, to the eternal destiny of Man. They form, like our physical needs, a necessary condition of our life on this earth. Which means to say that if they are not satisfied, we fall little by little into a state more or less resembling death, more or less akin to a purely vegetative existence.

They are much more difficult to recognize and to enumerate than are the needs of the body. But every one recognizes that they exist. All the different forms of cruelty which a conqueror can exercise over a subject population, such as massacre, mutilation, organized famine, enslavement or large-scale deportation, are generally considered to be measures of a like description, even though a man's liberty or his native land are not physical necessities. Every one knows that there are forms of cruelty which can injure a man's life without injuring his body. They are such as deprive him of a certain form of food necessary to the life of the soul.

Obligations, whether unconditional or relative, eternal or changing, direct or indirect with regard to human affairs, all stem, without exception, from the vital needs of the human being. Those which do not directly concern this, that or the other specific human being all exist to serve requirements which, with respect to Man, play a rôle analogous to food.

We owe a cornfield respect, not because of itself, but because it is food for mankind.

In the same way, we owe our respect to a collectivity, of whatever kind—country, family or any other—not for itself, but because it is food for a certain number of human souls.

Actually, this obligation makes different attitudes, actions necessary according to different situations. But, taken by itself, it is absolutely identical for everybody. More particularly is this so for all those outside such a collectivity.

The degree of respect owing to human collectivities is a very high one, for several reasons.

To start with, each is unique, and, if destroyed, cannot be

7

replaced. One sack of corn can always be substituted for another sack of corn. The food which a collectivity supplies for the souls of those who form part of it has no equivalent in the entire universe.

Secondly, because of its continuity, a collectivity is already moving forward into the future. It contains food, not only for the souls of the living, but also for the souls of beings yet unborn which are to come into the world during the immediately succeeding centuries.

Lastly, due to this same continuity, a collectivity has its roots in the past. It constitutes the sole agency for preserving the spiritual treasures accumulated by the dead, the sole transmitting agency by means of which the dead can speak to the living. And the sole earthly reality which is directly connected with the eternal destiny of Man is the irradiating light of those who have managed to become fully conscious of this destiny, transmitted from generation to generation.

Because of all this, it may happen that the obligation towards a collectivity which is in danger reaches the point of entailing a total sacrifice. But it does not follow from this that collectivities are superior to human beings. It sometimes happens, too, that the obligation to go to the help of a human being in distress makes a total sacrifice necessary, without that implying any superiority on the part of the individual so helped.

A peasant may, under certain circumstances, be under the necessity, in order to cultivate his land, of risking exhaustion, illness or even death. But all the time he will be conscious of the fact that it is solely a matter of bread.

Similarly, even when a total sacrifice is required, no more is owed to any collectivity whatever than a respect analogous to the one owed to food.

It very often happens that the rôles are reversed. There are collectivities which, instead of serving as food, do just the opposite: they devour souls. In such cases, the social body is diseased, and the first duty is to attempt a cure; in certain circumstances, it may be necessary to have recourse to surgical methods.

With regard to this matter, too, the obligation for those inside as for those outside the collectivity is an identical one.

It also happens that a collectivity supplies insufficient food for the souls of those forming part of it. In that case, it has to be improved.

Finally, there are dead collectivities which, without devouring souls, don't nourish them either. If it is absolutely certain that they are well and truly dead, that it isn't just a question of a temporary lethargy, then and only then should they be destroyed.

The first thing to be investigated is what are those needs which are for the life of the soul what the needs in the way of food, sleep and warmth are for the life of the body. We must try to enumerate and define them.

They must never be confused with desires, whims, fancies and vices. (We must also distinguish between what is fundamental and what is fortuitous.) Man requires, not rice or potatoes, but food; not wood or coal, but heating. In the same way, for the needs of the soul, we must recognize the different, but equivalent, sorts of satisfaction which cater for the same requirements. We must also distinguish between the soul's foods and poisons which, for a time, can give the impression of occupying the place of the former.

The lack of any such investigation forces governments, even when their intentions are honest, to act sporadically and at random.

Below are offered a few indications.

ORDER

The first of the soul's needs, the one which touches most nearly its eternal destiny, is order; that is to say, a texture of social relationships such that no one is compelled to violate imperative obligations in order to carry out other ones. It is only where this, in fact, occurs that external circumstances have any power to inflict spiritual violence on the soul. For he for whom the threat of death or suffering is the one thing standing in the way of the performance of an obligation, can overcome this disability, and will only suffer in his body. But he who finds that circumstances, in fact, render the various acts necessitated by a series of strict obligations incompatible with one another is, without being able to offer any resistance thereto, made to suffer in his love of good.

At the present time, a very considerable amount of confusion and incompatibility exists between obligations.

Whoever acts in such a way as to increase this incompatibility is a trouble-maker. Whoever acts in such a way as to diminish it is an agent of order. Whoever, so as to simplify problems, denies the existence of certain obligations has, in his heart, made a compact with crime.

Unfortunately, we possess no method for diminishing this incompatibility. We cannot even be sure that the idea of an order in which all obligations would be compatible with one another isn't itself a fiction. When duty descends to the level of facts, so many independent relationships are brought into play that incompatibility seems far more likely than compatibility.

Nevertheless, we have every day before us the example of a universe in which an infinite number of independent mechanical actions concur so as to produce an order that, in the midst of variations, remains fixed. Furthermore, we love the beauty of the world, because we sense behind it the presence of something akin to that wisdom we should like to possess to slake our thirst for good.

In a minor degree, really beautiful works of art are examples of *ensembles* in which independent factors concur, in a manner impossible to understand, so as to form a unique thing of beauty.

Finally, a consciousness of the various obligations always

proceeds from a desire for good which is unique, unchanging and identical with itself for every man, from the cradle to the grave. This desire, perpetually stirring in the depths of our being, makes it impossible for us ever to resign ourselves to situations in which obligations are incompatible with one another. Either we have recourse to lying in order to forget their existence, or we struggle blindly to extricate ourselves from them.

The contemplation of veritable works of art, and much more still that of the beauty of the world, and again much more that of the unrealized good to which we aspire, can sustain us in our efforts to think continually about that human order which should be the subject uppermost in our minds.

The great instigators of violence have encouraged themselves with the thought of how blind, mechanical force is sovereign throughout the whole universe.

By looking at the world with keener senses than theirs, we shall find a more powerful encouragement in the thought of how these innumerable blind forces are limited, made to balance one against the other, brought to form a united whole by something which we do not understand, but which we call beauty.

If we keep ever-present in our minds the idea of a veritable human order, if we think of it as of something to which a total sacrifice is due should the need arise, we shall be in a similar position to that of a man travelling, without a guide, through the night, but continually thinking of the direction he wishes to follow. Such a traveller's way is lit by a great hope.

Order is the first need of all; it even stands above all needs properly so-called. To be able to conceive it, we must know what the other needs are.

The first characteristic which distinguishes needs from desires, fancies or vices, and foods from gluttonous repasts or poisons, is that needs are limited, in exactly the same way as are the foods corresponding to them. A miser never has enough gold, but the time comes when any man provided with an unlimited supply of bread finds he has had enough. Food brings satiety. The same applies to the soul's foods.

The second characteristic, closely connected with the first, is that needs are arranged in antithetical pairs and have to combine together to form a balance. Man requires food, but also an interval between his meals; he requires warmth and coolness, rest and exercise. Likewise in the case of the soul's needs.

What is called the golden mean actually consists in satisfying neither the one nor the other of two contrary needs. It is a caricature of the genuinely balanced state in which contrary needs are each fully satisfied in turn.

LIBERTY

One of the indispensable foods of the human soul is liberty. Liberty, taking the word in its concrete sense, consists in the ability to choose. We must understand by that, of course, a real ability. Wherever men are living in community, rules imposed in the common interest must necessarily limit the possibilities of choice.

But a greater or lesser degree of liberty does not depend on whether the limits set are wider or narrower. Liberty attains its plenitude under conditions which are less easily gauged.

Rules should be sufficiently sensible and sufficiently straightforward so that any one who so desires and is blessed with average powers of application may be able to understand, on the one hand the useful ends they serve, and on the other hand the actual necessities which have brought about their institution. They should emanate from a source of authority which is not looked upon as strange or hostile, but loved as something belonging to those placed under its direction. They should be sufficiently stable, general and limited in number for the mind to be able to grasp them once and for all, and not find itself brought up against them every time a decision has to be made.

Under these conditions, the liberty of men of goodwill, though limited in the sphere of action, is complete in that of conscience. For, having incorporated the rules into their own being, the prohibited possibilities no longer present themselves to the mind, and have not to be rejected. Just as the habit, formed by education, of not eating disgusting or dangerous things is not felt by the normal man to be any limitation of his liberty in the domain of food. Only a child feels such a limitation.

Those who are lacking in goodwill or who remain adolescent are never free under any form of society.

When the possibilities of choice are so wide as to injure the commonweal, men cease to enjoy liberty. For they must either seek refuge in irresponsibility, puerility and indifference —a refuge where the most they can find is boredom—or feel themselves weighed down by responsibility at all times for fear of causing harm to others. Under such circumstances, men, believing, wrongly, that they are in possession of liberty, and feeling that they get no enjoyment out of it, end up by thinking that liberty is not a good thing.

OBEDIENCE

Obedience is a vital need of the human soul. It is of two kinds: obedience to established rules and obedience to human beings looked upon as leaders. It presupposes consent, not in regard to every single order received, but the kind of consent that is given once and for all, with the sole reservation, in case of need, that the demands of conscience be satisfied.

It requires to be generally recognized, and above all by leaders themselves, that consent and not fear of punishment or hope of reward constitutes, in fact, the mainspring of obedience, so that submission may never be mistaken for servility. It should also be realized that those who command, obey in their turn, and the whole hierarchy should have its face set in the direction of a goal whose importance and even grandeur can be felt by all, from the highest to the lowest.

Obedience being a necessary food of the soul, whoever is definitely deprived of it is ill. Thus, any body politic governed by a sovereign ruler accountable to nobody is in the hands of a sick man.

That is why wherever a man is placed for life at the head of the social organism, he ought to be a symbol and not a ruler, as is the case with the king of England; etiquette ought also to restrict his freedom more narrowly than that of any single man of the people. In this way, the effective rulers, rulers though they be, have somebody over them; on the other hand, they are able to replace each other in unbroken continuity, and consequently to receive, each in his turn, that indispensable amount of obedience due to him.

Those who keep masses of men in subjection by exercising force and cruelty deprive them at once of two vital foods, liberty and obedience; for it is no longer within the power of such masses to accord their inner consent to the authority to which they are subjected. Those who encourage a state of things in which the hope of gain is the principal motive take away from men their obedience, for consent which is its essence is not something which can be sold.

There are any number of signs showing that the men of our age have now for a long time been starved of obedience. But advantage has been taken of the fact to give them slavery.

RESPONSIBILITY

Initiative and responsibility, to feel one is useful and even indispensable, are vital needs of the human soul.

Complete privation from this point of view is the case of the unemployed person, even if he receives assistance to the extent of being able to feed, clothe and house himself. For he represents nothing at all in the economic life of his country, and the voting paper which represents his share in its political life doesn't hold any meaning for him.

The manual labourer is in a scarcely better position.

For this need to be satisfied it is necessary that a man should often have to take decisions in matters great or small affecting interests that are distinct from his own, but in regard to which he feels a personal concern. He also requires to be continually called upon to supply fresh efforts. Finally, he requires to be able to encompass in thought the entire range of activity of the social organism to which he belongs, including branches in connexion with which he has never to take a decision or offer any advice. For that, he must be made acquainted with it, be asked to interest himself in it, be brought to feel its value, its utility and, where necessary, its greatness, and be made fully aware of the part he plays in it.

Every social organism, of whatever kind it may be, which does not provide its members with these satisfactions, is diseased and must be restored to health.

In the case of every person of fairly strong character, the need to show initiative goes so far as the need to take command. A flourishing local and regional life, a host of educational activities and youth movements, ought to furnish whoever is able to take advantage of it with the opportunity to command at certain periods of his life.

EQUALITY

Equality is a vital need of the human soul. It consists in a recognition, at once public, general, effective and genuinely expressed in institutions and customs, that the same amount of respect and consideration is due to every human being because this respect is due to the human being as such and is not a matter of degree.

It follows that the inevitable differences among men ought

never to imply any difference in the degree of respect. And so that these differences may not be felt to bear such an implication, a certain balance is necessary between equality and inequality.

A certain combination of equality and inequality is formed by equality of opportunity. If no matter who can attain the social rank corresponding to the function he is capable of filling, and if education is sufficiently generalized so that no one is prevented from developing any capacity simply on account of his birth, the prospects are the same for every child. In this way, the prospects for each man are the same as for any other man, both as regards himself when young, and as regards his children later on.

But when such a combination acts alone, and not as one factor amongst other factors, it ceases to constitute a balance and contains great dangers.

To begin with, for a man who occupies an inferior position and suffers from it to know that his position is a result of his incapacity and that everybody is aware of the fact is not any consolation, but an additional motive of bitterness; according to the individual character, some men can thereby be thrown into a state of depression, while others can be encouraged to commit crime.

Then, in social life, a sort of aspirator towards the top is inevitably created. If a descending movement does not come to balance this ascending movement, the social body becomes sick. To the extent to which it is really possible for the son of a farm labourer to become one day a minister, to the same extent should it really be possible for the son of a minister to become one day a farm labourer. This second possibility could never assume any noticeable proportions without a very dangerous degree of social constraint.

This sort of equality, if allowed full play by itself, can make social life fluid to the point of decomposing it.

There are less clumsy methods of combining equality with differentiation. The first is by using proportion. Proportion can be defined as the combination of equality with inequality, and everywhere throughout the universe it is the sole factor making for balance.

Applied to the maintenance of social equilibrium, it would impose on each man burdens corresponding to the power and well-being he enjoys, and corresponding risks in cases of incapacity or neglect. For instance, an employer who is incapable or guilty of an offence against his workmen ought to be made to suffer far more, both in the spirit and in the flesh, than a workman who is incapable or guilty of an offence against his employer. Furthermore, all workmen ought to know that this is so. It would imply, on the one hand, a certain rearrangement with regard to risks, on the other hand, in criminal law, a conception of punishment in which social rank, as an aggravating circumstance, would necessarily play an important part in deciding what the penalty was to be. All the more reason, therefore, why the exercise of important public functions should carry with it serious personal risks.

Another way of rendering equality compatible with differentiation would be to take away as far as possible all quantitative character from differences. Where there is only a difference in kind, not in degree, there is no inequality at all.

By making money the sole, or almost the sole, motive of all actions, the sole, or almost the sole, measure of all things, the poison of inequality has been introduced everywhere. It is true that this inequality is mobile; it is not attached to persons, for money is made and lost; it is none the less real.

There are two sorts of inequality, each with its corresponding stimulant. A more or less stable inequality, like that of ancient France, produces an idolizing of superiors—not without a mixture of repressed hatred—and a submission to their commands. A mobile, fluid inequality produces a desire to better oneself. It is no nearer to equality than is stable inequality, and is every bit as unwholesome. The Revolution of 1789, in putting forward equality, only succeeded in reality in sanctioning the substitution of one form of inequality for another.

The more equality there is in a society, the smaller is the

action of the two stimulants connected with the two forms of inequality, and hence other stimulants are necessary.

Equality is all the greater in proportion as different human conditions are regarded as being, not more nor less than one another, but simply as other. Let us look on the professions of miner and minister simply as two different vocations, like those of poet and mathematician. And let the material hardships attaching to the miner's condition be counted in honour of those who undergo them.

In wartime, if an army is filled with the right spirit, a soldier is proud and happy to be under fire instead of at headquarters; a general is proud and happy to think that the successful outcome of the battle depends on his forethought; and at the same time the soldier admires the general and the general the soldier.

Such a balance constitutes an equality. There would be equality in social conditions if this balance could be found therein. It would mean honouring each human condition with those marks of respect which are proper to it, and are not just a hollow pretence.

HIERARCHISM

Hierarchism is a vital need of the human soul. It is composed of a certain veneration, a certain devotion towards superiors, considered not as individuals, nor in relation to the powers they exercise, but as symbols. What they symbolize is that realm situated high above all men and whose expression in this world is made up of the obligations owed by each man to his fellow-men. A veritable hierarchy presupposes a consciousness on the part of the superiors of this symbolic function and a realization that it forms the only legitimate object of devotion among their subordinates. The effect of true hierarchism is to bring each one to fit himself morally into the place he occupies.

HONOUR

Honour is a vital need of the human soul. The respect due to every human being as such, even if effectively accorded, is not sufficient to satisfy this need, for it is identical for every one and unchanging; whereas honour has to do with a human being considered not simply as such, but from the point of view of his social surroundings. This need is fully satisfied where each of the social organisms to which a human being belongs allows him to share in a noble tradition enshrined in its past history and given public acknowledgment.

For example, for the need of honour to be satisfied in professional life, every profession requires to have some association really capable of keeping alive the memory of all the store of nobility, heroism, probity, generosity and genius spent in the exercise of that profession.

All oppression creates a famine in regard to the need of honour, for the noble traditions possessed by those suffering oppression go unrecognized, through lack of social prestige.

Conquest always has that effect. Vercingetorix was no hero to the Romans. Had France been conquered by the English in the fifteenth century, Joan of Arc would be well and truly forgotten, even to a great extent by us. We now talk about her to the Annamites and the Arabs; but they know very well that here in France we don't allow their heroes and saints to be talked about; therefore the state in which we keep them is an affront to their honour.

Social oppression has the same effects. Guynemer and Mermoz have become part of the public consciousness, thanks to the social prestige of aviation; the sometimes incredible heroism displayed by miners or fishermen barely awakes an echo among miners or fishermen themselves.

Deprivation of honour attains its extreme degree with that total deprivation of respect reserved for certain categories of human beings. In France, this affects, under various forms, prostitutes, ex-convicts, police agents and the sub-proletariat composed of colonial immigrants and natives. Categories of this kind ought not to exist.

Crime alone should place the individual who has committed it outside the social pale, and punishment should bring him back again inside it. ✓

PUNISHMENT

Punishment is a vital need of the human soul. There are two kinds of punishment, disciplinary and penal. The former offers security against failings with which it would be too exhausting to struggle if there were no exterior support. But the most indispensable punishment for the soul is that inflicted for crime. By committing crime, a man places himself, of his own accord, outside the chain of eternal obligations which bind every human being to every other one. Punishment alone can weld him back again; fully so, if accompanied by consent on his part; otherwise only partially so. Just as the only way of showing respect for somebody suffering from hunger is to give him something to eat, so the only way of showing respect for somebody who has placed himself outside the law is to reinstate him inside the law by subjecting him to the punishment ordained by the law.

The need of punishment is not satisfied where, as is generally the case, the penal code is merely a method of exercising pressure through fear.

So that this need may be satisfied, it is above all necessary that everything connected with the penal law should wear a solemn and consecrated aspect; that the majesty of the law should make its presence felt by the court, the police, the accused, the guilty man—even when the case dealt with is of minor importance, provided it entails a possible loss of liberty. Punishment must be an honour. It must not only wipe out the stigma of the crime, but must be regarded as a supplementary form of education, compelling a higher devotion to the public good. The severity of the punishment must also be in keeping with the kind of obligation which has been violated, and not with the interests of public security.

The discredit attaching to the police, the irresponsible conduct of the judiciary, the prison system, the permanent social stigma cast upon ex-convicts, the scale of penalties which provides a much harsher punishment for ten acts of petty larceny than for one rape or certain types of murder, and which even provides punishments for ordinary misfortune—all this makes it impossible for there to exist among us, in France, anything that deserves the name of punishment.

For offences, as for crimes, the relative degree of immunity should increase, not as you go up, but as you go down the social scale. Otherwise the hardships inflicted will be felt to be in the nature of constraints or even abuses of power, and will no longer constitute punishments. Punishment only takes place where the hardship is accompanied at some time or another, even after it is over, and in retrospect, by a feeling of justice. Just as the musician awakens the sense of beauty in us by sounds, so the penal system should know how to awaken the sense of justice in the criminal by the infliction of pain, or even, if need be, of death. And in the same way as we can say of the apprentice who injures himself at his trade, that it is the trade which is getting into *him*, so punishment is a method for getting justice into the soul of the criminal by bodily suffering.

The question of the best means to employ to prevent a conspiracy from arising in high places with the object of obtaining immunity from the law, is one of the most difficult political problems to solve. It can only be solved if there are men whose duty it is to prevent such a conspiracy, and whose situation in life is such that they are not tempted to enter it themselves.

FREEDOM OF OPINION

Freedom of opinion and freedom of association are usually

classed together. It is a mistake. Save in the case of natural groupings, association is not a need, but an expedient employed in the practical affairs of life.

On the other hand, complete, unlimited freedom of expression for every sort of opinion, without the least restriction or reserve, is an absolute need on the part of the intelligence. It follows from this that it is a need of the soul, for when the intelligence is ill-at-ease the whole soul is sick. The nature and limits of the satisfaction corresponding to this need are inscribed in the very structure of the various faculties of the soul. For the same thing can be at once limited and unlimited, just as one can produce the length of a rectangle indefinitely without it ceasing to be limited in width.

In the case of a human being, the intelligence can be exercised in three ways. It can work on technical problems, that is to say, discover means to achieve an already given objective. It can provide light when a choice lies before the will concerning the path to be followed. Finally, it can operate alone, separately from the other faculties, in a purely theoretical speculation where all question of action has been provisionally set aside.

When the soul is in a healthy condition, it is exercised in these three ways in turn, with different degrees of freedom. In the first function, it acts as a servant. In the second function, it acts destructively and requires to be reduced to silence immediately it begins to supply arguments to that part of the soul which, in the case of any one not in a state of perfection, always places itself on the side of evil. But when it operates alone and separately, it must be in possession of sovereign liberty; otherwise something essential is wanting to the human being.

The same applies in a healthy society. That is why it would be desirable to create an absolutely free reserve in the field of publication, but in such a way as for it to be understood that the works found therein did not pledge their authors in any way and contained no direct advice for readers. There it would be possible to find, set out in their full force, all the arguments in favour of bad causes. It would be an excellent and salutary thing for them to be so displayed. Anybody could there sing the praises of what he most condemns. It would be publicly recognized that the object of such works was not to define their authors' attitudes *vis-à-vis* the problems of life, but to contribute, by preliminary researches, towards a complete and correct tabulation of data concerning each problem. The law would see to it that their publication did not involve any risk of whatever kind for the author.

On the other hand, publications destined to influence what is called opinion, that is to say, in effect, the conduct of life, constitute acts and ought to be subjected to the same restrictions as are all acts. In other words, they should not cause unlawful harm of any kind to any human being, and above all, should never contain any denial, explicit or implicit, of the eternal obligations towards the human being, once these obligations have been solemnly recognized by law.

The distinction between the two fields, the one which is outside action and the one which forms part of action, is impossible to express on paper in juridical terminology. But that doesn't prevent it from being a perfectly clear one. The separate existence of these two fields is not difficult to establish in fact, if only the will to do so is sufficiently strong.

It is obvious, for example, that the entire daily and weekly press comes within the second field ; reviews also, for they all constitute, individually, a focus of radiation in regard to a particular way of thinking; only those which were to renounce this function would be able to lay claim to total liberty.

The same applies to literature. It would solve the argument which arose not long ago on the subject of literature and morals, and which was clouded over by the fact that all the talented people, through professional solidarity, were found on one side, and only fools and cowards on the other.

But the attitude of the fools and cowards was none the less, to a large extent, consistent with the demands of reason. Writers have an outrageous habit of playing a double game.

Never so much as in our age have they claimed the rôle of directors of conscience and exercised it. Actually, during the years immediately preceding the war, no one challenged their right to it except the savants. The position formerly occupied by priests in the moral life of the country was held by physicists and novelists, which is sufficient to gauge the value of our progress. But if somebody called upon writers to render an account of the orientation set by their influence, they barricaded themselves indignantly behind the sacred privilege of art for art's sake.

There is not the least doubt, for example, that André Gide has always known that books like the *Nourritures Terrestres* and the *Caves du Vatican* have exercised an influence on the practical conduct of life of hundreds of young people, and he has been proud of the fact. There is, then, no reason for placing such books behind the inviolable barrier of art for art's sake, and sending to prison a young fellow who pushes somebody off a train in motion.* One might just as well claim the privileges of art for art's sake in support of crime. At one time the Surrealists came pretty close to doing so. All that has been repeated by so many idiots *ad nauseam* about the responsibility of our writers in the defeat of France in 1940 is, unfortunately, only too true.

If a writer, thanks to the complete freedom of expression accorded to pure intelligence, publishes written matter which goes contrary to the moral principles recognized by law, and if later on he becomes a notorious focus of influence, it is simple enough to ask him if he is prepared to state publicly that his writings do not express his personal attitude. If he is not prepared to do so, it is simple enough to punish him. If he lies, it is simple enough to discredit him. Moreover, it ought

* *'d'emprisonner un garçon qui jette quelqu'un hors d'un train en marche'*: a reference to a gratuitous act performed by Lafcadio, hero of André Gide's *Caves du Vatican*, who pushes somebody off a train in Italy to prove to himself that he is capable of committing any act whatever, however motiveless, unrelated to preceding events. [Translator.]

to be recognized that the moment a writer fills a rôle among the influences directing public opinion, he cannot claim to exercise unlimited freedom. Here again, a juridical definition is impossible; but the facts are not really difficult to discern. There is no reason at all why the sovereignty of the law should be limited to the field of what can be expressed in legal formulae, since that sovereignty is exercised just as well by judgments in equity.

Besides, the need of freedom itself, so essential to the intellect, calls for a corresponding protection against suggestion, propaganda, influence by means of obsession. These are methods of constraint, a special kind of constraint, not accompanied by fear or physical distress, but which is none the less a form of violence. Modern technique places extremely potent instruments at its service. This constraint is, by its very nature, collective, and human souls are its victims.

Naturally, the State is guilty of crime if it makes use of such methods itself, save in cases where the public safety is absolutely at stake. But it should, furthermore, prevent their use. Publicity, for example, should be rigorously controlled by law and its volume very considerably reduced; it should also be severely prohibited from ever dealing with subjects which belong to the domain of thought.

Likewise, repression could be exercised against the press, radio broadcasts, or anything else of a similar kind, not only for offences against moral principles publicly recognized, but also for baseness of tone and thought, bad taste, vulgarity or a subtly corrupting moral atmosphere. This sort of repression could take place without in any way infringing on freedom of opinion. For instance, a newspaper could be suppressed without the members of its editorial staff losing the right to go on publishing wherever they liked, or even, in the less serious cases, remain associated to carry on the same paper under another name. Only, it would have been publicly branded with infamy and would run the risk of being so again. Freedom of opinion can be claimed solely—and even then with certain reservations—by the journalist, not by the paper; for it is only the journalist who is capable of forming an opinion.

Generally speaking, all problems to do with freedom of expression are clarified if it is posited that this freedom is a need of the intelligence, and that intelligence resides solely in the human being, individually considered. There is no such thing as a collective exercise of the intelligence. It follows that no group can legitimately claim freedom of expression, because no group has the slightest need of it.

In fact the opposite applies. Protection of freedom of thought requires that no group should be permitted by law to express an opinion. For when a group starts having opinions, it inevitably tends to impose them on its members. Sooner or later, these individuals find themselves debarred, with a greater or lesser degree of severity, and on a number of problems of greater or lesser importance, from expressing opinions opposed to those of the group, unless they care to leave it. But a break with any group to which one belongs always involves suffering —at any rate of a sentimental kind. And just as danger, exposure to suffering are healthy and necessary elements in the sphere of action, so are they unhealthy influences in the exercise of the intelligence. A fear, even a passing one, always provokes either a weakening or a tautening, depending on the degree of courage, and that is all that is required to damage the extremely delicate and fragile instrument of precision which constitutes our intelligence. Even friendship is, from this point of view, a great danger. The intelligence is defeated as soon as the expression of one's thoughts is preceded, explicitly or implicitly, by the little word 'we'. And when the light of the intelligence grows dim, it is not very long before the love of good becomes lost.

The immediate, practical solution would be the abolition of political parties. Party strife, as it existed under the Third Republic, is intolerable. The single party, which is, moreover, its inevitable outcome, is the worst evil of all. The only remaining possibility is a public life without parties. Nowadays, such an idea strikes us as a novel and daring proposition. All the better, since something novel is what is wanted. But, in point of fact, it is only going back to the tradition of 1789. In the eyes of the people of 1789, there was literally no other possibility. A public life like ours has been over the course of the last half-century would have seemed to them a hideous nightmare. They would never have believed it possible that a representative of the people should so divest himself of all personal dignity as to allow himself to become the docile member of a party.

Moreover, Rousseau had clearly demonstrated how party strife automatically destroys the Republic. He had foretold its effects. It would be a good thing just now to encourage the reading of the *Contrat Social*. Actually, at the present time, wherever there were political parties, democracy is dead. We all know that the parties in England have a certain tradition, spirit and function making it impossible to compare them to anything else. We all know, besides, that the rival teams in the United States are not political parties. A democracy where public life is made up of strife between political parties is incapable of preventing the formation of a party whose avowed aim is the overthrow of that democracy. If such a democracy brings in discriminatory laws, it cuts its own throat. If it doesn't, it is just as safe as a little bird in front of a snake.

A distinction ought to be drawn between two sorts of associations: those concerned with interests, where organization and discipline would be countenanced up to a certain point, and those concerned with ideas, where such things would be strictly forbidden. Under present conditions, it is a good thing to allow people to group themselves together to defend their interests, in other words, their wage receipts and so forth, and to leave these associations to act within very narrow limits and under the constant supervision of the authorities. But such associations should not be allowed to have anything to do with ideas. Associations in which ideas are being canvassed should be not so much associations as more or less fluid social mediums. When some action is contemplated within them, there is no reason why it need be put into execution by any persons other than those who approve of it.

In the working-class movement, for example, such a distinction would put an end to the present inextricable confusion. In the period before the war, the working-man's attention was being continually pulled in three directions at once. In the first place, by the struggle for higher wages; secondly, by what remained—growing ever feebler, but still showing some signs of life—of the old trade-union spirit of former days, idealist and more or less libertarian in character; and, lastly, by the political parties. Very often, when a strike was on, the workmen who struggled and suffered would have been quite incapable of deciding for themselves whether it was all a matter of wages, a revival of the old trade-union spirit, or a political manoeuvre conducted by a party; and nobody looking on from the outside was in any better position to judge.

That is an impossible state of affairs. When the war broke out, the French trade-unions were dead or moribund, in spite of their millions of members—or because of them. They again took on some semblance of life, after a prolonged lethargy, when the Resistance against the invader got under way. That doesn't prove that they are viable. It is perfectly clear that they had been all but destroyed by two sorts of poison, each of which by itself is deadly.

Trade-unions cannot flourish if at their meetings the workmen are obsessed by their earnings to the same extent as they are in the factory, when engaged in piece-work. To begin with, because the result is that sort of moral death always brought about by an obsession in regard to money. Next, because the trade-union, having become, under present social conditions, a factor continually acting upon the economic life of the country, ends up inevitably by being transformed into a single, compulsory, professional organization, obliged to toe the line in public affairs. It has then been changed into the semblance of a corpse.

Besides, it is no less evident that trade-unions cannot live in intimate contact with political parties. There is something resulting from the normal play of mechanical forces which makes such a thing quite impossible. For an analogous reason, moreover, the Socialist Party cannot live side by side with the Communist Party, because the latter's party character is, as it were, marked to a so much greater degree.

Furthermore, the obsession about wages strengthens Communist influence, because questions to do with money, however closely they may affect the majority of men, produce at the same time in all men a sensation of such deadly boredom that it requires to be compensated by the apocalyptic prospect of the Revolution, according to Communist tenets. If the middle-classes haven't the same need of an apocalypse, it is because long rows of figures have a poetry, a prestige which tempers in some sort the boredom associated with money; whereas, when money is counted in sixpences, we have boredom in its pure, unadulterated state. Nevertheless, the taste shown by *bourgeois*, both great and small, for Fascism, indicates that, in spite of everything, they too can feel bored.

Under the Vichy Government, single and compulsory professional organizations for workmen have been created. It is a pity that they have been given, according to the modern fashion, the name of corporation, which denotes, in reality, something so very different and so beautiful. But it is a good thing that such dead organizations should be there to take over the dead part of trade-union activity. It would be dangerous to do away with them. It is far better to charge them with the day-to-day business of dealing with wages and what are called immediate demands. As for the political parties, if they were all strictly prohibited in a general atmosphere of liberty, it is to be hoped their underground existence would at any rate be made difficult for them.

In that event, the workmen's trade-unions, if they still

retain a spark of any real life, could become again, little by little, the expression of working-class thought, the instrument of working-class integrity. According to the traditions of the French working-class movement, which has always looked upon itself as responsible for the whole world, they would concern themselves with everything to do with justice—including, where necessary, questions about wages; but only at long intervals and to rescue human beings from poverty.

Naturally, they would have to be able to exert an influence on professional organizations, according to methods of procedure defined by law.

There would, perhaps, only be advantages to be gained by making it illegal for professional organizations to launch a strike, and allowing trade-unions—with certain restrictions—to do so, while at the same time attaching risks to this responsibility, prohibiting any sort of coercion, and safeguarding the continuity of economic life.

As for the lock-out, there is no reason why it should not be entirely suppressed.

The authorized existence of associations for promoting ideas could be subject to two conditions. First, that excommunication may not be applied. Recruitment would be voluntary and as a result of personal affinity, without, however, making anybody liable to be invited to subscribe to a collection of assertions crystallized in written form. But once a member had been admitted, he could not be expelled except for some breach of integrity or undermining activities; which latter offence would, moreover, imply the existence of an illegal organization, and consequently expose the offender to a more severe punishment.

This would, in fact, amount to a measure of public safety, experience having shown that totalitarian States are set up by totalitarian parties, and that these totalitarian parties are formed by dint of expulsions for the crime of having an opinion of one's own.

The second condition could be that ideas must really be put

into circulation, and tangible proof of such circulation given in the shape of pamphlets, reviews or typed bulletins in which problems of general interest were discussed. Too great a uniformity of opinion would render any such association suspect.

For the rest, all associations for promoting ideas would be authorized to act according as they thought fit, on condition that they didn't break the law or exert any sort of disciplinary pressure on their members.

As regards associations for promoting interests, their control would, in the first place, involve the making of a distinction, namely, that the word 'interest' sometimes expresses a need and at other times something quite different. In the case of a poor working-man, interest means food, lodging and heating. For an employer, it means something of a different kind. When the word is taken in its first sense, the action of the authorities should be mainly to stimulate, uphold and defend the interests concerned. When used in its second sense, the action of the authorities should be continually to supervise, limit and, whenever possible, curb the activities of the associations representing such interests. It goes without saying that the severest restrictions and the hardest punishments should be reserved for those which are, by their nature, the most powerful.

What has been called freedom of association has been, in fact, up to now, freedom for associations. But associations have not got to be free; they are instruments, they must be held in bondage. Only the human being is fit to be free.

As regards freedom of thought, it is very nearly true to say that without freedom there *is* no thought. But it is truer still to say that when thought is non-existent, it is non-free into the bargain. There has been a lot of freedom of thought over the past few years, but no thought. Rather like the case of a child who, not having any meat, asks for salt with which to season it.

SECURITY

Security is an essential need of the soul. Security means that the soul is not under the weight of fear or terror, except as the result of an accidental conjunction of circumstances and for brief and exceptional periods. Fear and terror, as permanent states of the soul, are wellnigh mortal poisons, whether they be caused by the threat of unemployment, police persecution, the presence of a foreign conqueror, the probability of invasion, or any other calamity which seems too much for human strength to bear.

The Roman masters used to place a whip in the hall within sight of their slaves, knowing that this spectacle reduced their hearts to that half-dead condition indispensable for slavery. On the other hand, according to the Egyptians, the just man should be able to say after death: 'I never caused any one any fear'.

Even if permanent fear constitutes a latent state only, so that its painful effects are only rarely experienced directly, it remains always a disease. It is a semi-paralysis of the soul.

RISK

Risk is an essential need of the soul. The absence of risk produces a type of boredom which paralyses in a different way from fear, but almost as much. Moreover, there are certain situations which, involving as they do a diffused anguish without any clearly defined risks, spread the two kinds of disease at once.

Risk is a form of danger which provokes a deliberate re-action; that is to say, it doesn't go beyond the soul's resources to the point of crushing the soul beneath a load of fear. In some cases, there is a gambling aspect to it; in others, where some definite obligation forces a man to face it, it represents the finest possible stimulant.

The protection of mankind from fear and terror doesn't imply the abolition of risk; it implies, on the contrary, the permanent presence of a certain amount of risk in all aspects of social life; for the absence of risk weakens courage to the point of leaving the soul, if the need should arise, without the slightest inner protection against fear. All that is wanted is for risk to offer itself under such conditions that it is not transformed into a sensation of fatality.

PRIVATE PROPERTY

Private property is a vital need of the soul. The soul feels isolated, lost, if it is not surrounded by objects which seem to it like an extension of the bodily members. All men have an invincible inclination to appropriate in their own minds anything which over a long, uninterrupted period they have used for their work, pleasure or the necessities of life. Thus, a gardener, after a certain time, feels that the garden belongs to him. But where the feeling of appropriation doesn't coincide with any legally recognized proprietorship, men are continually exposed to extremely painful spiritual wrenches.

Once we recognize private property to be a need, this implies for everyone the possibility of possessing something more than the articles of ordinary consumption. The forms this need takes can vary considerably, depending on circumstances; but it is desirable that the majority of people should own their house and a little piece of land round it, and, whenever not technically impossible, the tools of their trade. Land and livestock figure among the tools necessary to the peasant's trade.

The principle of private property is violated where the land is worked by agricultural labourers and farm-hands under the orders of an estate-manager, and owned by townsmen who receive the profits. For of all those who are connected with that land, there is not one who, in one way or another, is not a stranger to it. It is wasted, not from the point of view of corn-production, but from that of the satisfaction of the property-need which it could procure.

Between this extreme case and that other one of the peasant who cultivates with his family the land he owns, there are a number of intermediate states where Man's need of appropriation is more or less unrecognized.

COLLECTIVE PROPERTY

Participation in collective possessions—a participation consisting not in any material enjoyment, but in a feeling of ownership—is a no less important need. It is more a question of a state of mind than of any legal formula. Where a real civic life exists, each one feels he has a personal ownership in the public monuments, gardens, ceremonial pomp and circumstance; and a display of sumptuousness, in which nearly all human beings seek fulfilment, is in this way placed within the reach of even the poorest. But it isn't just the State which ought to provide this satisfaction; it is every sort of collectivity in turn.

A great modern factory is a waste from the point of view of the need of property; for it is unable to provide either the workers, or the manager who is paid his salary by the board of directors, or the members of the board who never visit it, or the shareholders who are unaware of its existence, with the least satisfaction in connexion with this need.

When methods of exchange and acquisition are such as to involve a waste of material and moral foods, it is time they were transformed.

There is no natural connexion between property and money. The connexion established nowadays is merely the result of a system which has made money the focus of all other possible motives. This system being an unhealthy one, we must bring about a dissociation in inverse order.

The true criterion in regard to property is that it is legitimate so long as it is real. Or, to be more precise, the laws concerning property are so much the better the more advantages they draw from the opportunities offered by the possessions of this world for the satisfaction of the property-need common to all men.

Consequently, the present modes of acquisition and possession require to be transformed in the name of the principle of property. Any form of possession which doesn't satisfy somebody's need of private or collective property can reasonably be regarded as useless.

That does not mean that it is necessary to transfer it to the State; but rather to try and turn it into some genuine form of property.

TRUTH

The need of truth is more sacred than any other need. Yet it is never mentioned. One feels afraid to read when once one has realized the quantity and the monstrousness of the material falsehoods shamelessly paraded, even in the books of the most reputable authors. Thereafter one reads as though one were drinking from a contaminated well.

There are men who work eight hours a day and make the immense effort of reading in the evenings so as to acquire knowledge. It is impossible for them to go and verify their sources in the big libraries. They have to take the book on trust. One has no right to give them spurious provender. What sense is there in pleading that authors act in good faith? *They* don't have to do physical labour for eight hours a day. Society provides for their sustenance so that they may have the leisure and give themselves the trouble to avoid error. A pointsman responsible for a train accident and pleading good faith would hardly be given a sympathetic hearing.

All the more reason why it is disgraceful to tolerate the existence of newspapers on which, as everybody knows, not one of the collaborators would be able to stop, unless he were prepared from time to time to tamper knowingly with the truth.

The public is suspicious of newspapers, but its suspicions don't save it. Knowing, in a general way, that a newspaper contains both true and false statements, it divides the news up into these two categories, but in a rough-and-ready fashion, in accordance with its own predilections. It is thus delivered over to error.

We all know that when journalism becomes indistinguishable from organized lying, it constitutes a crime. But we think it is a crime impossible to punish. What is there to stop the punishment of activities once they are recognized to be criminal ones? Where does this strange notion of non-punishable crimes come from? It constitutes one of the most monstrous deformations of the judicial spirit.

Isn't it high time it were proclaimed that every discernible crime is a punishable one, and that we are resolved, if given the opportunity, to punish all crimes?

A few straightforward measures of public salubrity would protect the population from offences against the truth.

The first would be to set up, with such protection in view, special courts enjoying the highest prestige, composed of judges specially selected and trained. They would be responsible for publicly condemning any avoidable error, and would be able to sentence to prison or hard labour for repeated commission of the offence, aggravated by proven dishonesty of intention.

For instance, a lover of Ancient Greece, reading in one of Maritain's books: 'The greatest thinkers of antiquity had not thought of condemning slavery', would indict Maritain before one of these tribunals. He would take along with him the only important reference to slavery that has come down to us—the one from Aristotle. He would invite the judges to read the sentence: 'Some people assert that slavery is absolutely contrary to nature and reason.' He would observe that there is nothing to make us suppose these particular 'people' were not among the greatest thinkers of antiquity. The court would censure Maritain for having published—when it was so easy for him to avoid falling into such a mistake—a false assertion, and one constituting, however unintentionally, an outrageous calumny against an entire civilization. All the daily papers, weeklies and others; all the reviews and the radio would be obliged to bring the court's censure to the notice of the public, and, if need be, Maritain's answer. In this particular case, it seems most unlikely there could be one.

On the occasion when *Gringoire*★ published *in extenso* a speech attributed to a Spanish anarchist, who had been announced as going to speak at a meeting in Paris, but who in fact, at the last minute, had been unable to leave Spain, a court of this kind would not have been out of place. Dishonesty being in such a case more patent than that two and two make four, no doubt prison or hard labour would not have been too severe a sentence.

Under this system, anybody, no matter who, discovering an avoidable error in a printed text or radio broadcast, would be entitled to bring an action before these courts.

The second measure would be to prohibit entirely all propaganda of whatever kind by the radio or daily press. These two instruments would only be allowed to be used for non-tendentious information.

The aforesaid courts would be there to see that the information supplied was not tendentious.

In the case of organs of information, they might have to pronounce judgment concerning not only erroneous assertions, but also intentional and tendentious omissions.

Circles in which ideas are discussed, and which desire to make them known, would only have a right to publish weekly, fortnightly or monthly journals. There is absolutely no need to appear more frequently in print, if one's object is to make people think instead of stupefying them.

★ *Gringoire*: a pre-war weekly of a virulent turn and politically reactionary. [Translator.]

The propriety of the methods of persuasion used would be guaranteed, thanks to the control exercised by the above courts, which would be able to suppress any publication guilty of too frequent a distortion of the truth; though the editors would be allowed to let it reappear under another name.

Nothing in all this would involve the slightest attack on public liberty. It would only mean satisfaction of the human soul's most sacred need—protection against suggestion and falsehood.

But, it will be objected, how can we guarantee the impartiality of the judges? The only guarantee, apart from that of their complete independence, is that they should be drawn from very different social circles; be naturally gifted with a wide, clear and exact intelligence; and be trained in a school where they receive not just a legal education, but above all a spiritual one, and only secondarily an intellectual one. They must become accustomed to love truth.

There is no possible chance of satisfying a people's need of truth, unless men can be found for this purpose who love truth.

PART TWO

UPROOTEDNESS

PART TWO

UPROOTEDNESS

To be rooted is perhaps the most important and least recognized need of the human soul. It is one of the hardest to define. A human being has roots by virtue of his real, active and natural participation in the life of a community which preserves in living shape certain particular treasures of the past and certain particular expectations for the future. This participation is a natural one, in the sense that it is automatically brought about by place, conditions of birth, profession and social surroundings. Every human being needs to have multiple roots. It is necessary for him to draw wellnigh the whole of his moral, intellectual and spiritual life by way of the environment of which he forms a natural part.

Reciprocal exchanges by which different sorts of environment exert influence on one another are no less vital than to be rooted in natural surroundings. But a given environment should not receive an outside influence as something additional to itself, but as a stimulant intensifying its own particular way of life. It should draw nourishment from outside contributions only after having digested them, and the human beings who compose it should receive such contributions only from its hands. When a really talented painter walks into a picture gallery, his own originality is thereby confirmed. The same thing should apply to the various communities throughout the world and the different social environments.

Uprootedness

Uprootedness occurs whenever there is a military conquest, and in this sense conquest is nearly always an evil. There is the minimum of uprootedness when the conquerors are migrants who settle down in the conquered country, intermarry with the inhabitants and take root themselves. Such was the case with the Hellenes in Greece, the Celts in Gaul and the Moors in Spain. But when the conqueror remains a stranger in the land of which he has taken possession, uprootedness becomes an almost mortal disease among the subdued population. It reaches its most acute stage when there are deportations on a massive scale, as in Europe under the German occupation, or along the upper loop of the Niger, or where there is any brutal suppression of all local traditions, as in the French possessions in the Pacific (if Gauguin and Alain Gerbault are to be believed).

Even without a military conquest, money-power and economic domination can so impose a foreign influence as actually to provoke this disease of uprootedness.

Finally, the social relations existing in any one country can be very dangerous factors in connexion with uprootedness. In all parts of our country at the present time—and setting aside the question of the conquest—there are two poisons at work spreading this disease. One of them is money. Money destroys human roots wherever it is able to penetrate, by turning desire for gain into the sole motive. It easily manages to outweigh all other motives, because the effort it demands of the mind is so very much less. Nothing is *so* clear *and so* simple as a row of figures.

UPROOTEDNESS IN THE TOWNS

There are social conditions in which an absolute and continuous dependence on money prevails—those of the wage-earning class, especially now that piece-work obliges each workman to have his attention continually taken up with the subject of his pay. It is in these social conditions that the disease of uprootedness is most acute. Bernanos has said that our workmen are not, after all, immigrants like those of Mr. Ford. The major social difficulty of our age proceeds from the fact that in a certain sense they *are* like them. Although they have remained geographically stationary, they have been morally uprooted, banished and then reinstated, as it were on sufferance, in the form of industrial brawn. Unemployment is, of course, an uprootedness raised to the second power. They are unable to feel themselves at home whether it be in the factories, their own dwellings, the parties and trade-unions ostensibly created on their behalf, places of amusement, or in intellectual activities if they attempt to acquire some culture.

For the second factor making for uprootedness is education as it is understood nowadays. The Renaissance everywhere brought about a break between people of culture and the mass of the population; but while abstracting culture from national tradition, it did at least cause it to be steeped in Greek tradition. Since then, links with the national traditions have not been renewed, but Greece has been forgotten. The result has been a culture which has developed in a very restricted medium, removed from the world, in a stove-pipe atmosphere—a culture very strongly directed towards and influenced by technical science, very strongly tinged with pragmatism, extremely broken up by specialization, entirely deprived both of contact with this world and, at the same time, of any window opening on to the world beyond.

Nowadays a man can belong to so-called cultured circles without, on the one hand, having any sort of conception about human destiny or, on the other hand, being aware, for example, that all the constellations are not visible at all seasons of the year. A lot of people think that a little peasant boy of the present day who goes to primary school knows more than Pythagoras did, simply because he can repeat parrot-wise that the earth moves round the sun. In actual fact, he no longer looks up at the heavens. This sun about which they talk to him in class hasn't, for him, the slightest connexion with the one he can see. He is severed from the universe surrounding him, just as little Polynesians are severed from their past by being forced to repeat : 'Our ancestors, the Gauls, had fair hair.'

What is called today educating the masses, is taking this modern culture, evolved in such a closed, unwholesome atmosphere, and one so indifferent to the truth, removing whatever it may still contain of intrinsic merit—an operation known as popularization—and shovelling the residue as it stands into the minds of the unfortunate individuals desirous of learning, in the same way as you feed birds with a stick.

Moreover, the desire to learn for the sake of learning, the desire for truth, has become very rare. The prestige of culture has become almost exclusively a social one, as much for the peasant who dreams of having a schoolteacher son, or the schoolteacher who dreams of having a son at the *Ecole Normale Supérieure*,* as for the society people who fawn upon savants and well-known writers.

The youth of our schools are as much obsessed by their examinations as our workmen engaged in piece-work are by their pay packets. There is something woefully wrong with the health of a social system, when a peasant tills the soil with the feeling that, if he is a peasant, it is because he wasn't intelligent enough to become a schoolteacher.

The mixture of confused and more or less false ideas known under the name of Marxism, a mixture to which, since Marx's day, it is, generally speaking, only very ordinary middle-class intellectuals who have contributed, is also for the working-class a completely outlandish doctrine, which they are incapable of assimilating, and which is, besides, devoid of any nutritive value, for it has been emptied of nearly all the truth contained

---

* *Ecole Normale Supérieure*: situated rue d'Ulm in Paris. Institution created by the Convention in 1794, reorganized under the Empire in 1808. Its object is to form an *élite* of teachers for secondary schools, and, in practice, teachers for all the higher branches of education are drawn from it. [Translator.]

44

in Marx's writings. From time to time, a scientific presentation for popular consumption is added. The effect of all this can only be to bring about the most intense uprootedness among the working-class.

Uprootedness is by far the most dangerous malady to which human societies are exposed, for it is a self-propagating one. For people who are really uprooted there remain only two possible sorts of behaviour: either to fall into a spiritual lethargy resembling death, like the majority of the slaves in the days of the Roman Empire, or to hurl themselves into some form of activity necessarily designed to uproot, often by the most violent methods, those who are not yet uprooted, or only partly so.

The Romans were a handful of fugitives who banded themselves together artificially to form a city, and deprived the Mediterranean peoples of their individual manner of life, their country, traditions, past history to such an extent that posterity has taken them, at their own valuation, for the founders of civilization in these conquered territories. The Hebrews were escaped slaves, and they either exterminated or reduced to servitude all the peoples of Palestine. The Germans, at the time Hitler assumed command over them, were really—as he was never tired of repeating—a nation of proletarians, that is to say, uprooted individuals. The humiliation of 1918, inflation, over-industrialization and above all the extreme gravity of the unemployment crisis had infected them with the moral disease to the acute point where irresponsibility takes possession. The Spaniards and Englishmen who, from the sixteenth century onwards, massacred or enslaved coloured peoples, were adventurers almost without any contact with the fundamental life of their own respective countries. The same may be said in regard to a part of the French Empire, which moreover was built up at a time when the French tradition was suffering from a decline. Whoever is uprooted himself uproots others. Whoever is rooted himself doesn't uproot others.

Under the same name of revolution, and often using identical slogans and subjects for propaganda, lie concealed two conceptions entirely opposed to one another. One consists in transforming society in such a way that the working-class may be given roots in it; while the other consists in spreading to the whole of society the disease of uprootedness which has been inflicted on the working-class. It must not be said or supposed that the second operation can ever form a prelude to the first; that is false. They are two opposite roads which do not meet.

The second conception is nowadays much more frequently met with than the first, both among militants and among the mass of the workers. It is obvious that it tends more and more to gain ground in proportion as uprootedness continues and increases its ravages. It can easily be realized that, from one day to another, the harm may become irreparable.

On the conservative side, a similar ambiguity prevails. A few really want the workers to become rooted again; only this desire of theirs is accompanied by imaginary pictures most of which, instead of having reference to the future, are borrowed from a past which is, moreover, partly fictitious. The rest want purely and simply to see maintained or reinforced that category of human material to which the proletariat has been reduced.

Thus those who really desire the good—and they are not very numerous—weaken their position still further by distributing themselves among two hostile camps with which they have nothing in common.

The sudden collapse of France in June 1940, which surprised every one all over the world, simply showed to what extent the country was uprooted. A tree whose roots are almost entirely eaten away falls at the first blow. If France offered a spectacle more painful than that of any other European country, it is because modern civilization with all its toxins was in a more advanced stage there than elsewhere, with the exception of Germany. But in Germany, uprootedness had taken on an aggressive form, whereas in France it was characterized by inertia and stupor. The difference is due to more or less hidden causes, some of which could no doubt be discovered were one to undertake the necessary search. On the other hand, the country which in face of the first wave of German terror behaved far and away the best, was the one where tradition is strongest and most carefully nurtured, that is to say, England.

In France, the uprootedness characterizing the proletariat had reduced vast numbers of workers to a state of apathetic stupor, and caused others to feel themselves at war with society. The same money which had brutally cut away the roots of the working-class, had at the same time gnawed at those of the middle-classes, for wealth is cosmopolitan; any feeble attachment to the country which these might still retain was very much outweighed, especially since 1936, by fear and hatred of the workers. Even the peasants had almost become uprooted since the 1914 war, demoralized by the rôle of cannon fodder they had played in it, by money which occupied an increasingly important place in their lives, and by far too frequent a contact with the corruption prevailing in the cities. As for intelligence, it was almost extinct.

This general malady throughout the country took the form of a sort of drowsiness, which alone prevented civil war from breaking out. France loathed the war which threatened to prevent her from continuing her sleep. Half stunned by the terrible blow of May and June 1940, she threw herself into the arms of Pétain in order to be able to continue to sleep with a semblance of security. Since then, enemy oppression has turned this sleep into such a grievous nightmare that she begins to toss about, anxiously awaiting outside help to come and waken her.

Under the effects of war, the disease of uprootedness has taken on such a sharp increase throughout Europe as to leave one legitimately appalled. The only thing which seems to offer any hope is this: that suffering will have to a certain extent restored to life memories which were lately almost dead, as in France those of 1789.

As for the Oriental countries, to which during the last few centuries, but especially in the last fifty years, the white man has carried the disease of uprootedness from which they are suffering, Japan gives ample proof of the intensity reached there by the active form of this disease. Indo-China offers an example of its passive form. India, where a living tradition still persists, has been sufficiently contaminated for even those who speak publicly in the name of this tradition to dream nevertheless of building in their land a nation according to the modern Western type. China remains very mysterious. Russia, which is, as always, half-European, half-Oriental, just as much so; for one cannot be sure whether the vigour that is covering her with glory proceeds, as in the case of the Germans, from uprootedness of an active nature, such as the history of the past twenty-five years would first lead one to expect, or whether it is above all a manifestation of the deep-flowing life of the people, going right back to the remotest times, and having remained subterraneously almost intact.

As for the American continent, since its population has for several centuries been founded above all on immigration, the dominating influence which it will probably exercise greatly increases the danger.

In this almost desperate situation, all we can look to for encouragement here below is in those historical atolls of the living past left upon the surface of the earth. Not that we should approve the fuss started by Mussolini over the Roman Empire, or try to make use of Louis XIV for the same sort of purpose. Conquests are not of life, they are of death at the very moment they take place. It is the distillations from the living past which should be jealously preserved, everywhere, whether it be in Paris or Tahiti, for there are not too many such on the entire globe.

It would be useless to turn one's back on the past in order simply to concentrate on the future. It is a dangerous illusion to believe that such a thing is even possible. The opposition of future to past or past to future is absurd. The future brings us nothing, gives us nothing; it is we who in order to build it have to give it everything, our very life. But to be able to give, one has to possess; and we possess no other life, no other living sap, than the treasures stored up from the past and digested, assimilated and created afresh by us. Of all the human soul's needs, none is more vital than this one of the past.

Love of the past has nothing to do with any reactionary political attitude. Like all human activities, the revolution draws all its vigour from a tradition. Marx felt this so strongly that he was determined to make this tradition go back to the remotest times by making class-war the one and only principle by which to explain history.

Up to the very beginning of this century, few things in Europe were closer to the Middle Ages than French trade-unionism, sole reflected ray, with us, of the guild spirit. The feeble remains of this trade-unionism are among the number of embers upon which it is most urgent that we should blow.

For several centuries now, men of the white race have everywhere destroyed the past, stupidly, blindly, both at home and abroad. If in certain respects there has been, nevertheless, real progress during this period, it is not because of this frenzy, but in spite of it, under the impulse of what little of the past remained alive.

The past once destroyed never returns. The destruction of the past is perhaps the greatest of all crimes. Today the preservation of what little of it remains ought to become almost an obsession. We must put an end to the terrible uprootedness which European colonial methods always produce, even under their least cruel aspects. We must abstain, once victory is ours, from punishing the conquered enemy by uprooting him still further; seeing that it is neither possible nor desirable to exterminate him, to aggravate his lunacy would be to show oneself more of a lunatic than he. We must also keep, above all, well to the fore in any political, legal or technical innovations likely to have social repercussions, some arrangement whereby human beings may once more be able to recover their roots.

This doesn't mean they should be fenced in. On the contrary, never was plenty of fresh air more indispensable. Rooting in and the multiplying of contacts are complementary to one another. For instance, if, wherever technical conditions permit —and as the result of a slight effort in this direction they could easily be made to do so—workmen were dispersed, each one owning his house, a bit of garden and a machine; and if, on the other hand, the *Tour de France** of former days were revived for the benefit of the young, if necessary on an international scale; if workmen were frequently given the opportunity of filling in periods of attendance at the assembly shops where the parts they make are combined with all the others, or of going off to help train apprentices; with, in addition, some satisfactory safeguard in the matter of wages—then the wretchedness of the proletarian lot would disappear.

We shall never put an end to the proletarian lot by passing laws, whether these be concerned with the nationalization of key industries, the abolition of private property, powers granted to the trade-unions to negotiate collective agreements, representation by factory delegates or the control of engagement. All the measures that are proposed, be they given a revolutionary or a reformist label, are purely legal, and it is not on a legal plane that working–class distress is situated, nor the remedy for this distress. Marx would perfectly well have understood this if he had been intellectually honest with himself, for it is a truth which bursts forth in the best pages of his *Capital*.

It is no use attempting to discover in the demands put forward by the workers the cure for their misfortune. Plunged in misfortune body and soul, including the imagination, how should they be able to imagine anything which didn't bear misfortune's mark? If they make a violent effort to extricate

---

* *Tour de France*: one of the last vestiges of the guild or corporation system. Young workmen serving their apprenticeship were known as *compagnons*, and in order to perfect themselves in their trade, used to undertake a journey on foot across France, following a fixed itinerary which took in the principal centres of production. The arrival of the railway gradually caused this very ancient custom to die out. [Translator.]

themselves therefrom, they fall into apocalyptic reverie, or seek compensation in a working-class imperialism which is no more to be encouraged than a national imperialism.

What one *can* look out for in their demands is the sign and token of their sufferings. Now, all, or nearly all, of these demands express the suffering caused by uprootedness. If they want control of engagement and nationalization, it is because they are obsessed by the fear of total uprootedness—that is, of unemployment. If they want the abolition of private property, it is because they have had enough of being admitted into wherever it is they work as immigrants allowed to enter on sufferance. This was also the psychological mainspring behind the workers' occupation of the factories in June 1936. For some days they experienced a pure, unmixed joy at finding themselves at home there where they spent their working-day; the joy of a child who doesn't want to think of tomorrow. Nobody could reasonably expect that tomorrow was going to be a particularly happy one.

The French working-class movement which came out of the Revolution was essentially a cry, less one of revolt than one of protest, in face of the pitiless hardship of the lot reserved for all the oppressed. Considering what can be expected from any kind of collective movement, this one certainly contained a relatively very high degree of purity of motive. It came to an end in 1914; ever since, there have been only echoes of it, the toxins generated by society in general having even corrupted the sense of misfortune. We must endeavour to recover its tradition; but nobody could wish to see it revived. However beautiful the sound of a cry of woe may be, one cannot wish to hear it again; it is more human to wish to cure the woe.

The actual list of workmen's woes supplies us with a list of the things that need changing. First of all, we must do away with the shock experienced by a lad who at twelve or thirteen leaves school and enters a factory. There are some workmen who could feel happy enough, had this shock not left behind it an ever-open wound; but they don't realize themselves that their suffering comes to them from the past. The child while at school, whether a good or a bad pupil, was a being whose existence was recognized, whose development was a matter of concern, whose best motives were appealed to. From one day to the next, he finds himself an extra cog in a machine, rather less than a thing, and nobody cares any more whether he obeys from the lowest motives or not, provided he obeys. The majority of workmen have at any rate at this stage of their lives experienced the sensation of no longer existing, accompanied by a sort of inner vertigo, such as intellectuals or *bourgeois*, even in their greatest sufferings, have very rarely had the opportunity of knowing. This first shock, received at so early an age, often leaves an indelible mark. It can rule out all love of work once and for all.

We must change the system concerning concentration of attention during working hours, the type of stimulants which make for the overcoming of laziness or exhaustion—and which at present are merely fear and extra pay—the type of obedience necessary, the far too small amount of initiative, skill and thought demanded of workmen, their present exclusion from any imaginative share in the work of the enterprise as a whole, their sometimes total ignorance of the value, social utility and destination of the things they manufacture, and the complete divorce between working life and family life. The list could well be extended.

Apart from the desire for reforms, three sorts of factors come into play in the process of production: technical, economic and military ones. Nowadays, the importance of the military factors in production corresponds to that of production itself in the conduct of war; in other words, it is very considerable.

From the military point of view, the crowding together of thousands of workmen into vast industrial prisons where the really qualified ones form a tiny minority is doubly absurd. Modern military conditions require, first, that industrial production should be dispersed; secondly, that the majority of workmen in peacetime should consist of trained professionals, under whose orders can be placed immediately, in an international crisis or during a war, a host of women, boys and old men, so as to increase at once the volume of production. Nothing helped so much to paralyse British war production for so long as the lack of qualified workmen.

But since it is impossible to have highly qualified professionals performing the work of machine-minders, this latter function must be done away with, save in time of war.

It so rarely happens that military requirements are in accordance, and not in contradiction, with the best human aspirations, that advantage ought to be taken of the fact.

From the technical point of view, the relative ease with which energy can be transmitted in the form of electricity certainly makes a high degree of decentralization possible.

As for the machines, they are not yet right for a transformation in the system of production; but the examples provided by adjustable automatic machines already in use would no doubt make it possible to effect such a transformation by dint of an effort, if the effort could only be made.

Speaking in general terms, a reform of an infinitely greater social importance than all the measures arrayed under the title of Socialism would be a transformation in the very conception of technical research. So far, no one has ever imagined that an engineer occupied in technical research on new types of machinery could have anything other than the following double objective in view: first, to increase the profits of the firm which has ordered the research, and secondly, to serve the interests of the consumer. For in such a case, when we talk about the interests of production, we mean producing more and at a cheaper rate; that is to say, these interests are really identical with those of the consumer. Thus, these two words are constantly being used the one for the other.

As for the workmen who will be spending their energies on this machine, nobody thinks twice about them. Nobody even thinks it possible to think about them. The most that ever happens is that from time to time some vague security apparatus is provided, although, in fact, severed fingers and factory stairs daily splashed with fresh human blood are such a common feature.

But this feeble show of interest is the only one. Not only does nobody consider the moral well-being of the workmen, which would demand too great an effort of the imagination; but nobody even considers the possibility of not injuring them in the flesh. Otherwise one might perhaps have found something else for the mines than that appalling automatic drill worked by compressed air, which sends an uninterrupted series of shocks for eight hours through the body of the man manipulating it.

No one thinks either of asking himself whether some new type of machine, by making capital less fluid and production more rigid, will not aggravate the general danger of unemployment.

What is the use of workmen obtaining as a result of their struggles an increase in wages and a relaxation of discipline, if meanwhile engineers in a few research departments invent, without the slightest evil intent, machines which reduce their souls and bodies to a state of exhaustion, or aggravate their economic difficulties? What use can the partial or total nationalization of economic production be to them, if the spirit of these research departments hasn't changed? And so far, as far as one can tell, it hasn't changed in places where nationalization has been introduced. Even Soviet propaganda has never claimed that Russia had discovered a radically new type of machine, worthy of being handled by an all-powerful proletariat.

And yet, if there is one conviction which stands out with irresistible force in the works of Marx, it is this one: that any change in the relationship between the classes must remain a pure illusion, if it be not accompanied by a transformation in technical processes, expressing itself in entirely new types of machinery.

From the workman's point of view, a machine needs to possess three qualities. First, it should be able to be worked without exhausting the muscles, or the nerves, or any organ whatever—and also without cutting or lacerating the flesh, save under very exceptional circumstances.

Secondly, in relation to the general danger of unemployment, the productive apparatus as a whole should be as flexible as possible, so as to be able to follow the fluctuations in demand. Consequently, the same machine ought to serve a variety of purposes, the more the better, and even to a certain extent indeterminate ones. This also forms a military requirement, for the greater ease in transferring from a peacetime to a wartime footing. Lastly, it is a factor which makes for happiness during working-hours, for it is thus possible to avoid that monotony so much feared by workmen because of the boredom and disgust it engenders.

Thirdly, it should normally be in keeping with the work of which a fully qualified man is capable. This again is a military necessity, and it is, furthermore, indispensable to the dignity and moral well-being of the workmen. A working-class composed almost entirely of competent professionals is not a proletariat.

A considerable development of the adjustable automatic machine, serving a variety of purposes, would go far to satisfy these needs. The first models of this type are already in existence, and it is certain that in this direction lie very great possibilities. Such machines make the work of a machine-minder obsolete. In a huge concern like Renault, few of the workmen look happy as they stand at work; amongst these few privileged beings are those in charge of automatic turrets with movable cam adjustment.

But what is essential is the idea itself of posing in technical terms problems concerning the effect of machines upon the moral well-being of the workmen. Once posed, the technicians have only to resolve them; just as they have resolved countless others. All that is necessary is that they should want to do so.

For this reason, the places where new machinery is devised should no longer fall entirely within the network of capitalist interests. It would be natural for the State to exercise some control over them by means of grants. And why shouldn't the workers' organizations do the same by giving bonuses? —without mentioning other means of bringing influence and pressure to bear. If the workers' unions could become really alive, they would be in perpetual contact with the research departments where new technical processes were being studied. Such a contact could be prepared in advance by fomenting a sympathetic atmosphere towards workmen in engineering schools.

Up to now, technicians have never had anything else in mind than the requirements of manufacture. If they were to start having always present before them the needs of those who do the manufacturing, the whole technique of production would be slowly transformed.

This ought to become a part of the instruction given in engineering schools and technical schools generally—but a part with some real substance to it.

There would no doubt be everything to be gained in putting in hand right away investigations concerning this type of problem.

The subject of such investigations would be easy enough to define. A pope once said: 'Material comes out of the factory ennobled, the workers come out of it debased.' Marx made exactly the same observation in still more vigorous terms. What is wanted is that all those who endeavour to carry out technical improvements should have continually present in their minds the conviction that among all the deficiencies of all kinds it is possible to detect in the present state of manufacturing, the one for which it is by far the most indispensably urgent to find a remedy is this one: that nothing must be done to make it worse; that everything must be done to make it less. This conception should henceforth form part of the sense of professional obligation, the sense of professional honour, with whosoever holds a responsible position in industry. One of the principal tasks before the workmen's trade-unions, if they were capable of carrying it out, would be to make this conception sink deep into the universal consciousness.

If the majority of workmen were highly qualified professionals, fairly frequently called upon to show inventiveness and initiative, each responsible for his production and machine, the present discipline in regard to work would no longer serve any useful purpose. Some men could work at home; others in small workshops, which could very often be organized on a co-operative basis. At present, the rule of authority is exercised in an even more intolerable fashion in small factories than in large ones; but that is because they try to imitate the large ones. Such workshops would not be small factories, they would be industrial organisms of a new kind, in which a new spirit could blow; though small, they would be bound together by organic ties strong enough to enable them to form as a whole a large concern. There is about large concerns, in spite of all their defects, a special sort of poetry, and one for which workmen have nowadays acquired a taste.

Payment by the piece would no longer hold any disadvantages, once the herding of the workers into prison-like structures had been abolished. It would no longer involve that obsession with speed at all costs. It would constitute the normal mode of remuneration for work freely carried out. Nor would obedience be any longer a matter of uninterrupted submissiveness. A workman or a group of workmen could have a certain number of orders to fulfil within a given time, and be left with a completely free hand in the actual layout of the work. It would be a different thing altogether from knowing tnat one had to go on repeating indefinitely the same movement, in obedience to an order, until the precise second when a new command came to impose a different movement for an equally unknown length of time. There is a certain relation to time which suits inert matter, and another sort of relation which suits thinking beings. It is a mistake to confuse the two.

Whether on a co-operative basis or not, these little work-shops would at any rate not be like prisons. A workman would be able now and again to show his wife where he works and his machine, as they were all so happy to do in June 1936, taking advantage of the occupation of the factories. The children would come along, after school, to join their father and learn how to work, at an age when work is by far the most exciting of all games. Thus, later on, when they came to start their apprenticeship, they would already be almost qualified in one trade, and could, according to their choice, perfect themselves in that particular one or acquire a second one. Work would be lit up by poetry for the rest of their lives by these wonders experienced in infancy, instead of wearing throughout life the gloomy aspect of a nightmare, simply because of the shock received on initiation.

If, even in the midst of the present demoralization, the peasants have far less need than the workmen of being continually goaded to activity by stimulants, the reason lies perhaps in this difference. A child can already find himself unhappy on a farm at the age of nine or ten; but nearly always there will have been a time when work was for him a marvellous game, reserved for the grown-ups.

If workmen, in their majority, could become reasonably happy, several seemingly essential and burning problems would not only be resolved but actually abolished. Without their having been resolved, people would forget that they had ever existed. Distress is a culture broth for false problems. It creates obsessions. The way to appease them is not to provide what they insist upon, but to bring about the disappearance of the distress. If a man is thirsty because of a wound in the stomach, drink is not what he requires, but to have his wound cured.

Unfortunately it is only the future of the young which can be changed. A great effort will have to be made in order to train working-class youth, and particularly in connexion with apprenticeship. The State will be obliged to take over the responsibility, because there is no other social entity capable of doing so.

Nothing demonstrates more clearly the essential failure of the capitalist class than the negligence shown by employers in the matter of apprenticeship. It is the sort which in Russia is termed criminal negligence. It would be impossible to insist too much on this point, to bring too much before the public notice this simple truth, easily grasped, incontrovertible. Employers have, during the past twenty or thirty years, forgotten to think about the training of sound professional workmen. The lack of qualified workmen contributed as much as any other single factor to the country's downfall. Even in 1934 and 1935, when the unemployment crisis had reached its height, when production was at dead-point, engineering and aviation works were looking for good professional workmen and couldn't find them. The workmen complained that the tests were too difficult; but it was they who hadn't received the necessary training so as to be able to carry out the tests. How, under such conditions, would it have been possible for us to have had sufficient arms? But, besides, even without a war, the lack of professionally trained men, becoming more serious as the years went by, was bound to end up by rendering economic life itself impossible.

Once and for all, the whole country and the interested parties themselves must be told that the employers showed themselves, in fact, incapable of shouldering the responsibilities which the capitalist system imposes on them. They have a function to fill, but it is not that one, for experience has shown that that one is too heavy and too vast for them. Once that has been thoroughly understood, we shall no longer be afraid of them, and they, for their part, will cease to oppose necessary reforms; they will stay within the modest limits of their natural function. That is their only chance of survival. It is because people are afraid of them that they so often think of getting rid of them.

They would say a workman didn't know how to look ahead

if they caught sight of him taking an aperitive; but their own common sense didn't extend to the point of looking far enough ahead to see that if no apprentices were trained, in twenty years' time there would no longer be any workmen, at least any deserving the name. Seemingly they are incapable of looking more than two or three years ahead. Doubtless, too, they were secretly inclined to prefer to have in their factories a drove of unfortunates, rootless individuals without the least claim to any sort of consideration. They didn't know that, though the submissiveness of slaves is greater than that of free men, their revolt is also a far more terrible one. They have had a certain experience of this, but without understanding what it was all about.

The lack of interest displayed by the workers' trade-unions in this matter of apprenticeship is just as scandalous from another point of view. *They* hadn't to concern themselves with questions of future production; but since their only title to existence lay in the defence of justice, they ought to have been moved to pity by the moral distress of the youngsters. In actual fact, the really wretched part of the factory population—the youths, women, immigrant workers, whether foreign or colonial—was abandoned to its wretchedness. The lump sum of all their sufferings counted for far less in trade-union circles than the problem of salary increases for categories of workmen already amply paid.

Nothing illustrates more clearly how difficult it is for any collective movement to be really set in the way of justice, and for the unfortunate to be really protected. They are unable to protect themselves, because they are prevented by misfortune; and they are not protected from the outside, because it is the tendency of human nature not to pay any attention to those in misfortune.

The J.O.C.* alone has concerned itself with the distress

---

* *J.O.C.* : stands for *Jeunesse Ouvrière Chrétienne*. Organization founded by the French Catholic clergy, chiefly concerned with exercising an influence on working-class youth from the professional and social points of view. In the latter respect, it bears a certain affinity to the Boy Scout Movement. [Translator.]

among youthful workers, the existence of such an organization being perhaps the only sure sign that Christianity is not dead in us.

Just as the capitalists have betrayed their calling by criminally neglecting not only the interests of the people, not only those of the nation, but even their own; so the workers' trade-unions have betrayed theirs by neglecting to protect the wretched ones among their ranks, in order to turn their attention to the defence of special interests. It is just as well that this should be known, too, in case the day should ever come when they found themselves in the position and under the temptation to commit abuses of power. Putting the curb on the trade-unions, transformed into single, compulsory organizations, was the natural and inevitable outcome of this change of spirit. In reality, the Vichy Government's action in this matter has been negligible. The C.G.T.* has not suffered rape at its hands. For some time now, the state of the latter has not been such as to make anything of the kind any longer possible.

The State is not particularly well qualified to take over the defence of the unfortunate. It is even wellnigh incapable of doing so, unless obliged to by some clear and urgent necessity in the public interest, and by a movement of opinion.

As far as the training of working-class youth is concerned, such a necessity in the public interest could not be clearer or more urgent. As for the movement of opinion, it must be created, and a beginning made now, by using the nuclei of

---

* C.G.T., or *Confédération Générale du Travail:* founded towards the end of the last century, a few years after the law of 1884 authorizing the existence of trade-unions. This organization has dominated the industrial workers' trade-union movement in France. At the height of the general strike of 1947, a split occurred between extremist and non-extremist elements, the latter regrouping themselves under the banner of *Force Ouvrière*. The C.G.T. still remains, however, the largest single industrial workers' trade-union organization; the second largest being the C.F.T.C. (*Confédération Française des Travailleurs Chrétiens*), with the aforesaid *Force Ouvrière* coming third. [Translator.]

genuine trade-union bodies, the J.O.C., research groups and youth movements, even official ones.

In Russia, the Bolsheviks have roused the enthusiasm of their people by proposing to them the building up of a vast industry. Couldn't we likewise rouse our own people's enthusiasm by proposing to them the building up of an industrial population of a new type? Such an objective would be well in accord with the French genius.

The training of an industrial youth should go beyond a purely professional training. It should, of course, admit of an education, like the training of any kind of youth; and for that reason it is desirable that the apprenticeship should not be done in the schools, where it is always badly done, but should be bathed right away in an atmosphere of production itself. At the same time, it cannot be allowed to be carried out in factories either. The subject requires the display of some inventiveness. Something is needed which combines the advantages of a training-school, those of apprenticeship in a factory, those of a *chantier de jeunesse**　on the present model, and many more besides.

But the training of an industrial youth, especially in a country like France, involves also access to a general education, a participation in an intellectual culture. They must be made to feel at home, too, in the world of thought.

What form is this participation to take? And what is this culture to be? That is a dispute which has been going on for a long time. At one time, in certain circles, people used to talk a lot about working-class culture. Others used to say there was no such thing as working-class or non-working-class culture, but just plain culture. The effect of the latter observation has been, on the whole, to cause the same treatment to be meted out to the most intelligent workmen and the ones most anxious to learn as is reserved for semi-imbecile boys in a *lycée*. Things have sometimes turned out somewhat better than that; but,

* *chantier de jeunesse:* type of instructional centre created by the Vichy Government with the object of giving young people on leaving school a supplementary education and practical experience in a trade. [Translator.]

by and large, that represents accurately enough the principle of vulgarization as it is understood at the present time. The term is as atrocious as the thing itself. When we have something reasonably satisfactory to denote, we shall have to think of another term.

Certainly, truth is one, but error is manifold; and in every culture, save in the case of the perfect one, which for Man can only constitute an extreme case, there is a mixture of truth and error. If our culture were close to perfection, it would be situated above the social classes. But since it is a mediocre culture, it is to a large extent one for middle-class intellectuals, and more especially, for some time now, one for intellectual government employees.

If one wanted to pursue the analysis in this direction, one would find that in some of Marx's ideas there is far more of truth than appears at first sight; but we need not expect Marxists themselves ever to go in for such an analysis; for they would first of all have to look at themselves in a mirror, which would be too painful an operation, and one for which the specifically Christian virtues alone are able to supply the necessary courage.

What makes it so difficult for our culture to be communicated to the people is not that it is too high, but that it is too low. We apply a strange remedy, indeed, by lowering it still further before distributing it to them in little doses.

There are two obstacles which make the people's access to culture a difficult matter. One is the lack of time and energy. The people have little leisure to devote to intellectual effort; and fatigue sets a limit to the intensity of such effort.

That particular obstacle is quite unimportant. At least, it would be so, if we didn't make the mistake of attributing importance to it. Truth lights up the soul in proportion to its purity, not in any sense to its quantity. It isn't the quantity of metal which matters, but the degree of alloy. In this respect, a little pure gold is worth a lot of pure gold. A little pure truth is worth as much as a lot of pure truth. Similarly, one perfect

Greek statue contains as much beauty as two perfect Greek statues.

Niobe's sin consisted in disregarding the fact that quantity has nothing to do with virtue, and she was punished for it by the death of her children. We commit the same sin every day, and are punished for it in the same way.

If a workman, in the course of a year's eager and persevering efforts, manages to learn a few geometrical theorems, as much truth will have entered into his soul as in that of a student who, during the same period, has shown a corresponding ardour in assimilating a portion of higher mathematics.

It is true that such a thing is scarcely believable, and would perhaps not be easy to prove. But for Christians at least it should be an article of faith, if they were to remind themselves that truth is amongst the number of pure blessings which the Gospel compares to bread, and that whoever asks for bread isn't given a stone.

Material obstacles—want of leisure, fatigue, lack of aptitude, sickness, physical pain—hinder the acquisition of the inferior or more ordinary elements of culture, not that of the most precious treasures it contains.

The second obstacle to working-class culture is that to the workman's social condition, as to any other kind, there corresponds a certain particular disposition of feeling. Consequently, there is something outlandish about what has been elaborated by other people and for other people.

The cure for that consists in an effort of translation; not of popularization, but of translation, which is a very different matter.

It isn't a question of taking truths—of already far too poor a quality—contained in the culture of the intellectuals, and then degrading them, mutilating them and destroying all their flavour; but simply of expressing them, in all their fullness, in a language which, to use Pascal's expression, makes them perceptible to the heart, for the benefit of people whose feelings have been shaped by working-class conditions.

The art of transposing truths is one of the most essential and the least known. What makes it difficult is that, in order to practise it, one has to have placed oneself at the centre of a truth and possessed it in all its nakedness, behind the particular form in which it happens to have found expression.

Furthermore, transposition is a criterion of truth. A truth which cannot be transposed isn't a truth; in the same way that what doesn't change in appearance according to the point of view isn't a real object, but a deceptive representation of such. In the mind, too, there is three-dimensional space.

The search for modes of transposition suitable for transmitting culture to the people would be very much more salutary still for culture than for the people. It would constitute an extremely precious stimulant for the former, which would in this way emerge from the appallingly stuffy atmosphere in which it is confined, and cease being merely something of interest to specialists. For that is all it is at present—a thing for specialists, from top to bottom, only more degraded the nearer you approach the bottom. Just as the workmen are treated as though they were rather stupid secondary schoolboys, so the secondary schoolboys are treated as though they were extremely tired students, and the students as though they were professional teachers suffering from amnesia and requiring to be re-educated. Culture—as we know it—is an instrument manipulated by teachers for manufacturing more teachers, who, in their turn, will manufacture still more teachers.

Amidst all the present forms of the uprooting malady, the uprooting of culture is not the least alarming. The first consequence of this malady, equally affecting all spheres, is generally that, relations being cut, each thing is looked upon as an end in itself. Uprooting breeds idolatry.

To take but one example of the deformation of our culture. The concern—a perfectly legitimate one—to preserve for geometrical reasoning its character of necessity, causes geometry to be presented to *lycée* boys as something without any relation at all to the outside world. The only interest they can take in it is as in some game, or else in order to get good marks. How could they be expected to see any truth in it?

The majority of them will always remain ignorant of the fact that nearly all our actions, the simple ones as well as the judiciously combined ones, are applications of geometrical principles; that the universe we inhabit is a network of geometrical relations, and that it is to geometrical necessity that we are in fact bound, as creatures enclosed in space and time. This geometrical necessity is presented to them in such a way that it appears arbitrary. Could anything be more absurd than an arbitrary necessity? By definition, necessity is something which is imposed.

On the other hand, when it is sought to popularize geometry and relate it to experience, the demonstrations are omitted. All that remains then is a few formulae totally devoid of interest. Geometry has then lost its savour, its very essence. For its essence lies in being a branch of study devoted to the subject of necessity—that same necessity which is sovereign in this material world.

Both these deformations could be easily avoided. There is no need to choose between demonstration and experience. It is as easy to demonstrate with some wood or iron as it is with a piece of chalk.

There is quite a simple way in which geometrical necessity could be introduced into training-schools, by associating theoretical study and the workshop. One would say to the children: 'Here are a certain number of tasks to be carried out (constructing objects fulfilling such and such requirements). Some of them are possible, others impossible. Carry out the ones that are possible, and as regards the ones you don't carry out, you must be able to force me to admit that they *are* impossible.' Through this crack, the whole of geometry can be made to pass into the sphere of practical work. Execution is a sufficient empirical proof of the possible; but as for the impossible, there is no empirical proof, and a demonstration is necessary. The impossible is necessity in its concrete shape.

As for the rest of Science, everything that belongs to standard Science—one cannot make Einstein and the quantum theory a part of working-class culture—is derived principally from an analogical method, consisting in transporting into the realm of nature the relations which govern human labour. Consequently, it is far more a natural concern of the workers, if one knows how to present it to them properly, than it is of secondary schoolboys.

This is even truer in the case of that branch of culture which comes under the title of 'Letters'. For the subject dealt with is always the human condition, and it is the people which has the truest, most direct experience of what this human condition is.

On the whole, and saving exceptions, second-class works and below are most suitable for the *élite*, and absolutely first-class works most suitable for the people.

For example, what an intensity of understanding could spring up from contact between the people and Greek poetry, the almost unique theme of which is misfortune! Only, one would have to know how to translate and present it. A workman, for instance, who bears the anguish of unemployment deep in the very marrow of his bones, would understand the feelings of Philoctetus when his bow is taken away from him, and the despair with which he stares at his powerless hands. He would also understand that Electra is hungry, which a *bourgeois*, except just at present, is absolutely incapable of understanding—including the publishers of the Budé Library.*

There is a third obstacle to working-class culture; that is slavery. The mind is essentially free and sovereign when it is really and truly exercised. To be free and sovereign, as a thinking being, for one hour or two, and a slave for the rest

---

* *Budé Library*: the Guillaume Budé Library was started some years ago by the association of the same name, with the object of providing the better-class reading public with the best possible texts in the Greek, Latin and French classics, translated or revised, as the case may be, and annotated by experts. [Translator.]

of the day, is such an agonizing spiritual quartering that it is almost impossible not to renounce, so as to escape it, the highest forms of thought.

If effective reforms were to be introduced, this obstacle would gradually disappear. Nay more, the memory of the recent state of slavery and the remains of it in process of disappearing would act as a powerful stimulant to the mind during the period of liberation.

A condition of any working-class culture is the mingling of what are called 'intellectuals'—an awful name, but at present they scarcely deserve a better one—with the workers. It is difficult to make something real out of such a mingling. However, the present situation provides an opportunity. Large numbers of young intellectuals have been driven into slavery to work in the factories and fields of Germany. Others have mixed with young workmen in the *camps de compagnons*.* But it is, above all, the former who have had a vital experience. Many have doubtless succumbed to it, or at any rate been too physically and spiritually weakened by it. Still, there may be some who will emerge having really profited therefrom.

This extremely valuable experience runs the risk of being wasted, due to the almost irresistible temptation to forget humiliation and misfortune as soon as one has left them behind. Now, straightaway, those among such prisoners who have returned should be approached and asked to keep up their contacts with the workers which had been begun by force, think over for themselves what this recent experience has meant, with the idea of effecting a *rapprochement* between culture and the people, thereby giving culture a new direction.

The trade-union Resistance organizations could at the present time be the means of effecting such a *rapprochement*. But, generally speaking, if the things of the mind are to play their

* *camps de compagnons:* see note on p. 62. These camps were apparently organized on a parallel basis to the *chantiers*, and were designed to replace the period of military service prohibited by the German occupants.

[Translator.]

belong to the minute workshops scattered about everywhere, and these would, in their turn, be the property of the workmen, either individually or collectively. Every workman would, besides, own a house and a bit of land.

This triple proprietorship comprising machine, house and land would be bestowed on him by the State as a gift on his marriage, and provided he had successfully passed a difficult technical examination, accompanied by a test to check the level of his intelligence and general culture.

The choice of a machine would be made to depend in the first place on the individual workman's tastes and natural abilities, and secondly on very general requirements from the point of view of production. It should be, of course, as far as possible, an adjustable automatic machine with a variety of uses.

This triple proprietorship could be neither transmitted by inheritance, nor sold, nor alienated in any way whatever. (The machine alone could, under certain circumstances, be exchanged.) The individual having the use of it would only be able to relinquish it purely and simply. In that event, it should be made difficult, but not impossible, for him later on to obtain an equivalent one elsewhere.

On a workman's death, this property would return to the State, which would, of course, if need be, be bound to maintain the well-being of the wife and children at the same level as before. If the woman was capable of doing the work, she could keep the property.

All such gifts would be financed out of taxes, either levied directly on business profits or indirectly on the sale of business products. They would be administered by a board composed of government officials, owners of business undertakings, trade-unionists and representatives of the Chamber of Deputies.

This right to property could be withdrawn on account of professional incapacity after sentence by a court of law. This, of course, presupposes the adoption of analogous penal measures for punishing, if necessary, professional incapacity on the part of the owner of a business undertaking.

A workman who wanted to become the owner of a small workshop would first have to obtain permission from a professional organization authorized to grant the same with discretion, and would then be given facilities for the purchase of two or three extra machines; but no more than that.

A workman unable to pass the technical examination would remain in the position of a wage-earner. But he would be able throughout the whole of his life, at whatever age, to make fresh attempts to satisfy the conditions. He would also at any age, and on several occasions, be able to ask to be sent on a free course of some months at a training-school.

These wage-earners through incapacity would work either in little workshops not run on a co-operative basis, as assistants to a man working on his own, or as hands in the assembly shops. But only a small number of them should be allowed to stay in industry. The majority should be sent to fill jobs as manual labourers and pen-pushers, which are indispensable to the carrying on of the public services and trade.

Up to the time he gets married and settles down somewhere for the remainder of his life—that is to say, depending on the individual character, up to the age of twenty-two, twenty-five or thirty—a young man would be regarded as being still in a state of apprenticeship.

During childhood, enough time should be left out of school to enable children to spend many, many hours pottering about in their father's company whilst at work. Semi-attendance at school—a few hours' study followed by a few hours' work—should then go on for some considerable time. Later, a very varied existence is what is needed: journeys of the *Tour de France** type, working courses spent, now with artisans working on their own, now in little co-operative workshops, now in assembly shops belonging to different concerns, now in youth

* *Tour de France*: see note p. 50. [Translator.]

associations of the *Chantiers* or *Compagnons*★ type; working courses which, according to individual tastes and capacities, could be several times repeated and further prolonged by attendance at workmen's colleges for periods varying between a few weeks and two years. The ability to go on such working courses should, moreover, under certain conditions, be made possible at any age. They should be entirely free of charge, and not carry with them any sort of social advantages.

When the young workman, gorged and glutted with variety, began to think of settling down, he would be ripe for planting his roots. A wife, children, a garden supplying him with a great part of his food, work associating him with an enterprise he could love, be proud of, and which was to him as a window opened wide on to the outside world—all this is surely enough for the earthly happiness of any human being.

Naturally, such a conception of the young working-man's development implies a complete recasting of the present prison-like system.

As for wages, it would be necessary to avoid, in the first place, of course, that they were so low as to cause actual distress—though there would scarcely be any fear of that under such conditions—since they absorb the workman's attention and prevent his attachment to the concern.

Corporative bodies, for purposes of arbitration, etc., ought to be created solely with this purpose in view: to function in such a way that no workman has hardly ever to think about money matters.

The profession of manager, like that of medical practitioner, is one whose practice the State, acting in the public interest, should license only after certain conditions have been fulfilled. Such conditions should concern not only capacity, but also moral character.

Capital sums involved would be much smaller than at present. A credit system could easily make it possible for any young man without capital who had the necessary

★ *Chantiers* or *Compagnons*: see notes pp. 62 and 68. [Translator.]

capacity and vocation for such a post to become a manager.

Business enterprise could thus be made again an individual thing. As for incorporated joint-stock companies, perhaps it would be just as well, while arranging for a suitable method of transition, to abolish them and declare them illegal.

Naturally, the variety of business undertakings would involve the consideration of very varied forms of administration. The plan sketched here is only presented as the final stage reached after long efforts, amongst which advances in technical invention would be indispensable.

At all events, such a form of social existence would be neither capitalist nor socialist.

It would put an end to the proletarian condition, whereas what is called Socialism tends, in fact, to force everybody without distinction into that condition.

Its goal would be, not, according to the expression now inclined to become popular, the interest of the consumer—such an interest can only be a grossly material one—but Man's dignity in his work, which is a value of a spiritual order.

The difficulty about such a social conception is that there is no possible chance of its emerging from the domain of theory unless a certain number of men can be found who are fired by a burning and unquenchable resolve to make it a reality. It is not at all certain that such men can be found or called into being.

Yet, otherwise, it really seems the only choice left is one between different, and almost equally abominable, forms of wretchedness.

Although such a conception can only become a reality over a long period of time, post-war reconstruction should at once adopt as its rule the dispersion of industrial activity.

UPROOTEDNESS IN THE COUNTRYSIDE

The problem of uprootedness in the countryside is no less serious than that of uprootedness in the towns. Although the disease is not so far advanced, there is something even more shocking about it; for it is contrary to nature that the land should be cultivated by uprooted individuals. Both problems require, therefore, to receive equal attention.

Besides, one should never bestow any public mark of attention on industrial workers, without bestowing another one of corresponding importance on the peasants. For they are ever ready to take offence, very susceptible, and always tortured by the thought that they are being forgotten. It is certain that amidst all this present suffering, they find comfort in the assurance that they are being thought about. It must be admitted that we think much more about them when we are hungry than when we have all we want to eat; and that is so even in the case of people who imagined they had placed their thoughts on a level very much above that of all ordinary physical needs.

Workmen have a tendency which ought not to be encouraged to think that, when one refers to the 'people', one is necessarily referring solely to them. There is not the slightest justification for this; unless one chooses to regard as such the fact that they kick up far more of a noise than the peasants. They have succeeded in convincing, in regard to this point, the intellectuals who display an interest in the people. The result has been among the peasants a sort of hatred for what is politically known as the Left, except in places where they have fallen under communist influence, or where anti-clericalism is the ruling passion; and doubtless in a few other cases besides.

In France, the opposition between peasants and workmen goes a long way back. In a complaint made at the end of the fourteenth century, the peasants enumerated in heart-rending accents the cruelties they were made to suffer at the hands of all classes of society, including the artisans.

In the history of popular movements in France, it has hardly ever happened, unless I am mistaken, that peasants and workmen have been found on the same side. Even in

1789, it was doubtless more of a coincidence than anything else.

In the fourteenth century, the peasants were far and away the most wretched among the population. But even when they are materially better off—and when such is the case, they scarcely ever realize it, because the workmen who come to spend a few days' holiday in the village cannot resist the temptation to boast—they are always tortured by the feeling that everything worth while happens in the towns, and that they are 'out of it'.*

Naturally, this state of mind is aggravated by the setting up of the wireless and cinemas in the villages, and by the sale of newspapers like *Confidences* and *Marie-Claire*,† compared with which cocaine is a harmless product.

Such being the situation, one must first invent and then put into execution something which will henceforth give the peasants the feeling that they are 'in it'.‡

It is perhaps a pity that in the broadcasts officially made over the London wireless, the workmen have always been referred to much more than the peasants. It is true that their part in the Resistance is a far, far smaller one. But this is possibly an additional reason for giving repeated proofs that one is aware of their existence.

It must be borne in mind that you cannot say the French people are behind a movement if this is not true of the majority of the peasants.

One should make it a rule never to promise new and better things to the workmen, without at the same time promising as much to the peasants. The great cunning shown by the Nazi Party before 1933 consisted in presenting itself to the workmen

* '*out of it*': as in text. [Translator.]

† *Confidences* and *Marie-Claire*: two illustrated weeklies addressed to the feminine public, whose apparently elevated tone fails to disguise their profound moral and intellectual mediocrity. [Translator.]

‡ '*in it*': as in text. [Translator.]

as a specifically working-class party, to the peasants as a specifically peasant one, to the lower middle-class as a specifically lower middle-class one, etc. That was easy enough for it to do, as it lied to everybody. We ought to do as much, but without lying to anybody. It isn't easy, but it isn't impossible.

Peasant uprootedness has been, over the course of the last few years, as mortal a danger for the country as working-class uprootedness. One of the most serious symptoms was, seven or eight years ago, the desertion of the land in the very middle of an unemployment crisis.

It is obvious that a depopulation of the countryside leads, finally, to social death. We can say it will not reach that point. But still, we don't know that it won't. So far, there seems to be nothing which is likely to arrest it.

With regard to this phenomenon, two things require to be noted.

The first is that the white man carries it about with him wherever he goes. The disease has even penetrated into the heart of the African continent, which had for thousands of years, nevertheless, been made up of villages. These black people at any rate, when nobody came to massacre them, torture them, or reduce them to slavery, knew how to live happily on their land. Contact with us is making them lose the art. That ought to make us wonder whether even the black man, although the most primitive of all colonized peoples, hadn't after all more to teach us than to learn from us. The benefits we have conferred on them resemble the one conferred by the financier on the shoemaker.* Nothing in the world can make up for the loss of joy in one's work.

The second thing to be noted is that the apparently unlimited powers of the totalitarian State are unavailing against this evil. In Germany, formal and official admissions of failure have been made over and over again regarding this matter.

* *the financier on the shoemaker:* reference to La Fontaine's fable 'Le Savetier et le Financier', vol. 8, fable no. 2. [Translator.]

In one way, that is all to the good, since it gives us the chance of doing better than them.

The destruction of stocks of wheat during the economic crisis had a profound effect on public opinion—and rightly so; but if one thinks it over, the desertion of the land in the middle of an industrial crisis has something about it of a still more shocking character, if such were possible. It is obvious that there is no hope of solving the workmen's problem separately from the peasants'. There is no means of preventing the working-class population from turning into a proletariat if it is constantly being increased by an afflux of peasants who have broken away from their past.

The war has shown how serious are the ravages of this disease among the peasants. For the soldiers were young peasants. In September 1939, one used to hear peasants say: 'Better to live as a German than die as a Frenchman.' What had been done to them to make them think that they had nothing to lose?

It is important to realize one of the greatest difficulties in the political sphere. If it is true that the workmen suffer cruelly through feeling themselves to be exiles in our present type of society, the peasants, for their part, are under the impression that in this society it is, on the contrary, only the workmen who are really in their element. In the eyes of the peasants, the intellectuals who champion the cause of the workmen don't appear as defenders of the oppressed, but as defenders of a privileged class. The intellectuals are far from suspecting the existence of such an attitude.

The inferiority complex in the countryside is such that you see peasant millionaires who find it natural to be treated by retired *petits bourgeois* with the sort of arrogance shown by colonials towards natives. An inferiority complex has to be very great for money not to be able to wipe it out.

Consequently, the more one sets about satisfying the moral needs of the workmen, the more necessary it is to take steps to make the same provision for the peasants. Otherwise the resultant disequilibrium will be dangerous for society and have unpleasant repercussions on the workmen themselves.

The need to feel rooted, with the peasants, takes first of all the form of a hunger for property. This is a real hunger with them, and a healthy and natural one. One is certain to make an impression on them by seriously putting forward hopes of this kind. And there is no reason why one should not do so, once it is the need of property which is recognized as sacred, and not the legal title laying down the form for holding property. There are any number of possible legal dispositions which would enable, little by little, the land not yet owned by peasants to be transferred to them. Nothing can justify the property rights of a townsman over a piece of land. Large agricultural estates are only justifiable in certain cases, for technical reasons; and even in such cases, one can well imagine peasants cultivating vegetables and similar products intensively, each on his own little strip, and at the same time, with modern equipment, applying extensive methods of cultivation co-operatively over vast areas owned by them in common.

A measure which would go straight to the heart of the peasants is one whereby land came to be regarded as raw material for carrying on work, and not as an asset in the distribution of an inheritance. In this way, we should no longer witness the shocking spectacle of a peasant in debt throughout the whole of his life to some brother in the government service doing less work and earning more money.

Pensions—even the smallest ones—for the old on retirement would doubtless have a great effect. The word 'pension' has, unfortunately, magic properties which attract young peasants to the towns. The humiliation suffered by the old is often great in the country, and the drawing of a little money, under honourable conditions, would bolster up their prestige.

Through the force of contrast, too great a stability produces in the peasant an uprooting effect. A youngster begins ploughing by himself at about the age of fourteen. The work is then pure poetry, an intoxicating pleasure for him, although he is barely strong enough to manage it. A few years later, that boyish enthusiasm has been exhausted, the job is familiar, the physical energy is overflowing, and far in excess of what is required for the work; and yet there is no more to do than what has been done day after day for several years. So the young man starts to spend the week dreaming about what he is going to do on Sunday. From that moment he is lost.

A peasant boy's first complete contact with work, at the age of fourteen, this initial rapture of his, ought to be hallowed by a solemn ritual celebration of a kind to leave an indelible impression in the depths of his soul. In the more Christian villages, this celebration should bear a religious character.

But besides this, three or four years later, some draught ought to be supplied to assuage his thirst for something new. For a young peasant, it can only take one form: travel. All young peasants should be given the opportunity to travel free of charge in France, or even abroad; not about the cities, but about the countryside. It would involve organizing for the peasants something resembling the *Tour de France*.* Cultural and educational facilities could be added. For very often the best among these young peasants, after having, at thirteen, abandoned school with a sort of violence in order to throw themselves into work, feel again towards eighteen or twenty a desire to learn. The same thing happens, by the way, to young workmen. Systems of exchange could make it possible for even young men regarded by their families as indispensable to go away. It goes without saying that such travels would be purely voluntary. But parents would not have the right to veto them.

It is difficult to realize how strong the travel obsession is with peasants, and what a moral effect such a reform could have, even before it became a fact, at the promissory stage, and all the more so once the thing had come to be a part of ordinary habit. The young man, after knocking about the

* *Tour de France*: see note p. 50. [Translator.]

world for a few years, but without ever ceasing to be a peasant, would return home, his longings appeased, to found a family.

Something of a similar nature is doubtless necessary for girls too. They certainly need something to take the place of *Marie-Claire*,* and they certainly cannot be left with *Marie-Claire*.

Life in barracks has been a terrible source of uprooting for young peasants. So contrary was the final effect of military training to the one intended, that young men, after learning military exercises, were in less of a condition to fight than they were before having learned them; for whoever left a barracks left it as an anti-militarist. This provides the practical proof that you cannot, in the interests of the military machine itself, allow the military authorities to have the sovereign disposal of two years out of each life, or even only one year. Just as you cannot leave Capitalism in sole charge of the professional training of youth, so you cannot leave the Army in sole charge of its military training. The civil authorities must have a share in the latter, and in such a way as to make it a source of education instead of a source of corruption.

Contact between young peasants and young workmen in the course of military service is not at all desirable. The latter seek to impress the former, which is bad for both of them. Contacts of this sort don't really have the effect of bringing people together. Only a course of action pursued in common can do that; and, in the nature of things, there *can* be no common action in barracks, since you are getting ready for war there in time of peace.

There is no reason why barracks should be installed in towns. For the use of young peasants, one could very well have barracks far away from any town.

It is true that the owners of brothels would suffer. But it is useless even to consider any kind of reform, unless one is absolutely determined to put a stop to the collusion between

* *Marie-Claire*: see note p. 76. [Translator.]

the public authorities and people of that sort, and to abolish an institution which is a disgrace to France.*

It may be mentioned, by the way, that we have paid dearly for this disgrace. Turning prostitution into an official institution, in the way this has been done in France, largely contributed towards demoralizing the army, and completely demoralized the police, which was bound to bring about the ruin of democracy. For it is not possible for a democracy to subsist when the police, who represent the law in the eyes of the citizens, are an open target for public contempt. People in England cannot imagine any true sort of democracy in which the police are not regarded with an affectionate respect. But their police haven't got a drove of prostitutes to amuse themselves with.

If it were possible to reckon up exactly the factors which have contributed to our defeat, it would doubtless be found that all these things which have been our shame—like that one, and our colonial greediness, and our ill-treatment of foreigners—have each brought their individual and effective weight to bear in our general undoing. A lot of things can be said about our misfortune, but not that it is undeserved.

Prostitution is a typical example of that natural ability possessed by this malady of uprootedness to propagate itself to the second power. The condition of professional prostitute constitutes the extreme degree of uprootedness, and, in connexion with this particular malady, a mere handful of prostitutes is sufficient to spread a tremendous amount of infection. It is clear that we shall never have a healthy peasant population so long as the State persists in bringing about of its own accord the meeting together of young peasants and prostitutes. And as long as our peasantry is unhealthy, our working-class cannot be healthy either, nor the rest of the population.

Moreover, nothing could be more popular with the peasants than a scheme for reforming the system of military service, paying special attention to their moral well-being.

* . . . "disgrace to France": prostitution ceased to be officially recognized in France in 1947. [Translator.]

Uprootedness in the Countryside

The problem concerning culture of the mind presents itself in the case of the peasants, as it does in that of the workmen. They also need to be provided with a translation suitable for them, and not the same as the one for the workmen.

In all matters connected with things of the mind, the peasants have been brutally uprooted by conditions in the modern world. In the past they had everything which a human being can require in the way of art and thought, in a form which was their own, and was of the highest quality. When you read all that Restif de la Bretonne has written about his childhood, you can only conclude that the lot of the most unfortunate peasants of that time was infinitely preferable to that of the most fortunate ones of today. But it is impossible to return to the past, however close. Means must be devised to prevent the peasants from remaining unresponsive to the culture of the mind which is offered them.

Science should be presented to peasants and workmen in very different ways. In the case of workmen, it is natural that mechanics should occupy the foremost place. In that of peasants, everything should be centred around the wonderful cycle whereby solar energy, poured down into plants, is retained in them by the action of chlorophyll, becomes concentrated in seeds and fruits, enters into Man in the form of food or drink, passes into his muscles and spends itself on preparing the soil. Everything connected with Science can be situated around this cycle, for the notion of energy is at the heart of everything. Were the thought of this cycle to sink deep into the minds of peasants, it would permeate their labour with poetry.

Generally speaking, the main object of all education in the villages should be to increase the feeling for the beauty of the world, the beauty of nature. Tourists have, it is true, discovered that peasants are not interested in landscapes. But when you spend whole days doing exhausting work side by side with peasants— which is the only way of being able to have heart-to-heart talks with them—you hear some of them regretting their work is so hard as to leave them no time to enjoy the beauties of nature.

Naturally, it isn't simply by exclaiming: 'Look, how beautiful it is!' that their feeling for beauty will be increased. It isn't quite so simple as that.

The movement in connexion with folk-lore which of late has been started in cultured circles should try to help the peasants to feel at home again in human thought. Under the present system, they are made to regard everything connected with thought as the exclusive property of the towns, in which one is willing to grant them a small, a very small, share, because they are incapable of conceiving for themselves a large one.

It is the colonial mentality again, only in a less acute form. And just in the same way as a native from the colonies, who has a smattering of European education, can be brought to despise his own people more than would a cultured European, so the same thing often happens with a schoolteacher who comes from a peasant family.

The first condition necessary for bringing about a moral re-rooting of the peasantry in the country is that the profession of rural schoolteacher should be something distinct, specific; not merely partially, but totally different from that of a schoolteacher in the towns. It is in the highest degree absurd to form in the same mould teachers for Belleville* and for some little village. It is one of the many absurdities of an age whose salient characteristic is stupidity.

The second condition is that the rural schoolteachers should know the peasants and not look down on them, which will not be obtained simply by recruiting them from among the peasantry. A very large part of their training ought to be devoted to the folk-lore of all countries, presented not as an object of curiosity, but as something superb. They should be told about the part played by shepherds in the first speculations made by the human mind, those concerning the stars, and also—as the comparisons which continually occur in ancient texts indicate—those concerning good and evil. They should

* *Belleville:* working-class quarter in the N.E. of Paris. [Translator.]

be made to read peasant literature—Hesiod, *Piers Plowman*, the complaints of the Middle Ages, the few contemporary works which are of authentically peasant inspiration; all this, of course, without forgetting the claims of general culture. After such a preparation, they could be sent to serve for a year as farm-hands, anonymously, in some other part of the country; then assembled again in training-colleges to help them to see their own experience in proper perspective. Schoolteachers going to working-class and factory districts should be given an appropriate course on the same lines. But such experiences must be morally prepared for beforehand; otherwise they arouse disdain and repulsion instead of compassion and love.

It would be of great advantage, too, if the Churches were to turn the rôle of village priest or pastor into something specific. It is shocking to observe to what extent, in a French village which is wholly Catholic, religion can be divorced from daily life and reserved for a few hours only on Sunday, when one remembers what a preference Christ showed for taking the theme of his parables from country scenes. But a great many of these parables don't figure in the liturgy, and the ones that do don't excite any attention. In just the same way as the sun and stars the schoolteacher talks about inhabit the text-books and exercise-books and have nothing to do with the sky, so the vine, the corn, the sheep to which reference is made in church on Sundays have nothing in common with the vine, the corn and the sheep which are in the fields and to which every day one has to sacrifice a little part of one's life. The peasants who are Christians are also uprooted so far as their religious life is concerned. The idea of showing a village without a church in the Exhibition of 1937 was not so absurd as many people said it was.

Just as the young *Jocistes** feel exalted at the thought of Christ as a working-man, so the peasants should take a similar

* *Jocistes:* members of the J.O.C. (*Jeunesse Ouvrière Chrétienne*). See note p. 60. [Translator.]

pride in the part devoted in the New Testament parables to the life of the fields and in the sacred function ascribed to bread and wine, and derive therefrom the feeling that Christianity is something which belongs to them.

Polemics on the subject of laicization have constituted one of the chief sources responsible for the poisoning of peasant life in France. Unfortunately, they are far from having neared their end. It is impossible to avoid taking up a definite attitude in this matter, and at first sight it appears almost impossible to light on one which is not extremely unsatisfactory in itself.

It is certain that neutrality is a lie. The laic (anti-clerical) system is not neutral. It inculcates in children a philosophy which is on the one hand very superior to religion of the Saint-Sulpice* type, and on the other hand very inferior to genuine Christianity. But the latter is, nowadays, extremely rare. Many schoolteachers evince a zeal in their attachment to this philosophy comparable to religious fervour.

Liberty of instruction is not a solution. The expression is meaningless. No one has any proprietary rights over the spiritual formation of a child: neither the child, for he is not in a position to act in the matter; nor the parents; nor the State. The rights of the family, so often invoked, are nothing but a handy weapon in the argument. Any priest who refrained from talking about Christ to a child belonging to a non-Christian family, when given a perfectly normal opportunity of doing so, would be one who had lost his faith. To keep the lay schools just as they are, and allow or even encourage, next door, competition on the part of the religious schools, is an absurdity, both from a theoretical and a practical point of view. Private schools, whether religious or not, should

* *Saint-Sulpice:* reference to former seminary situated close to church of that name in Paris, and historically one of the most renowned centres of ecclesiastical education in France, where Ernest Renan studied to become a priest. Here the implication is an excessively orthodox religious outlook, lacking in spiritual spontaneity. [Translator.]

be authorized, not in virtue of any principle of liberty, but for reasons of public utility in every individual case where the school is a good one, and be subject only to public inspection.

To let the clergy have a share in public education is not a solution either. Even if it were possible, it would not be desirable, and it is not possible in France without a civil war.

To order the schoolteachers to talk about God to the children—as happened for some months under the Vichy Government, upon the recommendation of M. Chevalier*— is a joke in extremely bad taste.

To allow laic philosophy to preserve its official status would be an arbitrary measure, and an unjust one, seeing that it fails to correspond to a true scale of values, and one which would hurl us straight into totalitarianism. For although laicization has produced a certain amount of fervour of an almost religious kind, it is, by the very nature of things, a strictly limited amount; and we are living at a time when passions are fanned to white heat. Totalitarianism's idolatrous course can only be arrested by coming up against a genuinely spiritual way of life. If children are brought up not to think about God, they will become Fascist or Communist for want of something to which to give themselves.

We perceive more clearly what justice demands in this matter, once the notion of right has been replaced by that of obligation related to need. The soul of a child, as it reaches out towards understanding, has need of the treasures accumulated by the human species through the centuries. We do injury to a child if we bring it up in a narrow Christianity which prevents it from ever becoming capable of perceiving that there are treasures of the purest gold to be found in non-Christian civilizations. Lay education does an even greater

* *M. Chevalier*: M. Jacques Chevalier was occupying the post of Professor of Philosophy at Grenoble University, when he was sent for by Marshal Pétain to become Minister of National Education, during the Occupation. [Translator.]

injury to children.   It covers up these treasures, and those of Christianity as well.

The only attitude public education can adopt, in France, with regard to Christianity, which is at once legitimate and practically realizable, consists in looking upon it as one treasury of human thought among many others. It is too absurd for words that a French university graduate should have read poetry of the Middle Ages, *Polyeucte*, *Athalie*, *Phèdre*, Pascal, Lamartine, philosophical doctrines impregnated with Christianity like those of Descartes and Kant, the *Divine Comedy* or *Paradise Lost*, and never once have opened a Bible.

Future professional teachers and schoolmasters should simply be told that religion has at all times and in all countries, save quite recently in certain parts of Europe, played a dominant rôle in the development of human culture, thought and civilization. An educational course in which no reference is made to religion is an absurdity. Furthermore, in the same way as when studying history little French children are told a lot about France, so it is natural that, being in Europe, when you talk about religion you should refer primarily to Christianity.

Consequently, we ought to include in the teaching of the bigger children, at every stage, courses which could be described as, for example, religious history. The children would be made to read passages from the Bible, and above all the Gospels. Comments would be made in the spirit of the text itself, as should always be the case.

One would talk about dogma as something which has played a rôle of the highest importance in our countries, and in which men of the very greatest eminence have believed whole-heartedly; without hiding the fact either that it has been the pretext for inflicting any number of cruelties. But, above all, one would try to make the children feel all the beauty contained therein. If they ask: 'Is it true?', we should answer:'It is so beautiful that it must certainly contain a lot of truth. As for knowing whether it is, or is not, absolutely true, try to become capable of deciding that for yourselves when you grow up.' It would be strictly forbidden to add, by way of commentary, anything implying either a negation of dogma or an affirmation of it. Any teacher or schoolmaster who wished and who had the necessary knowledge and teaching ability would be free to talk to the children not only about Christianity, but also, though laying far less stress on it, about no matter what genuine current of religious thought. Religious thought is genuine whenever it is universal in its appeal. (Such is not the case with Judaism, which is linked to a racial conception.)

If such a solution were applied, religion would cease by degrees, it is to be hoped, being something one takes sides about for or against, in the same way as one takes sides in politics. Thus, we should abolish those two opposing camps—the schoolmaster's and the *curé's*—which foster a sort of latent civil war in so many French villages. Contact with the beauty of Christianity, presented simply as a beautiful thing to be savoured, would imperceptibly imbue the mass of the population with spirituality, if it is still capable of being so imbued, far more effectively than any amount of dogmatic teaching of religious beliefs.

The use of the word beauty doesn't in the least imply that religious questions should be considered after the manner of the aesthetes. The aesthetes' point of view is sacrilegious, not only in matters of religion but even in those of art. It consists in amusing oneself with beauty by handling it and looking at it. Beauty is something to be eaten; it is a food. If we are going to offer the people Christian beauty purely on account of its beauty, it will have to be as a form of beauty which gives nourishment.

In rural schools, the careful and regular reading, with frequent commentaries and repetitions, of those parts of the New Testament describing scenes of rural life, could do a lot to give back to the life of the fields its lost poetry. If on the one hand the whole spiritual life of the soul, and on the other hand all the scientific knowledge acquired concerning the material universe, are made to converge upon the act of work, work occupies its rightful place in a man's thoughts. Instead of being a kind of prison, it becomes a point of contact between this world and the world beyond.

For example, surely there is no reason why a peasant engaged in sowing shouldn't have at the back of his mind, without shaping words—even unspoken ones—on the one hand certain similes drawn by Christ, such as: 'Unless the seed die . . . ', 'The seed is the Word of God . . . ', 'The grain of mustard seed . . . which is the least of all seeds . . . ', and on the other hand the double mechanism of growth; the one whereby the seed, by consuming itself and with the aid of bacteria, reaches the surface of the soil; and the other whereby solar energy pours down in rays of light, is captured by the green colouring matter of the plant-stalk, and rises upward in an irresistible ascending movement. The analogy which makes the mechanism of this world a reflection of the supernatural mechanism, if one may use that expression, then becomes luminously clear, and the fatigue induced by work, to use ordinary popular speech, gets it into the body. The toil always more or less associated with the work effort becomes the pain which makes the beauty of the world penetrate right to the very core of the human being.

A similar method could charge the workman's labour with a similar significance. It is just as easy to conceive.

Thus only would the dignity of work be fully established. For, if we go to the heart of things, there is no true dignity without a spiritual root and consequently one of a supernatural order.

The popular school's job is to give more dignity to work by infusing it with thought, and not to make of the working-man a thing divided up into compartments which sometimes works and sometimes thinks. Naturally, a peasant who is sowing has to be careful to cast the seed properly, and not to be thinking about lessons learnt at school. But the object which engages our attention doesn't form the whole content of our thoughts. A happy young woman, expecting her first child, and busy sewing a layette, thinks about sewing it properly. But she never forgets for an instant the child she is carrying inside her. At precisely the same moment, somewhere in a prison workshop, a female convict is also sewing, thinking, too, about sewing properly, for she is afraid of being punished. One might imagine both women to be doing the same work at the same time, and having their attention absorbed by the same technical difficulties. And yet a whole gulf of difference lies between one occupation and the other. The whole social problem consists in making the workers pass from one to the other of these two occupational extremes.

What is required is that this world and the world beyond, in their double beauty, should be present and associated in the act of work, like the child about to be born in the making of the layette. Such an association can be achieved by a mode of presenting thoughts which relates them directly to the movements and operations peculiar to each sort of work, by a process of assimilation sufficiently complete to enable them to penetrate into the very substance of the individual being, and by a habit impressed upon the mind and connecting these thoughts with the work movements.

We are not, at present, either intellectually or spiritually capable of such a transformation. We should be doing well if we were able to set about preparing for it. Naturally, schools alone would not be enough. All sections of the community in which something resembling thought still operates would have to take part: the Churches, trade-unions, literary and scientific circles. One hardly dare mention in this category political circles.

Our age has its own particular mission, or vocation—the creation of a civilization founded upon the spiritual nature of work. The thoughts relating to a presentiment of this vocation, and which are scattered about in Rousseau, George Sand, Tolstoy, Proudhon and Marx, in papal encyclicals, and elsewhere, are the only original thoughts of our time, the only ones we haven't borrowed from the Greeks. It is because we have been unequal to this mighty business which was being conceived in us that we have thrown ourselves into the abyss presented by totalitarian systems. But if Germany is beaten, possibly our moral bankruptcy will not be final. Maybe we still have a chance. One cannot think about it without anguish. ... If, indeed, we have a chance, mediocre as we are, how shall we do so as not to miss it?

Such a vocation is the only thing great enough to put before the peoples instead of the totalitarian idol. If it is not put before them in such a way as to make them feel its grandeur, they will remain in the grip of the idol; only it will be painted red instead of brown. When men are offered the choice between guns and butter, although they prefer butter so very much more than guns, a mysterious fatality compels them, in spite of themselves, to choose guns. There isn't enough poetry about butter—at least, when you have some; for it does take on a certain poetry when you haven't any. But we dare not admit our preference for it.

At the present moment, the United Nations, particularly America, spend their time saying to the starving populations of Europe: With our guns, we're going to give you butter. This produces only one reaction, the thought that they don't seem to be in any particular hurry about it. The day they *are* given this butter, the people will literally throw themselves upon it; and immediately after that will turn towards whoever has some lovely guns, all nicely wrapped in their coverings, to show them, to no matter what ideology they may belong. Don't let us imagine that being worn out, all they will ask for is a comfortable existence. Nervous exhaustion caused by some recent misfortune makes it impossible for those concerned to settle down to enjoy a comfortable existence. It forces people to seek forgetfulness, sometimes in a dizzy round of exacerbated enjoyment—as was the case after 1918—at other times in some dark and dismal fanaticism. When misfortune bites too deeply, it creates a disposition towards misfortune, which makes people plunge headlong into it themselves, dragging others along with them. Germany is an example of this.

The unhappy peoples of the European continent are in need of greatness even more than of bread, and there are only two sorts of greatness: true greatness, which is of a spiritual order, and the old, old lie of world conquest. Conquest is an *ersatz* greatness.

The contemporary form of true greatness lies in a civilization founded upon the spirituality of work. It is a conception that can be propagated without running the risk of promoting the slightest discord. The word spirituality doesn't imply any particular affiliation. Even the Communists, in the present state of things, would probably not reject it. Besides, it would not be difficult to find in Marx quotations that can all be brought back to the reproach of a lack of spirituality levelled at capitalist society; which implies that there ought to be some in the new society. The conservative parties wouldn't dare to reject such a conception; nor would radical, laical or masonic circles either. Christians would seize on it with joy. It could create unanimity.

But one can only lay hold of such a conception in fear and trembling. How can we touch it without soiling it, turning it into a lie? Our age is so poisoned by lies that it converts everything it touches into a lie. And we are of our age, and have no reason to consider ourselves better than our age.

To bring discredit on words like these, by launching them among the general public without taking infinite precautions beforehand, would be to cause irreparable harm; it would amount to killing all remaining hope that the thing itself should ever materialize. They must not be attached to a cause or a movement, nor even to a régime, nor to a nation either. We must not do them the sort of harm Pétain has done to the words 'Work, Family, Country'*, nor the harm either which

* '*Work, Family, Country*': 'Travail, Famille, Patric' was the motto adopted by the Pétain Government on taking over power. [Translator.]

the Third Republic has done to the words 'Liberty, Equality, Fraternity'. They must not be made a slogan.

If they are presented to the public, it must be solely as the expression of a thought which reaches very far beyond the men and the societies of today, and which one proposes in all humility to keep ever before the mind as a guide in all things. If such modesty has less power to carry the masses with it than more ostentatious attitudes have, it cannot be helped. It is better to fail than succeed in doing harm.

But this thought would not have to be trumpeted about in order to permeate little by little people's minds, because it is an answer to the uneasy feelings of all people at the present time. Everybody is busy repeating, in slightly different terms, that what we suffer from is a lack of balance, due to a purely material development of technical science. This lack of balance can only be remedied by a spiritual development in the same sphere, that is, in the sphere of work.

The only difficulty lies in the painful mistrust—alas, only too well founded—of the masses, who look upon any slightly elevated proposition as a snare set to trap them.

A civilization based upon the spirituality of work would give to Man the very strongest possible roots in the wide universe, and would consequently be the opposite of that state in which we find ourselves now, characterized by an almost total uprootedness. Such a civilization is, therefore, by its very nature, the object to which we should aspire as the antidote to our sufferings.

UPROOTEDNESS AND NATIONHOOD

There is still another kind of uprootedness to be considered so as to be able to have a rough idea of our principal disease. It is the kind one might call geographical, that is to say, concerned with human collectivities occupying clearly defined territorial limits. The actual significance of these collectivities has wellnigh disappeared, except in one case only—that of the nation. But there are, and have been, very many other examples; some on a smaller, sometimes quite a small, scale, in the shape of a town, collection of villages, province or region; others comprising many different nations; and yet others comprising bits of many different nations.

The nation, single and separate, has taken the place of all that—the nation, or in other words, the State; for there is no other way of defining the word nation than as a territorial aggregate whose various parts recognize the authority of the same State. One may say that, in our age, money and the State have come to replace all other bonds of attachment.

For a long time now, the single nation has played the part which constitutes the supreme mission of society towards the individual human being, namely, maintaining throughout the present the links with the past and the future. In this sense, one may say that it is the only form of collectivity existing in the world at the present time. The family doesn't exist. What nowadays goes by that name is a minute collection of human beings grouped around each of us: father and mother, husband or wife, and children; brothers and sisters being already a little remote. Latterly, in the midst of the general distress, this little nucleus has developed an almost irresistible force of attraction, to the extent sometimes of making people cast aside every kind of duty; but that is because there alone people could find a little living warmth against the icy cold which all of a sudden had descended on them. It was an almost animal reaction.

But no one thinks nowadays about his ancestors who died fifty or even only twenty or ten years before his birth; nor about his descendants who will be born fifty or even only twenty or ten years after his death. Consequently, from the point of view of the collectivity and its particular function, the family no longer counts.

Looked at from this point of view, a profession doesn't count either. A corporation, or guild, was a link between the dead, the living and those yet unborn, within the framework of a certain specified occupation. There is nothing today which can be said to exist, however remotely, for the purpose of carrying out such a function. French trade-unionism, around 1900, may possibly have shown a certain tendency in this direction, but it never came to anything.

Finally, the village, district, province or region—all the geographical units smaller than the nation—have almost ceased to count; as have all geographical units composed of many nations or bits of many nations, too. When one used to say, for example, a few centuries ago, 'Christendom', the word had quite a different affective implication from that of the present-day 'Europe'.

To sum up, Man has placed his most valuable possession in the world of temporal affairs, namely, his continuity in time, beyond the limits set by human existence in either direction, entirely in the hands of the State. And yet it is just in this very period when the nation stands alone and supreme that we have witnessed its sudden and extraordinarily rapid decomposition. This has left us stunned, so that we find it extremely difficult to think clearly on the subject.

The French people, in June and July 1940, were not a people waylaid by a band of ruffians, whose country was suddenly snatched from them. They are a people who opened their hands and allowed their country to fall to the ground. Later on—but after a long interval—they spent themselves in ever more and more desperate efforts to pick it up again; but some one had placed his foot on it.

Now a national sense has returned. The words 'to die for France' have again taken on a meaning which they hadn't possessed since 1918. But in the movement of opposition which has seized hold of the French people, hunger, cold, the always hateful presence of foreign soldiers exercising complete authority, the breaking-up of families, for some exile, captivity—all these sufferings have at least played a very large part, most likely a decisive one. The best proof of this lies in the difference in spirit distinguishing the occupied from the unoccupied zone. Nature has not dispensed any greater amount of patriotic fervour to those living north than to those living south of the Loire. Different situations have simply produced different states of mind. The example set by England, hopes of a German defeat, have also been important contributory factors.

France's only reality today consists in memories and hopes. The Republic never seemed so beautiful as under the Empire; one's native land never seems so beautiful as when under the heel of a conqueror, if there is hope of seeing it again intact. That is why one shouldn't take the present intensity of national feeling for a guide as to its actual efficacy, once liberation has been effected, for ensuring the stability of public life.

The memory of the sudden dissolution of this feeling in June 1940 is one so charged with shame, that one prefers not to think about it, to rule it out altogether and only to think about how to set things to rights again for the future. In private life also, each of us is always tempted to set his own failings, to a certain extent, on one side, relegate them to some attic, invent some method of calculation whereby they turn out to be of no real consequence. To give way to this temptation is to ruin the soul; it is the one that, above all, has to be conquered.

We have all succumbed to this temptation, on account of the public shame which has been so deep that each one of us has felt wounded to the quick in his own feelings of personal honour. Without this temptation, reflections concerning so extraordinary an event would already have given rise to some new patriotic doctrine, some new patriotic conception.

From the social point of view, more especially, it will be impossible to avoid considering the notion of patriotism. Not considering it afresh, but considering it for the first time; for, unless I am mistaken, it never has been considered. Strange indeed, for a notion which has played and still plays so important a rôle, isn't it? That just shows what sort of a place we really accord to thought.

The idea of patriotism had lost all credit among French workmen during the last quarter of a century. The Communists put it into circulation again after 1934, to the accompaniment of plentiful tricolour flags and singing of the *Marseillaise*. But they hadn't the least compunction in withdrawing it and placing it on the shelf again a little before the war. It is not in the name of patriotism that they started setting up a resistance. They only began adopting it again about nine months after the defeat. Little by little they have adopted it entirely. But only simpletons would take that to mean a veritable reconciliation between the working-class and the country. Workmen are dying for their country—that is only too true. But we live in an age so impregnated with lies that even the virtue of blood voluntarily sacrificed is insufficient to put us back on the path of truth.

For very many years, workmen were taught that internationalism was the most sacred of all duties, and patriotism the most shameful of all *bourgeois* prejudices. Then more years were spent teaching them that patriotism was a sacred duty, and anything that wasn't patriotism a betrayal. How, at the end of all that, could they be expected to react otherwise than crudely and in obedience to propaganda?

A healthy working-class movement is out of the question, unless it be given a doctrine assigning a place to the idea of patriotism, and a clearly defined, that is, a limited, place. Moreover, this need is only more evident in working-class circles than elsewhere because the problem of patriotism has been so much discussed in them for so long. But it is a need common to the whole country. It is unpardonable that a word which nowadays is almost always to be found coupled with the word duty should hardly ever have been made the subject of any investigation. As a rule, all people can find to quote in connexion with it is a mediocre page of Renan's.

The nation is a recent innovation. In the Middle Ages, allegiance was owed to the lord, or the city, or both, and by extension to territorial areas not very clearly defined. The sentiment we call patriotism certainly existed, often to a very intense degree; only its object was not set within territorial limits. The sentiment covered variable extensions of land, according to circumstances.

Actually, patriotism has always existed, as far back as we can go in history. Vercingetorix really died for Gaul; the Spanish tribes which resisted conquest by the Romans, sometimes to the point of extermination, died for Spain, knowing they were doing so, and declaring it; those who died at Marathon and Salamis died for Greece; at a time when Greece, not having yet been reduced to a province, was in relation to Rome in the same position as Vichy France is to Germany, children in the Greek towns used openly to pelt collaborators with stones and call them traitors, with the same indignation which we feel today.

What had never existed right up to recent times was some definite, circumscribed thing, permanently installed as an object of patriotic devotion. Patriotism was something diffuse, nomadic, which expanded or contracted according to degrees of similarity and common danger. It was mixed up with different kinds of loyalty—loyalty to other men, a lord, a king, or a city. The whole formed something very complicated, but also very human. To express the sense of obligation every one feels towards his country, people would usually talk about 'the public' or 'the public good', an expression which can serve equally well to indicate a village, town, province, France, Christendom or Mankind.

People also talked about the kingdom of France. In the latter expression, the sense of obligation towards the country was mingled with that of fidelity to the king. But two obstacles have prevented this sentiment from ever being a pure one, not even in the time of Joan of Arc. It must be remembered that the population of Paris was against Joan of Arc.

The first obstacle was that, on the death of Charles V, France, to use Montesquieu's words, ceased to be a monarchy and fell into the state of despotism from which she only emerged in the eighteenth century. Nowadays, we find it so natural to pay taxes to the State, that we have difficulty in imagining the moral upheaval in the midst of which this custom was first introduced. In the fourteenth century, to pay any taxes other than exceptional levies acquiesced in for war purposes was looked upon as dishonourable, a disgrace reserved for conquered countries, and the manifest sign of slavery. The same feeling is found expressed in the Spanish *Romancero*, and also in Shakespeare: 'That England . . . hath made a shameful conquest of itself'.

Charles VI, during his minority, aided and abetted by his uncles, by using corruption and the vilest cruelty, brutally compelled the people of France to accept a perfectly arbitrary tax, renewable at will, which literally reduced the poor to starvation, whilst the noblemen frittered away the proceeds. It is for this reason that the English of Henry V's day were first of all welcomed as liberators, at a time when the Armagnacs represented the side of the rich and the Burgundians that of the poor.

The French people, brutally and at one fell swoop made to submit to the yoke, thereafter, right up to the eighteenth century, gave only spasmodic signs of independence. Throughout the whole of this period they were looked upon by other Europeans as the perfect example of an enslaved people, a people who could be treated like cattle by their sovereign.

But, meanwhile, there arose deep down in the heart of this people a suppressed hatred of the king—all the more bitter for remaining unexpressed—a traditional hatred never to be extinguished. One senses it already in a heartrending complaint by the peasants under Charles VI. It must have played a part in the mysterious popularity of the League in Paris. After Henry IV's assassination, a child of twelve was put to death for having publicly declared that he would do as much to the little Louis XIII. Richelieu began his career by a speech in which he called upon the clergy to proclaim that all regicides would be damned, giving as his reason the fact that those would protest, if they were able, at being subjected to the authority of the king of France. A Catalan historian of the same period, in telling the story of the Sicilian Vespers, writes: 'The French, who, wherever they exercise power, are as cruel as it is possible to be . . .'

The Bretons were in despair when their sovereign Anne was forced to marry the king of France. If these same Bretons could return today, or better have returned some years ago, would they find or have found very strong reasons for thinking they had been mistaken? However discredited the Breton autonomist movement may be by the type of people manipulating it and the sinister ends they pursue, there is no doubt that this propaganda stands for something real both in fact and in the minds of the population concerned. There are hidden treasures in these people which have never managed to see the light of day. French culture doesn't suit them; their own is unable to put forth shoots; hence they find themselves, as a people, relegated to the very bottom of the lower social strata. A large proportion of illiterate soldiers are Breton men, and, so it is said, a large proportion of Parisian prostitutes are Breton women. Autonomy would not be a remedy; but this doesn't mean that the disease doesn't exist.

Franche-Comté, which lived freely and happily under the very distant suzerainty of the Spanish, fought in the seventeenth century in order not to become French. The people of Strasburg wept when they saw the troops of Louis XIV entering their city in time of peace, without a previous declaration of any kind, through a violation of a solemn undertaking worthy of Hitler.

Paoli, the last Corsican hero, battled heroically to prevent his country from coming under French rule. There is a monument to his honour in a church in Florence; in France he is hardly remembered. Corsica is an example of the danger of infection involved in uprootedness. After having conquered, colonized, corrupted and debased the people of that island, we have now had to put up with them in the shape of prefects

of police, police narks, sergeant-majors, *pions**★* and other functions of a like nature, in pursuit of which they, in their turn,
have treated the French like a more or less conquered people.
They have also contributed towards giving France in the
minds of numerous natives belonging to the colonies a reputation for cruelty and brutality.

Although the kings of France are praised for having assimilated the countries they conquered, the truth is that they to a
large extent uprooted them. This is an easy method of
assimilation, within the reach of anybody. People who have
their culture taken away from them either carry on without
any at all, or else accept the odds and ends of the culture one
condescends to give them. In either event, they don't stand out
individually, so they appear to be assimilated. The real marvel
is to assimilate populations so that they preserve their culture,
though necessarily modified, as a living thing. It is a marvel
which very seldom takes place.

It is true that, under the *Ancien Régime*, the French showed
themselves to be intensely conscious of their French-ness in
all periods of particular splendour for France: in the thirteenth
century, when the whole of Europe flocked to the University
of Paris; in the sixteenth century, when the Renaissance,
already extinguished or not yet lighted elsewhere, had its
seat in France; in the early part of Louis XIV's reign, when
arms and letters enjoyed a dual prestige. It is none the less
certain that it was not the kings who welded together these
disparate territories. It was solely the Revolution.

Already during the eighteenth century there existed in
France, in very different ranks of society, alongside the grossest
forms of corruption, a bright, pure flame of patriotism. Take
for example the brilliantly gifted young peasant, brother of
Restif de la Bretonne, who was hardly more than a child
when he became a soldier out of pure love for the public weal,

★ *pions:* a slang term for supervisors or under-masters in secondary
schools. Used in a more general sense, it implies a coarse, narrow-minded,
aggressive type of person. [Translator.]

and was killed at the age of seventeen. But that was already the Revolution at work. People felt a presentiment of it, waited for it, longed for it, right throughout the century.

The Revolution melted all the peoples subject to the French Crown into one single mass, and that by their enthusiasm for national sovereignty. Those who had been Frenchmen by force, became so by free consent; many of those who were not French wanted to become so. For to be French, thenceforward, meant belonging to the sovereign nation. If all the peoples, everywhere, had become sovereign—as was hoped—none could take away from France the honour of having been the first to begin. Besides, frontiers no longer counted. Foreigners were only people who went on being the slaves of tyrants. Foreigners of a genuinely republican spirit were willingly accepted as honorary Frenchmen.

Thus, in France, there has been this paradox of a patriotism founded, not on love of the past, but on the most violent break with the country's past. And yet, the Revolution had a past in the more or less underground part of French history: everything connected with the freeing of the serfs, liberties of the towns, social struggles; the revolts in the fourteenth century, the beginnings of the Burgundian movement, the Fronde; and then writers like d'Aubigné, Théophile de Viau, Retz. Under François I, a project for creating a people's militia was set aside, because the noblemen objected that if it was put into operation the militiamen's grandsons would find themselves noblemen and their own grandsons serfs. So great was the dynamic force thrusting beneath the surface of this people.

But the influence of the *Encyclopédistes*, all of them uprooted intellectuals, all obsessed with the idea of progress, killed any chance of inspiration being sought in a revolutionary tradition. Besides, the prolonged terror under Louis XIV had left a gap difficult to bridge. It is because of this that, in spite of Montesquieu's efforts in a contrary sense, the liberating current of the eighteenth century found itself without historical roots: 1789 really was an open break.

The sentiment which then went by the name of patriotism was solely concerned with the present and the future. It was the love of the sovereign nation, based to a large extent on pride in belonging to it. The quality of being French seemed to be not so much a natural fact as a choice on the part of the will, like joining a party or church in our own day.

As for those who remained attached to the past history of France, their attachment took the form of a personal and dynastic fidelity to the king. They saw nothing wrong in looking to foreign kings to send them armed help. They were not traitors. They remained faithful to what they thought they owed faithfulness, exactly like the men who brought about the death of Louis XVI.

The only people at that time who were patriots, in the sense that word took on later, were those who appeared in the eyes of their contemporaries—and have since appeared in those of posterity—as arch-traitors; men like Talleyrand, who served, not, as has been said, every régime, but France behind every régime. But for such men France was neither the sovereign nation nor the king; it was the French State. Subsequent events have shown how right they were.

For, when the illusion of national sovereignty showed itself to be manifestly an illusion, it could no longer serve as an object of patriotism; on the other hand, kingship was like one of those severed plants one doesn't replant again. Patriotism had to change its meaning and turn itself towards the State. But thereby it straightway ceased to be popular. For the State was not something brought into being in 1789; it dated from the beginning of the seventeenth century, and shared some of the hatred nursed by the people against the monarchy. Thus it happened that, by an historical paradox which at first sight seems surprising, patriotism changed to a different social class and political camp. It had been on the Left; it went over to the Right.

The change-over was completed following upon the Commune and the inauguration of the Third Republic. The May massacre of 1871 was a blow from which, morally, French workmen have perhaps never recovered. And it is not so long ago as all that. A workman of fifty at the present time can well have listened to horrified accounts of it from the lips of his father, then a child. The nineteenth-century French army was a specific creation of the Revolution. Even soldiers in the service of the Bourbons, Louis-Philippe or Napoleon III must certainly have fired on the people very much against their own inclination. In 1871, for the first time since the Revolution, leaving out the brief interlude of 1848, France possessed a republican army. This same army, composed of decent young fellows from the French countryside, set about massacring workmen with an extraordinary display of sadistic pleasure. It was enough to produce a considerable shock.

The principal cause of this was doubtless the need of compensation for the disgrace of the defeat, that same need which led us a little later on to conquer the unfortunate Annamites. Everything points to the fact that, unless supernatural grace intervenes, there is no form of cruelty or depravity of which ordinary, decent people are not capable, once the corresponding psychological mechanisms have been set in motion.

The Third Republic was another shock. It is easy to believe in national sovereignty so long as wicked kings or emperors hold the nation in thrall; people think: if only they weren't there!... But when they *are* no longer there, when democracy has been installed and nevertheless the People is indubitably not sovereign, bewilderment is inevitable.

The year 1871 was the last year of that particular sort of French patriotism born in 1789. Frederick, the German Prince Imperial—afterwards Frederick II—a humane, reasonable and intelligent man, was very much surprised by the intensity of this patriotism, which he encountered everywhere throughout the course of the campaign. He couldn't understand why the Alsatians, hardly knowing a word of French, speaking a dialect closely allied to German, brutally conquered at a relatively recent date, refused to have anything to do with

Germany. He discovered that the motive for this was the pride felt in belonging to the country which had produced the French Revolution, to the sovereign nation. Their annexation, by separating them from France, doubtless helped them to preserve this state of mind, at any rate partially, right up to 1918.

The Paris Commune was not, to begin with, a social movement at all, but an outburst of patriotism and even of extreme chauvinism. All through the nineteenth century, moreover, the aggressive turn taken by French patriotism had alarmed the rest of Europe. The war of 1870 was the direct outcome of this; for though France had not made preparations for war, she had none the less declared it without any plausible reason. Dreams of imperial conquest had remained alive among the people right throughout the century. At the same time, toasts were drunk to world independence. Conquering the world and liberating the world are, in fact, two incompatible forms of glory, but which can be easily reconciled with one another in reverie.

All this bubbling-up of popular feeling died away after 1871. Two things, nevertheless, caused an appearance of patriotic continuity to be maintained. One was the resentment at being defeated. There was not yet at that time any real reason for bearing the Germans a grudge. They had not been the aggressors; they had pretty well refrained from committing atrocities; and it was not our place to reproach them with violating the rights of peoples in connexion with Alsace-Lorraine, whose population is largely Germanic, from the moment we began sending our first expeditions into Annam. But we bore them a grudge for having beaten us, just as though they had violated some divine, eternal, imprescriptible right to victory on the part of France.

In our present hatred of them, for which, unfortunately, there exist only too many legitimate reasons, this curious sentiment also plays its part. It was also one of the motives behind the action of certain collaborationists right at the beginning. If France found herself on the side of the vanquished, they thought, it could only be because of some faulty deal, some mistake, some misunderstanding; her natural place was on the side of the victors; therefore, the easiest, least arduous, least painful method of bringing about the indispensable rectification was to change sides. This state of mind was very prevalent in certain circles at Vichy in July 1940.

But what above all prevented French patriotism from disappearing altogether under the Third Republic, after losing nearly all its vital sap, was the fact that there was nothing else. The French had nothing except France to which to remain faithful; and when they abandoned her for a while, in June 1940, one saw how hideous and pitiful could be the spectacle of a people no longer attached by bonds of fidelity to anything whatever. That is why, later on, they once again clung on exclusively to France. But if the French People recovers its sovereignty—at least, what nowadays goes by that name—the same difficulty as before 1940 will reappear, namely, that the reality designated by the word France will be above all a State.

The State is a cold concern which cannot inspire love, but itself kills, suppresses everything that might be loved; so one is forced to love it, because there is nothing else. That is the moral torment to which all of us today are exposed.

Here lies perhaps the true cause of that phenomenon of the leader which has sprung up everywhere nowadays and surprises so many people. Just now, there is in all countries, in all movements, a man who is the personal magnet for all loyalties. Being compelled to embrace the cold, metallic surface of the State has made people, by contrast, hunger for something to love which is made of flesh and blood. This phenomenon shows no signs of disappearing, and, however disastrous the consequences have been so far, it may still have some very unpleasant surprises in store for us; for the art, so well known in Hollywood, of manufacturing stars out of any sort of human material, gives any sort of person the opportunity of presenting himself for the adoration of the masses.

Unless I am mistaken, the idea of making the State an object of loyalty appeared for the first time in France and in Europe with Richelieu. Before his time, people used to talk in religious-like tones about the public weal, the country, the king or the local lord. It was he who first adopted the principle that who-ever exercises a public function owes his entire loyalty, in the exercise of that function, not to the public, or to the king, but to the State and nothing else. It would be difficult to give an exact definition of the State. But it is, unfortunately, only too obvious that the word stands for something very real.

Richelieu, who possessed the intellectual clarity so common at that time, defined in luminous terms the difference between politics and morals, over which there has subsequently arisen so much confused thinking. Here is more or less what he said : We should beware of applying the same rules to the welfare of the State as to that of the soul; for the welfare of souls is attended to in the world above, whereas that of States is only attended to in this world.

That is cruelly exact. A Christian ought to be able to draw therefrom but one conclusion: that whereas to the welfare of the soul, or in other words to God, a total, absolute and unconditional loyalty is owed; the welfare of the State is a cause to which only a limited and conditional loyalty is owed.

But although Richelieu believed himself to be a Christian, and no doubt sincerely, his conclusion was a totally different one, namely, that a man responsible for the welfare of the State, and the men under him, must employ to this end all useful means, without any exception, and, if necessary, sacrifice thereto their own lives, their sovereign, their people, foreign countries, and any and every species of obligation.

It represents—but in a much nobler form—Maurras' doctrine: '*Politique d'abord*'. But Maurras, with perfect logic, is an atheist. The Cardinal, in postulating something whose whole reality is confined to this world as an absolute value, committed the sin of idolatry. Nor, in this connexion, is it metal, stone or wood which are really dangerous. The real sin of idolatry is always committed on behalf of something similar to the State. It was this sin which the devil wanted Christ to commit when he offered him the kingdoms of this world. Christ refused. Richelieu accepted. He had his reward. But he always believed himself to be acting solely out of devotion, and in a sense it was true.

His devotion to the State uprooted France. His policy was to kill systematically all spontaneous life in the country, so as to prevent anything whatsoever being able to oppose the State. If certain limits seem to have been set to his action in this sense, that is only because he was beginning and was astute enough to proceed gradually. All one needs to do is to read Corneille's dedicatory prefaces to realize to what vile depths of servility he had managed to reduce people's minds. Later on, to shield our national glory from shame, some people hit on the idea of saying that all this was merely the polite language of the time. But it's a lie. To convince oneself of the fact, all one has to do is to read what Théophile de Viau has written. Only, Théophile died prematurely as a result of an arbitrary imprisonment, whereas Corneille lived to a grand old age.

Literature is only useful to us here as a sign; but it is a sure sign. Corneille's servile language shows that Richelieu wanted to enslave people's very minds; not for his own benefit, for in his self-abnegation he was probably sincere, but for that of the State he represented. His conception of the State was already totalitarian. He applied it as much as he was able to by subjecting the country, to the full extent the means of the time allowed, to a police régime. He thus destroyed a considerable part of the moral life of the country. If France submitted herself to be gagged in this way, it is because the nobility had so laid her waste by nonsensical and atrociously cruel civil wars that she consented to buy civil peace at that price.

After the Fronde outburst, which in its beginnings, from many points of view, was a forerunner of 1789, Louis XIV set himself up in power far more in the spirit of a dictator than in that of a legitimate sovereign. That is what his phrase '*L'Etat, c'est moi*' indicates. It is not a kingly conception. Montesquieu has explained all this very clearly, in roundabout terms. But what he couldn't yet perceive in his time was that there have been two stages in the decline of the French monarchy. After Charles V, the monarchy degenerated into a personal despotism. But from Richelieu onwards, it was replaced by a State machine with totalitarian tendencies, which, as Marx points out, has not only outlasted all changes of régime, but has been strengthened and perfected by each succeeding change.

During the Fronde and under Mazarin, France, in spite of the general distress, was morally able to breathe. Louis XIV found her full of brilliant men of genius whom he recognized and encouraged. But at the same time he carried on, to a much higher degree of intensity, the policy of Richelieu. In this way he reduced France in a very short time to a desert from the moral point of view, not to mention one of fearful material poverty.

If one reads Saint-Simon, not as a literary and historical curiosity, but as a document dealing with the lives of human beings who actually lived, one is overcome with horror and disgust at such a turgid atmosphere of mortal *ennui*, such widespread spiritual, moral and intellectual baseness. La Bruyère, the letters of Liselotte—all the documents of the time, read in the same spirit, leave the same impression. Going back even a little further, one should certainly realize, for example, that Molière didn't write his *Misanthrope* just for fun.

Louis XIV's régime was really already totalitarian. The country was ravaged by terrorism and denunciation. The idolizing of the State in the person of the sovereign was organized with an impudence which was an outrage to all Christian consciences. The art of propaganda was already thoroughly understood, as is shown by that ingenuous admission by the chief of police to Liselotte regarding the orders received not to allow any book on any subject to appear which didn't contain an extravagant eulogy of the king.

Under this régime, uprootedness in the French provinces, the suppression of all local life, reached a far higher degree of intensity. The eighteenth century provided a lull. The operation whereby national sovereignty was substituted for royal sovereignty under the Revolution had only this drawback, the non-existence of national sovereignty. As in the case of Orlando's mare,* that was the only defect to be found. In point of fact, there existed no known means of creating something concrete corresponding to these words. Thenceforward, there remained only the State, which naturally reaped the benefit of the strong desire for unity—'unity or death'—which had developed around the belief in national sovereignty. Whence, further destruction in the sphere of local life. With the aid of war—war having been from the very start the mainspring of all this business—the State, under the Convention and the Empire, became ever more and more totalitarian.

Louis XIV had debased the Gallic Church by associating it with the cult of his own person and by imposing obedience on it even in matters of religion. This servile attitude of the Church towards the sovereign was very largely responsible for the anti-clericalism of the following century.

But when the Church committed the irreparable mistake of making common cause with the monarchy, it thereby cut itself off from the general life of the nation. Nothing was better able to serve the totalitarian designs of the State. The only result could be the laical system, prelude to that open adoration of the State as such which is now so much in favour.

Christians are defenceless against the laical spirit. For either they must throw themselves entirely into political action, party politics, to put temporal power back again into the hands of the clergy, or the supporters of the clergy; or else they must resign themselves to being irreligious, in their turn, in all that appertains to the secular side of their own lives,

* *Orlando's mare:* reference to Ariosto's *Orlando Furioso*. The mare in question possessed every quality except that she happened to be dead. [Translator.]

which is what usually happens today, to a far greater extent than those concerned realize themselves. In either case, they set aside the proper function of religion, which is to suffuse with its light all secular life, public or private, without ever in any way dominating it.

During the nineteenth century, the railways caused frightful havoc from the point of view of uprootedness. George Sand was still able to see in her native Berry customs which maybe went back for several thousand years, the very memory of which would have been entirely lost but for the hasty notes she took down concerning them.

Loss of the past, whether it be collectively or individually, is the supreme human tragedy, and we have thrown ours away just like a child picking off the petals of a rose. It is above all to avoid this loss that peoples will put up a desperate resistance to being conquered.

Now, the totalitarian phenomenon of the State arises through a conquest carried out by the public authorities of the people under their care, without being able to spare them the evils necessarily accompanying all conquests, in order to possess a better instrument for carrying out foreign conquest. This is what happened formerly in France and has happened more recently in Germany, not to mention Russia.

But the development of the State exhausts a country. The State eats away its moral substance, lives on it, fattens on it, until the day comes when no more nourishment can be drawn from it, and famine reduces it to a condition of lethargy. That was the condition France had reached. In Germany, on the other hand, the centralization of the State is quite a recent development, consequently there the State possesses all the aggressiveness supplied by a superabundance of food of high energizing content. As for Russia, popular life is so intensely strong there, that one wonders whether, in the end, it isn't the people that will devour the State, or rather re-absorb it.

The Third Republic, in France, was a very curious affair; one of its most curious features being that its entire structure,

outside the actual arena of parliamentary life, was derived from
the Empire. The love Frenchmen have for abstract logic makes
it very easy for them to be deceived by labels. The English
have a kingdom with a republican content; we had a republic
with an imperial content. Moreover, the Empire itself was
linked, over and beyond the Revolution, back in an unbroken
chain to the monarchy; not the ancient French monarchy, but
the totalitarian, police-ridden one of the seventeenth century.

The personality of Fouché is a symbol of this continuity.
The repressive apparatus of the French State continued on
throughout all changes without being troubled or interrupted,
with an ever-increasing power of action. That is why the
State, in France, remained a target for people's resentment,
hatred and aversion, which, in the past, had been aroused by
royal government turned tyrannical. We have actually lived
through this strange paradox, so strange that one couldn't even
be aware of it at the time: a democracy in which all public
institutions, and all things connected with them, were openly
hated and despised by the entire population.

No Frenchman had the slightest qualms about robbing or
cheating the State in the matter of customs, taxes, subsidies or
anything else. We must except certain ranks of civil servants;
but they formed part of the State machine. If the middle-
classes went much further than anybody else in the country
in dealings of this sort, it was solely because far more opportunities came their way. The police, in France, are held in such
profound contempt that many Frenchmen regard this attitude
as one necessarily built into the everlasting moral structure
of the respectable citizen. Guignol* forms part of genuine
French folk-lore, which goes back to the *Ancien Régime* and
has never grown out of date. The epithet '*policier*' constitutes

* *Guignol*: figure of popular French comedy. Dates from towards the end
of the eighteenth century. Originated in Lyons, like Punch in London.
Occupied in directing pointed sallies, though tinged with benevolence,
at humanity in general, and in verbally castigating the powers that be.
[Translator.]

in French one of the most scathing insults, and it would be interesting to know if exact equivalents exist in other languages.* But, of course, the police are really nothing other than the active instrument at the service of the authorities. The feelings of the French people with regard to this instrument have remained the same as they were in the days when peasants were obliged, as Rousseau noted, to conceal the fact that they had a piece of ham in the house.

Similarly, the whole series of political institutions were the object of disgust, derision and disdain. The very word politics had taken on a profoundly pejorative meaning incredible in a democracy. 'Oh, he's a politician,' 'all that, that's just politics': such phrases expressed final and complete condemnation. In the eyes of a number of French people, even the parliamentary profession itself—for it was a profession—had something ignominious about it. Some Frenchmen prided themselves on keeping away from all contact with what they termed '*la politique*', except on the day of the elections, or even on that day too; others looked upon their local deputy as a sort of servant, a being created and put into the world specially to serve their own private interests. The only feeling which tempered the contempt for public affairs was the party spirit, at any rate among such as had caught this disease.

One would seek in vain to find a single aspect of public life that was able to arouse in the French the remotest feelings of loyalty, gratitude or affection. In the heyday of laical enthusiasm, there had been public education; but for a long time now education has ceased to be anything, both in the eyes of parents and children alike, except a machine for producing diplomas, in other words, jobs. As to items of social legislation, never had the French people, to the extent to which their appetite in that direction was satisfied, regarded them as other than concessions extorted from niggardly authorities as a direct result of bringing violent pressure to bear.

* Epithet '*policier*': translator's note in answer to implied query by author of book: Not in English, at any rate.

No other interest replaced the one lacking for public affairs. Each successive régime having destroyed at an ever-increasing rate local and regional life, it had finally ceased to exist. France was like a dying man whose members are already cold, and whose heart alone goes on beating. Hardly anywhere was there any real throb of life except in Paris; but even there, as soon as you reached the suburbs, an atmosphere of moral decay began to make itself felt.

In those outwardly peaceful days before the war, the *ennui* of the little French provincial towns constituted perhaps as real a form of cruelty as that of more visible atrocities. Isn't it as cruel to condemn human beings to spend those unique, irreplaceable years between the cradle and the grave in a dismal atmosphere of *ennui*, as to have them starved or massacred? It was Richelieu who started throwing this pall of *ennui* over France, and since his time the atmosphere has only grown stuffier and stuffier. When war broke out, a state of asphyxiation had been reached.

If the State has morally killed everything, territorially speaking, smaller than itself, it has also turned territorial frontiers into prison walls to lock up people's thoughts. As soon as one examines history a little closely, and outside of the ordinary manuals, one is amazed to see to what extent certain periods almost without material means of communication surpassed ours in the wealth, variety, fertility and vitality of their exchanges of thought over the very widest expanses. That is the case with the Middle Ages, pre-Roman antiquity, the period immediately preceding historical times. In our day, with our wireless, aeroplanes, latest developments in transport of all kinds, printing and the press, the modern phenomenon of the nation keeps shut up in separate little compartments even so naturally universal a thing as Science. Frontiers, of course, are not impassable; but just as they subject the traveller to an unending series of irritating and laborious formalities, so in the same way all contact with foreign ways of thinking, in no matter what sphere, demands a mental effort in order to get across the frontier. The effort required is considerable, and quite a number of people are not prepared to make it. Even in the case of those who do, the fact that such an effort *has* to be made prevents the formation of organic links across the frontiers.

It is true that there are international Churches and parties. But as for the Churches, they offer us the supreme scandal of clergy and faithful asking God at the same time, with the same rites, the same words, and it must be supposed, an equal amount of faith and purity of heart, to grant a military victory to one or other of two warring camps. This shocking spectacle has been going on for a long time; but in our century religious life has been subordinated to that of the nation as never before. And as for parties, their internationalism is either a pure fiction, or else it takes the form of a total subserviency to one particular nation.

Lastly, the State has also broken all the bonds which could, outside the sphere of public life, provide a goal for the exercise of loyalty. Much as the French Revolution did, by suppressing the trades-corporations, to encourage technical progress, morally speaking it created a corresponding amount of evil, or at any rate finally sealed an evil already partly accomplished. It cannot be too often repeated that nowadays, whenever people refer to such organizations, in no matter what circles, the last thing they have in mind is anything resembling the old trades-corporations.

Once the trades-corporations had disappeared, labour became, in the individual lives of men, a means whose corresponding end was money. There is somewhere in the Charter of the League of Nations a sentence declaring that henceforth labour shall no longer be regarded as a commodity. It was a joke in the worst possible taste. We live in an age when a host of worthy people, who judge themselves to be very far removed from what Lévy-Bruhl called the pre-logical mentality, have believed in the magical efficacy of words far more than any savage from the depths of Australia ever did. When you take some indispensable commercial product off the market, you have to arrange for it to be distributed in some other way. Nothing of the kind was attempted in connexion with labour, which, naturally, has continued being a commodity.

Hence, professional loyalty becomes merely a form of commercial honesty. In a society founded on exchange, the heaviest form of social reprobation falls on robbery and swindling, and especially swindling by a dealer who sells poor quality goods guaranteeing them all the time to be first-class. Accordingly, when one sells one's labour, honesty demands that one should furnish goods of a quality corresponding to the price paid. But honesty is not the same as loyalty. A wide distance separates these two virtues.

A strong current of loyalty flows through working-class association, which was for a long time the dominant impulse behind trade-union activity. But several obstacles have prevented this loyalty from forming a solid buttress to moral life. On the one hand, the commercial side of social life has penetrated into the working-class movement, by wage questions being given first place; and the more questions of money dominate, the quicker the spirit of loyalty disappears. On the other hand, to the extent to which the working-class movement is a revolutionary one, it has escaped from this drawback, but has acquired the weaknesses inherent in all forms of rebellion.

Richelieu, some of whose observations are so extraordinarily lucid, declares having learnt from experience that, all other things being equal, rebels are always half as strong as the defenders of official power. Even if people think they are upholding a good cause, the feeling that they are in rebellion weakens them. Without some psychological mechanism of this sort, there could be no stability about human societies. This mechanism explains the firm hold obtained by the Communist Party. Revolutionary workmen are only too thankful to have a State at the back of them—a State which gives an official character, legitimacy and reality to their actions that only a State can confer, and which at the same time is situated too far away from them, geographically, to be able to disgust them. In just the same way, the *Encyclopédistes*, feeling deeply uncomfortable at finding themselves in conflict with their own ruler, showed desperate anxiety to obtain the favour of the rulers of Prussia and Russia. One can also understand, making use of this analogy, why more or less revolutionary workmen who had resisted the attraction of Russian prestige were not able to prevent themselves succumbing to the German variety.

Apart from those who have given themselves entirely to the Communist Party, workmen cannot find in loyalty towards their own class a sufficiently concrete, sufficiently clearly defined aim to satisfy their need of inner stability. Few notions are so vague as that of social class. Marx, who built up the whole of his system upon it, never attempted to define it, nor even simply to investigate it. The only information to be extracted from his works on the subject of social classes is that they are things which engage in strife. That is not enough. Besides, it is not one of those notions which, without being able to be defined in words, are clear to the mind. It is even harder to conceive it or feel it without some definition than it is to define it.

The loyalty implicit in adherence to some religious form also counts little enough—strange though this may be—in modern life. In spite of great and obvious differences, a result which is in a sense analogous is produced by the English system of a national Church and the French system of the separation of Churches and State. Only the latter seems the more destructive.

Religion has been proclaimed a private affair. According to present-day habits of mind, this doesn't mean that it resides in the secret places of the soul, in that inner sanctuary where even the individual conscience doesn't penetrate. It means that it is a matter of choice, opinion, taste, almost of caprice, something like the choice of a political party, or even that of a tie; or else that it is a matter to do with one's family, education, personal surroundings. Having become a private concern, it has lost the obligatory character associated with public manifestations, and consequently can no longer lay claim to loyalty unchallenged.

A number of revealing remarks show that this is so. How often, for instance, we hear the following commonplace repeated: 'Whether Catholics, Protestants, Jews or Free-Thinkers, we're all Frenchmen,' exactly as though it were a question of small territorial fragments of the country, as who should say: 'Whether from Marseilles, Lyons or Paris, we're all Frenchmen.' In a document promulgated by the Pope, one may read: 'Not only from the Christian point of view; but, more generally, from the human point of view . . .', as though the Christian point of view—which either has no meaning at all, or else claims to encompass everything in this world and the next—possessed a smaller degree of generality than the human point of view. It is impossible to conceive a more terrible admission of religious bankruptcy. That is how the *anathema sit* have to be paid for. To sum up, religion, degraded to the rank of a private matter, reduces itself to the choice of a place in which to spend an hour or two every Sunday morning.

What is comical about the situation is that religion, that is to say, Man's relationship to God, is not nowadays regarded as too sacred a matter to be interfered with by any outside authority, but is placed among the things which the State leaves to each one's own particular fancy, as being of small importance from the point of view of public affairs. At least, that has been the case in the recent past, and that is the contemporary meaning attached to the word ' tolerance'.

Thus there exists nothing, apart from the State, to which loyalty can cling; which is why up to 1940 loyalty had not been withdrawn from it. For men feel that there is something hideous about a human existence devoid of loyalty. Amidst the general debasement of all words in the French vocabulary which have anything to do with moral concepts, the words *traître* and *trahison* have lost none of their forcefulness. Men feel also that they are born for sacrifice; and the only form of sacrifice remaining in the public imagination was military sacrifice, that is, a sacrifice offered to the State.

Indeed, all that was left was the State. The ideal of the Nation, in the sense in which the men of 1789 or 1792 understood the word, which then used to bring tears of joy to people's eyes—all that belonged irremediably to the past. Even the word nation had changed its meaning. In our day, it no longer denotes the sovereign people, but the sum total of peoples recognizing the authority of the same State; it is the political structure created by a State and the country under its control. When one talks about national sovereignty nowadays, all it really means is the sovereignty of the State. A conversation between a contemporary of ours and a man of 1792 would lead to some highly comic misunderstandings. For not only is the State in question not the sovereign people, but it is the very self-same inhuman, brutal, bureaucratic, police-ridden State bequeathed by Richelieu to Louis XIV, by Louis XIV to the Convention, by the Convention to the Empire, and by the Empire to the Third Republic. And what is more, it is instinctively recognized and hated as such.

Thus we have witnessed this strange spectacle—a State, the object of hatred, repugnance, derision, disdain and fear, which, under the name of *patrie*, demanded absolute loyalty, total self-abnegation, the supreme sacrifice, and obtained them, from 1914 to 1918, to an extent which surpassed all expectations. It set itself up as an absolute value in this world, that is, as an object of idolatry; and it was accepted and served as such, honoured with the sacrifice of an appalling number of human lives. A loveless idolatry—what could be more monstrous, more heartrending?

When anybody goes much further in his devotion than his heart prompts him to do, a violent reaction, a sort of revulsion of feeling sets in later on inevitably. This is frequently observable in families where an invalid requires things to be done for him which exceed the affection he inspires. His relatives harbour a resentment which is suppressed as too unworthy to admit, but which is ever-present, like some secret poison.

That is exactly what happened between Frenchmen and France, after 1918. They had given too much to France, more than they had it in them to give to her.

All the flow of anti-patriotic, pacifist and internationalist ideas after 1918 claimed to be in the name of those killed in the war and the veterans; and in the case of the latter, a good deal of it really had its source among themselves. There were also, it is true, extremely patriotic veterans' associations. But the expression of their patriotism had a hollow ring, and was lacking altogether in persuasive force. It reminded one of the language of people who, having suffered too much, continually feel the need to remind themselves that they haven't suffered in vain. For too high a degree of suffering in relation to what the heart prompts can produce one or other of two attitudes: either the violent rejection of the object to which too much has been sacrificed, or else the clinging to it in a sort of despair.

Nothing did more harm to patriotism than the reminder, repeated *ad nauseam*, of the part played by the police behind the battle front. Nothing was more calculated to wound the susceptibilities of Frenchmen, by pointing out to them, standing behind their country, that police-ridden State, the traditional object of their hatred. At the same time, extracts from the sensational press during the war years, read over again later on quite calmly and with appropriate feelings of disgust, and connected up with the rôle of the police, left them with the impression that they had been hoaxed. There is nothing that a Frenchman is less able to forgive. Since the very words which expressed patriotic feeling had become discredited, the feeling itself became relegated, in a sense, to the category of feelings one is ashamed to talk about. There was a time, not so long ago either, when to have expressed patriotic sentiments in working-class circles—at least, in some of them—would have seemed to those present like a breach of propriety.

All the evidence points to the fact that the most courageous soldiers in 1940 were veterans of the previous war. One can only conclude that their post-1918 reactions had a deeper influence over the minds of their children than over their own. This is a very frequent phenomenon and quite easy to understand. Those who were eighteen in 1914 had had their characters formed in the years preceding the war.

It has been said that the schools at the beginning of the century had formed a generation for victory, and that those after 1918 turned out a beaten one. There is undoubtedly a lot of truth in this. Still, the schoolmasters from 1918 onwards were mostly veterans, and very many children who reached the age of ten between 1920 and 1930 must have had such men as teachers.

If the effect of this reaction was felt in France more than in other countries, this was because of a far more acute form of uprootedness there, resulting from a far older and more intense form of State centralization, the demoralizing effects of victory, and the complete licence allowed in the field of propaganda.

The balance was also upset in regard to the notion of patriotism, but compensated in an inverse sense, this compensation taking place in the realm of pure speculation. Owing to the fact that the State had remained, in the midst of a total void, the only reality entitled to demand of Man his loyalty and sacrifice, the notion of patriotism presented itself to the mind as an absolute value. The country was beyond good and evil. It is what is expressed in the English saying: 'Right or wrong, my country'.* But people often go farther. They refuse to admit that their country can ever be wrong.

However small the inclination of men of all classes may be for making an effort of critical examination, a patent absurdity, even if they refuse it conscious recognition, throws them into

---

* '*Right or wrong, my country*': as in text. [Translator.]

a state of uneasiness which weakens the spirit. In reality, nothing is more mixed up with ordinary, daily human affairs than philosophy, but it is an implied philosophy.

To posit one's country as an absolute value that cannot be defiled by evil is manifestly absurd. Country is merely another name for nation; and the nation is a self-contained unit composed of various territorial areas and peoples assembled together as a result of historical events in which chance has played a great part, so far as human intelligence is able to judge, and where good and evil are always mingled with one another. The nation is a fact, and a fact is not an absolute value. It is just one fact amongst other similar facts. More than one nation exists on the earth's surface. Ours is certainly unique. But each of the others, considered by itself and with affection, is unique in the same degree.

It was the fashion before 1940 to talk about 'eternal France'. Such words are a sort of blasphemy. One is compelled to say the same about the moving pages which have been written by great French Catholic writers on the vocation of France, the eternal salvation of France and other similar themes. Richelieu showed a much clearer perception when he said that the salvation of States was only brought about in this world. France is something which is temporal, terrestrial. Unless I am mistaken, it has never been suggested that Christ died to save nations. The idea of a nation being chosen by God for itself simply belongs to the old Mosaic law.

So-called pagan antiquity would never have blundered into so gross a confusion. The Romans regarded themselves as specially chosen, but solely for world dominion. They were not concerned with the next world. Nowhere does it appear that any city, or people, should have thought itself chosen for a supernatural destiny. The Mysteries which represented, to a certain extent, the official road to salvation, as the Churches do today, were local institutions, but recognized as being on an equal footing among themselves. Plato describes how Man, assisted by the power of grace, passes out of the cavern of this world; but he doesn't say that a whole city can pass out of it. On the contrary, he depicts the collectivity as something animal, which hinders the soul's salvation.

Antiquity is often accused of having only been able to recognize collective values. In fact, this mistake was only made by the Romans, who were atheists, and by the Hebrews; and in the latter case, only up to the time of the Babylonian exile. But if it is wrong to attribute this mistake to pre-Christian antiquity, it is also wrong not to recognize that we are continually committing it ourselves, corrupted as we are by the dual Roman-Hebrew tradition, which all too often carries the day with us as against pure Christian inspiration.

Christians today find it awkward to have to recognize that, if the word patriotism is used in its strongest possible sense, its complete sense, a Christian has only one country that can be the object of such patriotism, and which is situated outside this world. For he has but one *Patros*, who lives outside this world. 'Lay up for yourselves treasures in heaven ... for where your treasure is, there will your heart be also.' It is therefore forbidden to have one's heart on this earth.

Christians today don't like raising the question of the respective rights over their heart enjoyed by God and their country. The German bishops ended one of their most courageous protests by saying that they refused ever to have to make a choice between God and Germany. And why did they refuse to do this ? Circumstances can always arise which make it necessary to choose between God and no matter what earthly object, and the choice must never be in doubt. But the French bishops would not have expressed themselves any differently. Joan of Arc's popularity during the past quarter of a century was not an altogether healthy business; it was a convenient way of forgetting that there is a difference between France and God. Yet this lack of inward courage to challenge the accepted notion of patriotism didn't make for greater energy in patriotic performance. Joan of Arc's statue was occupying a prominent place in every church throughout the country, all through those terrible days when Frenchmen abandoned France to her fate.

'If any man come to me, and hate not his father and mother, and wife, and children, and brethren, and sisters, yea, and his own life also, he cannot be my disciple.' If it is commanded to hate all that, using the word 'hate' in a certain sense, it is certainly forbidden also to love one's country, using the word 'love' in a certain sense. For the proper object of love is good-ness, and 'God alone is good'.

Such facts are self-evident, but, by some magic spell or other, go altogether unrecognized in our age. Otherwise it would have been impossible for a man like Father de Foucauld—who, out of charity, had chosen to bear witness to Christ among non-Christian populations—to consider that he had the right at the same time to supply the *Deuxième Bureau* with informa-tion on the subject of these same populations.

It would be salutary for us to ponder the devil's terrible words with reference to the kingdoms of this world, as he showed them all to Christ: 'All this power . . . is delivered unto me . . .'. Not a single kingdom is excepted.

What didn't shock the Christians shocked the workmen. A tradition still sufficiently recent so as not to be quite dead, makes the love of justice the central inspiration behind the French working-class movement. During the first half of the nineteenth century it was a passionate love, which took the side of the oppressed all over the world.

As long as the People constituted as a sovereign nation were synonymous with the Country, no problem arose concerning their relationship to justice. For it was agreed—quite arbitrarily, and on the flimsiest interpretation of the *Contrat Social*—that a sovereign nation doesn't commit acts of injustice towards either its members or its neighbours; it being supposed that the causes making for injustice were all bound up with the non-existence of the sovereign nation.

But as soon as, behind the country, there stands the old State, justice is far away. In the modern form of patriotism, justice hasn't much of a part to play, and above all nothing is said which might encourage any relationship between patriotism and justice to be drawn. One dare not assert that there is an equivalence between the two conceptions; one wouldn't dare, in particular, make such an assertion before a gathering of workmen, who, beneath their social oppression, feel the State's cold, metallic touch, and realize in a confused sort of way that the same cold touch must prevail in international relations. When a lot is talked about patriotism, little is heard about justice; and the sense of justice is so strong amongst workmen, even if they are materialists, owing to the fact that they are always under the impression they are being deprived of it, that any form of moral education in which justice hardly figures cannot possibly exercise any hold over them. When they die for France, they always need to feel that at the same time they are dying for something very much greater, taking part in the universal struggle against injustice. For them, to use a now famous expression, patriotism is not enough.

The same thing applies wherever a flame, a spark, however indistinct, of truly spiritual life burns. By its light, patriotism is not enough. And for those in whom this light is absent, patriotism, in its highest aspects, is far too exalted; it can then only constitute a sufficiently strong incentive in the form of the blindest national fanaticism.

It is true that men are capable of dividing their minds into compartments, in each of which an idea lives a sort of life of its own, undisturbed by other ideas. They don't care for either critical or synthetical effort, and won't submit to making either, unless obliged.

But in situations of fear, anguish, when the flesh draws back before the prospect of death, or too great a degree of suffering or danger, in the mind of every man, even if he is completely uneducated, a manufacturer of arguments suddenly stands forth, who elaborates proofs to demonstrate why it is legitimate and right to avoid that particular death, suffering or danger. Such proofs can be either good or bad, depending on the particular case. At all events, at the time, the body's disturbed condition gives them an intensity of persuasive force that no orator has ever succeeded in acquiring.

There are people to whom things do not happen in this way. That is either because their natures protect them from fear, that their flesh, blood and bowels remain unaffected by the presence of death or suffering; or else because their minds have attained such a degree of unity that this manufacturer of arguments has no opportunity of getting to work in them. With others, again, he is able to get to work, and makes his arguments felt, but they are scorned nevertheless. That in itself presupposes either an already high degree of inward unity, or else powerful outward incentives.

Hitler's profound remark on the subject of propaganda, namely that brute force is unable to prevail over ideas if it is alone, but that it easily manages to do so by taking unto itself a few ideas of no matter how base a nature, provides also the key to the inner life. The tumults of the flesh, however violent they may be, cannot prevail over a thought in the mind, if they act alone. But their victory is an easy one if they communicate their persuasive force to some other thought, however inferior it may be. That is the important point. No thought is of too inferior a quality for this rôle of ally of the flesh. But the flesh needs thought of some kind as an ally.

That is why, whereas in normal times people—even cultured ones—live, without the slightest inconvenience, with the most colossal inward contradictions, in times of supreme crisis the least flaw in the realm of consciousness acquires the same importance as if the most lucid of philosophers were at hand, maliciously ready to take advantage of the fact; and this happens to everybody, however ignorant he or she may be.

In times of greatest stress, which are not necessarily those of greatest danger, but those when Man finds himself, in face of the tumult raging in his flesh and blood and bowels, alone and bereft of all outward support, those whose inward lives depend entirely on one idea are the only ones capable of resisting. Which is why totalitarian systems form men able to withstand anything.

Patriotism can only become a single idea of this sort in a régime of the Hitlerian type. This could easily be proved, in detail, but it isn't worth while since the evidence is so overwhelming. If patriotism is not such an idea, and yet, all the same, has a part to play, then either there must exist disorder in the inward consciousness, and some hidden weakness of the spirit, or else there must be some other idea, dominating all the rest, and in relation to which patriotism has a perfectly clearly recognized rôle, but a limited and subordinate one.

This latter was not the case under the Third Republic—not in any class of society. What there was everywhere was moral incoherence; which is why a pet argument manufacturer was busy in everybody's mind between 1914 and 1918. Most people resisted by making a supreme effort, thanks to that sort of reaction which often encourages men to rush blindly, through fear of bringing dishonour upon themselves, to the opposite extreme to that to which fear urges them. But when the mind is exposed to danger and suffering as a result of obeying this impulse alone, it quickly becomes worn out. The agonized arguments which were unable to bring their influence to bear on personal conduct, go gnawing away all the more surely in the very depths of the mind, and make their influence felt retrospectively. That is what happened after 1918. And those who had not made any sacrifice and were ashamed of it were very quick, for other reasons, to catch the infection. In such an atmosphere were children brought up who, a little later on, were to be asked to go out and die.

One can realize how far this inward disintegration had proceeded with the French, when one reflects that even today* the idea of collaboration with the enemy is not entirely out

* *even today* . . . : written in 1943. [Translator.]

of favour. On the other hand, if encouragement is sought in the spectacle of the Resistance, if one tells oneself that the resisters find no difficulty at all in deriving inspiration from patriotism and from a host of other motives, one must at the same time go on reminding oneself that France, as a nation, finds herself at the moment on the side of justice, the general good and things of that kind, that is to say, among the beautiful things which don't exist. The allied victory will take her out of this category, and put her back into the realm of facts; many difficulties which seemed to be disposed of will reappear. In a sense, affliction simplifies everything. The fact that France entered along the path of resistance more slowly, later than most of the other occupied countries, shows that it would be a mistake to be without apprehensions as to the future.

One can see clearly to what a point of moral incoherence our régime had attained if one considers the schools. Moral philosophy forms part of the curriculum, and even those teachers who didn't care to make it the subject of dogmatic teaching, taught it inevitably in a diffuse sort of way. And the central conception of morals is justice and the obligations it imposes towards one's neighbour.

But when it is a question of history, morals ceases to play any part. The question is never raised as to France's obligations abroad. Sometimes she is referred to as being just and generous, as though that were something supererogatory, a feather in her cap, a crown to her glory. The conquests she has made and then allowed to slip from her grasp can, perhaps, be regarded with a certain doubt, like those of Napoleon; but never the ones she has managed to hold on to. The past is nothing else but the story of France's growth, and it is considered that this growth must necessarily be a good thing from every point of view. No one ever asks himself whether in the course of her growth she hasn't brought about destruction. To look into the possibility of her having at some time or another destroyed things which were worth as much as she would seem the most appalling blasphemy. Bernanos says that the people of *Action Française** look upon France as a prime baby who has only to grow and put on flesh to satisfy his parents' every wish. But there are others besides them. It is the general opinion which, without ever being expressed, is always implied in the way in which the country's past history is regarded. And, besides, the comparison with a baby is too flattering. The living things that are only asked to put on flesh are rabbits, pigs and chickens. Plato found the right expression when he compared the collectivity to an animal. And those who are blinded by its prestige, which means every one except for a few predestined individuals, 'call just and beautiful the things that are necessary, being incapable of discerning and teaching what a distance separates the essence of what is necessary from the essence of what is good'.

Everything is done to make children feel—not that they don't feel it naturally—that things concerning the country, the nation, the nation's growth have a degree of importance which sets them apart from other things. And it is precisely in regard to those things that justice, consideration for others, strict obligations assigning limits to ambitions and appetites—all that moral teaching one is trying to instil into the lives of little boys—never get mentioned.

What conclusion is there to be drawn other than that morals are among the number of less important things, which, like religion, a trade, the choice of a doctor or a grocer, belong to the lower plane of private life?

But with morals, properly speaking, thus relegated to a lower plane, no other system is advanced as a substitute. For the superior prestige of the nation is bound up with the exaltation of war. It furnishes no motives for action in peace-time, except in a régime which constitutes a permanent preparation for war, like the Nazi régime. Save in such a régime

---

* *the people of 'Action Française'*: militant royalists, convinced that the salvation of France depended on the overthrow of the Republic and its replacement by a monarchy, if necessary by violence. See also note p. 101. [Translator.]

as the latter, it would be dangerous to remind people too much that this country of theirs which asks its children to lay down their lives has a reverse side—the State, with its taxes, customs, police. This is carefully avoided, and so it never occurs to anybody that to hate the police or defraud the customs and income-tax authorities is to display a lack of patriotism. A country like England forms to a certain extent an exception, on account of a centuries-old tradition of liberty guaranteed by the authorities. Thus, this dual system or morals, in time of peace, weakens the power of the unchanging moral law, without putting anything in its place.

This duality is present at all time, everywhere, and not only in the schools. For nearly every day, in normal times, when a Frenchman reads the paper, discusses things at home or in the local *bistrot*, he is moved to think for France, in the name of France. From that moment, and until he enters again into his own private self, he loses even all recollection of the virtues which, in a more or less vague and abstract way, he recognizes it is his personal duty to practise. When it is a question of one-self, and even of one's family, it is a more or less recognized thing that one mustn't be too boastful; that one must beware of one's judgments when one is at the same time judge and prosecutor; that one must ask oneself whether opposition on the part of others may not be at least partly justified; that one mustn't try to occupy the whole stage, or think solely of oneself; in short, that limits must be set to egoism and pride. But when it comes to national egoism, national pride, not only is the field unlimited, but the highest possible degree of it seems to be imposed by something closely resembling an obligation. Regard for others, recognition of one's own faults, modesty, the voluntary limitation of one's desires—all are now turned into so many crimes, so many sacrileges. Among several sublime sentiments which the Egyptian *Book of the Dead* puts into the mouth of the just man after death, perhaps the most moving is the following: 'I have never turned a deaf ear to just and true words'. But in international affairs, every one regards it as a sacred duty to turn a deaf ear to just and true words, if they go contrary to the interests of France. Or else, do we admit that words contrary to the interests of France can never be just and true ones? That would come to exactly the same thing.

There are certain errors of taste which good breeding, in the absence of morality, prevents people from falling into in private life, and which seem perfectly natural on a national scale. Even the most odious of patronesses would hesitate to assemble together all their protégés to remind them of the huge benefits they had received and of the corresponding gratitude they owed in return. But a French Governor of Indo-China doesn't hesitate, in the name of France, to talk in that fashion, even immediately after the most atrocious acts of repression or the most scandalous famines; and he expects to hear himself echoed, and, indeed, insists upon it.

This is a custom inherited from the Romans. They never committed any acts of cruelty, never granted any favours, without boasting in each case of their generosity and clemency. No one was ever received in audience, no matter what the subject might be, even a simple alleviation of some terrible form of oppression, without first beginning by the familiar catalogue of praise. In this way they brought dishonour upon entreaty, which before then had been an honourable act, by burdening it with lies and flattery. In the *Iliad*, you never find a Trojan on his knees before a Greek and imploring for his life, putting the remotest trace of flattery in his words.

Our patriotism comes straight from the Romans. That is why French children are encouraged to seek inspiration for it in Corneille. It is a pagan virtue, if these two words are compatible. The word pagan, when applied to Rome, really possesses the significance charged with horror which the early Christian controversialists gave it. The Romans really were an atheistic and idolatrous people; not idolatrous with regard to images made of stone or bronze, but idolatrous with regard to themselves. It is this idolatry of self which they have bequeathed to us in the form of patriotism.

This duality in the moral sphere is a far more appalling scandal if, instead of lay morality, one thinks of the Christian virtues, of which lay morality is in any case simply an edition for general public use, a diluted solution. The essential fact about the Christian virtues, what lends them a special savour of their own, is humility—the freely accepted movement towards the bottom. It is through this that the saints resemble Christ. 'Who, being in the form of God, thought it not robbery to be equal with God.... He humbled himself.... Though he were a Son, yet learned he obedience by the things which he suffered.'*

But when a Frenchman thinks about France, pride, for him, is a duty, according to present notions; humility would be a betrayal. It is this betrayal which is perhaps what the Vichy Government is most bitterly reproached with. People are right in that, for its humility is of a debased kind; it is that of the slave who cringes and lies to avoid receiving blows. But in matters of this sort, a humility of a really high order is something unknown to us. We cannot even conceive such a thing possible. In order merely to be able to conceive it, we should have to make a special effort of the imagination.

In the soul of a Christian, the presence of the pagan virtue of patriotism acts as a dissolvent. We received it from the hands of Rome without giving it baptism. It is strange to reflect that the barbarians, or those who were so named, were baptized almost without any difficulty at the time of the invasions; but the heritage of ancient Rome never was, no doubt because it was impossible for it to be, and that in spite of the fact that the Roman Empire turned Christianity into a State religion.

It would be difficult, moreover, to imagine a more cruel

* '... *which he suffered*': reference: Philippians ii, 6 and 8, and Hebrews v, 8. [Translator.]

injury. As for the barbarians, it is not surprising that the Goths accepted Christianity without difficulty, if, as their contemporaries thought, they were of the same blood as those Getae, the noblest of the Thracians, whom Herodotus calls immortalizers because of their intense faith in eternal life. The barbarian heritage became mingled with the Christian spirit to form that unique, inimitable, perfectly homogeneous product known as chivalry. But between the spirit of Rome and that of Christ there has never been any fusion. If fusion had been possible, the Apocalypse would have lied in representing Rome as the woman seated on the beast, the woman full of the names of blasphemy.

The Renaissance was first of all a resurrection of the Greek spirit and then of the Roman spirit. It is only in this second stage that it acted as a dissolvent of Christianity. It is in the course of this second stage that there came into being the modern form of nationality, the modern form of patriotism. Corneille was right to dedicate his *Horace* to Richelieu, and to do so in terms whose baseness provides a suitable accompaniment to the almost delirious pride which permeates this tragedy. Such baseness and such pride are inseparable: we see that well enough in Germany today. Corneille himself is an excellent example of the sort of asphyxia which seizes Christian morality when it comes into contact with the Roman spirit. His *Polyeucte* would seem to us comical if habit had not blinded us. Polyeucte, according to his version, is a man who suddenly realizes that there is a far more glorious kingdom to conquer than any of a terrestrial kind, and that a particular technique exists for doing so. He immediately feels obliged to set out on this conquest, without giving a thought to anything else, and in the same frame of mind as when he used formerly to wage war in the service of the Emperor. Alexander wept, we are told, because he had only the terrestrial globe to conquer. Corneille apparently thought Christ had come down to earth to make up for this deficiency.

If patriotism acts invisibly as a dissolvent of morality,

whether Christian or lay, in time of peace, the contrary takes place in wartime; and this is perfectly natural. Where there is a moral duality, it is always the morality the actual circumstances require that suffers injury. The line of least resistance naturally gives the advantage to the type of morality which, in point of fact, there is no need to exercise: a war morality in peacetime, a peace morality in wartime.

In peacetime, justice and truth, because of the water-tight compartment separating them individually from patriotism, are degraded to the rank of purely private virtues, such as for example politeness; but when the country demands the supreme sacrifice, this very separation deprives patriotism of that total validity which alone can call forth a total effort.

When one has got into the habit of considering as an absolute good, free of any shadow of doubt, this growth in the course of which France devoured and digested so many lands, is it surprising that propaganda inspired by precisely the same idea, and only substituting the name of Europe in place of that of France, should be able to penetrate into a corner of the mind? Present-day patriotism consists in an equation between absolute good and a collectivity corresponding to a given territorial area, namely France; any one who changes in his mind the territorial term of the equation, and substitutes for it a smaller term, such as Brittany, or a larger term, such as Europe, is looked upon as a traitor. Why? It is all perfectly arbitrary. Habit makes it impossible for us to realize how exceedingly arbitrary it is. But at a time of supreme crisis, this arbitrary notion offers a hold to the manufacturer of sophistries inside us.

The present collaborators* have as regards the new Europe which a German victory would create the same attitude the inhabitants of Provence, Brittany, Alsace and Franche-Comté are expected to have towards the past, so far as the conquest of their country by the king of France is concerned. Why should the difference between these two historical periods

* *The present collaborators . . . :* written in 1943. [Translator.]

change what is good and what is bad? Between 1918 and 1919 one would frequently hear worthy people who looked forward to peace argue as follows: 'Formerly, provinces used to go to war with one another, then they became united and formed themselves into nations. In the same way the nations are going to unite in each continent, then throughout the whole world, and that will be the end of all war'. It was a very widely held platitude, and derived from that type of reasoning by extrapolation which exercised such an influence in the nineteenth century and was carried over into the twentieth. The good people who talked thus had a general idea of the history of France, but they didn't pause to think, when they were speaking, that the national unity had been brought about almost exclusively by the most brutal conquests. Yet if they did remember this in 1939, they must also have remembered that those conquests had always seemed to them a good thing. Is it surprising, therefore, that with a part at least of their mind they should have thought: 'For the purposes of progress and the fulfilment of History, it may be we have to pass through this experience'? They can well have said to themselves: 'France was victorious in 1918; she was unable to bring about European unity. Now Germany is trying to do so; we mustn't interfere with her'. The cruelties accompanying the German system ought, it is true, to have stopped them. But they may either not have heard anything about them, or supposed them to have been invented by a lying propaganda, or regarded them as of little importance, because the victims were peoples of inferior category. Is it not just as easy to be ignorant of the cruelties of the Germans towards the Jews or the Czechs as it is of those of the French towards the Annamites?

Péguy used to say: Blessed are they who die in a just war. It must follow that those who kill them unjustly are cursed. If it is true that the French soldiers of 1914 died in a just war, then it must certainly also be true, to at least the same extent, for Vercingetorix. If one thinks thus, what must one's feelings be towards the man who kept him chained up in a dungeon, in complete darkness, for six years, and then offered him as a public spectacle to the Romans before finally cutting his throat? But Péguy was a fervent admirer of the Roman Empire. If one admires the Roman Empire, why be angry with Germany which is trying to reconstitute it on a vaster scale by the use of almost identical methods? This didn't stop Péguy from going to his death in 1914. But it is this contradiction, though unformulated, unrecognized, which stopped a good many young men in 1940 from facing the enemy fire in the same spirit as Péguy.

Either conquest is always an evil thing, or it is always a good thing, or again it is sometimes a good, sometimes an evil thing. In this last case, a criterion is needed for judging. To suggest as a criterion that conquest is a good thing when it increases the power of the nation to which one belongs by the accident of birth, an evil thing when it diminishes this power, is something so entirely contrary to reason that it can only be acceptable to people who, of their own accord and once and for all, have banished reason altogether, as is the case with Germany. But Germany is able to do this, because she lives by a romantic tradition. France is not, because her attachment to reason forms part of the national heritage. A certain proportion of Frenchmen may well declare themselves hostile towards Christianity ; but, before as after 1789, all movements in the realm of ideas which have taken place in France have claimed to be based on reason. It is impossible for France to set aside reason in the name of patriotism.

That is why France feels uncomfortable in her patriotism, in spite of the fact that it was she who, in the eighteenth century, invented the modern form of patriotism. It must not be imagined that what has been called the universal vocation of France renders a conciliation between patriotism and universal values easier for Frenchmen than for other people. It is, indeed, the contrary which is true. It is more difficult for Frenchmen, because they are unable completely to succeed in either suppressing the second term of the contradiction, or separating the two terms by a water-tight compartment. They find this contradiction within their own patriotism. But because of this they are as it were obliged to invent a new sort of patriotism. If they do so, they will be fulfilling what has been up to a point, in the past, the function of France, namely, to think out what it is the world requires. The world requires at the present time a new patriotism. And it is now that this inventive effort must be made, just when patriotism is something which is causing bloodshed. We mustn't wait until it has become once more just a subject for conversation in drawing-rooms, learned societies and open-air cafés.

It is easy to say, with Lamartine: '*Ma patrie est partout où rayonne la France . . . La vérité, c'est mon pays.*' Unfortunately, this would only make sense if France and truth were synonymous. France sometimes resorts to lying and committing injustice; this has happened, is happening and will happen again. For France is not God, not by a long chalk. Christ alone was able to say: 'I am the truth'. No one else on this earth has the right to say that, whether speaking as an individual or in the name of a collectivity, but with far less reason still in the latter case. For it is possible for a man to attain such a degree of holiness that it is no longer he who lives, but Christ in him. Whereas there is no such thing as an holy nation.

There was once a nation which believed itself to be holy, with the direst consequences for its well-being; and in connexion with this, it is strange indeed to reflect that the Pharisees were the resisters in this nation, and the publicans the collaborators, and then to remind oneself what were Christ's relations with each of these two national groups.

This would seem to oblige us to consider that our resistance would be a spiritually dangerous, even a spiritually harmful, position, if amidst the motives which inspire it we did not manage to restrain the patriotic motive within the necessary bounds. It is precisely this danger which, in the extremely clumsy phraseology of our time, is meant by those who, sincerely or not, say they are afraid this movement may turn into something Fascist; for Fascism is always intimately connected with a certain variety of patriotic feeling.

France's vocation in the universe cannot, unless we lie to ourselves, be recalled with unmixed pride. If we lie to ourselves, we betray it in the very words with which we seek to recall it; if we remind ourselves of the truth, shame should always temper our pride, for every historical example of it which is offered to us has its embarrassing side. In the thirteenth century, France was a centre of inspiration for the whole of Christendom. Yet it was, nevertheless, at the beginning of this century that she utterly destroyed, south of the Loire, a budding civilization which already shone with a remarkable splendour; and it was in the course of this military operation, and in co-operation with the military power, that the Inquisition first became established. That is certainly an ineradicable blot on her reputation. The thirteenth century was the one in which Gothic replaced Romanesque, polyphonic music the Gregorian chant, and, in theology, constructions derived from Aristotle replaced Platonic sources of inspiration, hence one is at liberty to doubt whether French influence in this century amounted to any real progress. In the seventeenth century, once more, France shed her light over Europe. But the military prestige connected with this spiritual radiance was obtained by methods which any lover of justice is ashamed to mention; besides, just in the same degree as the French classical conception produced marvellous works in the French language, so was its influence destructive in other countries. In 1789, the hopes of all peoples were centred on France. But three years later she started going to war, and from her earliest victories onwards, her liberating expeditions became transformed into conquering ones. Without England, Russia and Spain to oppose her, she would have imposed on Europe a unity perhaps hardly less stifling than the one Germany is seeking to impose today. In the latter half of the last century, when people began to realize that Europe was not the whole world, and that there were quite a few continents on this planet, France was again seized with the desire to play a universal rôle. But all she managed to do was to carve out for herself a colonial empire copied from the British model, and in the hearts of not a few coloured peoples her name is now linked with feelings which it is unbearable to have to think about.

Thus the contradiction inherent in French patriotism is visible also throughout the whole of French history. It must not be concluded from this that just because France has gone on living so long with this contradiction, she can go on doing so indefinitely. In the first place, once one has recognized a contradiction, it is disgraceful to put up with it. Then, as a matter of brute fact, France very nearly died from a crisis in French patriotism. Everything leads one to suppose that she *would* have died from it, but for the fact that British patriotism was, fortunately, made of sterner stuff. But we cannot transfer the latter over to France. It is our own kind we have to remake. It is waiting to be remade. It is again showing signs of life because German soldiers on French soil are the very best propaganda agents for French patriotism; only they won't always be there.

A terrible responsibility rests with us. For it is nothing less than a question of refashioning the soul of the country, and the temptation is so strong to do this by resorting to lies or half-lies that it requires more than ordinary heroism to remain faithful to the truth.

The patriotic crisis took on a double aspect. In political parlance, one might say that there was both a Leftist and a Rightist crisis.

On the Right, amongst the younger middle-class generation, the break between patriotism and morals had, in conjunction with other causes, completely discredited all morality; but the prestige of patriotism was scarcely any greater. The attitude of mind expressed in the phrase '*Politique d'abord*' had spread considerably further than the actual influence of Maurras. The phrase was, of course, absurd; for politics are simply a technique, a specialized method of procedure. It is as if one were to say: 'Mechanics first'. The question which immediately poses itself is this: 'Politics for what?' Richelieu would answer: 'For the greater glory of the State'. And why for this purpose and not for some other one? To this question, no answer is forthcoming.

That is the question which mustn't be asked. So-called realist politics, handed down from Richelieu to Maurras, not without being seriously impaired on the way, only make sense if this question is not put. A simple condition exists for it not to be. When the beggar said to Talleyrand: 'Milord, I've got to live somehow', Talleyrand replied: 'I don't see that that is necessary'. But the beggar himself saw the necessity for it all right. In just the same way, Louis XIV saw well enough how necessary it was that the State should be served with blind devotion, because the State was, in fact, himself. Richelieu only looked upon himself as being the State's servant No. 1; all the same, in a sense he possessed it, and for that reason identified himself with it. Richelieu's political attitude only makes sense for those who, whether individually or collectively, feel either that they are masters of their country or else capable of becoming so.

The younger middle-class generation could no longer, from 1924 onwards, have the feeling that France was their domain. The working-classes made far too much noise for that. Besides which, it suffered from that mysterious exhaustion that swept over France after 1918, the causes of which were no doubt largely physical. Whether the fault is attributable to alcoholism, the nervous condition of the parents at the time their children were born and during their upbringing, or some other factor, the fact remains that for a long time now French youth has shown every indication of fatigue. German youth, even in 1932, when the authorities were doing nothing for them, gave evidence of an incomparably greater vitality, in spite of the very hard and long-drawn-out privations they had been through.

This fatigue prevented the middle-class youth in France from feeling in a condition to impose themselves on the country. Hence, to the question: 'Politics for what?' the necessary answer was: 'For the purpose of being placed in power in this country by other people'—that is to say, people from abroad, foreigners. There was nothing in the moral code of these young people to stop them having such a desire. The shock they received in 1936 only sharpened this desire in them to an irreparably acute degree. Nobody had done them any harm; but they had received a nasty fright, been made to eat humble pie, and, what was an unpardonable crime in their eyes, precisely by those whom they regarded as their social inferiors. In 1937, the Italian press quoted an article from a French students' review in which a French girl expressed the hope that, surrounded as he was by innumerable cares of State, Mussolini would somehow find time to come and restore order in France.

Whatever antipathy we may feel towards people of this class, however criminal their subsequent attitude may have been, they are human creatures, and unhappy human creatures too. The problem in their case presents itself in these terms: how to reconcile them with France without delivering her into their hands?

On the Left, that is to say, above all among the workmen and the intellectuals who lean in their direction, there are two absolutely distinct currents of opinion, although occasionally, but by no means necessarily, the two currents are found in the same person. One of these is the current emanating from French working-class tradition, which can clearly be traced back to the eighteenth century, when so many workmen read Jean-Jacques Rousseau, but which maybe has underground connexions linking it up with the first movements on behalf of communal freedom. Those who are influenced by this current alone, devote themselves entirely to the thought of justice. Unfortunately, nowadays, such a thing is rare enough among the workmen and extremely rare among the intellectuals.

There are people of this sort to be found in all so-called Leftist groups—Christian, trade-unionist, anarchist, socialist, and particularly among Communist workmen, for Communist propaganda talks a lot about justice. In this it carries out the teachings of Lenin and Marx, strange as this may seem to those who have not studied all the ins and outs of the doctrine.

These men all feel profoundly internationalist in time of peace, for they know that justice recognizes no national boundaries. They often feel the same even in wartime, so long as their country escapes being defeated. But their country's defeat immediately causes a pure, steady flame of patriotism to light up in the depths of their consciousness. Men like this will be permanently reconciled with their country if they are offered a type of patriotism subordinated to the cause of justice.

The other current is a retort to the middle-class attitude. Marxism, by offering to the working-class the supposedly scientific certainty that they will shortly become the lords and masters of the terrestrial globe, has created a working-class imperialism very similar to the nationalist imperialisms. Russia has provided, as it were, the experimental proof of this, and furthermore she is being relied upon to undertake the most arduous part of the action which is to result in the overthrow of established institutions.

For people who are morally exiled and in the position of immigrants, in contact above all with the repressive side of the State, and who for generations have found themselves on the border line of those social categories which provide fair game for the police, and are themselves treated as such each time the State swings over towards reaction, this offers an irresistible temptation. A huge, powerful, sovereign State, governing a territory much vaster than that of their own country, says to them: 'I am yours, I am your possession, your property. I exist only to serve you, and before long I will make you the undisputed masters in your own country'.

On their side, to refuse such a friendly offer would be just about as easy as to refuse a cup of water when you haven't had anything to drink for two days. Some, who made a terrific effort of self-control in order to do this, so exhausted themselves in the process that they immediately succumbed to the first exercise of pressure on the part of Germany. Many of the others are only resisting in appearance, and in reality are simply standing on one side, for fear of the risks which action necessarily brings in its train once a formal engagement has been entered into. Such people, whether numerous or otherwise, can never make up a force.

The U.S.S.R., outside Russia, is really the spiritual home of the working-class, their 'country'. In order to realize this, all one had to do was to watch the French workmen's eyes as they gathered round the newspaper stalls and scanned the headlines announcing the first big Russian reverses. It was not the thought of the repercussions these defeats might have on Franco-German relations which filled their eyes with despair, for British reverses never affected them in this way. They felt they were threatened with the loss of more than France. They felt rather in the same way as the early Christians would have felt if some one had supplied them with material proofs showing Christ's resurrection to have been a fiction. In a general way, there is no doubt quite a lot of resemblance between the state of mind of the early Christians and that of many Communist workmen. The latter, too, are looking forward to some approaching Day of Judgment which shall establish absolute righteousness at one single stroke and for-ever on this earth, and at the same time their own glory. Martyrdom came easier to the early Christians than to those of succeeding centuries, and infinitely easier than to Christ's immediate disciples, who, at the moment of supreme crisis, were unable to face it. So today, sacrifice is easier for a Communist than for a Christian.

Since the U.S.S.R. is a State, patriotic feeling for it is subject to the same contradictions as is patriotic feeling anywhere. But it doesn't result in the same weakening. Quite the reverse. The presence of a contradiction, when it is felt, even in a dull sort of way, wears down the feelings; when it isn't felt at all, the feelings are thereby intensified, since they derive benefit at the same time from incompatible motives. Thus the U.S.S.R. has all the prestige attaching to a State, and to that cold brutality which permeates the politics of a State, especially a totalitarian one; while at the same time it has all the prestige attaching to a champion of justice. If the contradiction is not felt, this is partly because of its remoteness, partly because it promises absolute power to all who faithfully love it. Such an expectation doesn't diminish the need for justice, but renders it a blind one. As each of us considers himself sufficiently capable of practising justice, each of us naturally thinks that a system under which he wielded power would be a reasonably just one. This is the temptation Christ underwent at the hands of the devil. Men are continually succumbing to it.

Although these workmen, animated by working-class imperialism, are very different from young middle-class Fascists, and make up a finer variety of humanity, the problem they pose is a similar one. How are they to be made to love their country sufficiently, without handing it over to them? For it can't be handed over to them, nor can they be given a privileged position in it; this would be a crying injustice towards the rest of the population, and more especially the peasants.

The present attitude of these workmen towards Germany must not blind us to the gravity of the problem. Germany happens to be the enemy of the U.S.S.R. Before she became so, agitation was already rife amongst them, it being a vital necessity for the Communist Party always to maintain agitation; and it took the form of agitation 'against German Fascism and British Imperialism'. France didn't appear in the picture at all. Furthermore, throughout a whole year which was a decisive one, from the summer of 1939 to the summer of 1940, Communist influence in France was entirely directed against the country. It will not be an easy thing to induce these workmen to turn their hearts towards their country.

Among the rest of the population, the crisis in the matter of patriotism has not been so acute; it hasn't gone so far as a renunciation in favour of something different; there has merely been a sort of melting away. In the case of the peasants, this was no doubt due to the fact that they felt they were of no account in the country, except in the shape of cannon fodder to serve interests which were alien to theirs; in that of the *petits bourgeois*, it must have been above all due to *ennui*.

To all such individual causes of want of patriotism there was added a very general cause which forms as it were the reverse side of idolatry. The State had ceased to be, under the title of nation or country, something infinitely valuable in the sense of something valuable enough to be served with devotion. On the other hand, it had become in everybody's eyes of unlimited value as something to be exploited. The quality of absoluteness which is bound up with idolatry remained with it, once the idolatry had ceased, and assumed this new aspect. The State appeared like an inexhaustible horn of plenty, pouring out its treasures in direct proportion to the pressure put upon it. So people always had a grudge against it for not providing more. Whatever it didn't supply seemed to be as a result of a deliberate refusal on its part. When it made demands, such insistence appeared paradoxical. When it imposed its will, this became at once an intolerable act of coercion. People's attitude towards the State was that of children, not towards their parents, but towards adults who are neither loved nor feared; children always demanding something and never wanting to obey.

How could people be expected to pass straightway from

such an attitude to that of unlimited devotion demanded by war? For even after war had begun, the French believed that the State had victory tucked away somewhere in a safe place, side by side with other treasures which it wasn't going to give itself the trouble to bring out. Everything was done to encourage this idea, as a slogan of the time testifies: 'We shall win because we're the stronger'.

Victory is going to liberate a country in which every one will have been almost exclusively occupied in disobeying, from either good or bad motives. People will have listened-in to London, read and distributed forbidden literature, travelled without a permit, hidden away supplies of corn, worked as badly as possible, done some blackmarketing, and will have boasted about all this to their friends and relations. How are people going to be made to understand that all this is finished, that henceforward they have to obey?

People will also have spent these years dreaming about eating their fill. Such dreams are the kind indulged in by beggars, in the sense that all one thinks about is receiving plenty of good things without giving anything in return. In point of fact, the authorities will have to guarantee proper distribution; how are we then to avoid this cheeky beggar's attitude, which already before the war was that of the public towards the State, becoming infinitely more accentuated? And if this attitude is adopted towards a foreign country, America for example, the danger becomes very much more serious still.

Another dream, and a very widespread one, is to kill; to kill invoking the highest possible motives, but in an underhand way and without any risk. Whether the State breaks up under the pressure of this diffused terrorism, as is to be feared, or whether it attempts to control it, in either case the repressive and police-ridden aspect of the State, which traditionally is so hated and despised in France, will occupy the forefront.

The government which arises in France after the liberation of the country will have to face a triple danger caused by this blood lust, this mendicity complex and this inability to obey.

As for a remedy, there is only one: to give French people something to love; and, in the first place, to give them France to love; to conceive the reality corresponding to the name of France in such a way that as she actually is, in her very truth, she can be loved with the whole heart.

The essence of the contradiction inherent in patriotism is that one's country is something limited whose demands are unlimited. In times of extreme peril, it demands everything. Why should one accord everything to something which is limited? On the other hand, not to be resolved to give it everything in case of need is to abandon it entirely, for its preservation cannot be assured at any lesser price. So one always seems to be either on the debit or the credit side of what is due to it, and if one remains too long on the credit side, one swings later on with all the greater force back on to the debit side, through a process of reaction.

The contradiction is only one in appearance. Or, to be more precise, it is a real one, but when thoroughly examined is seen to be one of those basic contradictions belonging to our human condition, which must be recognized, accepted and used as a footboard for hoisting oneself above what is simply human. Never in this world can there be any dimensional equality between an obligation and its subject. The obligation is something infinite, the subject of it is not. This contradiction presses down upon the daily lives of all men, without exception, including those who would be quite incapable of formulating it even confusedly in words. All the devices men have thought they had discovered for avoiding it have turned out to be lies.

One of them consists in only being prepared to recognize obligations towards what is not of this world. One variety of this particular device is spurious mysticism, spurious contemplation. Another is the practice of good works carried out in a certain spirit, 'for the love of God', as they say, the unfortunate objects of compassion being but the raw material for the action, an anonymous means whereby one's love of God can be manifested. In either case there is a lie, for 'he who loveth not his brother whom he hath seen, how should he love God whom he hath not seen?' It is only through things and individual beings on this earth that human love can penetrate to that which lies beyond.

Another device consists in admitting that there are on this earth one or more objects enshrining this absolute value, this infinitude, this perfection which are essentially bound up with the obligation as such. That is the lie propagated by idolatry.

The third device consists in denying any sort of obligation. You cannot prove this by a mathematical demonstration to be an error, for obligation belongs to an order of certainty very superior to that of formal proof. Actually, such a negation is impossible. It amounts to spiritual suicide. And Man is so made that in him spiritual death is accompanied by psychological diseases in themselves fatal. So that, in fact, the instinct of self-preservation prevents the soul from doing more than draw closer to such a state; and even so it is seized with a *taedium vitae* which turns it into a desert. Almost always, or rather, almost certainly always, he who denies all obligations lies to others and to himself; in actual fact, he recognizes some amongst them. There isn't a man on earth who doesn't at times pronounce an opinion on good and evil, even if it be only to find fault with somebody else.

We have to accept the situation provided for us, and which subjects us to absolute obligations in regard to things that are relative, limited and imperfect. So as to be able to discern what these things are and the form in which their demands upon us are likely to be made, we need only to see clearly what their actual relationship is to goodness.

So far as our country is concerned, the conceptions of rootedness, of vital medium, suffice in this connexion. They have no need to be established by documentary proof, for of late years they have been verified experimentally. Just as there are certain culture-beds for certain microscopic animals, certain types of soil for certain plants, so there is a certain part of the soul in every one and certain ways of thought and action communicated from one person to another which can only exist in a national setting, and disappear when a country is destroyed.

Today every Frenchman knows what it was he missed as soon as France fell. He knows it as well as he knows what is missing when one is forced to go hungry. He knows that one part of his soul sticks so closely to France, that when France is taken away it remains stuck to her, like the skin does to some burning object, and is thus pulled off. There is something, then, to which a part of every Frenchman's soul sticks, and is the same for all, unique, real though impalpable, and real in the sense of something one is able to touch. Hence, what threatens France with destruction—and in certain circumstances an invasion is a threat of destruction—is equivalent to a threat of physical mutilation for all Frenchmen, and for their children and grandchildren, and for their descendants to the end of time. For there are peoples which have never recovered after having once been conquered.

That is sufficient for the obligation owed to one's country to impose itself as something self-evident. It co-exists with other obligations. It does not require that we should give everything always; but that we should give everything sometimes. Just as a miner has sometimes to give everything, when an accident happens in the mine and his companions are in danger of death. It is an accepted, a recognized thing. The obligation owed to one's country is every bit as clear, once the country is actually felt as something real and tangible—as it is being felt today. All Frenchmen have come to feel the reality of France through being deprived of her.

People have never ventured to deny the obligation towards one's country otherwise than by denying the reality of the country. Extreme pacifism of the type advocated by Gandhi is not a denial of this obligation, but a particular method for discharging it. This method has never yet been applied, so far as we know; it has certainly not been applied by Gandhi, who is far too much of a realist. If it had been applied in

France, the French would not have used any armed force to resist the invader; but they would never have been prepared to do anything, of any kind, which might assist the army of occupation; they would have done everything possible to hinder it, and they would have persisted indefinitely, inflexibly in that attitude. It is clear that, in so doing, far greater numbers would have perished, and in far more frightful circumstances. This would be an imitation of Christ's passion realized on a national scale.

If there were any nation, in the aggregate, sufficiently close to perfection for one to be able to suggest to it that it should imitate Christ's passion, such a thing would certainly be well worth doing. As a nation it would disappear; but this disappearance would be worth infinitely more than the most glorious survival. However, it isn't that way these things are done. Most likely, almost certainly, they cannot be done that way. It can only be given to the individual soul, in its most secret manifestations, to follow the path leading to such perfection.

At the same time, if there are men whose vocation it is to bear witness to this unattainable perfection, the authorities are in duty bound not to obstruct them, and, in fact, to give them every assistance. In England, conscientious objectors are recognized.

But that is not enough. For men like these, we should go to the trouble of inventing something which, without constituting any direct or indirect participation in strategic operations, would involve being present in some way at the actual scene of war, and present in a much more arduous and more perilous fashion than is demanded of the soldiers themselves.

That is the unique remedy for the inconveniences arising out of pacifist propaganda. For that would make it possible, without being unjust, to bring discredit on those who, while professing an out-and-out pacifism, or what amounts to the same, refused to stand up for their principles in this way. Pacifism is only capable of causing harm when a confusion arises between two sorts of aversion: the aversion to kill, and the aversion to be killed. The former is honourable, but very weak; the latter, almost impossible to acknowledge, but very strong. When mixed together, they supply a motive force of extraordinary power, which is not restrained by any feeling of shame, and where the latter sort of aversion is alone operative. French pacifists of recent years had an aversion to being killed, but none to killing; otherwise they would not have rushed so hastily, in July 1940, to collaborate with Germany. The very few who were amongst them out of a real aversion to killing were sadly deceived.

By separating these two aversions, we eliminate all danger. The influence of the aversion to kill is not dangerous; in the first place, it is a good influence, for it has its origin in goodness; secondly, it is weak, and, unfortunately, there is no chance that it should ever be otherwise. As for those whom the fear of death renders weak, they should be treated with compassion, for every human being, unless he has been turned into a fanatic, is, at any rate at times, liable to this weakness; but if they turn their weakness into a doctrine to be propagated, that is criminal, and it is then necessary, and not difficult, to discredit them.

In defining one's native country as a certain particular vital medium, one avoids the contradictions and lies which corrode the idea of patriotism. There is one's own particular vital medium; but there are others besides. It has been produced by a network of causes in which good and evil, justice and injustice have been mixed up together, and so it cannot be the best possible one. It may have arisen at the expense of some other combination richer in vital properties, and if such has been the case, it would be right to regret the fact; but past events are over and done with; the particular medium happens to be in existence, and, such as it is, deserves to be guarded like a treasure for the good it contains.

The peoples conquered by the soldiers of the king of France in many cases suffered a wrong. But so many organic ties have grown up in the course of centuries that a surgical operation would but add a further wrong to the wrong already done. It is only possible partially to repair the past, and this can only be done through a recognized local and regional life receiving the unreserved encouragement of the authorities within the setting of the French nation. Moreover, the disappearance of the French nation, far from repairing in the slightest bit the wrong resulting from past conquest, would aggravate it in a far more serious manner. Admitting that certain peoples underwent, a few centuries ago, a loss of vitality as a result of French aggression, they would be altogether morally destroyed by a further wound brought about by German aggression. In this sense only is the commonplace true, according to which no incompatibility exists between the love for one's native heath and that for one's native land. For in this way a man from Toulouse can passionately regret the fact that his city should some centuries ago have become French; that so many marvellous Romanesque churches should have been destroyed to make way for a second-rate imported Gothic; that the Inquisition should have cut short a spiritual blossoming there; and can still more passionately vow never to permit that this same city of his should ever become German.

The same thing applies to relations with foreign countries. If one's native land is regarded as a vital medium, there is no need for it to be protected from foreign influences, save only in so far as that may be necessary for it to be able to remain such, that is to say, not in any rigorous fashion. The State could cease to be the absolute ruler by divine right over the territories under its control; and a reasonable and limited authority over these territories exercised by international organizations dealing with essential problems whose scope is an international one would cease to wear the appearance of a crime of *lèse-majesté*. Nuclei could also be established for the free circulation of ideas, on a vaster scale than France and incorporating France, or connecting certain bits of French territory with certain bits of non-French territory. For instance, wouldn't it be a natural thing for Brittany, Wales, Cornwall and Ireland to feel themselves, in regard to certain things, to be parts of the same environment?

But once again, the more attachment one shows for such non-national nuclei, the more one will want to preserve the national liberty; for this sort of intercourse over frontier boundaries doesn't exist for enslaved peoples. That is why the cultural exchanges between Mediterranean countries were incomparably greater and more vital before than after the Roman conquest; whereas all these countries, when reduced to the unfortunate state of provinces, fell into a dull uniformity. Exchange is only possible where each one preserves his own genius, and that is not possible without liberty.

In a general way, if the existence of a great number of life-giving nuclei is recognized, one's own particular country only constituting one among them, nevertheless, should the latter be threatened with annihilation, all the obligations implied by loyalty towards all these separate nuclei unite in the single obligation to go to the assistance of one's country. For the members of a population which is enslaved to a foreign State are deprived of all these nuclei at once, and not merely of the national nucleus. Thus, when a nation finds itself in peril to this extent, the military obligation becomes the unique way of expressing all one's loyalties in this world. This is true even for conscientious objectors, if sufficient trouble is taken to find for them an equivalent to actual participation in fighting.

Once this is recognized, certain modifications in the manner of considering war ought to follow, where peril threatens the nation. In the first place, the distinction between soldiers and civilians, which the pressure of circumstances has already almost obliterated, should be entirely abolished. This was what had, to a large extent, brought about the anti-patriotic reaction after 1918. Every individual in the population owes his country the whole of his strength, his resources, and his life itself, until the danger has been removed. It is desirable that the sufferings and perils should be shared by all categories of the population, young and old, men and women, the healthy and the sick, to the full extent to which this is technically possible, and even a bit more besides. Lastly, personal honour is so intimately bound up with the performance of this obligation, and external means of compulsion are so contrary to principles of honour, that all those who desire to escape it should be allowed to do so; they would be made to lose their nationality, and, in addition, either banished and forbidden ever to set foot in the country again, or be made to suffer some permanent form of indignity as a public mark that they had forfeited their right to personal honour.

It is shocking that want of personal honour should be punished in the same way as robbery or assassination. Those who don't want to defend their country should be made to lose, not life or liberty, but purely and simply their country.

If the state of the country is such that for a great many the latter is but a trifling punishment, then the military code also proves itself to be without efficacy. We cannot be ignorant of the fact.

If at certain times the military obligation comprehends all earthly loyalties, the State is under the reciprocal duty, at all times, to protect every nucleus, whether in or outside national territory, from which a part of the population, large or small, draws some of its spiritual life.

The State's most obvious duty is to keep efficient watch at all times over the security of the national territory. Security doesn't mean absence of danger, for in this world danger is ever-present; it means a reasonable chance of being able to weather any storms which should arise. But that is only the State's most elementary duty. If it does no more than that, it is as though it did nothing at all; for if that *is* all it does, it cannot even succeed in doing that.

The State's duty is to make the country, in the highest possible degree, a reality. The country was not a reality for very many Frenchmen in 1939. It has again become one as a result of deprivation. It must be made to remain so in possession, and for that to happen it must really become, in fact, a life-giving agent, really be turned into good, root-fixing ground. It must also be made a favourable setting for participation in and loyal attachment to all other sorts of environmental expression.

Today, whilst Frenchmen have recovered the feeling that France is a reality, they have at the same time become far more conscious than before of local differences. The dividing up of France into separate portions, the censorship of correspondence which limits exchanges of thought to a restricted area, have each played their part, and paradoxically enough, the forcible throwing together of the population has also greatly contributed to this. People have now in a much sharper, more permanent form than before the feeling that they belong to Brittany, Lorraine, Provence or Paris. There is an element of hostility in this feeling which we should try to get rid of; just as it is urgent also to get rid of xenophobia. But this feeling in itself ought not to be discouraged; on the contrary. It would be disastrous to declare it anti-patriotic. In the atmosphere of anguish, confusion, solitude, uprootedness in which the French find themselves, all loyalties, all attachments are worth preserving like treasures of infinite value and rarity, worth tending like the most delicate plants.

That the Vichy Government should have put forward a regionalist doctrine is neither here nor there. Its only mistake in this connexion has been in not applying it. Far from always preaching the exact opposite of its various battle-cries, we ought to adopt many of the ideas launched by the propaganda services of the National Revolution, but turn them into realities.

In the same way, the French, because of their isolation, have come to realize that France is a small country, that shut up inside her it is stifling and they require a wider range. The idea of Europe, of European unity, contributed a good deal towards the success of collaborationist propaganda in the early days. We cannot do too much to encourage, nourish such sentiments as these. It would be disastrous to create any opposition between them and patriotic sentiments.

Lastly, we cannot do too much to encourage the existence of progressive associations not forming wheels within the wheels of public administration; for that is the only condition on which they won't just become corpses. The trade-unions are a case in point, when they are not burdened with day-to-day responsibilities in the matter of economic organization. The same can be said of Christian associations, Protestant or Catholic, and particularly of organizations like the J.O.C.*; but should the State allow itself to be influenced the least little bit by clerical wishes, it would assuredly kill them on the spot. The same can also be said of associations which arose after the defeat in 1940, some of them officially, like the *chantiers de jeunesse* and *camps de compagnons*,† others clandestinely, like the resistance groups. The former possess a certain amount of life, in spite of their official character, thanks to an exceptional conjunction of circumstances; but if their official rôle were to be maintained, they would just lose every spark of vitality. The latter have arisen in opposition to the State, and if one were to yield to the temptation to grant them an official existence in the public life of the country, such a thing would ravage them morally to a terrible degree.

On the other hand, if associations of this sort are out of contact with public affairs, they cease to exist. It is necessary, therefore, that while not forming part of the public administration, they should yet at the same time not lose all contact with it. A method of effecting this might be, for example, for representatives of such associations to be frequently chosen by the State to carry out special missions on a temporary basis. But the State would, on the one hand, have to select these representatives itself, and, on the other hand, all their associates would

* *J.O.C.*: see note p. 60. [Translator.]

† *Chantiers de jeunesse* and *camps de compagnons*: see notes pp. 62 and 68. [Translator.]

have to regard their having been selected as a matter for pride. Such a method could gradually develop into an institution.

Here again, whilst every effort is made to eliminate violent antagonisms, differences should be encouraged. In a country like ours, the perpetual stirring of ideas can never do any harm. It is mental inertia which is fatal to it.

The duty which falls to the State to ensure that the people are provided with a country to which they really feel they belong can never be regarded as a condition precedent to the carrying out of the military obligation by the population in times of national peril. For if the State fails in its duty, if the country is allowed to fall into ruin, nevertheless, whilst national independence subsists, there is always hope of a resurrection; if we look closely, we find in the history of all countries the most surprising ups and downs, sometimes following quite swiftly upon one another. But if the country is subdued by foreign arms, there is nothing left to hope for, save the possibility of a rapid liberation. Hope alone, it is worth dying to preserve, when nothing else is left.

Thus, although one's country is a fact, and, as such, subject to external conditions, to hazards of every kind, in times of mortal danger there is none the less an unconditional obligation to go to its assistance. But it is obvious that, in fact, the people will show all the greater ardour in its/defence the more they will have been made to feel its reality.

The patriotic conception as defined above is incompatible with present-day views about the country's history, its national grandeur, and above all with the way in which one talks at present about the Empire.

France possesses an empire, and consequently, whatever attitude one may adopt with regard to it, it poses certain factual problems which are highly complex and vary considerably according to the different localities. But we mustn't mix everything up together. First of all, there is a question of principle, and even something less definite than that, a question of sentiment. On the whole, has a Frenchman the right to be proud that France possesses an empire, and to think and talk about it with pride and joy, and in the tones of a legitimate owner?

Certainly, if he happens to be a French patriot after the style of Richelieu, Louis XIV or Maurras. But not if the Christian ethic and the spirit of 1789 are indissolubly mixed into the actual substance of his patriotism. Every other nation might possibly have had the right to carve out an empire for itself, but not France; for the same reason which made the temporal sovereignty of the Pope a scandal in the eyes of Christendom. When one takes upon oneself, as France did in 1789, the function of thinking on behalf of the world, of defining justice for the world, one may not become an owner of human flesh and blood. Even if it be true that if we hadn't done so, others would have got hold of these unfortunate native peoples and would have treated them still worse, that was not a legitimate motive; when all is said and done, the total amount of harm would have been less. Motives of this kind are more often than not bad ones. It is not for a priest to become the owner of a brothel on the supposition that its inmates would be worse treated by some bully. It was not for France to surrender her self-respect out of compassion. Besides, that is not what she did. Nobody would seriously venture to claim that she went out to conquer these peoples to prevent other countries ill-treating them: all the less so since it was she who, in the nineteenth century, was largely responsible for bringing these colonial adventures back into fashion.

Amongst those she has reduced to submission, there are some who feel very keenly how scandalous it is that she of all countries should have done this; their resentment towards us is aggravated by a terribly grievous kind of bitterness and by a sort of bewilderment.

It may be that France now has to choose between her attachment to her Empire and the need to have a soul of her own again; or, in more general terms, between having a soul of her own and the Roman or Corneille-esque conception of greatness.

If she chooses wrongly, if we ourselves force her to choose wrongly, which is only too likely, she will have neither the one nor the other, but only the most appalling adversity, which she will undergo with astonishment, without anybody being able to discover any reason for it. And all those who are now in a position to get up and speak, or to wield a pen, will be eternally responsible for having committed a crime.

Bernanos has understood and declared that Hitlerism is a return to pagan Rome. But has he forgotten, have we forgotten, what an influential part Rome has played in our history, our culture, and still plays today in our everyday thoughts? If, out of horror for a certain form of evil, we have taken the terrible decision to make war, with all the atrocities war necessarily involves, can we be forgiven if we make less pitiless war against that same form of evil in our own hearts? If all the grandeur after the style of Corneille attracts us by its heroic glamour, Germany can equally well attract us too, for the German soldiers are undoubtedly 'heroes'. In the present confusion of thought and feeling over the subject of patriotism, is there any guarantee at all that a French soldier in Africa is inspired by a purer ideal of sacrifice than a German soldier in Russia? Actually, there isn't any. If we do not feel what a terrible responsibility this places on us, we cannot remain innocent in the midst of this unleashing of crime throughout the world.

If there is one thing for which it is necessary to face everything, set everything at naught for love of the truth, it is that one. We are all brought together in the name of patriotism. What is the use of us, what scorn shall we not deserve, if in our thoughts on this subject the least vestige of a lie is found?

But if feelings of a Corneille-esque type don't inspire our patriotism, one may well ask what motive there is to replace them.

Yet, there is one, no less vital, absolutely pure, and corresponding exactly to present circumstances. It is compassion for our country. We have a glorious respondent. It was Joan of

Arc who used to say she felt pity for the kingdom of France.

But we can quote an infinitely higher authority. In the Gospels, there is not the least indication that Christ experienced anything resembling love for Jerusalem and Judaea, save only the love which goes wrapped in compassion. He never showed any other kind of attachment to his country. But his compassion he expressed on more than one occasion. He wept over the city, foreseeing, as it was not difficult to do at that time, the destruction which should shortly fall upon it. He spoke to it as to a person. 'Oh, Jerusalem, Jerusalem . . . how often would I have gathered . . .' Even as He was carrying the cross, He showed once again the pity He felt for it.

Let no one imagine that compassion for one's country excludes warlike energy. It fired the Carthaginians to perform one of the most prodigious deeds of heroism in the whole of history. After being conquered and reduced to very little by Scipio Africanus, they subsequently underwent over the course of fifty years a process of demoralization compared with which the French capitulation at Munich is as nothing at all. They were mercilessly exposed to whatever injuries the Numidians cared to inflict on them, and, having renounced by treaty the right to go to war, they vainly implored Rome for permission to defend themselves. When they finally did so without permission, their army was utterly wiped out. They then had to implore the pardon of the Romans. They agreed to hand over three hundred children of the nobility and all the arms they possessed. Then their delegates were ordered to evacuate the city entirely and definitively, so that it could be razed to the ground. They burst into cries of indignation, then into the bitterest tears. 'They called upon their native city by name, and, addressing it as though it were a person, uttered the most heartrending things.' Then they begged the Romans, if they were determined to do them injury, only to spare their city, its stones, its temples, to which no possible guilt could be attached, and instead, if necessary, exterminate the entire population; they declared that such a course would bring less shame upon the Romans and would be infinitely preferable for the people of Carthage. The Romans remained inflexible; whereupon the city rose in rebellion, although devoid of resources, and it took Scipio Africanus, at the head of a large army, three whole years to reduce it and lay it waste.

This poignantly tender feeling for some beautiful, precious, fragile and perishable object has a warmth about it which the sentiment of national grandeur altogether lacks. The vital current which inspires it is a perfectly pure one, and is charged with an extraordinary intensity. Isn't a man easily capable of acts of heroism to protect his children, or his aged parents? And yet no vestige of grandeur is attached to these. A perfectly pure love for one's country bears a close resemblance to the feelings which his young children, his aged parents, or a beloved wife inspire in a man. The thought of weakness can inflame love in just the same way as can the thought of strength, but in the former case the flame is of an altogether different order of purity. The compassion felt for fragility is always associated with love for real beauty, because we are keenly conscious of the fact that the existence of the really beautiful things ought to be assured for ever, and is not.

One can either love France for the glory which would seem to ensure for her a prolonged existence in time and space; or else one can love her as something which, being earthly, can be destroyed, and is all the more precious on that account.

These are two distinct ways of loving; perhaps, most probably, incompatible with each other, although in speech they become mixed up together. Those whose hearts are made so as to experience the latter way can yet find themselves sometimes, through force of habit, using forms of speech which are really only suitable in the case of the former.

But the latter is alone legitimate for a Christian, for it alone wears the Christian badge of humility. It alone belongs to that species of love which can be given the name of charity. Nor should it be supposed that the object of such love need necessarily be confined to an unhappy country. Happiness is as much an object for compassion as unhappiness, because it belongs to this earth, in other words is incomplete, frail and fleeting. Moreover, there is, unfortunately, always a certain amount of unhappiness in the life of any country.

Let no one imagine either that a love of this nature would run the risk of ignoring or rejecting what there is of pure and genuine grandeur in the past history of France, or in the country's present hopes and ideals. Quite the opposite. Compassion is all the more tender, all the more poignant, the more good one is able to discern in the being who forms the object of it, and it predisposes one to discern the good. When a Christian represents to himself Christ on the Cross, his compassion is not diminished by the thought of the latter's perfection, nor the other way about. But, on the other hand, such a love can keep its eyes open on injustices, cruelties, mistakes, falsehoods, crimes and scandals contained in the country's past, its present and in its ambitions in general, quite openly and fearlessly, and without being thereby diminished; the love being only rendered thereby more painful. Where compassion is concerned, crime itself provides a reason, not for withdrawing oneself, but for approaching, not with the object of sharing the guilt, but the shame. Mankind's crimes didn't diminish Christ's compassion. Thus compassion keeps both eyes open on both the good and the bad and finds in each sufficient reasons for loving. It is the only love on this earth which is true and righteous.

Just now it is the only sort of love that is suitable for the French. If the events we have recently been living through are not sufficient warning to us of the need to change our way of loving our country, what sort of lesson is there which could teach us? What more can one receive to awaken one's interest than a heavy blow with a club on the head?

Compassion for our country is the only sentiment which doesn't strike a false note at the present time, suits the situation in which the souls and bodies of Frenchmen actually find themselves, and possesses at once the humility and dignity appropriate to misfortune, and also that simplicity which misfortune requires above everything else. To call up before people's minds at this time France's historic greatness, her past and future glories, the splendour which has surrounded her existence, none of that is possible without a sort of inward contraction which gives something forced to one's tone. Nothing that in any way resembles pride can be suitable for those in misfortune.

For the French who are suffering, recollections of this sort fall into the category of compensations. To seek compensations in misfortune is a bad thing. If the past is recalled too often, if it is turned into the unique source of comfort, such proceedings can cause immeasurable harm. The French are being starved of greatness. But for the unfortunate, greatness after the Roman manner is not what is wanted; for either it seems to them a mockery, or else their minds become poisoned by it, as was the case in Germany.

Compassion for France is not a compensation for, but a spiritualization of, the sufferings being undergone; it is able to transfigure even the most purely physical sufferings, such as cold and hunger. Whoever feels cold and hunger, and is tempted to pity himself, can, instead of doing that, from out of his own shrunken frame, direct his pity towards France; the very cold and hunger themselves then cause the love of France to enter into the body and penetrate to the depths of the soul. And this same compassion is able, without hindrance, to cross frontiers, extend itself over all countries in misfortune, over all countries without exception; for all peoples are subjected to the wretchedness of our human condition. Whereas pride in national glory is by its nature exclusive, non-transferable, compassion is by its nature universal; it is only more potential where distant and unfamiliar things are concerned, more real, more physical, more charged with blood, tears and effective energy where things close at hand are concerned.

National pride is far removed from the affairs of daily life. In France, its only means of expression is through the resistance;

but there are many who either have not the opportunity to take any effective part in the resistance, or can only devote some of their time to it. Compassion for France is an incentive charged with at least as much active value for the purposes of the resistance; but one which can besides find daily, uninterrupted expression, on every possible sort of occasion, in a fraternal note marking the relations between Frenchmen. Fraternal feelings flourish readily in the midst of compassion for misfortune, which, while inflicting on each his share of suffering, endangers something far more precious than the well-being of each. National pride, whether it be in good times or in bad, is incapable of creating any real, ardent sense of fraternity. This didn't exist among the Romans. They didn't know what really tender feelings were.

A patriotism inspired by compassion gives the poorest part of the population a privileged moral position. National glory only acts as a stimulant among the lower orders of society at times when every one can, while looking forward to his country's glory, look forward at the same time to having as large a personal share therein as he can wish for. Such was the case at the beginning of Napoleon's reign. Any little French lad, no matter where he hailed from, could legitimately carry in his heart any sort of dreams as to the future; no ambition could be regarded as great enough to be absurd. Every one knew that all ambitions would not be realized, but each one in particular had a chance of being, and many of them could be partially so. A noteworthy document of the period states that Napoleon's popularity was due, less to the devotion Frenchmen felt for his person, than to the possibilities of advancement, the opportunities of carving out a career for themselves which he offered them. That is exactly the feeling which appears in *Le Rouge et le Noir*. The Romantics were children who felt bored because they no longer had before them the prospect of unrestricted social advancement. They sought literary glory as a substitute.

But this particular stimulant is only found in times of

upheaval. Nor can one say that it ever takes the form of an invitation to the people as such. Every man of the people who partakes of it, dreams of emerging from amongst the people, leaving behind him the anonymity which characterizes humanity in the mass. This ambition, when it is widely held, is the result of a disturbed social condition, and the cause of more serious disturbances to follow; for it sees in social stability an obstacle. Although it happens to be a stimulant, it cannot be said that it is a healthy one, either for the individual soul or for the country. It is quite likely that this stimulant plays a large part in the present resistance movement; for as far as France's future is concerned, hopes are readily entertained; and as for the individual's own future, any one, no matter who it is, who has proved his mettle in the midst of danger, can look forward to no matter what in the state of latent revolution in which the country finds itself. But if this is so, it presents a terrible danger for the period of reconstruction, and another stimulant needs to be discovered immediately.

In times of social stability, in which, save in exceptional cases, those who form part of the anonymous mass remain in it more or less, never even seeking to emerge therefrom, the people cannot feel themselves at home in a patriotism founded upon pride and pomp-and-glory. It is as strange and unfamiliar to them as are the salons of Versailles, which constitute one of its expressions. Glory is the reverse of anonymity. If to military glory we add literary, scientific and other sorts of glory, the people will continue to feel themselves strangers. The knowledge that certain Frenchmen who have covered themselves with glory have come out of their ranks will not, in stable periods, afford the people any comfort; for if the former have come out of the people, they have ceased to form part of the people.

On the other hand, if their country is presented to them as something beautiful and precious, but which is, in the first place, imperfect, and secondly, very frail and liable to suffer misfortune, and which it is necessary to cherish and preserve, they will rightly feel themselves to be more closely identified with it than will other classes of society. For the people have a monopoly of a certain sort of knowledge, perhaps the most important of all, that of the reality of misfortune; and for that very reason, they feel all the more keenly the preciousness of those things which deserve to be protected from it, and how incumbent it is on each of us to cherish and protect them. Melodrama reflects this popular state of feeling. Why it happens to be such a dreadful literary form would be worth while taking the trouble to examine. But far from being a false form of expression, it is very close, in a certain sense, to reality.

Were such a relationship to be established between the people and the country, the former would no longer regard their own personal sufferings as crimes committed by the country against themselves, but as ills suffered by the country in and through themselves. The difference is immense. In another sense, it is slight, and very little would be required to effect the change. But that little would have to come from another world. This presupposes a dissociation between the country and the State. Which is possible if grandeur in the Corneille style is abolished. But it would involve anarchy if, to compensate for this, the State were unable to manage to inspire of its own accord an increased public esteem.

To do that, it ought certainly not to return to the old methods of parliamentary life and party struggle. But what is most important of all, perhaps, is a complete overhaul of the police system. Circumstances would lend themselves to this. The English police system might be studied with advantage. At all events, the liberation of the country will, it is to be hoped, bring with it the liquidation of the personnel composing the police force, except for those who have taken a personal part against the enemy. They must be replaced by men who enjoy public esteem, and since that is, unfortunately, chiefly founded nowadays on money and diplomas, a fairly high standard of education must be demanded even beginning with ordinary policemen and inspectors, and further up really high qualifications, with correspondingly high pay. It would even be necessary, if the vogue for having *Grande Ecoles** continues in France—which is perhaps not to be desired—to have one for the police, candidates being selected by examination. These are certainly clumsy methods; but something of the kind is indispensable. Furthermore—and this is still more important— we must do away entirely with social categories like those of prostitutes and ex-convicts, which play officially the part of a defenceless herd delivered over to the whims of the police, and providing the latter at the same time with both victims and accomplices; for a mutual contamination is under such conditions inevitable, collaboration having a debasing effect on both sides. We must abolish, in law, both these two categories of persons.

Criminal dishonesty in matters connected with the State on the part of men in public life must also be effectively punished, and more severely so than armed robbery.

The State in its administrative function should appear as the manager of the country's resources; a more or less capable manager, who is expected to be on the whole rather less capable than otherwise, because his task is a difficult one and carried out under morally unfavourable conditions. Obedience is none the less obligatory, not because of any particular right to issue commands possessed by the State, but because obedience is essential for the country's preservation and tranquillity. We must obey the State, however it happens to be, rather like loving children left by their parents, gone abroad, in the charge of some mediocre governess, but who obey her nevertheless out of love for their parents. If the State happens not to be mediocre, so much the better; besides, the pressure of public opinion must always be exercised in the manner of a stimulant encouraging it to leave the path of mediocrity; but whether

---

* *Grandes Ecoles*: the so-called 'Grandes Ecoles' are all the State-directed centres of higher education for training the *élite* of the majority of the leading professions—for example, the Ecole Polytechnique, Ecole Militaire de St. Cyr, Ecole Normale Supérieure, etc. [Translator.]

mediocre or not, the obligation of obedience remains the same.

It is certainly not an unlimited obligation, but its only valid limit is a revolt on the part of conscience. No criterion can be offered indicating exactly what this limit is; it is even impossible for each of us to prescribe one for himself once and for all: when you feel you can't obey any longer, you just have to disobey. But there is at least one necessary condition, although insufficient of itself, making it possible to disobey without being guilty of crime; this is to be urged forward by so imperious an obligation that one is constrained to scorn all risks of whatever kind. If one feels inclined to disobey, but one is dissuaded by the excessive danger involved, that is altogether unpardonable, whether it be because one contemplated an act of disobedience, or else because one failed to carry it out, as the case may be. Besides, whenever one isn't strictly obliged to disobey, one is under the strict obligation to obey. A country cannot possess liberty unless it is recognized that disobedience towards the authorities, every time it doesn't proceed from an overriding sense of duty, is more dishonourable than theft. That means to say that public order ought to be regarded as more sacred than private property. The authorities could popularize this way of looking at things by means of education and other suitable methods which would have to be thought out.

But it is only compassion for our country, the watchful and tender concern to keep it out of harm's way, which can give to peace, and especially to civil peace, what civil or foreign war possesses, unfortunately, of itself — something stirring, touching, poetic and sacred. This compassion alone can give us back that feeling we have lacked for so long, and so rarely experienced throughout the course of history, and which Théophile* expressed in the beautiful line: '*La sainte majesté des lois*'.

When Théophile wrote that line, it was perhaps the last time

* *Théophile*: i.e. Théophile de Viau, early seventeenth-century poet. [Translator.]

171

such a feeling was deeply experienced in France. Afterwards came Richelieu, then the Fronde, then Louis XIV, and so on. Montesquieu vainly sought to re-establish it in the public imagination by means of a book. The men of 1789 laid claim to it, but they didn't really feel it in their hearts, otherwise the country wouldn't have slithered so easily into war, both domestic and foreign.

Since then, even our language has become unsuitable to express it. It is, nevertheless, this sentiment which people are trying to revive, or its pale counterpart, when they talk about '*légitimité*'.* But giving a sentiment a name is not sufficient to call it to life. That is a fundamental truth which we are too apt to forget.

Why lie to ourselves? In 1939, just before the war, under the régime of decree-laws, republican *légitimité* already no longer existed. It had departed like Villon's youth '*qui son partement m'a celé*', noiselessly, without any warning, and without any one having done or said anything to stop it. As for the feeling for *légitimité*, it was completely dead. That it should now re-appear in the thoughts of those in exile, that it should occupy a certain place, in company with other feelings in fact incompatible with it, in dreams for curing a sick people, all that means nothing at all, or very little. If it was dead in 1939, how should it suddenly become effective again after years of systematic disobedience?

On the other hand, the Constitution of 1875 can no longer serve as a basis for *légitimité*, after having come crashing down in 1940 amid general public indifference and even contempt, after being abandoned to its fate by the French People. For that is exactly what they did do. Neither the resistance groups nor the French in London can do anything about it. If a shadow of regret was expressed, it was not by any section of the people, but by parliamentary men in whom their profession kept alive an interest in republican institutions, elsewhere non-existent. Once again, it makes no difference that some considerable time

* '*légitimité*': legitimacy, that is, in accordance with law. [Translator.]

afterwards the feeling for *légitimité* should have reappeared to a certain extent. At the present moment, hunger invests the Third Republic with all the poetry associated with a time when there was enough to eat. It is a fugitive kind of poetry. Moreover, the disgust felt for so many years and which attained its maximum in 1940 still persists.

It is nevertheless certain that as and when the Vichy business falls to pieces, and to the extent to which revolutionary, possibly Communist, institutions don't arise, a return will be made to the political structure of the Third Republic. But that will only be because there is a void which has to be filled with something. That is a question of necessity, not of *légitimité*, and corresponds to the people's attitude, which is not one of loyal enthusiasm, but of dull resignation. On the other hand, the date 1789 certainly awakens a really deep echo; but all there is attached to it is an inspiration, there are no institutions.

Seeing that we have, in fact, recently experienced a break in historical continuity, constitutional legality can no longer be regarded as having an historical basis; it must be made to derive from the eternal source of all legality. The men who offer their services to the country to govern it will have to publicly recognize certain obligations corresponding to essential aspirations of the people eternally inscribed in the depths of popular feeling; the people must have confidence in the word and in the capacity of these men, and be provided with means of expressing the fact; they must also be made to feel that, in accepting these men, they give an undertaking to obey them.

Since the people's obedience towards the public authorities is a necessity for the country, this obedience becomes a sacred obligation, and one which confers on the public authorities themselves, seeing that they form the object of it, the same sacred character. This doesn't mean an idolizing of the State in association with patriotism in the Roman style. It is the exact opposite of this. The State is sacred, not in the way an idol is sacred, but in the way common objects serving a religious purpose, like the altar, the baptismal water or anything else of the kind, are sacred. Everybody knows they are only material objects; but material objects which are regarded as sacred because they serve a sacred purpose. That is the sort of majesty appropriate for the State.

If we are unable to inspire the people of France with a conception of this nature, they will have only the choice between anarchy and idolatry. Idolatry might take a communist form. That is probably what would happen. It might also take a nationalist form, in which case it would presumably have as its object the pair of idols so characteristic of our age, composed of a man acclaimed as leader and at his side the iron-bound machine of State. But we mustn't forget that, first, publicity is able to manufacture leaders, and secondly, if circumstances place a man of genuine ability in such a situation, he rapidly becomes a prisoner of his rôle. In other words, in the language of today, the absence of a pure source of inspiration would leave the French people no other alternatives than anarchy, Communism or Fascism.

There are some people, in America for example, who ask themselves whether the French in London might not have leanings towards Fascism. That is not putting the question in the proper way. Intentions, by themselves, are not of any great importance, save when their aim is directly evil, for to do evil the necessary means are always within easy reach. But good intentions only count when accompanied by the corresponding means for putting them into effect. St. Peter hadn't the slightest intention of denying Christ; but he did so because the grace was not in him which, had it been there, would have enabled him not to do. And even the energy, the categorical tone he employed to underline the contrary intention, helped to deprive him of this grace. It is a case which is worth pondering in all the trials life sets before us.

The thing is to know whether the French in London possess the necessary means to prevent the people of France from sliding into Fascism, and at the same time stop them from falling into either Communism or anarchy. Fascism, Communism and anarchy being all scarcely different, almost equivalent, expressions of the self-same evil, what we want to know is whether they have any remedy for this evil.

If they haven't one, their *raison d'être*, which is to keep France in the war, is brought entirely to an end by victory, which will then plunge them back again among the mass of their fellow-countrymen. If they have one, they should already have begun applying it to a great extent, and efficiently so, long before victory. For a treatment of this description cannot be started in the midst of all the nervous tension which will, both in each individual and in the mass, necessarily accompany the liberation of the country. Still less can it be started once people's nerves have quietened down again—supposing one day such a thing to happen; it would be much too late: any sort of treatment would then be entirely out of the question.

The important thing, then, is not for them to assert before the world their right to govern France; any more than it is for a doctor to publicly assert his right to prescribe treatment for a patient. The essential thing is to have rightly diagnosed the case, conceived a cure, chosen the right medicaments, and made sure the patient is supplied with them. When a doctor knows how to do all that, not without a certain risk of making mistakes, but with a reasonable chance of being right, then, if other people try to prevent him exercising his function, and to put a charlatan in his place, it is his duty to oppose them with all his might. But if, in some place where there isn't a doctor, a lot of ignoramuses busy themselves about the bedside of a sick man whose condition calls for the most precise, most up-to-date form of treatment, what does it matter in whose particular hands among that lot he happens to be when it comes to dying, or else being saved by a stroke of luck? No doubt, it must in any case always be better that he should find himself in the hands of those who love him. But those who love him won't inflict on him the additional suffering of a battle royal raging at his pillow, unless they know themselves to be in possession of a likely means of saving his life.

PART THREE
THE GROWING OF ROOTS

PART THREE

THE GROWING OF ROOTS

THE problem of a method for breathing an inspiration into a people is quite a new one. Plato alludes to it in his *Politics* and elsewhere; doubtless there were precepts on this subject among the secret stores of knowledge accumulated in pre-Roman antiquity, of which no trace has been left. Possibly this problem and others akin to it continued to be discussed in such circles as those of the Templars and early free masons. Montesquieu, unless I am mistaken, was unaware of it. Rousseau, with his powerful mind, clearly recognized its existence, but didn't go any further. The men of 1789 do not appear to have had any inkling of it. In 1793, without people having gone to the trouble of raising the problem, still less of investigating it, hasty solutions were improvised, such as festivals in honour of the Supreme Being, of the Goddess of Reason, which were just ridiculous and odious. In the nineteenth century, the level of general intelligence had descended very far below the point at which such questions are raised.

In our own day, people have investigated and penetrated deeply into the problem of propaganda. Hitler, in particular, has made lasting contributions on this subject to the store of human knowledge. But it is an altogether different problem. Propaganda is not directed towards creating an inspiration: it closes, seals up all the openings through which an inspiration might pass) it fills the whole spirit with fanaticism. Its measures cannot be suitable for obtaining a contrary objective. Nor is it just a question of adopting reverse measures: the causal connexion is not so simple.

It must not be thought either that the inspiring of a people is a mystery reserved to God alone, and for which, consequently, no method exists. The supreme and perfect state of mystical contemplation is something that is infinitely more mysterious still, and yet St. John of the Cross wrote treatises on the method of attaining to such a state, which, by their scientific precision, are far and away superior to anything produced by the psychologists or professors of our own time. If he felt called upon to do this, he was doubtless right, for he was certainly competent; the beauty of his writings is a sufficiently clear indication of their authenticity. Actually, from remote antiquity, long before Christianity, right up to the latter half of the Renaissance, it was always universally recognized that there is a method to be followed in spiritual matters and in everything connected with the soul's welfare. The ever greater and greater methodical control which men have exercised over matter since the sixteenth century has led them to believe, by way of contrast, that the things of the soul are either arbitrary or else bound up with some form of magic, with the immediate efficacy of intentions and words.

Such is not the case. Everything in creation is dependent on method, including the points of intersection between this world and the next. That is what the word *Logos* indicates, signifying connexion even more than word. The method merely differs according to the different sphere. The higher one goes, the more rigorous and precise it becomes. It would be strange, indeed, if the order of material things were to reflect more of divine wisdom than that of spiritual things. The contrary is true.

It is unfortunate for us that this problem, in regard to which, unless I am wrong, we have nothing we can look to for guidance, should be precisely the one that requires today the most urgent solution on our part, under pain not so much of disappearing altogether as of never having really existed.

Besides, if Plato, for example, had devised a general solution for it, we should require to do more than make a study of his solution in order to get ourselves out of the quandary; for we have to face a situation in regard to which history is of little help to us. We cannot find in history any reference to anything even remotely resembling the situation in which France is likely to find herself as a result of a German defeat. Furthermore, we don't even know what that situation will be. All we know is that it will be an unprecedented one. Thus, even if we knew how an inspiration can be breathed into a country, we should still not know how to proceed in the case of France.

On the other hand, since it is a question of a practical problem, the knowledge of a general solution is not indispensable for dealing with a particular case. When a machine stops, a workman, a foreman or an engineer can perceive a means of making it go again without possessing any general knowledge of the principles governing the repair of machinery. The first thing to be done in such a case is to have a look at the machine. Nevertheless, in order to look at it to some purpose, one must carry in one's mind a definite notion of mechanical relationships. In the same way, looking on day by day at the changing situation in France, one must carry in one's mind a definite notion of public action as a mode of education for the country.

It is not enough to have perceived such a notion, given it one's attention, understood it; it must be given a permanent place in the mind, so that it may be present even when one's attention is directed towards something else.

It demands an all the greater effort seeing that it is, for us, a completely new idea. Since the Renaissance, public activities have never been visualized in this light, but solely as a means of establishing a particular form of power regarded as desirable for one reason or another.

Education—whether its object be children or adults, individuals or an entire people, or even oneself—consists in creating motives.) To show what is beneficial, what is obligatory, what is good—that is the task of education. Education concerns itself with the motives for effective action. For no action is ever carried out in the absence of motives capable of supplying the indispensable amount of energy for its execution.

To want to direct human creatures—others or oneself—towards the good by simply pointing out the direction, without making sure the necessary motives have been provided, is as if one tried, by pressing down the accelerator, to set off in a motor-car with an empty petrol tank. Or again, it is as if one were to try to light an oil lamp without having put in any oil. This mistake was pointed out in a celebrated passage that has been read, re-read and alluded to over and over again for the last twenty centuries. In spite of which, we still go on making it.

It is fairly easy to classify the means of education contained in public action:

First, fear and hope, brought about by threats and promises.

Suggestion.

Expression, either officially or under official sanction, of some of the thoughts which, before ever being publicly expressed, were already in the hearts of the people, or in the hearts of certain active elements in the nation.

Example.

The modalities themselves of action, and those of organizations created for purposes of action.

The first means is the grossest, and it is always employed. The second is also employed by everybody nowadays: it is the one in the handling of which Hitler has displayed such genius.

The other three are unknown.

We must try to conceive them in relation to the three successive forms our public action is capable of assuming: its present form; the actual taking over of power at the moment of liberation; and the exercise of power on a provisional basis during the immediately succeeding months after liberation.

The Growing of Roots

At present we have only two mediatory instruments at our disposal, the radio and the underground movement. For the great mass of French people, it is practically the radio alone which counts.

The third of the five means enumerated above must on no account be confused with the second. Suggestion constitutes, as Hitler saw, an ascendancy. It is a form of coercion. A great part of its efficacity is due, on the one hand to repetition, and on the other hand to the strength at the command of the group whence the suggestion originates, or which it aims to acquire.

The efficacity of the third means is of an altogether different kind. Its foundations are laid in the hidden structure of human nature.

It sometimes happens that a thought, either formulated to oneself or not formulated at all, works secretly on the mind and yet has but little direct influence over it.

If one hears this thought expressed publicly by some other person, and especially by some one whose words are listened to with respect, its force is increased an hundredfold and can sometimes bring about an inner transformation.

It can also happen that one needs, whether one realizes it or not, to hear certain words, which, if they are effectively pronounced, and in a quarter whence one would normally expect good to come from, infuse comfort, energy and as it were a food.

In private life these two word functions are theoretically filled by friends or natural guides, though, in fact, rarely enough.

But there are certain occasions when the march of public events occupies so much more important a place in the personal life of each of us than does the course of individual affairs, that a number of hidden thoughts and hidden needs of this sort are found to be the same with practically all the human beings which go to make up a people.

This provides the opportunity for carrying out an action,

which, while it is directed towards a whole people, remains essentially a personal, not a collective, one. Thus, far from stifling the resources concealed in the depths of each mind, which is what all collective action, in the nature of things, inevitably does, however lofty the ends pursued may be, this type of action awakens them, stirs them up and stimulates their growth.

But who or what is able to exercise such an action?

In normal circumstances, there is perhaps nowhere whence it could be exercised. Very powerful obstacles stand in the way of its being done, save partially and to a feeble extent, by any government. Other obstacles make it similarly difficult for it to be done anywhere than by the State.

However, from this point of view, the circumstances in which France actually finds herself happen to be wonderfully, providentially favourable.

From many other points of view it has been disastrous that France should not have had, like other countries, a regular government in London. But from this point of view it is exceptionally fortunate; and it is even fortunate from this point of view that the North African affair should not have led to the transformation of the National Committee into a regular government.

The hatred of the State, which has existed in a latent, secret, but very powerful form in France since the days of Charles VI, makes it impossible for words emanating directly from a government to be welcomed by every individual Frenchman like the voice of a friend.

On the other hand, in an action of this kind, words must have an official character if they are to be really effective.

The leaders of Fighting France constitute something analogous to a government to the precise degree necessary so that their words should have an official character.

The movement preserves enough of its original nature—that of a revolt springing up out of the depths of a few faithful hearts acting completely independently—for the words which issue from it to have in the ears of every Frenchman the close, intimate, warm and tender accents of the voice of a friend.

And above all General de Gaulle, surrounded by those who have followed him, is a symbol. He symbolizes France's faithfulness to herself, which for a moment was concentrated almost entirely in him, and above all everything in Man which revolts against the servile adoration of force.

Everything spoken in his name has, in France, the authority attaching to a symbol. Consequently, whoever speaks in that name can, as he chooses, and according to what seems to be best at the particular time in question, take his inspiration from the level of those feelings and thoughts which are actually simmering in the minds of Frenchmen, or from a higher level, and in that case as high a level as he wishes; there being nothing to prevent him taking it sometimes from that region situated above the skies. Just as much as it would be out of place for such words to issue from a government necessarily tainted by all the meannesses associated with the exercise of power, so it is in order in the case of words emanating from a symbol which represents what is highest in the eyes of every individual.

A government which uses words, thoughts too lofty for it, far from gaining any prestige thereby, discredits them and at the same time makes itself ridiculous. That is what happened in connexion with the principles of 1789 and the formula 'Liberty, Equality, Fraternity' during the course of the Third Republic. That is what also happened as regards the words, often in themselves of a very high moral level, proclaimed by the so-called National Revolution.* In the latter case, it is true, the stigma of the betrayal caused them to be discredited with a lightning rapidity. But almost certainly the same thing would have happened even otherwise, though much more slowly.

The French movement in London has at this moment, but

* *National Revolution:* a reference to the Vichy Government's declared programme of a '*Révolution Nationale*', that is to say, a national regeneration. [Translator.]

not for long perhaps, this extraordinary privilege that being to a large extent symbolical, it is able to disseminate the most lofty inspirations without discrediting them or impropriety on its part.

Thus, out of the very unreality which has been its lot since the beginning—on account of the initial isolation in which those who launched it found themselves—it can draw, if it knows how to make use of it, a far greater abundance of reality.

'His strength is made perfect in weakness', says St. Paul.

It is a strange blindness that has brought about in a situation charged with such marvellous possibilities the desire to descend to the vulgar, banal position of an *émigré* government. It is providential that this desire has not been satisfied.

In regard to foreign countries, moreover, the situation offers similar advantages.

Since 1789, France has, in fact, occupied a unique place among the nations. This is something recent; for 1789 is not far away. From the end of the fourteenth century, which witnessed the most ferocious repressions carried out in the Flemish and French cities under the minority of Charles VI, up to 1789, France had scarcely represented in the eyes of the foreigner, from the political point of view, anything other than the tyranny of absolutism and the servility of a subject people. When du Bellay wrote: '*France, mère des arts, des armes et des lois*', the last word was *de trop*. As Montesquieu so ably pointed out, and as Retz before him had explained with such marvellous lucidity, there were no laws at all in France from the death of Charles VI onwards.

Between 1715 and 1789, France, filled with an humble enthusiasm, went to school in England. At that time, the English seemed to be the only people worthy of the name of citizens in the midst of slave populations. But after 1792, when France, having stirred the hearts of all the oppressed, found herself engaged in a war in which she had England for an enemy, all the prestige attaching to the ideas of justice and liberty was concentrated on her; with the result that during the following century a species of exaltation filled the French people which other peoples didn't experience directly, but caught from the French its illuminating beam.

The French Revolution, unfortunately enough, was responsible for such a violent break with the past all over the European continent that any tradition going back to 1789 is in practice equivalent to one stemming from antiquity.

The war of 1870 showed what France meant in the eyes of the world. In that war, the French were the aggressors, in spite of the Ems despatch ruse; indeed, this ruse is itself proof that the aggression came from the French side. The Germans, disunited as they were, and shuddering still at the memory of Napoleon, expected to be invaded. They were very surprised to find cutting into France was like cutting into a pile of butter. But they were still more surprised to find themselves an object of horror in the eyes of Europe, when their only fault had been to defend themselves victoriously. But the vanquished country was France, and in spite of Napoleon, and because of 1789, that was enough to cause the victors to be regarded with horror.

One can see in the personal diary of the Prince Imperial, Frederick, what a painful surprise for the best of the Germans was this, to them, incomprehensible condemnation.

Perhaps it is possible to date from that time the German inferiority complex, an apparently contradictory mixture of a bad conscience and the feeling that they are suffering from an injustice, and their ferocious reaction to it. At all events, from that moment, it was the Prussian who, in the European consciousness, took the place of what had hitherto been looked upon as the typical German, namely, a dreamy, blue-eyed musician, *gutmütig*, a pipe-smoker and beer-drinker, completely harmless—the type which is still found in the pages of Balzac. And Germany went on becoming more and more like this new picture of herself.

France underwent a hardly less serious moral injury. Her recovery after 1871 is admired. But it is not seen at what a price it was achieved. France had become a realist. She had ceased to believe in herself. The massacre during the Commune, so startling by reason of the number of victims and its ferocious character, gave the workmen the permanent feeling that they were outcasts in their own country, and the middle class, as a result of a bad conscience, a sort of physical fear of the workmen. This was still evident in June 1936;* and the collapse in June 1940 is in a sense a direct result of that extraordinarily brief yet bloody civil war of May 1871, which continued secretly for nearly three-quarters of a century. The consequence was that the feeling of friendship between the youth of the big *Ecoles*† and the people, from which feeling the whole of French nineteenth century thought had derived, as it were, its nourishment, became nothing but a memory. On the other hand, the humiliation of the defeat turned the thoughts of middle-class youth, by a process of reaction, towards a thoroughly mediocre conception of national greatness. Obsessed by the conquest she had suffered and which had belittled her in her own eyes, France no longer felt capable of any vocation higher than that of conquering in her turn.

Thus France became just like any other nation, thinking only of carving out for herself her share of black or yellow human flesh and of obtaining for herself the hegemony of Europe.

After a life of such intense exaltation, the sudden drop to such a low level could not take place without precipitating a profound *malaise*. June 1940 marks the extreme limit reached by this *malaise*.

It must be said at once, because it is true, that after the disaster the first reaction on the part of France was to vomit up her own past, her immediate past. This was not the result of Vichy propaganda. On the contrary, it was the cause of the National Revolution having, to begin with, an appearance of

---

*. . . *in June* 1936: a reference to the big sitdown strike of that year, when important factories and industrial plants, such as the Renault works, were occupied by the employees for some days. [Translator.]

† *Ecoles*: see note p. 170. [Translator.]

success. And it was a right and wholesome reaction. The only side to the disaster which could be looked upon as a good thing was the opportunity it afforded to vomit up a past of which it was itself the final outcome; a past during which France had done nothing except claim the privileges consonant with a mission that she had renounced because she didn't believe in it any longer.

Abroad, the collapse of France was only deeply felt in places where the spirit of 1789 had left behind a legacy.

The temporary laying low of France as a nation gives her the opportunity of becoming once again among the nations what she was in the past, and what for a long time now people were hoping to see her become again—an inspiration. And for France to be able to recover her prestige in the world— a prestige which is indispensable to the very health of her inner life—she must become an inspiration before she has become again, thanks to the defeat of her enemies, a nation. Afterwards, it would probably be impossible for several reasons.

There again, the French movement in London is in the best possible position imaginable, if only it knows how to make use of it. The movement is neither more nor less official than what is required in order to be able to speak in the name of the country. Not possessing any governmental authority—even a nominal, fictitious authority—over the French people, based entirely upon free consent, it has something of a spiritual power about it. The unswerving loyalty displayed in the darkest hours, the blood spilt freely every day in its name, give it the right freely to use the most exalted words in the language. Its position is exactly as it should be for making known to the world the voice of France; a voice whose authority is not based on physical power, which was destroyed by the defeat, nor on glory, which was wiped out in shame; but, first, on an elevated plane of thought in keeping with the present tragedy, and, secondly, on a spiritual tradition graven in the hearts of all peoples.

It is not difficult to define this movement's double mission: to help France to discover in the depths of her misfortune an inspiration in keeping with her genius and with the actual needs of mankind in distress, and to spread this inspiration, once recovered or at any rate glimpsed, throughout the world.

If we stick to this double mission, many things of a less lofty order will be granted to us in addition; (if we stick in the first place to these lesser things, even they will be refused to us.)

Naturally, it is not just a question of a verbal inspiration. Every real inspiration passes into the muscles and emerges in the form of actions; and at the present time the only actions possible to Frenchmen are those which contribute towards driving out the enemy.

All the same, it would be wrong to suppose that the only mission of the French movement in London lay in raising the energy of the French to the highest possible pitch in their struggle against the enemy.

Its mission is to help France to find again a genuine inspiration, which, because of its very genuineness, naturally finds an outlet in efforts and acts of heroism on behalf of the liberation of the country.

This doesn't amount to the same thing.

It is because it is necessary to carry out a mission of so lofty a nature that the clumsy but efficacious means of threats, promises and suggestions would not be adequate.

On the other hand, the use of words answering the secret thoughts and needs of the human beings composing the French people is a method marvellously well adapted to the task to be accomplished, provided it be used in the correct manner.

For that, there must first of all be in France a receiving organization, that is to say, people whose primary duty it is to discover these secret thoughts, these secret needs, and pass the information on to London.

What is indispensable for this task is a passionate interest in human beings, whoever they may be, and in their minds and souls; the ability to place oneself in their position and to recognize by signs thoughts which go unexpressed; a certain intuitive sense of history in process of being enacted; and the faculty of expressing in writing delicate shades of meaning and complex relationships.

In view of the extent and complexity of the field to be kept under observation, there ought to be a good many of these observers; but in fact that is impossible. However, anybody who can be used in this way should be used at once, without exception.

On the supposition that there exists a receiving organization in France, an inadequate—it cannot be otherwise—but a genuine one, the next operation, by far the more important of the two, takes place in London. It consists in making a selection, in being able to mould the spirit of the country.

The knowledge of what words are likely to find an echo in the hearts of Frenchmen, because they correspond to something which is already there—that knowledge is solely one of fact. It contains no indication at all of a good objective, and politics, like every human activity, is an activity directed towards a good objective.

The state of mind of the French is nothing else than a fact. In principle it constitutes something that is neither good nor bad; in fact it is made up of a mixture of good and bad, according to proportions which can vary greatly.

That is a self-evident truth, but one which it is as well to remind oneself of, because the sentimental feelings which naturally correspond to a state of exile might cause it to be more or less forgotten.

From among all the words likely to awaken an echo in the hearts of the French, the ones to choose are those which it is right to wish should be echoed; they ought to be repeated over and over again, leaving out the others, so as to bring about the disappearance of what may advantageously be made to disappear.

What criteria of selection should be adopted?

One can think of two. First, the good, in the spiritual sense of the word; secondly, the useful—that is to say, of course, useful from the point of view of the war and the national interests of France.

In connexion with the first criterion, there is to start with a postulate to be considered. It must be weighed very carefully, very deliberately, in one's mind and conscience, then adopted or rejected once and for all.

A Christian cannot do otherwise than adopt it.

It is the postulate that what is spiritually good is good in every respect, at all times, in all places, under all circumstances.

It is what Christ expressed in the words: 'Do men gather grapes of thorns, or figs of thistles? Even so every good tree bringeth forth good fruit; but a corrupt tree bringeth forth evil fruit. A good tree cannot bring forth evil fruit, neither can a corrupt tree bring forth good fruit.'*

The meaning of these words is this. Above the earthly, carnal sphere in which our thoughts habitually move, and which is on every side an inextricable mixture of good and evil, there is another, a spiritual sphere, where good is only good and, even at the inferior level, produces only good; where evil is only evil and can produce nothing but evil.

It is a direct consequence of faith in God. The absolute good is not only the very best good of all—it would then be a relative good—but the unique, total good, which comprises within itself in a superlative degree all forms of the good, including those which are sought by men who deviate from the path of absolute good.

All forms of pure good issuing directly from the absolute good possess similar properties to the latter.

And so amongst the list of echoes capable of being awakened in French hearts by London, we must first of all choose everything which is purely and genuinely good, without the slightest consideration for expediency, applying no other test than that

* Quotation: Matt. vii, 16-18. [Translator.]

192

of genuineness; and we must let them have all that very often, untiringly, using words as simple and clear-cut as possible.

Naturally, everything which is only concerned with evil, hatred, meanness must in like manner be rejected, without any consideration for expediency.

There remain the medium-quality motives, which are inferior to spiritual good without being of themselves necessarily bad, and in connexion with which the question of expediency arises.

In the case of each of these, a thorough examination must be made if possible, going really carefully into the subject, of all the effects it is likely to produce in this, that or the other respect; this, that or the other possible bunch of circumstances.

Unless this precaution is taken, one might by mistake encourage what one didn't want instead of what one did.

For example, after 1918, pacifists thought they ought to appeal to the love of security, of comfort, in order to be readily listened to. They thus hoped to attain sufficient influence to be able to direct the country's foreign policy, in which case they reckoned they would direct it in such a way as to ensure peace.

They didn't ask themselves what the consequences of such incitations would be should they attain an influential position which yet was not enough to place the direction of foreign policy in their hands.

If they had only asked themselves this question, the answer would at once have been plain to them. In such an event, the incitations in question would be unable either to prevent or to postpone war, but only make it possible for any war to be won by the more aggressive, the more bellicose side, and so bring into disrepute for a long time to come the love of peace itself.

It may be observed, incidentally, that in the very working of democratic institutions, according to our notions, there lies a perpetual open invitation to commit this sort of criminal and fatal negligence.

To avoid committing it, in the case of every incitation we must say to ourselves: this incitation is able to produce certain effects in this, that or the other social group, and in what other ones besides? It is able to produce certain effects in this, that or the other sphere; and in what other ones besides? This, that or the other situation is able to result; what other ones besides? In each case, what effects would it be likely to produce in each group, in each sphere, at once, a little later, or later on still? In what respects would each of these possible effects be beneficial, in what respects detrimental? What appears to be the degree of probability in the case of each of these possibilities?

We must carefully consider each of these points and all of them together; suspend for a moment any inclination to choose between them; then decide, and, as in all human decisions, run the risk of making a mistake.

Having made our choice, we must put it to a practical test, and, of course, the registering apparatus set up in France will endeavour to perceive progressively the results obtained.

But words are only a beginning. Action is a more powerful tool for moulding people's minds.

It possesses a double property with respect to incitations. To begin with, an incitation only becomes real to the mind when it has brought about an action performed by the body.

It isn't enough to foster this, that or the other incitation, actual or embryonic, in the hearts of Frenchmen, counting upon the latter to translate of their own accord their own incitations into actions.

We must, in addition, from London, as far as is humanly possible, as continuously as possible, with the greatest possible number of details, and by every appropriate means, radio or otherwise, suggest actions.

A soldier once said, recounting his own behaviour during a campaign: 'I obeyed all the orders, but I felt how impossible it would have been for me, how infinitely above what my courage was capable of, to place myself voluntarily and without orders in the path of danger'.

A very profound truth is contained in that remark. An order is an incredibly efficacious stimulant. Under certain circumstances, it contains within itself the energy necessary for carrying out the action which it lays down.

Incidentally, to find out what these circumstances are, what it is which determines them, what different aspects they can assume, and to draw up a complete list of them, would provide one with a key for the solution of the most essential and most urgent problems of war and politics.

Any clearly recognized responsibility, imposing certain precise and absolutely strict obligations, incites one to brave danger in the same way as an order. It only makes its presence felt once the action is in full swing and as a result of the particular circumstances corresponding to the latter. The ability to recognize such a responsibility is all the greater according to the superior degree of intelligence; it depends still more on intellectual honesty, an infinitely precious virtue which prevents one from lying to oneself in order to avoid discomfort.

Those who are able to expose themselves to danger without the constraint imposed by an order or some definite responsibility are of three kinds. Those who have a lot of natural courage, with a temperament to a large extent a stranger to fear and an imagination little exposed to nightmarish impressions; such people often go to meet danger lightheartedly, in an adventurous spirit, without paying much attention to the precise sort of danger involved. Those who find it difficult to display courage, but who derive the necessary impetus to do so from impure motives. Medal-hunting, vengeance, hatred are examples of this type of motive; there are a great many more, and they vary very much according to different characters and sets of circumstances. Those who obey a direct and individual order come from God.

This last case is not so rare as one might be led to suppose; for where it exists it is often hidden, even hidden from the individual himself concerned, those whose case it is being sometimes numbered among the ones who think they don't believe in God. All the same, though less rare than one supposes, it is, unfortunately, not very frequent.

The two other categories have a courage which, while often very spectacular and rewarded by the name of heroism, is very inferior in human quality to that of the soldier who obeys the orders of his superiors.

The French movement in London possesses exactly the requisite degree of official character for its directives to have the stimulating properties attaching to orders, yet without diminishing that sort of pure and lucid frenzy which accompanies the free acceptance of sacrifice. Its opportunities and corresponding responsibilities are, therefore, immense.

The more actions there are in France carried out by its orders, the more people there are acting under its orders, the more chance France will have of recovering a spirit which will enable her to make a triumphant re-entry into the war—not only militarily speaking, but spiritually speaking also—and to set about the reconstruction of the country after the war.

Over and above the question of number, it is the choice of actions which is essential.

It is essential from several points of view, some of which are so highly important that the present partitioning which places this sphere entirely in the hands of technicians in the subversive arts must be looked upon as disastrous.

Speaking quite generally, in any sort of sphere, it is inevitable that evil should dominate wherever the technical side of things is either completely or almost completely sovereign.

Technicians always tend to make themselves sovereign, because they feel they alone know what they are about; and this is perfectly natural on their part. The responsibility for any evil overtaking them, as a necessary consequence, has to be exclusively borne by those who have allowed them full rein. When they are allowed to have full rein, it is always solely for want of keeping continually in mind a clear and absolutely precise conception of the particular ends to which this, that or the other technique should be subordinated.

The direction given by London to the action being carried out in France must correspond to a series of different objectives.

The most obvious is the strictly military and immediate objective, as far as information and sabotage are concerned.

In regard to this, the French in London can only act as a connecting link between England's requirements and the good-will of the French in France.

The extreme importance of such matters is obvious, when one considers how it becomes clearer and clearer every day that it is communications far more than battles which is going to be decisive in this war. The twin proposition locomotives-sabotage is proportionately identical with the twin proposition boat-submarine. The destruction of locomotives is as important as that of submarines; the relationship between these two forms of destruction being that of offensive and defensive action.

The disorganization of production is no less essential.

The volume, the amount of our influence on the action being carried out in France depends chiefly on the material means placed at our disposal by the British. Our influence over France, the influence we already possess and still more the influence we are able to acquire, can be of immense service to the British. There is thus a mutual need of each other's services; but ours is by far the greater, at least so far as the immediate future is concerned, which is too often the only aspect considered.

Such being the case, if between them and us there do not exist not only good, but warm, genuinely friendly and in some sort intimate relations, that is something which cannot be allowed to continue and must be made to cease immediately. Wherever human relations are not what they should be, there is generally fault to be found on both sides. But it is always far more to the purpose to consider one's own faults, so as to put a stop to them, than those of the other party. Besides, the need is far greater on our side—at any rate the immediate need. And then, we are *émigrés* who have been given shelter, and so we owe them a debt of gratitude. Lastly, it is a well-known fact that the British have no aptitude for getting outside their skins and placing themselves in the position of other people; their best qualities, their particular function on this planet, are almost incompatible with the possession of such an aptitude. The same aptitude is actually, and unfortunately, almost as rare with us; but it belongs in the nature of things to what is recognized as being France's vocation. For all these reasons, it is for us to make the necessary effort to bring our relations up to a suitable degree of warmth; a sincere desire on our part to understand—free, naturally, from any suspicion of servility—must pierce beneath their reserve to the real capacity for friendship which it conceals.

Personal feelings play in all big world events a part that can never be discerned to its full extent. The fact that a state of friendship exists or doesn't exist between two men, or two groups of men, can in certain cases prove decisive for the destiny of the human race.

This is perfectly understandable. A truth can only present itself to the mind of a particular human being. How is he going to communicate it? If he tries to expound it, he won't be listened to; for other people have never heard of that particular truth, won't recognize it as such; they won't realize that what he is saying is true; they won't pay enough attention to enable them to see that it is so; for they won't have received any inducement to make the necessary effort of concentration.

But friendship, admiration, sympathy or any other sort of benevolent feeling would naturally predispose them to give a certain amount of their attention. A man who has something new to say—for as far as platitudes are concerned no effort of attention is necessary—can only be listened to, to begin with, by those that love him.

So it is that the transmission of truths among men depends entirely on the state of their feelings; and the same applies to no matter what kind of truth.

With exiles who are ever thinking of their country—and

those who forget it are lost—the heart is so irresistibly turned towards the homeland in distress that few emotional resources are left for friendship for the land they happen to be living in. Such friendship cannot really germinate and spring up in their hearts unless they do themselves a sort of violence. But this violence is an obligation on their part.

Frenchmen who are in London have no more imperative obligation towards the French people, who live with their eyes turned in their direction, than that of seeing that between themselves and the *élite* of Englishmen there exists a real, living, warm, close and effective friendship.

Apart from strategic utility, still further considerations should play their part in the choice of actions to be undertaken. They are of far greater importance even, but come second in order, because strategic utility is a necessary condition for giving reality to the action in question; where it is absent, there is confusion, non-action, and the indirect virtue of action, which gives it its chief value, is likewise absent.

This indirect virtue is, once again, a double one.

Action gives the fullness of reality to the incitations which have inspired it. The expression of such incitations, as heard on the outside, only gives them as yet a semi-reality. Action possesses a virtue of quite another order.

Many different feelings can co-exist in the heart. The choice of those which must, after having been discovered in the hearts of Frenchmen, be accorded the degree of reality which official expression confers—that choice is already limited by questions of material necessity. If, for example, you speak to the French every evening for a quarter of an hour, and if you are obliged to repeat yourself frequently because jamming makes it impossible to be certain of having been heard, and because in any case repetition is a pedagogical necessity, you are only able to say a limited number of things.

As soon as you step into the sphere of action, the limits are even narrower. You are obliged to effect a new choice, in accordance with the criteria already outlined above.

The Growing of Roots

The manner in which an incitation becomes transformed into an act is something that requires to be studied. The same act may be produced by this, that or the other incitation, or by a mixture of incitations; on the other hand, some other incitation may not be capable of producing it.

To bring people not only to carry out a given action, but, furthermore, to carry it out under the impulse of a given incitation, the best means, perhaps the only means, appears to consist in the association established between the two by means of speech. That is to say that, each time a certain action is advised by radio, this advice should be accompanied by one or more incitations towards it; each time the advice is repeated, the incitation, or incitations, should again be mentioned.

It is true that precise instructions are communicated by means other than the radio. But they ought all to be backed up by words of encouragement transmitted by radio, bearing on the same subject, to be specified only in so far as discretion permits; minus the details, but plus the mention of incitations.

Action possesses a second virtue within the sphere of incitations. It not only confers reality upon incitations which, previously, existed in a semi-phantasmal state: it also causes incitations and feelings to arise in the mind which previously didn't exist at all.

That happens every time either the enthusiasm of the moment or the force of circumstances causes the action to go beyond the sum total of energy contained in the incitation which has produced the action.

This mechanism—knowledge of which is as essential for the conduct of one's own life as for its action upon men in general—is equally capable of producing evil or good.

For instance, it often happens that in a family a chronic invalid, tenderly nursed as a result of a sincere affection, ends up by arousing among his relatives a secret, hidden hostility, because they have been obliged to expend more energy on him than was contained in their affection for him.

The Growing of Roots

Among the common people, on whom such obligations, added to habitual sources of fatigue, weigh so heavily, the impression is sometimes conveyed of insensibility, or even of cruelty, incomprehensible to an outsider. It is for this reason that, as *Gringoire** so charitably remarked on one occasion, cases of child martyrdom are more often found among the common people than elsewhere.

The resources which this mechanism possesses for producing good are illustrated in an admirable Buddhist tale.

A Buddhist tradition has it that Buddha promised to cause whoever should pronounce his name with the desire to be saved to ascend to heaven and join him there. On this tradition rests the practice known as 'reciting the name of the Lord', which consists in repeating a certain number of times a few Sanskrit, Chinese or Japanese syllables meaning: 'Glory to the Lord of Light'.

A young monk was anxious about the eternal salvation of his father, an old miser whose every thought was about money. The Prior of the monastery sent for the old man and promised to give him a penny every time he should recite the Lord's name; he had only to present himself every evening and tell them how many pennies were owing to him, and he would be paid on the spot. The old man, thoroughly delighted, now spent all his leisure moments in this occupation, and used to come to the monastery every evening to be paid. All of a sudden, they missed him. After a week, the Prior sent the young man to find out how his father was. It was then discovered that the old man had now become so absorbed in reciting the name of the Lord that he could no longer keep count of the number of times he did so; which was what had prevented him from coming to claim his money. The Prior advised the young monk not to do anything further and simply to wait. Some little while afterwards, the old man arrived at the monastery with shining eyes, and related how he had had an illumination.

* *Gringoire:* see note p. 37. [Translator.]

It is to phenomena of this sort that Christ refers in his precept: 'Lay up to yourselves treasures in heaven . . . for where your treasure is, there will your heart be also'.

Which means to say that there are certain actions which have the virtue of transporting from earth to heaven part of the love that lies in a man's heart.

A miser is not a miser when he first starts hoarding money. No doubt he is urged on, to begin with, by the thought of all the pleasures which money can buy. But the efforts and privations to which he daily subjects himself come to have an allurement. When the sacrifice surpasses by far the original impulse, the treasure, the object of his sacrifices, becomes for him an end in itself, and he subordinates himself to it. The collector's mania rests upon a similar mechanism. A host of other examples might be cited.

Thus, when the sacrifices made on behalf of an object greatly surpass the impulse which induced them, the result is, as regards this object, either a movement of repulsion or else an attachment of a new and more intense kind, unconnected with the initial impulse.

In the second case, the result is either good or bad according to the nature of the object.

If in the case of the invalid there is often repulsion, that is because this type of effort doesn't lead to anything; there is no external result to show for the internal accumulation of fatigue. The miser, on the other hand, is able to watch his treasure grow.

There are also, however, situations, combinations of character, which makes it so that a family invalid inspires, on the contrary, a fanatical attachment. By investigating all this sufficiently thoroughly, one would doubtless be able to discern the appropriate laws.

But even a summary acquaintance with these phenomena can furnish us with certain practical rules.

In order to avoid the effect of repulsion, the possible exhaustion of incitations must be foreseen; from time to time the authority of official utterance must be lent to new incitations for carrying out the same actions, to incitations representing what has been able to germinate in the secret places of the heart.

Above all, we must see to it that the transference mechanism which attaches the miser to his treasure works in such a way as to produce good and not evil; avoid or at least limit to the strictest minimum all the evil which could thus be brought about.

It is not difficult to understand how.

The mechanism in question consists in this, that an action, after having been conducted with difficulty from motives unrelated to itself, becomes by itself an object of attachment. The result is either good or evil, according to whether the action is in itself a good or an evil one.

If you kill German soldiers in order to serve France and then at the end of a certain time you acquire a taste for assassinating human beings, it is clearly an evil thing.

If, in order to serve France, you offer your assistance to workmen avoiding transportation to Germany and then at the end of a certain time you acquire a taste for helping those in misfortune, it is clearly a good thing.

Not every case is so clear as are the above two, but all can be examined in this fashion.

Moreover, all things being equal, one should always choose methods of action which contain in themselves an impulsion towards the good. Indeed, one should even do so very often when all things are not equal. It should be done not only because the purpose served is a good one, which would be a sufficient reason, but because it is a useful one into the bargain.

Evil becomes an operative motive far more easily than good; but once pure good has become an operative motive in the mind, it forms there the fount of a uniform and inexhaustible impulsion, which is never so in the case of evil.

It is quite possible for one to become a double-acting secret service agent out of patriotism, in order the better to serve one's country by deceiving the enemy. But if the efforts expended in this form of activity are in excess of the energy supplied by the patriotic motive, and if one later on acquires a taste for this form of activity for its own sake, there comes a time almost inevitably when one no longer knows oneself whom one is serving and whom one is deceiving, when one is ready to serve or to deceive anybody.

On the other hand, if out of patriotism one is impelled to perform actions which cause the love of some higher good than that of one's country to take root and develop, then the mind takes on that cast which produces martyrs, and the country reaps the benefit.

Faith is more realist than is realist policy. Whoever isn't convinced of this doesn't possess faith.

One should therefore examine and weigh extremely carefully, each time looking at the problem from every angle, the several methods of action which go to form the subversive resistance movement in France.

Careful observations on the spot, carried out solely from this point of view, are indispensable in this connexion.

Nor should we rule out the possibility of its being necessary to invent new forms of action, bearing in mind at the same time the above considerations and immediate objectives.

(For instance, the immediate setting afoot of a vast conspiracy to *destroy all official documents* relating to the control of individuals by the State, which destruction can be carried out by very varied means, such as provoking fires, etc.—that is something which could have very great immediate and long-term advantages.)

A degree of reality superior even to that of action is attained by the organization which co-ordinates actions, when such an organization has not been formed artificially, but has grown up like a plant in the midst of day-to-day necessities, having at the same time been moulded with patient vigilance and with some particular good clearly kept in view. This constitutes, perhaps, the highest possible degree of reality.

Organizations already exist in France. But there are also—which is of infinitely greater interest still—embryonic, germinal, roughly sketched organizations in process of growth.

They must be examined, viewed on the spot, and the authority emanating from London must be used like a tool to shape them discreetly and patiently, like a sculptor who divines the shape contained in the block of marble in order to bring it forth.

This shaping must be guided at once by immediate and non-immediate considerations.

Everything that has been said hitherto about verbal propositions and action applies equally here.

An organization which can crystallize and seize upon the words launched officially, translate their inspiration into different words entirely of its own, realize them in co-ordinated actions for which it offers an ever-increasing guarantee of efficacity; can be a living, warm environment, full of friendly intercourse, companionship and kindness—that is the sort of humus in which the unfortunate French, uprooted by the disaster, can live and find their salvation both in war and in peace.

It must be done now. Once victory is attained, in the irresistible unleashing of individual appetites seeking happiness or power, it will be absolutely impossible to start anything of the kind.

It must be done immediately. It is something indescribably urgent. To miss the opportunity now would be to lay oneself open to what would almost amount perhaps to criminal guilt.

The unique source of salvation and greatness for France lies in regaining contact with her genius in the depths of her distress. This must be accomplished now, immediately; whilst the distress is still a crushing one; whilst France still has before her, in the future, the opportunity of making real the first conscious glimmerings of her recovered genius by expressing them through warlike action.

After victory has been won, this opportunity would no longer exist, and peace would not offer its equivalent. For it is infinitely more difficult to imagine, to conceive a peacetime action than it is a wartime one. In order to penetrate and infuse a peacetime action, an inspiration must already have a high degree of consciousness, radiance, reality. Such will only be the case with France, when peace dawns, if the last phase of the war has produced this effect. The war must be made the teacher to develop and nourish this inspiration; and for this to happen a deep, authentic inspiration, a veritable illumination of the spirit must arise whilst the war is in full swing.

France must once more be fully present in this war, share in the victory at the cost of her blood; but that is not enough. Such a thing could take place in the shadows, and the real profit derived therefrom would then be small.

What is wanted besides is that what goes to nourish her war effort should be nothing less than her veritable genius, discovered once more in the depths of her misfortune, although with an inevitably weak proportion of consciousness at first, after such a night.

The war itself can then fan it into a flame.

The true mission of the French movement in London is, by reason even of the military and political circumstances, a spiritual mission before being a military and political one.

It could be defined as being that of director of conscience on a national plane.

The mode of political action outlined in these pages requires that every choice made be preceded by the simultaneous review of several considerations of a very different nature. This implies a high degree of concentration, more or less of the same standard as that required for creative work in art or science.

But why should politics, which decide the fate of peoples and whose object is justice, demand any less concentration than art or science, whose respective objects are beauty and truth?

Politics have a very close affinity to art—to arts such as poetry, music and architecture.

Simultaneous composition on several planes at once is the law of artistic creation, and wherein, in fact, lies its difficulty.

A poet, in the arrangement of words and the choice of each word, must simultaneously bear in mind matters on at least five or six different planes of composition. The rules of versification—number of syllables and rhymes—in the poetic form he has chosen; the grammatical sequence of words; their logical sequence from the point of view of the development of his thought; the purely musical sequence of sounds contained in the syllables; the so to speak material rhythm formed by pauses, stops, duration of each syllable and of each group of syllables; the atmosphere with which each word is surrounded by the possibilities of suggestion it contains, and the transition from one atmosphere to another as fast as the words succeed each other; the psychological rhythm produced by the duration of words corresponding to such and such an atmosphere or such and such a movement of thought; the effects of repetition and novelty; doubtless other things besides; and finally a unique intuition for beauty which gives all this a unity.

Inspiration is a tension on the part of the soul's faculties which renders possible the indispensable degree of concentration required for composition on a multiple plane.

Whoever finds himself incapable of such concentration will one day acquire the capacity for it, if he perseveres humbly and patiently, and if he is impelled by a violent and unshakable desire.

If he is not the prey of such a desire, it is not absolutely imperative that he should make verses.

Politics, in their turn, form an art governed by composition on a multiple plane. Whoever finds himself with political responsibilities, if in his heart he hungers and thirsts after justice, must desire to possess this faculty of composition on a multiple plane, and consequently is bound, in the end, to receive it.

However, at the moment, there is no time to lose. A host of things need urgent attention.

The method of political action outlined here goes beyond the possibilities of the human intelligence, at least as far as those possibilities are known. But it is precisely that which lends it its value. It is no use asking ourselves whether we are or are not capable of applying it. The answer would always be no. It is something which must be perfectly clearly conceived in the mind, pondered over long and often, planted permanently in that part of the mind where thoughts take root, and brought up whenever decisions have to be taken. There is then, perhaps, the chance that the decisions, though imperfect, will be good ones.

Whoever writes verse with the ambition of composing a beautiful lines as those of Racine, will never write a beautiful line; and still less so if he doesn't even harbour that hope.

In order to write verse that contains some beauty, one must have had the ambition to equal by the arrangement of words that pure and divine beauty which, according to Plato, lies on the other side of the skies.

One of the fundamental truths of Christianity is that progress towards a lesser imperfection is not produced by the desire for a lesser imperfection. Only the desire for perfection has the virtue of being able to destroy in the soul some part of the evil which defiles it. Hence Christ's commandment: 'Be ye therefore perfect, even as your Father which is in heaven is perfect'.

To the extent to which human language falls short of divine beauty, to that extent Man's sentient and intellectual faculties fall short of truth, and the necessities of social life fall short of justice. Consequently, politics cannot but be as much in need of efforts of creative invention as are art and science.

That is why almost the entire sum of political opinions and discussions in which these opinions get bandied about has as little to do with politics as has the clash of aesthetic opinions in the cafés of Montparnasse to do with art. The politician in the one case, as the artist in the other, can only find in such activity a certain stimulant, which ought to be taken in very small doses

Politics are practically never looked upon as an art of so high a category. But that is because we have for centuries been accustomed to regard them solely, or at least principally, as a technique for acquiring and holding on to power.

Now, power is not an end. By nature, in essence and by definition, it constitutes exclusively a means. It is to politics what a piano is to musical composition. A composer who requires a piano in order to be able to invent his melodies will find himself in an embarrassing situation if he happens to be staying in a village where there isn't one. But if one is procured for him, it is then up to him to compose.

Fools that we are, we had confused the manufacture of a piano with the composition of a sonata.

An educational method which is not inspired by the conception of a certain form of human perfection is not worth very much. When it is a matter of educating a whole people, this conception should be that of a civilization. It must not be sought in the past, which only contains imperfect models; far less still in our dreams of the future, which are necessarily as mediocre as we ourselves are, and consequently vastly inferior to the past. The inspiration for such an education must be sought, like the method itself, among the truths eternally inscribed in the nature of things.

Here are a few indications on this subject.

Four obstacles above all separate us from a form of civilization likely to be worth something: our false conception of greatness; the degradation of the sentiment of justice; our idolization of money; and our lack of religious inspiration. We may use the first person plural without any hesitation, for it is doubtful whether at the present moment there is a single human being on the surface of the globe who is free from that quadruple defect, and more doubtful still whether there is a single one belonging to the white race. But if there are one or two, which, in spite of everything, is to be hoped, they remain hidden.

Our conception of greatness is the most serious defect of all, and the one concerning which we are least conscious that it is a defect: at least, a defect in ourselves; for in our enemies it shocks us. But in spite of the warning contained in Christ's parable of the mote and the beam, it never occurs to us to recognize it as ours.

Our conception of greatness is the very one which has inspired Hitler's whole life. When we denounce it without the remotest recognition of its application to ourselves, the angels must either cry or laugh, if there happen to be angels who interest themselves in our propaganda.

It appears that as soon as Tripolitania was occupied, the teaching of the Fascist version of history was stopped there. That is excellent. But it would be interesting to know in what, as regards ancient times, the Fascist teaching of history differed from that of the French Republic. The difference can hardly have been very noticeable, since the great authority in republican France on matters of ancient history, J: Carcopino, gave a series of lectures in Rome on the subject of Ancient Rome and Gaul which were perfectly suitable to be given in that city and were very warmly applauded.

At the present moment, the French in London hold certain things against J. Carcopino, but it is not on account of his historical views. Another historian belonging to the Sorbonne said in January 1940 to some one who had written something rather harsh about the Romans: 'If Italy comes in against us, you will have been right.' As a basis for historical judgment, it seems insufficient.

Those who have been defeated often benefit from a sentimentalism which is even sometimes unjust, but only those defeated provisionally. Affliction confers an immense prestige so long as it is accompanied by strength. The affliction of the weak is not even an object of attention—when, indeed, it is not an object of repulsion. When the early Christians had become solidly convinced that Christ, in spite of having been crucified, had subsequently risen from the dead and was to return before very long in his glory to recompense his own and punish all the rest, no tortures had any further terrors for them. But previously, when Christ had only been an absolutely pure being, as soon as misfortune overtook him, he was abandoned. Those who loved him most could not find in their hearts the courage to run risks on his behalf. Torture gets the better of courage when in order to face it there isn't the stimulus of a revenge. The revenge need not be a personal one. A martyred Jesuit in China is sustained by the temporal grandeur of the Church, in spite of the fact that he cannot expect it to assist him personally in any way. There is no other force on this earth except force. That could serve as an axiom. As for the force which is not of this earth, contact with it cannot be bought at any lesser price than the passing through a kind of death.

There is not on earth any other force except force, and it is this which communicates force to the feelings, including compassion. Any number of examples could be given. Why did the pacifists after 1918 feel so much more pity for Germany than for Austria? Why did the necessity for holidays with pay seem to so many people an axiom of mathematical clarity in 1936 and not in 1935?* Why are there so many more people who take an interest in factory workers than in agricultural workers? And so on.

The same in the case of history. The heroic resistance of the vanquished is admired when time brings with it a certain revenge, not otherwise. No compassion is felt for things which have been utterly destroyed. Who is there who accords any to Jericho, Gaza, Tyre, Sidon; to Carthage, Numantia, Sicily under the Greeks, or Peru before the time of Columbus?

But, it will be objected, why lament the disappearance of things about which we know, as it were, nothing at all? We know nothing about them because they have disappeared. Those who destroyed them didn't consider it necessary to become the guardians of the culture they represented.

Generally speaking, the most serious mistakes, those which

* See first footnote on page 188. [Translator.]

warp completely the mental processes, destroy the soul, placing it outside the reach of truth and goodness, cannot be discerned. For they are caused by the fact that certain things escape the scrutiny of the mind. If they escape such a scrutiny, how could they be scrutinized, however hard one were to try? That is why truth is, in its essence, a supernatural good.

It is the same with history. No attention is paid to the defeated. It is the scene of a Darwinian process more pitiless still than that which governs animal and vegetable life. The defeated disappear. They become naught.

The Romans, so it is said, civilized Gaul. There was no art there before Gallo-Roman art; no thought before the Gauls had the privilege of reading the philosophical productions of Cicero; and so on.

We know, as it were, nothing about Gaul; but the scanty indications we do possess are sufficient to prove all that to be a lie.

Gaulish art runs no risk of being made the subject of written accounts on the part of our archaeologists, since the material used was wood. But the town of Bourges was such a marvel of pure beauty that the Gauls lost their last campaign because they couldn't find the courage to destroy it of their own accord. Caesar, of course, destroyed it, and at the same time massacred the entire forty thousand human beings found therein.

We have it from Caesar that the course of study pursued by the Druids lasted twenty years, and consisted in learning by heart poems about the divine nature and the universe. Gaulish poetry must, therefore, at any rate have contained a sufficient number of religious and metaphysical poems for it to be the subject of twenty years' study. Compared with the incredible imaginative riches suggested by this fact alone, Latin poetry, in spite of Lucretius, seems a miserable affair.

Diogenes Laërtius says that a tradition attributed several foreign origins to Greek wisdom, and amongst others the Druids of Gaul. Other texts indicate that the thought of the Druids was related to that of the Pythagoreans.

Thus this people possessed a whole ocean of sacred poetry whose inspiration we are only able to form some idea of through the works of Plato.

All that disappeared when the Romans wiped out the entire collection of Druids for being guilty of the crime of patriotism.

It is true that the Romans put a stop to human sacrifice practised, so they said, in Gaul. We know nothing about the actual form this took, the manner and spirit in which it was practised, if it was a method of executing criminals or simply consisted in putting to death innocent people, and, in the latter case, if it was done with consent or not. The testimony of the Romans is very vague and cannot be accepted with entire confidence. But what we do know for certain is that the Romans themselves instituted in Gaul and everywhere else the putting to death of thousands of innocent people, not in order to do honour to the gods, but in order to amuse the crowds. That was a Roman institution *par excellence*, one they set up wherever they went; and yet we dare to regard them as civilizers.

Nevertheless, if one were to state publicly that pre-Roman Gaul was much more civilized than Rome, it would sound like an absurdity.

That is simply a characteristic example. In spite of the fact that on the same soil which was that of Gaul a nation has arisen, which is our own; that patriotism has with us, as elsewhere, a marked tendency to spread itself in the direction of the past; that the few documents which have been preserved provide an irrefutable testimony, the military defeat of the Gauls is an unsurmountable obstacle to our recognizing the high spiritual qualities of this civilization which was destroyed.

There have, all the same, been one or two attempts on the right lines, like that of Camille Jullian.* But Trojan territory having never again served as the abode of a nation, who has ever gone to the trouble to discern the truth which blazes forth

* *Camille Jullian:* historian (1859-1933), and the author of a remarkable *Histoire de la Gaule.* [Translator.]

in the clearest possible fashion in the *Iliad*, in Herodotus and in the *Agamemnon* of Aeschylus—namely, that Troy possessed a level of civilization, culture and spiritual development far superior to that of those by whom it was unjustly attacked and destroyed, and that its disappearance was a disaster in the history of humanity?

Up to June 1940, various articles appeared in the French press, by way of patriotic encouragement, comparing the Franco-German conflict to the Trojan war, and explaining how the latter was already then a struggle between civilization and barbarism, the barbarians being the Trojans. Now, there is nothing to account for this mistake save the fact that Troy was defeated.

If one cannot help falling into such a mistake in connexion with the Greeks, who were haunted by remorse for the crime committed and themselves bore witness in favour of their victims, how much more so in the case of other nations, whose invariable practice it is to vilify those whom they have exterminated?

History is founded upon documents. The professional historian won't allow himself to form hypotheses which don't rest upon something. That seems to be very reasonable; but in reality it is far from being so. For, since there are holes in documents, a balanced judgment requires that hypotheses which haven't any basis should be present to the mind, provided they be there in that capacity, and that there be several of them in connexion with each particular point.

All the more reason why when dealing with documents it is necessary to read between the lines, allow oneself to be transported entirely, with a complete forgetfulness of self, into the atmosphere of the events recalled, keep the attention fixed for a very long time on any little significant details and discover exactly what their full meaning is.

But the respect for documents and the professional spirit of historians do not incline their minds towards this type of exercise. What is called the historical spirit doesn't pierce through the paper to discover real flesh and blood; it consists in a subordination of the mind to documents.

Now, according to the nature of things, documents originate among the powerful ones, the conquerors. History, therefore, is nothing but a compilation of the depositions made by assassins with respect to their victims and themselves.

What is called the tribunal of History, seeing that its information is derived in this fashion, cannot possibly judge in any other way than the one followed in the fable of 'The animals smitten with the plague'.

On the subject of the Romans, we have absolutely nothing except what the Romans themselves wrote and what was written by their Greek slaves. The latter, poor devils, amidst their servile reticences, have said quite enough about them, if only we took the trouble to read really attentively what they have to say. But why should we take that trouble? There is nothing to induce us to make the effort. It isn't the Carthaginians who allot the prizes of the Academy* or the professorships at the Sorbonne.

Why, for the same reason, should we bother to cast doubts upon the information supplied by the Hebrews concerning the inhabitants of Canaan whom they either exterminated or enslaved? It isn't the people of Jericho who control nominations to the *Institut Catholique*.†

We know from one of Hitler's biographies that one of the books which exercised a profound influence on him in his youth was a tenth-rate work on Sulla. The fact that it was tenth-rate is neither here nor there. What matters is that it reflected the attitude of what is known as the *élite*. Who would be found to write contemptuously about Sulla? If Hitler desired the sort of greatness which he saw glorified in this book and everywhere else, he certainly made no mistake about it. For that is exactly the sort of greatness he has achieved, the very

* *Academy:* the Académie Française. [Translator.]

† *Institut Catholique:* famous Catholic centre of higher education in Paris, situated rue d'Assas. [Translator.]

sort before which we all bow down in servile admiration as soon as our eyes are turned towards the past.

We don't go beyond a base submission of the mind in regard to it; we haven't tried, like Hitler, to seize it with both hands. But in this respect he is a better man than any of us. Once one recognizes something as being a good, one should want to seize it. Not to want to do so is cowardly.

Let us just imagine for a moment that wretched, uprooted youth wandering about in the streets of Vienna, athirst for greatness. It well became him to be athirst for greatness. Was it his fault if he was unable to perceive any form of greatness except the criminal form? Ever since the common people have become literate and no longer possess oral traditions, it is those capable of wielding a pen who have supplied the public with conceptions of greatness and with examples serving to illustrate them.

The author of this mediocre book on Sulla, all those who in writing about Sulla or about Rome had made possible the atmosphere in which this book was written, and, more generally, all those who, being in a position to voice their thoughts in speech or writing, contributed towards the intellectual and spiritual atmosphere in which the youthful Hitler grew up—all those people are perhaps more guilty of Hitler's crimes than he is himself. Most of them are now dead; but those of today are no better than their elders and cannot be rendered more innocent by the purely accidental date of birth.

People talk about punishing Hitler. But he cannot be punished. He desired one thing alone, and he has it: to play a part in History. He can be killed, tortured, imprisoned, humiliated, History will always be there to shield his spirit from all the ravages of suffering and death. What we inflict on him will be, inevitably, an historical death, an historical suffering—in fact, History. Just in the same way as for any one who has reached the perfect love of God, whatever happens is good as coming from God; so for this idolizer of History, everything connected with History must be good. Moreover, he has a very considerable advantage; for the pure love of God inhabits the centre of the soul, leaves the sensibility exposed to injury, doesn't form an armour. Idolatry is an armour, prevents pain from entering the soul. Whatever Hitler is made to suffer, that will not stop him from feeling himself to be a superb figure. Above all, it will not stop, in twenty, fifty, a hundred or two hundred years' time, some solitary little dreamer, whether German or otherwise, from seeing in Hitler a superb figure, with a superb destiny from beginning to end, and desiring with all his soul to have a similar destiny. In which case, woe betide his contemporaries.

The only punishment capable of punishing Hitler, and deterring little boys thirsting for greatness in coming centuries from following his example, is such a total transformation of the meaning attached to greatness that he should thereby be excluded from it.

It is chimerical and due to the blindness induced by national hatred to imagine that one can exclude Hitler from the title to greatness without a total transformation, among the men of today, of the idea and significance of greatness. And in order to be able to contribute towards such a transformation, one must have accomplished it in oneself. Each of us can at this very moment commence Hitler's punishment inside his own mind, by modifying the scope of the sentiment attaching to greatness. This is far from being an easy matter, for a social pressure as heavy and enveloping as the surrounding atmosphere stands opposed thereto. So as to be able to carry it out, one has to exclude oneself spiritually from the rest of society. Which is why Plato said that the ability to discern the good only exists in predestined souls that have been directly trained by God.

It is nonsense to try to make out how far Hitler and Napoleon may be said to resemble and differ from each other. The only problem of any interest is to know whether you can legitimately exclude one from greatness without at the same time excluding the other; whether their titles to admiration are similar or essentially different. And if, after having clearly posed the question and looked at it squarely in the face for some time, you allow yourself to slip into untruthfulness, you are lost.

Marcus Aurelius said, using more or less these words, with reference to Alexander and Caesar: if they were not just, nothing forces me to imitate them. Similarly, nothing forces us to admire them.

Nothing forces us to do this, except the sovereign influence of force.

Can one possibly admire without loving? And if admiration is a form of love, how can one bring oneself to love anything other than the good?

It would not be difficult to make a pact with oneself to admire in history only those actions and lives through which shines the spirit of truth, justice and love; and, at a much lower level, those in which it is possible to discern a genuine foretaste of this spirit at work.

That would exclude, for example, St. Louis himself, on account of the regrettable advice he gave his friends to plunge their swords into the belly of any one who in their presence should air opinions tainted with heresy or incredulity.

People will, of course, say in his defence that it was the spirit of the times, which, being situated seven centuries before our own day, were proportionately unenlightened. It's a lie. Shortly before St. Louis' day, the Catholics of Béziers, far from plunging their swords into the bodies of the heretics in their town, all suffered death rather than consent to hand them over. The Church has forgotten to place them in the ranks of her martyrs, a distinction which she accords to inquisitors put to death by their potential victims. Nor have lovers of tolerance, enlightenment and laicization, during the past three centuries, done anything to commemorate this event either; so heroic a form of the virtue they label so insipidly tolerance they would have found disconcerting.

But even if it were true, even if fanatical cruelty had dominated the minds of all in the Middle Ages, the sole conclusion to be drawn therefrom would be that there was nothing to love or admire in that epoch. It would not place St. Louis so much as a millimetre closer to righteousness. The spirit of truth, justice and love has nothing whatever to do with questions of date; it is eternal; evil constitutes the distance which separates actions and thoughts from it; an act of cruelty in the tenth century is exactly as cruel, neither more nor less so, than an act of cruelty in the nineteenth.

In identifying an act of cruelty, it is necessary to bear in mind the circumstances, the different meanings attached to acts and words, the symbolic language peculiar to each environment; but once an act has been indubitably recognized as being cruel, it is a horrible one, whenever and wherever it happens to have been committed.

We should feel it irresistibly if we loved as ourselves all the unfortunate beings who two or three thousand years ago suffered cruelties at the hands of their fellow-men.

We wouldn't then be able to write, as does M. Carcopino, that slavery had become mild in Rome under the Empire, seeing that it was rarely accompanied by any harsher punishment than beating with a rod.

The modern superstition in regard to progress is a by-product of the lie thanks to which Christianity became turned into the official Roman religion; it is bound up with the destruction of the spiritual treasures of those countries which were conquered by Rome, with the concealment of the perfect continuity existing between these treasures and Christianity, with an historical conception concerning the Redemption, making of the latter a temporal operation instead of an eternal one. Subsequently, the idea of progress became laicized; it is now the bane of our times. In laying down that inhuman acts in the fourteenth century were great and good things, but horrible things in the nineteenth century, how could a little chap of the twentieth century, fond of reading history, be prevented from saying to himself: 'I feel certain that the time when humanity was a virtue is now over and that we are returning to an age of inhumanity?' What is there to prevent one imagining a cyclical succession instead of an uninterrupted straight line? The dogma of progress brings dishonour upon goodness by turning it into a question of fashion.

It is, moreover, solely because the historical mind consists in accepting the word of murderers unquestioningly that this dogma seems to correspond so admirably to the facts. When from time to time a shaft of horror manages to pierce the opaque insensibility of a reader of Livy, he says to himself: 'Those were the customs of the time'. The writings of Greek historians leave one, nevertheless, with the clearest impression that the brutality of the Romans horrified and paralysed their contemporaries in exactly the same way as that of the Germans does today.

If I am not mistaken, amidst all the facts concerning the Romans which we find in ancient history, there is only one example of a perfectly pure act of goodness. Under the triumvirate, at the time of the proscriptions, the consular personages, consuls, praetors whose names were on the list embraced the knees of their own slaves, imploring their help and calling them their masters and saviours; for Roman pride wasn't made to resist misfortune. The slaves, rightly enough, spurned these advances. There were very few exceptions in this matter. But a certain Roman, without having had to degrade himself, was hidden in his own house by his slaves. Some soldiers, who had seen him entering it, put these slaves to the torture to compel them to give up their master. The slaves submitted to it all without giving way. But the master, from his hiding-place, could see their tortures, and, unable to put up with the sight of them, came out and handed himself over to the soldiers and was immediately put to death.

Whoever has his heart in the right place, if he had to choose between several different destinies, would choose to be either this master or one of these slaves, rather than one of the Scipios, a Caesar, a Cicero, an Augustus, a Virgil or even one of the Gracchi.

Here is an example of what it is legitimate to admire. In history, there are few perfectly pure things. Most of them concern persons whose names have not been recorded, like this Roman, like those inhabitants of Béziers at the beginning of the thirteenth century. If one were to look for names which are associated with real purity, one would find very few. In Greek history, one would only be able to name Aristides, Dio, Plato's friend, and Agis, the little socialist king of Sparta, put to death at the age of twenty. In French history, would one be able to find any other name besides that of Joan of Arc? It is doubtful.

But that is not the point. Are we obliged to admire many things? The essential thing is to admire what one can find to admire with one's whole soul. Who can admire Alexander with his whole soul whose soul is not base?

There are people who suggest that the teaching of history should be suppressed. It is true we ought to suppress the absurd custom of learning history lessons, apart from a bare minimum summary of dates and landmarks, and apply to history the same species of attention we give to literature. But as for suppressing the study of history, that would be disastrous. Without history there can be no sense of patriotism. We have only to look at the United States to see what it is to have a people deprived of the time-dimension.

Others suggest teaching history by placing wars in the background. That would be lying. We know only too well today, and it is equally true of the past, that no subject is more important from the point of view of the peoples than that of war. We must talk about war just as much as, if not more than, we do at present ; but in a different way.

No other method exists for acquiring knowledge about the human heart than the study of history coupled with experience of life, in such a way that the two throw light upon each other. It is our duty to supply this food to the mind of youth, the mind of Man. But it must be a truth-giving food. Facts must not only be correct, so far as one is able to verify them, but must be shown in their true perspective relatively to good and evil.

History is a tissue of base and cruel acts in the midst of which a few drops of purity sparkle at long intervals. If such is the case, it is first of all because there is very little purity amongst men; and secondly because the greater part of what little there is remains hidden. One must try and seek out if possible indirect testimony of its existence. The Romanesque churches, the Gregorian chant can only have arisen amongst peoples in whom much more purity was to be found than there has been in succeeding centuries.

In order to love France, we must feel that she has a past; but we must not love the historical wrapper of that past. We must love the part which is inarticulate, anonymous, which has vanished.

It is absolutely false to imagine that there is some providential mechanism by which what is best in any given period is transmitted to the memory of posterity. By the very nature of things, it is false greatness which is transmitted. There is, indeed, a providential mechanism, but it only works in such a way as to mix a little genuine greatness with a lot of spurious greatness; leaving us to pick out which is which. Without it we should be lost.

The transmission of spurious greatness down the centuries is not peculiar to history. It is a general law, and governs equally well, for example, literature and the other arts. There is a certain domination of literary talent over the centuries which corresponds to the domination of political talent in space; they are forms of domination of a like kind, equally temporal, equally attached to the realm of matter and force, equally base. They can, furthermore, form the subject of sale or exchange in open market.

Ariosto didn't blush to say to his patron, the Duke of Este, in the course of his poem, what more or less amounts to this: I am in your power during the course of my life, and you can decide whether I am to be rich or poor. But in my power lies your future good name, and I can decide whether, three hundred years hence, people will say good or evil of you, or nothing at all. It is in our mutual interest to come to an understanding. Give me your patronage and riches, and I will make you illustrious.

Virgil had far too deep a sense of the proprieties to publicly place on record a commercial transaction of this nature. Nevertheless, this was, in fact, the transaction which took place between him and Augustus. His verse is often delightful to read; but in spite of that, for him and others like him, another name should be found than that of poet. Poetry is not something for sale. God would be unjust if the *Aeneid*, which was composed under these conditions, were worth as much as the *Iliad*. But God is not unjust, and the *Aeneid* is very far indeed from being on an equality with the *Iliad*.

It is not only in the study of history, it is in all forms of study put before children that the good is held up to contempt, and when they grow up, all they can find in the nourishment offered to their minds are motives for persisting in this contemptuous attitude.

It is obvious—that is a truth which has long since become a platitude with children and men—that talent has nothing to do with morality. But in all spheres nothing *but* talent is held up to the admiration of children and men. In all manifestations of talent, whatever they may be, they see shamelessly flaunted before them the lack of all those virtues which it is recommended they should practise. What conclusion is to be drawn other than that virtue is in keeping with mediocrity? So far has this conviction penetrated, that the very word virtue has now something ridiculous about it—that word which at one time held so much meaning, like the words honesty and goodness also. The British are closer to the past than people in other countries; also there are no words today in the French language for translating 'good' and 'wicked'.*

How should a child who sees cruelty and ambition glorified

* '*good*' and '*wicked*': as in text. [Translator.]

in his history lessons; egoism, pride, vanity, passion for self-advertisement glorified in his literature lessons; all the discoveries that have unsettled the lives of men glorified in his science lessons, without any account being taken of either the method of discovery or the effect of the unsettlement produced —how should he be expected to learn to admire the good? Everything which tries to go against this universal current, for instance the homage paid to Pasteur, has a false ring about it. In an atmosphere of false greatness, it is useless to try to restore the true variety. False greatness must first be despised.

It is true that talent has no connexion with morality; but then, there is no greatness about talent. It is untrue that there is no connexion between perfect beauty, perfect truth, perfect justice: they are far more than just connected: they form a single mysterious unity, for the good is one.

There exists a focal point of greatness where the genius creating beauty, the genius revealing truth, heroism and holiness are indistinguishable. Already, as one approaches this point, one can see the different forms of greatness tending to flow into one another. In Giotto, it is not possible to distinguish between the genius of the painter and the Franciscan spirit; nor in the pictures and poems produced by the Zen sect in China between the painter's or poet's genius and the state of mystical ecstasy; nor, when Velasquez places on the canvas his kings and beggars, between the painter's genius and the burning and impartial love that pierces to the very depths of people's souls. The *Iliad*, the tragedies of Aeschylus and those of Sophocles bear the clearest indication that the poets who produced them were in a state of holiness. From the purely poetic point of view, without taking into account anything else, it is infinitely preferable to have written the Canticle of St. Francis of Assisi, that jewel of perfect beauty, than the entire works of Victor Hugo. Racine wrote the only work* in the whole of French literature which can almost be placed on a par with the great Greek masterpieces at a time when his spirit

* . . . *the only work* . . . : *Phèdre:* see p. 225. [Translator.]

was racked by the problem of his conversion. He was far from being in a state of holiness when he wrote his other plays, but then, nor do we find in them the same heartrending beauty. A tragedy like *King Lear* is the direct fruit of the pure spirit of love. Holiness irradiates the Romanesque churches and the Gregorian chant. Monteverdi, Bach, Mozart were beings whose lives were pure even as were their works.

If there are geniuses whose genius is pure to the extent of being manifestly very close to the greatness characteristic of the most perfect among the saints, why waste one's time admiring others? One can make use of others, derive instruction and pleasure from them; but why love them? Why give one's heart to anything other than the good?

In French literature there is a discernible current of purity. In poetry, we must begin with Villon, the first, the greatest. We know nothing about his faults, nor even if there were any such on his part; but his purity of soul is clearly manifest through the heart-breaking expression of misfortune. The last, or almost the last, is Racine, on account of *Phèdre* and the *Cantiques spirituels*. Between them one can name Maurice Scève, d'Aubigné, Théophile de Viau, who were three great poets and three human beings of a rare nobility. In the nineteeth century, all the poets were more or less men-of-letters, which shamefully pollutes poetry; though Lamartine and Vigny at any rate really aspired after something pure and genuine. There is also a little true poetry in Gérard de Nerval. At the end of the century, Mallarmé was admired no less as a sort of saint than as a poet, and these two marks of greatness were, in fact, indistinguishable in him the one from the other. Mallarmé is a true poet.

In prose, there is perhaps a mysterious purity in Rabelais, in whom, moreover, everything is mysterious. There is certainly some in Montaigne, in spite of his numerous failings, because there always dwelt within him a pure being, but for whom he would doubtless not have emerged from mediocrity, that is to say La Boétie. In the seventeenth century, one can think of Descartes, Retz, of Port-Royal, above all of Molière. In the eighteenth century, there are Montesquieu and Rousseau. That is perhaps all.

On the supposition that the above list is fairly accurate, this doesn't mean that we shouldn't read what is left, but only that we shouldn't read it expecting to find there the genius of France. The genius of France only resides in that which is pure.

It is perfectly correct to say that it is a Christian and Hellenic genius. Which is why it would be right to accord a far smaller share in the education and culture of Frenchmen to things specifically French than to Romanesque art, the Gregorian chant, liturgical poetry, and to Greek art, poetry and prose of the best period. There one is able to drink in torrents of absolutely pure beauty from every point of view.

It is unfortunate that Greek should be regarded as an erudite subject for specialists only. If we were to cease subordinating the study of Greek to that of Latin, and try to make a child capable of reading easily and with enjoyment an easy Greek text with the translation by the side of it, it would be possible to diffuse a slight knowledge of Greek to a very appreciable extent, even below the secondary school grade. Thus, every child of any ability at all would be able to enter into direct contact with the civilization whence we have derived our very notions of beauty, truth and justice.

The love of the good will never spring up in the hearts of the population in general, as it is necessary it should do for the salvation of the country, so long as people believe that in no matter what sphere greatness can be the result of something other than the good.

That is why Christ said: 'A good tree bringeth forth good fruit, but a corrupt tree bringeth forth evil fruit'. Either a perfectly beautiful work of art is an evil fruit, or the inspiration which produced it is akin to holiness.

If pure good were never capable of producing on this earth true greatness in art, science, theoretical speculation, public enterprise, if in all these spheres there were only false greatness, if in all these spheres everything were despicable, and consequently condemnable, there would be no hope at all for the affairs of this world; no possible illumination of this world by the other one.

But it is not so; which is why it is absolutely necessary to distinguish true from false greatness, and to set up the former only as an object of love. True greatness is the good fruit which grows on the good tree, and the good tree is a disposition of the soul akin to holiness. The other forms of so-called greatness have to be examined dispassionately, in the same way as one examines natural curiosities. If, in point of fact, this separation under two distinct headings can give rise to mistakes, it is none the less essential to let the principle of separation itself sink into the depths of the soul.

The modern conception of science is responsible, as is that of history and that of art, for the monstrous conditions under which we live, and will, in its turn, have to be transformed, before we can hope to see the dawn of a better civilization.

This is all the more vital in that, although science is strictly speaking a matter for specialists only, the prestige which science and savants have acquired over people's minds is immense, and in non-totalitarian countries far and away surpasses any other kind. In France, at the outbreak of the war, it was perhaps the only form of prestige remaining; nothing else was any longer accorded any respect. There was about the atmosphere of the *Palais de la Découverte*, in 1937,* at the same time a mixture of publicity and something almost religious, using the latter word in its most vulgar sense. Science, with its technical side which is but the application of it, constitutes our only claim to be proud of ourselves as Westerners, men of the white race, modern men.

The missionary who persuades a Polynesian to give up his ancestral traditions, which are so poetic and so beautiful, concerning the creation of the world, in favour of those contained

* *Palais de la Découverte*: one of the main attractions of the French Exhibition of 1937. [Translator.]

in Genesis, imbued with a very similar poetic feeling—that missionary derives his persuasive force from the consciousness he has of his superiority as a white man, a consciousness which is based on science. He is, nevertheless, as much a stranger to science as is the Polynesian; for whoever isn't a specialist remains absolutely a stranger to it. Genesis remains even more of a stranger to it. A village schoolteacher who makes fun of the *curé*, and whose attitude dissuades children from going to Mass, derives his persuasive force from the consciousness he possesses of his superiority as a modern individual over a dogma of the Middle Ages, which consciousness is based upon science. All the same, as far as possibilities for its verification go, Einstein's theory is at least as little founded upon reason and as much opposed to common sense as is the Christian tradition concerning the conception and birth of Christ.

In France, people question everything, respect nothing; some show a contempt for religion, others for patriotism, the State, the administration of justice, property, art, in fact everything under the sun; but their contempt stops short of science. The crudest scientism has no more fervent adepts than the anarchists. Le Dantec* is their saint. Bonnot's *bandits tragiques*† took their inspiration from him, and the greatest hero among them, in the eyes of his comrades, was nicknamed 'Raymond la Science'. At the other extreme, one comes across priests and monks so absorbed by the religious life that they display a sovereign contempt for all secular values; but their contempt stops short of science. In all the arguments in which religion and science appear to be in conflict, the Church displays an intellectual inferiority which is almost comic, for it is due, not

* *Le Dantec:* Félix Le Dantec (1869-1917), biologist, and amongst other things the author of a little work on atheism. [Translator.]

† *Bonnot's 'bandits tragiques'*: the name given by the press of the time (1912) to a gang of terrorists led by a certain Bonnot. These men, some of whom professed anarchistic tenets, committed a whole series of crimes in various parts of Paris, before being finally overcome by police forces armed with dynamite. [Translator.]

to the force of the arguments adduced by the other side, usually of a very mediocre order, but solely to an inferiority complex.

So far as the prestige of science is concerned, there are no such people nowadays as unbelievers. That places on savants, and also on philosophers and writers to the extent to which these write about science, a responsibility equal to that which the priests had in the thirteenth century. They are both, now as then, human beings whose material wants are attended to by society in order that they may have the leisure to explore, discover and communicate what is truth. In the twentieth century as in the thirteenth, the bread spent on this purpose is no doubt, unfortunately, bread thrown away, or perhaps even worse than that.

The Church in the thirteenth century had Christ; but it also had the Inquisition. Science in the twentieth century has no Inquisition; but neither has it Christ, nor anything equivalent to Christ.

The responsibility which savants and all who write about science have assumed in these days is such a heavy one that they also, like the historians and even to a greater degree, are possibly guiltier of Hitler's crimes than Hitler himself.

This is what would appear from a passage in *Mein Kampf*: 'Man must never fall into the error of believing himself to be the lord and master of creation. . . . He will then feel that in a world in which planets and suns follow circular trajectories, moons revolve round planets, and force reigns everywhere and supreme over weakness, which it either compels to serve it docilely or else crushes out of existence, Man cannot be subject to special laws of his own'.

These lines express in faultless fashion the only conclusion that can reasonably be drawn from the conception of the world contained in our science. Hitler's entire life is nothing but the putting into practice of that conclusion. Who can reproach him for having put into practice what he thought he recognized to be the truth? Those who, having in themselves the foundations of the same belief, haven't embraced it consciously and haven't translated it into acts, have only escaped being criminals thanks to the want of a certain sort of courage which he possesses.

Once more, it is not the forlorn youth, the wretched vagabond, with the hungry soul, whom it is right to accuse, but those who fed him upon lies. And those who fed him upon lies were our elders, whom we resemble.

In the catastrophe of our time, the executioners and their victims are, both together, before anything else, the involuntary bearers of a testimony against the appalling wretchedness in which we wallow.

In order to have the right to punish the guilty, we ought first of all to purify ourselves of their crimes, which we harbour under all sorts of disguises in our own hearts. But if we manage to perform this operation, once it has been accomplished we shall no longer feel the least desire to punish, and if we consider ourselves obliged to do so, it will be as little as possible and with extreme sorrow.

Hitler has clearly perceived the absurdity of the eighteenth century conception, still in favour today, and which already had its roots in Descartes. For the last two or three centuries, people have believed that force rules supreme over all natural phenomena, and at the same time that men can and should base their mutual relations upon justice, recognized as such through the application of reason. This is a flagrant absurdity. It is inconceivable that everything in the universe should be entirely subjected to the rule of force and that Man should be able to escape the effects of this, seeing that he is made of flesh and blood and that his mind wanders here and there at the mercy of sensory impressions.

There is only one possible choice to be made. Either we must perceive at work in the universe, alongside force, a principle of a different kind, or else we must recognize force as being the unique and sovereign ruler over human relations also.

In the first case, one places oneself in radical opposition to modern science as founded by Galileo, Descartes and several others, pursued throughout the eighteenth century, notably by Newton, then in the nineteenth, and now in the twentieth. In the second case, one places oneself in radical opposition to the humanism which arose at the time of the Renaissance, triumphed in 1789, and which, in a considerably degenerated form, served as inspiration for the whole of the Third Republic.

The philosophy which has inspired the laical spirit and political radicalism is founded at the same time on this science and on this humanism, which are, as can be seen, manifestly incompatible with each other. You cannot, therefore, say that Hitler's victory over France in 1940 was the victory of a lie over a truth. An incoherent lie was vanquished by a coherent lie. That is why, as their arms gave way, people's spirits did likewise.

During the course of the last few centuries, the contradiction between science and humanism has been felt confusedly, although the intellectual courage has always been lacking to look it squarely in the face. Attempts have been made to resolve it, without first bringing it into the light of day. Such intellectual dishonesty is always punished by a lapse into error.

Utilitarianism was the fruit of one of these attempts. It rests upon the supposed existence of a wonderful little piece of mechanism thanks to which force, on entering into the sphere of human relations, becomes an automatic producer of justice.

The economic liberalism of the nineteenth century middle-classes rests entirely upon the belief in such a mechanism; the only proviso being that in order to possess this property of being an automatic producer of justice, force must take the form of money to the exclusion of all use either of arms or of political power.

Marxism is nothing else than a belief in a mechanism of this sort. There, force is given the name of history; it takes the form of the class struggle; justice is relegated to some future time which has to be preceded by a sort of apocalyptic cataclysm.

And Hitler, too, after his brief moment of intellectual courage and perspicacity, fell into believing in this little piece of mechanism. But what he needed was a brand-new model of a machine. He hasn't, however, either the taste or the capacity for intellectual invention, apart from a few flashes of intuitive genius. So he borrowed the model for his machine from the people who obsessed him continually by the repulsion with which they inspired him. He simply selected as his machine the notion of a chosen race, a race destined to make everything bow before it, and then to establish among its slaves the type of justice suitable to the condition of slavery.

With regard to all these conceptions, in appearance so diverse and at bottom so similar, there is only one drawback, which is the same for all: they are lies.

Force is not a machine for automatically creating justice. It is a blind mechanism which produces indiscriminately and impartially just or unjust results, but, by all the laws of probability, nearly always unjust ones. Lapse of time makes no difference; it doesn't increase in the functioning of this mechanism the infinitesimal proportion of results which happen by chance to be in conformity with justice.

Where force is absolutely sovereign, justice is absolutely unreal. Yet justice cannot be that. We know it experimentally. It is real enough in the hearts of men. The structure of a human heart is just as much of a reality as any other in this universe, neither more nor less of a reality than the trajectory of a planet.

It doesn't lie within the power of any man absolutely to exclude all justice whatsoever from the ends which he assigns to his actions. The Nazis themselves have not been able to do this. If it were possible for men to do so, they would no doubt have managed it.

(Let this be remarked in parenthesis. Their conception of a just order which is to be the final outcome of their victories rests upon the conviction that, for all who are slaves by nature, servitude is the condition which is at the same time the happiest and the most just. Now, this is precisely the conviction Aristotle held, and which inspired his great argument in justification of slavery. St. Thomas Aquinas, although he didn't approve of slavery, looked upon Aristotle as the greatest authority on all subjects of study accessible to human reason, amongst which is justice. Consequently, the existence in contemporary Christianity of a Thomistic current constitutes a bond of complicity—amongst many others, unfortunately—between the Nazis and their adversaries. For, even if we reject that particular notion of Aristotle's, we are necessarily led in our ignorance to accept others which must have lain in him at the root of that one. A man who takes the trouble to draw up an apology for slavery cannot be a lover of justice. The age in which he lived has nothing to do with it. To accept as authoritative the ideas of a man who doesn't love justice constitutes an offence against justice, inevitably punished by a decrease in powers of discernment. If St. Thomas committed that offence, nothing obliges us to repeat it.)

If justice is inerasable from the heart of Man, it must have a reality in this world. It is science, then, which is mistaken.

Not science, to be perfectly exact, but modern science. The Greeks possessed a science which is the foundation of our own. It comprised arithmetic, geometry, algebra in a form peculiar to them, astronomy, mechanics, physics and biology. The sum total of knowledge accumulated was naturally very much less. But by its scientific character, according to the full significance we attach to that term, and judged by what we hold to be valid standards, that science equalled and even surpassed our own. It was more exact, precise, rigorous. The use of demonstration and of the experimental method were alike perfectly conceived.

If this is not generally recognized, it is solely because the subject itself is little known. It will occur to few people, unless urged on by some particular vocation, to plunge into the atmosphere of Greek science as into something real and vital. But those who have done so have had no difficulty in recognizing the truth.

The generation of mathematicians now approaching the age of forty is aware that after a long dearth of the scientific spirit in the development of mathematics, a return to the exactitude indispensable for savants is in process of taking place by the use of methods almost identical with those practised by Greek geometricians.

As for technical applications, if Greek science didn't produce many, it isn't because it was incapable of doing so, but because the Greek savants didn't wish it. These men, obviously very much less advanced than we are, as is natural seeing that they lived twenty-five centuries ago, feared the effects of technical inventions which could be made use of by tyrants and conquerors. So, instead of delivering to the public the greatest possible number of technical discoveries and selling them to the highest bidder, they kept rigorously secret all the ones they happened to make for their own amusement; and, apparently, themselves remained poor. However, Archimedes, on one occasion, put his technical knowledge to use in order to defend his country. He did it all by himself, without revealing the smallest secret to anybody. Even today, we still find the account given of the marvellous things he managed to accomplish very largely incomprehensible. But he succeeded so well that the Romans only entered into Syracuse thanks to an act of semi-treachery.

This science, which was as scientific as our own, if not more so, had no trace of materialism about it. What is more, it was not a subject of profane study. The Greeks regarded it as a religious subject.

The Romans killed Archimedes. Shortly afterwards they killed Greece, just as the Germans, had it not been for England, would have killed France. Greek science disappeared completely. In Roman civilization not a trace of it remained. If the memory of it was transmitted to the Middle Ages, this was by means of so-called Gnostic thought, in very closed circles of initiates. Even so, it seems clear that it was only a question of preservation, not of any creative continuation; except perhaps as far as alchemy was concerned, about which so little is known.

At all events, Greek science didn't make any public reappearance until the beginning of the sixteenth century (if I am not mistaken in the date) in Italy and France. It very rapidly acquired an enormous prestige and penetrated into the whole life of Europe. Today, nearly all our thoughts, customs, reactions and ways of behaviour as Europeans bear the impress either of its spirit or of its material applications.

This is true more particularly of the intellectuals, even if they don't happen to be what are called 'scientific' men, and even truer still of the workmen, who spend all their lives in an artificial universe formed by the applications of science.

However, as in certain fairy tales, this science which was awakened after lying dormant for nearly two milleniums was no longer the same. It had been changed. It was of another kind, absolutely incompatible with anything of a religious spirit.

That is why religion is nowadays something we relegate to Sunday morning. The rest of the week is dominated by the spirit of science.

Unbelievers, who give their entire week up to it, have a triumphant feeling of inward unity. But they are mistaken, for their moral attitude is no less in contradiction with science than is the religion of the others. Hitler has clearly perceived this. Moreover, he is making a lot of other people perceive it also, wherever the presence or threatened presence of the S.S. is felt, and even further afield. Today, it is only belonging unconditionally to some brown, red or other totalitarian system which is able to give, as it were, a solid illusion of inward unity. Which is why it constitutes such a strong temptation for so many distraught minds.

Among Christians, the absolute incompatibility between the spirit of religion and that of science, to both of which they cling, leaves the soul in a permanent state of secret, unacknowledged uneasiness. In certain cases it is hardly felt at all; in others to a greater or lesser extent, depending on the individual; but it is, of course, practically never admitted. It prevents inward cohesion. It makes it impossible for the Christian spirit to permeate all their thoughts. By an indirect effect of its continual presence, the most fervent Christians express every hour of their lives judgments, opinions, which, unknown to them, are based on standards which go contrary to the spirit of Christianity. But the most disastrous consequence of this uneasiness is to make it impossible for the virtue of intellectual probity to be exercised to the fullest extent.

The modern phenomenon of irreligion among the population can be explained almost entirely by the incompatibility between science and religion. It developed when the population of the towns began to be installed in an artificial world, the material expression of science. In Russia, the transformation was hastened by means of propaganda which, in order to uproot the faith, relied almost exclusively upon the spirit of science and technical progress. Everywhere, once the people in the towns had become irreligious, the country people, ever exposed to influence through their inferiority complex in regard to the towns, followed their example, though to a more limited extent.

Due to the very fact of the people's desertion of the Churches, religion was automatically transferred to the Right, became a middle-class affair, something for respectable people. For, in fact, an institutional religion is necessarily bound to rely upon those who go to church. It cannot rely upon those who stay outside. It is true that some time before this desertion took place, the servile attitude of the clergy towards the temporal power caused them to commit some grave mistakes. But these could have been put right but for this desertion. If they were in part responsible for bringing about this desertion, that part was only a very small one. It is almost solely science which has emptied the churches.

If a section of the bourgeoisie was less disturbed in its piety by science than was the working-class, that is because, in the first place, it was in a less permanent, less bodily contact with the applications of science. But it was above all because it hadn't any religious faith. Whoever hasn't any religious faith cannot lose it. Save for a few rare exceptions, the practice of religion was amongst such people a matter of what was socially fitting. A scientific conception of the world doesn't prevent one from observing what is socially fitting.

Thus, Christianity is, in effect, apart from a few isolated centres of inspiration, something socially in accordance with the interests of those who exploit the people.

It is then not surprising that it should play on the whole such a mediocre part at this time in the struggle against the modern form of evil.

All the more so seeing that, even in places, in hearts where religious activity is sincere and intense, there lies all too often at their core a source of impurity owing to a lack of the spirit of truth. The fact of the existence of science gives Christians a bad conscience. Few of them dare be quite certain that if they started from scratch and examined every problem, leaving out all personal preference, in an absolutely impartial critical spirit, the Christian dogma would seem to them to be manifestly and totally the truth.

This uncertainty might be expected to loosen their ties with religion; but this doesn't happen, and the reason why it doesn't happen is because religious life supplies them with something of which they stand in need. They themselves feel more or less confusedly that it is a need which attaches them to religion. But need is not a legitimate bond between Man and God. As Plato remarks, a great distance separates the nature of necessity from that of good. God gives Himself to Man gratuitously and by way of addition; but Man should not desire to receive. He should give himself utterly, unconditionally, and for the only reason that after having strayed from illusion to illusion in his uninterrupted search for the good, he is certain he has found the truth in turning himself to God.

Dostoievsky uttered the most frightful blasphemy when he said: 'If Christ is not the truth, I prefer to remain outside the truth with Christ'. Christ said: 'I am the truth.' He also said that He was bread and wine; but He added: 'I am the true bread, the true wine', that is to say, the bread which is nothing but truth, the wine which is nothing but truth. They must first of all be desired as truth, only afterwards as food.

It is clear that all these things must have been completely forgotten, since people have been able to take Bergson for a Christian—the man who thought he saw in the spiritual energy displayed by the mystics the perfect expression of that *élan vital* which he turned for himself into an idol. Whereas what is really marvellous, in the case of the mystics and the saints, is not that they have more life, a more intense life than that of other people, but that in them truth should have become life. In this world of ours life, the *élan vital* so dear to Bergson, is but a lie; only death is true. For life constrains one to believe what one requires to believe in order to live; this servitude has been raised to the rank of a doctrine under the name of Pragmatism, and Bergson's philosophy is a form of Pragmatism. But those beings who have, in spite of flesh and blood, spiritually crossed a boundary equivalent to death, receive on the farther side another life, which is not primarily life, which is primarily truth; truth which has become living; as true as death and as living as life. A life, as Grimm's fairy tales put it, as white as snow and as red as blood. It is that which is the breath of truth, the divine Spirit.

Pascal had already been guilty of lack of probity in his search for God. Having had his mind formed by the practice of science, he didn't dare hope that by allowing it full play it would find certitude in the Christian dogma. He didn't dare run the risk either of having to do without Christianity. So he undertook an intellectual research having decided beforehand where it was to lead him. To avoid all possible risk of landing himself elsewhere, he allowed his mind to be dominated by a conscious and deliberately entertained suggestion. After which, he sought for proofs. In the sphere of probability, significant indication, he discovered some very weighty things. But as for proofs properly so called, he only advanced wretched enough ones; the argument of the wager, the prophecies, the miracles. What is more serious for him is that he never did reach certitude. He never did receive the gift of faith, and that is because he had tried to take possession of it.

Most of those who embrace Christianity, or else who, having been born into it and never having left it, remain sincerely and fervently attached to it, are attracted and afterwards held by a need of the heart. They would be unable to do without religion. At least they would be unable to do without it and at the same time avoid experiencing a sort of degradation. But for religious feeling to emanate from the spirit of truth, one should be absolutely prepared to abandon one's religion, even if that should mean losing all motive for living, if it should turn out to be anything other than the truth. In this state of mind alone is it possible to discern whether there is truth in it or not. Otherwise, one doesn't venture even to propound the problem in all its rigour.

God ought not to be for a human heart a reason for living, like his treasure is for a miser. Harpagon and Grandet loved their treasure; they would have allowed themselves to be killed for it; they would have died of grief because of it; they would have performed miracles of courage and energy on behalf of it. It is possible to love God in this way. But one ought not to do so. Or rather it is only to a certain part of the soul that such a love is permissible, because it cannot understand any other kind; but it should remain subject to, in the hands of, that other part of the soul which is worth more.

One can say without fear of exaggeration that today the spirit of truth is almost absent from religious life.

This is observable amongst other things in the nature of the arguments adduced in favour of Christianity. Many of them are of the publicity type associated with 'Pink' pills. It is the case with Bergson and all that draws its inspiration from him. In Bergson, religious faith appears after the manner of a 'Pink' pill of a superior kind, which imparts an astonishing amount of vitality. The same thing applies to the historical argument, which runs in this sort: 'Look what a miserable lot men were before Christ. Christ came, and see how men, in spite of their backslidings, afterwards became, on the whole, a good lot!' That is absolutely contrary to the truth. But even if it were true, it reduces apologetics to the level of advertisements for pharmaceutical products, which describe the state of the patient before and after. It is measuring the effectiveness of Christ's Passion, which, if it is not fictitious, is necessarily infinite, by an historical, temporal and human result which, even if it were real, which it isn't, would necessarily be finite.

Pragmatism has encroached upon and profaned the very conception of faith.

If the spirit of truth is almost absent from religious life, it would be strange indeed if it were to be present in secular life. It would be the turning upside down of an eternal hierarchy. But such is not the case.

The savants insist that the public should regard science with that religious respect which is owed to truth, and the public accepts to do so. But it is being deceived. Science is not a fruit of the spirit of truth, and this is obvious as soon as one looks into the matter.

For the effort of scientific research, such as it has been understood since the sixteenth century, cannot possess as its motive the love of truth.

That rests on a criterion which is universal and sure in its application. It consists, in order to form an opinion about anything, to endeavour to discern the proportion of good contained, not in the thing itself, but in the motives for the effort which has produced it. For the amount of good in the thing itself is the same as the amount of good in the motive behind it, neither more nor less. Christ's words on the subject of the trees and their fruits are a guarantee of this.

God alone, it is true, can discern the motives hidden in people's hearts. But the conception which governs any particular activity, and which is generally no secret, is compatible with certain motives and not with others; there are some which it necessarily excludes, in the nature of things.

It is a question, therefore, of an analysis leading to an evaluation of the product of any particular human activity by examining the motives compatible with the conception which governs it.

From this analysis a method may be derived for making men —peoples and individuals, and oneself to begin with—better, by modifying the conceptions in such a way as to bring the purest motives into play.

The conviction that every conception incompatible with really pure motives is itself tainted with error, is the first necessary article of faith. Faith is above all the conviction that the good is one. To believe that there are several distinct and mutually independent forms of good, like truth, beauty and morality—that is what constitutes the sin of polytheism, and not just simply allowing the imagination to play with the notions of Apollo and Diana.

On applying this method to the analysis of science during the past three or four centuries, one is bound to recognize that the beautiful word truth stands infinitely above it. The savants, in the efforts they put forth day by day throughout the course of their lives, cannot be urged on by the desire to possess truth. For what they acquire is simply knowledge, and knowledge is not in itself an object of desire.

A little boy learns his geography lesson so as to have good marks, or in obedience to orders received, or to please his parents, or because he feels that far-off places and their names have a poetry about them. If none of these motives exists, he just doesn't learn his lesson.

Supposing at a given moment he doesn't know the name of the capital of Brazil, and the next moment he learns what it is, he has acquired an additional item of knowledge. But he is no whit nearer to truth than he was before. There are certain cases in which the acquisition of knowledge causes one to approach truth, there are other cases in which it doesn't. How to distinguish between the two sets of cases?

If a man surprises his wife whom he loves and in whom he has perfect confidence being flagrantly unfaithful to him, he is suddenly brought into brutal contact with a piece of truth. If he happens to hear that some woman whom he doesn't know, whose name he hears mentioned for the first time, in a town which he doesn't know either, has deceived her husband, that fact doesn't alter his relationship to truth in the slightest.

This latter example furnishes the key. The acquisition of knowledge causes us to approach truth when it is a question of knowledge about something we love, and not in any other case.

Love of truth is not a correct form of expression. Truth is not an object of love. It is not an object at all. What one loves is something which exists, which one thinks on, and which may hence be an occasion for truth or error. A truth is always the truth with reference to something. Truth is the radiant manifestation of reality. Truth is not the object of love but reality. To desire truth is to desire direct contact with a piece of reality. To desire contact with a piece of reality is to love. We desire truth only in order to love in truth. We desire to know the truth about what we love. Instead of talking about love of truth, it would be better to talk about the spirit of truth in love.

Pure and genuine love always desires above all to dwell wholly in the truth whatever it may be, unconditionally. Every other sort of love desires before anything else means of satisfaction, and for this reason is a source of error and falsehood. Pure and genuine love is in itself spirit of truth. It is the Holy Spirit. The Greek word which is translated spirit means literally fiery breath, breath mingled with fire, and it represented, in antiquity, the notion which science represents today by the word energy. What we translate by 'spirit of truth' signifies the energy of truth, truth as an active force. Pure love is this active force, the love which will not at any price, under any condition, have anything to do with either falsehood or error.

For such a love as this to be able to be the motive of the

savant in his exhausting task of research, he would have to have something to love. It would be necessary for the conception which he forms of the object of his studies to contain an aspect of the Good. But just the opposite is the case. Since the Renaissance—or to be more exact, since the second half of the Renaissance—the very conception of science has been that of a branch of study whose object is placed beyond good and evil, especially beyond good; viewed without any relation either to good or evil, but especially without any relation to good. Science only studies the facts as such, and the mathematicians themselves regard mathematical relations simply as facts of the mind. Facts, force, matter, isolated, considered singly, without reference to anything else—there is nothing here that a human mind can love.

It follows that the acquisition of fresh knowledge is not a sufficient stimulant to encourage savants in their efforts. Other stimulants are needed. To start with, they have the stimulant which is found in hunting, sport, games. One often hears mathematicians comparing their speciality to a game of chess. Some of them compare it to activities in which flair, psychological intuition is necessary, because they say they have to guess in advance which mathematical concepts will prove to be, if adopted, sterile or fruitful. That is certainly playing a game, and almost a game of chance. Very few savants penetrate sufficiently deeply into science for their hearts to be stirred by beauty. There is a certain mathematician who readily compares mathematics to sculpture in a particularly hard stone. People who present themselves to the public as the high-priests of truth strangely degrade the rôle they have assumed by comparing themselves to chess players; the comparison with a sculptor is at any rate more becoming. But if one's vocation is to be a sculptor, it is better to be a sculptor than a mathematician. On closer examination, the latter comparison, according to the present conception of science, doesn't make sense. It represents a very blurred anticipation of a different conception.

Technical application plays such a large part in the prestige of science that one would be inclined to expect savants to derive a powerful stimulant from reflecting upon the different forms of application. In fact, what provides a stimulant is not that but the actual prestige such applications confer on science. Just as the idea of making history goes to the heads of the politicians, so the savants become intoxicated at feeling themselves to be taking part in something really great. Great in the sense of false greatness, certainly; a greatness independent of any consideration for the good.

At the same time, certain among them, those whose researches are above all theoretical, while tasting the pleasures of this intoxication, are proud to announce themselves to be indifferent to technical application. They thus enjoy two advantages which are really incompatible but are compatible in the realm of fancy, which is always a most agreeable situation in which to be. They are among the ones who direct men's destiny, so their indifference towards this destiny promptly reduces mankind to the proportions of race of ants. It is a god-like state. They do not realize that, according to the present conception of science, if you take away its technical applications, nothing else is left which it is possible to look upon as a good. Skill at a game similar to chess is something of no value at all. Were it not for its technical applications, no member of the public today would take any interest in science; and if the public didn't take an interest in science, those who follow a scientific career would have had to choose another one. They have no right to take up the detached attitude which they do. But though it isn't a legitimate attitude, it acts as a stimulant.

For others, on the contrary, reflecting upon technical applications provides a stimulant. But all they are concerned about is their importance, not their good or evil effects. A savant who feels himself to be on the point of making a discovery which may quite well seriously upset human existence, will nevertheless strain every effort in order to carry his researches to a successful conclusion. It seems that it hardly ever, if ever, happens that he should stop to weigh up the probable effects of the upsetting change from the point of view of good and evil, and give up his researches if evil should seem the more likely to result. Such heroism would even appear to be out of the question; and yet it ought to be an understood thing. But here, as elsewhere, it is false greatness which dominates, the kind represented by quantity and not by the good.

Finally, savants are perpetually spurred on by social considerations which are so paltry as to make them almost too shameful to be acknowledged, and which do not play a large ostensible rôle, but are extremely powerful. Anyone who saw the French, in June 1940, letting their country drop so easily, and then a few months later, before they had really been made to feel the pinch of hunger, performing miracles of endurance, defying fatigue and cold for hours, in order to procure themselves an egg, cannot be unaware of what an incredible source of energy lies in paltry considerations.

The primary social consideration for savants is purely and simply one of professional duty. Savants are people who are paid to manufacture science; they are expected to manufacture some; they feel it to be their duty to manufacture some. But that is insufficient for them as a stimulant. Professional advancement, professorships, rewards of all kinds, honours and money, receptions abroad, the esteem and admiration of colleagues, reputation, fame, titles—all that counts for a great deal.

The habits of savants provide the best proof of this. In the sixteenth and seventeenth centuries, savants used to fling challenges at one another. When they published their discoveries, they used purposely to omit various links in the chain of proof, or else they would upset the order of them, so as to prevent their colleagues from being able to understand exactly what it was all about; in this way they protected themselves against the danger of some rival being able to claim to have previously made the same discovery. Descartes himself admits having done this in his *Géométrie*. Which proves that he was not a philosopher in the sense in which this word was understood by Pythagoras and Plato—a lover of divine Wisdom. Since Greece disappeared there hasn't been such a thing as a philosopher.

Nowadays, as soon as a savant has discovered anything, before even having allowed himself the time to test its value, he rushes off to send what is called a *note au compte rendu** in order to make quite sure of his prior claim. A case like that of Gauss is perhaps unique in our science. He would push manuscripts containing the most marvellous discoveries into the backs of drawers and forget about them; then when somebody produced something altogether sensational, he would remark casually: 'All that is so, I discovered it fifteen years ago; but one can go very much farther in this direction and propound this, that or the other theorem in addition'. But, of course, he was a genius of the first order. Perhaps there have, indeed, been a few like that, just a mere handful, in the course of the last three or four centuries. What science meant to them has remained their secret. Inferior motives have played a very great part in the daily efforts of all the rest.

Today the ease of communications all over the world in peacetime and specialization carried to an extreme have made it so that savants of each speciality, who themselves constitute reciprocally their one and only public, form the equivalent of a village. Professional tittle-tattle goes the rounds unceasingly; everybody knows everybody else, has a personal like or dislike for the other fellow. Different generations and nationalities run up against each other; other people's private affairs, politics, professional jealousies play an important part. It follows that the collective opinion of this village is bound to be vitiated; it represents, notwithstanding, the sole species of control over the savant; for neither laymen, nor savants belonging to other branches, take any interest in his researches. The

* *note au compte rendu:* advance notification of a report; term apparently used in scientific circles. [Translator.]

force of social considerations causes the savant's mind to be subservient to this collective opinion; he endeavours to please it. Whatever it is prepared to admit in science, is admitted; whatever it is not prepared to admit, is rejected. There is not a single disinterested judge amongst them, since each specialist, owing to the very fact that he is a specialist, is an interested party.

It will be said that the fertility of a theory is an objective criterion. But this criterion is only valid in the case of such theories as are admitted. A theory which is rejected by the collective opinion of the village of savants is perforce sterile, because no attempt is then made to draw any results from it. This happens especially in the case of physics, where the actual means of research and control are a monopoly in the hands of a very closed circle. If people hadn't taken such a great fancy to the quantum theory when it was first launched by Planck, and that in spite of the fact that it was absurd—or perhaps because it happened to be so, for everyone was tired of reason—nobody would ever have known that it was a fertile one. At the time it became so popular, there was absolutely no solid data for giving one any reason to suppose that it would be. Hence we find a Darwinian process operating in science. Theories spring up as it were at random, and there is survival of the fittest. Such a science as this can well be a form of *élan vital*, but certainly not a form of the search for truth.

The general public itself cannot be, nor is it, ignorant of the fact that, science, like every other product of a collective opinion, is subject to fashion. The savants inform it at fairly frequent intervals that such-and-such theories are old-fashioned. We should regard this as a scandal, if we were not too brutish to be sensitive to any scandal at all. How can one possibly accord a religious respect to something subjected to fashion? The Negro fetishists are very superior to us; they are infinitely less idolatrous than we. They have a religious respect for a piece of carved wood which is beautiful, and to which beauty imparts an eternal significance.

The Growing of Roots

We are really and truly suffering from the disease of idolatry, and it is so deeply rooted that it takes away from Christians the power to bear witness to the truth. No deaf men's dialogue could possibly equal in comical force the polemic between the modern spirit and the Church. The unbelievers select, in the name of the scientific spirit, and to use them as arguments against the Christian faith, truths which constitute indirectly, or even directly, manifest proofs of that faith. The Christians never notice this, and make feeble attempts, with a bad conscience and a distressing lack of intellectual honesty, to deny such truths. Their blindness is their punishment for the crime of idolatry.

No less comical is the embarrassment of the worshippers of the idol when they seek to express their enthusiasm. They look for something to praise and cannot find anything. It is easy enough to praise scientific applications; only scientific applications are something technical, they are not science. What is there to praise in science itself? And more precisely, seeing that science is incarnate in men, what is there to praise in the savants? It is not very easy to perceive. When people want to hold up a savant to the admiration of the public, they always choose Pasteur, at any rate in France. He serves as a cloak to the idolatry of science just as Joan of Arc does to nationalist idolatry.

He is chosen because he did a great deal to relieve the physical ills of mankind. But if his intention to succeed in doing this was not the primary motive of his efforts, the fact that he did succeed in doing it must be regarded as a mere coincidence. If that actually was the primary motive, the admiration owed to him has nothing to do with the greatness of science; it is a question of a practical virtue; and in that case, Pasteur would need to be placed in the same category as a hospital nurse devoted to the point of heroism, and would only differ from her in the range of the results achieved.

Since the spirit of truth is absent from the motives behind science, it cannot be present in science. If one were to expect to find it, on the other hand, to any considerable extent in philosophy and literature, one would be disappointed.

Are there many books or articles which leave us with the impression that the author, first before ever beginning to write, and then again before handing the manuscript to the printer, asked himself with any real concern: 'Am I in line with truth?' Are there many readers who, before opening a book, ask themselves with any real concern: 'Am I going to find truth in here?' If all those whose profession it is to think —priests, pastors, philosophers, writers, savants, teachers of all kinds—were offered the choice, at this very instant, between two destinies: either to sink immediately and irrevocably into a state of idiocy, in the literal sense of the word, with all the humiliations attendant on such a collapse, and retaining only just sufficient lucidity to be able to feel the full bitterness of their plight; or else a sudden and prodigious development of the intellectual faculties, such as to guarantee them immediate world-wide fame and after their death glory for thousands of years to come, but with this drawback, that their thought would always remain a little bit out of line with truth— is it possible to suppose that there would be many who in regard to such a choice would experience even a momentary hesitation?

The spirit of truth is nowadays almost absent from religion and from science and from the whole of thought. The appalling evils in the midst of which we struggle, without even managing to understand quite how tragic they are, are due entirely to that. '*Cet esprit de mensonge et d'erreur—De la chute des rois funeste avant-coureur*',* which Racine spoke about, is today no longer the monopoly of sovereigns. It embraces all classes of the population; it takes possession of whole nations and drives them into a frenzy.

The remedy is to bring back again among us the spirit of

* '*Cet esprit de mensonge . . .* ': from *Athalie*, Act 1, sc. 2. The exact quotation is: '*Répandre cet esprit d'imprudence et d'erreur*,' etc. [Translator.]

truth, and to start with in religion and science; which implies that the two of them should become reconciled.

The spirit of truth can dwell in science on condition that the motive prompting the savant is the love of the object which forms the stuff of his investigations. That object is the universe in which we live. What can we find to love about it, if it isn't its beauty? The true definition of science is this: the study of the beauty of the world.

As soon as one thinks about it, it becomes obvious. Matter, blind force are not the object of science. Thought is incapable of reaching out to them; they fly ahead of it. The savant's thought is never able to reach beyond relations in which matter and force are knit into an invisible, impalpable and unalterable pattern of order and harmony. 'Heaven's net is vast', says Lao-Tse; 'its meshes are wide; yet nothing gets through.'

How should human thought ever have any other object but thought? That is so well-known a difficulty in the theory of knowledge that one gives up trying to fathom it, leaving it on one side as an accepted fact. But there is an answer. It is that the object of human thought is itself thought. The savant's true aim is the union of his own mind with the mysterious wisdom eternally inscribed in the universe. That being so, how should there be any opposition or even separation between the spirit of science and that of religion? Scientific investigation is simply a form of religious contemplation.

This was certainly the case in Greece. What, then, has happened since? How is it that this science, which when is was cut down by the Roman sword was essentially religious in spirit, should have woken up materialistic after coming out of its long lethargy? What had happened in the interval?

A transformation had taken place in religion. I do not refer to the advent of Christianity. Early Christianity, as we can still find it in the New Testament, and particularly in the Gospels, was, like the Mystery religions of antiquity, perfectly capable of becoming the central inspiration behind a strictly genuine science. But Christianity suffered a transformation, probably connected with its transition to the rank of the official Roman religion.

After this transformation, Christian thought, except in the case of a very few mystics, always exposed to the danger of being condemned, no longer admitted any other conception of divine Providence than that of a personal Providence.

This conception is found in the Gospels, for God is there referred to as the Father. But the conception of an impersonal Providence, and one in a sense almost analogous to a mechanism, is also to be found there. 'That ye may be the children of your Father which is in heaven; for he maketh his sun to rise on the evil and on the good, and sendeth rain on the just and on the unjust. . . . Be ye therefore perfect, even as your Father which is in heaven is perfect' (Matt. v, 45, 48).

Thus it is that blind impartiality characteristic of inert matter, it is that relentless regularity characterizing the order of the world, completely indifferent to men's individual quality, and because of this so frequently accused of injustice—it is that which is held up as a model of perfection to the human soul. It is a conception of so profound a significance that we are not even today capable of grasping it; contemporary Christianity has completely lost touch with it.

All the parables about the seed are connected with this notion of an impersonal Providence. Grace descends from God upon all beings; what becomes of it depends on what they are; there where it really penetrates, the fruit it bears is the result of a process similar to a mechanical one, and which, like a mechanical one, takes place in a time continuum. The virtue of patience, or to translate the Greek word more accurately, of immobile expectancy, is relative to this necessity of duration.

The non-intervention of God in the operation of grace is expressed as clearly as it possibly can be: 'So is the kingdom of God, as if a man should cast seed into the ground; and should sleep, and rise night and day, and the seed should spring and grow up, he knoweth not how. For the earth bringeth forth fruit of herself; first the blade, then the ear, after that the full corn in the ear' (Mark iv, 26-28).

Everything which has to do with asking is suggestive also of something similar to a piece of mechanism. All real desire for pure good, after a certain degree of intensity has been reached, causes the good in question to descend. If this result is not attained, either the desire is not real, or it is too weak, or the good desired is imperfect, or it is mixed with evil. When the conditions have been fulfilled, God never refuses. Like the germination of grace, it is a process that takes place in a time continuum. Which is why Christ commands us to be importunate. The similes which he uses in this connexion are also suggestive of a mechanism. It is a psychological mechanism which compels the judge to give satisfaction to the widow: 'Yet because this widow troubleth me, I will avenge her, lest by her continual coming she weary me' (Luke xviii, 5), and the man who has gone to bed to open the door to his friend: 'Though he will not rise and give him, because he is his friend, yet because of his importunity he will rise and give him . . .' (Luke xi, 8). If we exercise a sort of compulsion upon God, it can only be a question of a mechanism instituted by God. Supernatural mechanisms are at least as dependable as are the laws of gravity; but natural mechanisms are the conditions necessary for producing events as such, without regard being had for any consideration of value; whereas supernatural mechanisms are the conditions necessary for producing pure good as such.

This is what is confirmed by the practical experience of the saints. They have observed, so it is said, that they could sometimes, by force of desire, cause more good to descend upon a soul than the latter really desired of its own accord. This shows that good descends from heaven upon earth only to the extent to which certain conditions are in fact fulfilled on earth.

The entire works of St. John of the Cross are nothing else but a strictly scientific study of supernatural mechanisms. Plato's philosophy also is nothing else than that.

The Growing of Roots

Even the judgment appears, in the Gospels, as something impersonal: 'He that believeth on him is not condemned: but he that believeth not is condemned already. . . . And this is the condemnation . . . every one that doeth evil hateth the light; . . . but he that doeth truth cometh to the light' (John iii, 18-21); 'As I hear, I judge, and my judgment is just' (John v, 30); 'If any man hear my words, and believe not, I judge him not: for I came not to judge the world, but to save the world. He that rejecteth me, and receiveth not my words, hath one that judgeth him: the word that I have spoken, the same shall judge him in the last day' (John xii, 47-48).

In the story of the labourers of the eleventh hour, there seems to be caprice on the part of the owner of the vineyard. But a closer examination shows the opposite to be the case. He pays only one type of wage because he possesses only one type of wage. He hasn't any change. St. Paul defined the wage thus: 'I shall know even as I am known'. That doesn't admit of degrees. Similarly, there are no degrees in connexion with the act which gives the right to receive the wage. One is called; one either comes running up, or one doesn't. No one is able to anticipate the call, even by so much as a second. The actual moment is of no importance; nor is the amount of work or the quality of the work performed in the vineyard. One enters or one doesn't enter into eternity, as the case may be, according to whether one has consented or refused.

'Whosoever exalteth himself shall be abased; and he that humbleth himself shall be exalted' (Luke xiv, 11): that conjures up a balance, as though the earthly part of the soul were in one of the scales, and the divine part in the other. There is a Good Friday hymn also comparing the Cross to a balance: '. . . Ceux-là ont reçu leur récompense'. God has, therefore, only the power to reward those efforts that cannot be rewarded in this world, those efforts carried out in the void; the void attracts grace. Efforts carried out in the void constitute the operation which Christ calls 'laying up treasures in heaven'.

One could find in the Gospels, in spite of the fact that they have transmitted to us but a small portion of Christ's teachings, what one might call a supernatural physics of the human soul. Like all scientific doctrine, this science only contains things which are clearly intelligible and experimentally verifiable. However, here verification takes the form of the march towards perfection, and consequently one has to accept the word of those who have accomplished it. But we readily accept the word of the savants, without the least check, concerning what takes place in their laboratories, although we don't know at all whether they love truth. It would be more reasonable to accept the word of the saints, at least of all the genuine ones, for it is certain they have a whole-hearted love of truth.

The problem of miracles only causes difficulty between religion and science because it is badly presented. To present it properly, it is necessary to give a definition of a miracle. To say that it is a fact contrary to the laws of nature is to say something completely devoid of significance. We do not know what the laws of nature are. We can only make suppositions in regard to them. If the laws we suppose are contradicted by facts, it shows that our supposition was at any rate in part erroneous. To say that a miracle is the effect of a particular act of volition on the part of God is no less absurd. Amidst all the events which take place, we have no right to maintain that certain of them rather than others are the result of God's will. All we know, in a general way, is that everything which happens, without any exception, is in accordance with the will of God considered as Creator; and that everything which contains at any rate a particle of pure good proceeds from the supernatural inspiration of God considered as Absolute Good. But when a saint performs a miracle, what is good is the saintliness, not the miracle. A miracle is a physical phenomenon necessitating as one of its prerequisites a total abandonment of the soul either to good or to evil.

One has to say either to good or to evil, for there are diabolical miracles: 'For false Christs and false prophets shall arise, and shall show signs and wonders, to seduce, if it were possible, even the elect' (Mark xiii, 22); 'Many will say to me in that day: Lord, Lord, have we not prophesied in thy name, and in thy name have cast out devils, and in thy name done many wonderful works? And then I will profess unto them: I never knew you; depart from me, ye that work iniquity' (Matt. vii, 22-23).

It is in no way contrary to the laws of nature that a total abandonment of the soul to either good or evil should be accompanied by physical phenomena which are only produced in such a case. It would be contrary to the laws of nature if it were otherwise. For every attitude of the human soul is accompanied by a certain particular physical state. Sorrow is accompanied by salt water in the eyes; then why not in certain states of mystical ecstasy, as is averred, a certain lifting up of the body above the ground? The fact may be true or not; it doesn't much matter. What is certain is that if the mystical ecstasy corresponds to something real in the soul, it must be accompanied in the body by phenomena which are not observable when the soul is in a different state. The connexion between mystical ecstasy and these phenomena is formed by a mechanism similar to that which connects sorrow with tears. We know nothing about the first mechanism. But we don't know any more about the second one.

The unique supernatural fact in this world is holiness itself and what lies near to it; it is the fact that the divine commandments should become for those who love God a motive, an active force, motor energy in the literal sense, like petrol in a motor-car. If three steps are taken without any other motive than the desire to obey God, those three steps are miraculous; they are equally so whether they take place on dry land or on water. Only that if they take place on dry land nothing extraordinary appears.

It is said that stories about walking upon water and the resurrection of the dead are so common in India that nobody, except out of vulgar curiosity, would go out of his way to see any performances of that kind. It is certain at any rate that accounts of such matters are very widespread there. They were also very widespread in Greece in its decline, as may be seen in Lucian. This singularly diminishes the apologetical value of miracles for Christianity.

A Hindu anecdote relates how an ascetic, after fourteen years spent in solitude, returned to see his family. His brother asked him what he had acquired in that time. So he led his brother down to a river and crossed it on foot before his very eyes. The brother hailed a ferryman, crossed by boat, handed over a penny, and said to the ascetic: 'Is it worth while spending fourteen years' efforts in order to acquire what I can obtain by the payment of a penny?' It is the attitude of common sense.

As far as the exactitude of the extraordinary acts related in the Gospels is concerned, all affirmations or denials on the subject can only be the result of guesswork, and the problem itself is without interest. It is certain that Christ possessed certain special powers; why should we doubt it, seeing that we are able to verify that Hindu and Tibetan saints possess them? To know the precise degree of exactitude of each particular event would not be of any use to us.

The powers exercised by Christ constituted, not a proof, but a link in the chain of a demonstration. They were the certain sign that Christ was placed outside the ordinary run of humanity, amongst those who have given themselves either to evil or to good. They didn't indicate which. But it was easy to see which it was by the manifest perfection of Christ, the purity of his life, the perfect beauty of his words, and the fact that he only exercised his powers in order to perform acts of compassion. All this was merely the proof that he was a saint. But those who were certain he was a saint, when they listened to him declaring himself to be the Son of God, might hesitate as to the precise meaning of these words, but were bound to believe that they contained a truth. For when a saint says such things, he cannot either be lying or be mistaken. We, in the same way, are bound to believe all that Christ has said, save where we have the right to suppose a faulty transcription; and what gives the proof its force is beauty. When the subject in question is the good, beauty is a rigorous and positive proof; and, indeed, there can be none other. It is absolutely impossible for there to be any other.

Christ said : 'If I had not done among them the works which none other man did, they had not had sin'; but he also said: 'If I had not come and spoken unto them, they had not had sin'.* Elsewhere he speaks about his 'mighty works'.* Acts and words are classed together. The exceptional character of the acts had no other object than to draw attention. Once the attention has been drawn, there can be no other form of proof than beauty, purity, perfection.

The words addressed to Thomas, 'Blessed are they that have not seen, and yet have believed',* cannot refer to those who, without having seen it, believe in the fact of the resurrection. That would be praising credulity, not faith. There are old women everywhere who are only too ready to believe no matter what tale about dead people returned to life. Surely those who are called blessed are they who have no need of the resurrection in order to believe, and for whom Christ's perfection and the Cross are in themselves proof.

Thus from the religious point of view the miracles are of secondary importance, and from the scientific point of view they enter naturally into the scientific conception of the world. As for the idea of proving God's existence by a violation of the laws of nature, it would doubtless have appeared to the early Christians as monstrous. It could only arise in our diseased minds, which think that the fixed order of the world is able to offer legitimate arguments to atheists.

The succession of events in the world also appears in the Gospels as though it were regulated by a Providence that is, in one sense at any rate, impersonal and comparable to a piece of mechanism. Christ said to his disciples: 'Behold the fowls of the

* Quotations: (1) John xv, 24 and 22; (2) Matt. xi, 21; (3) John xx, 29. [Translator.]

air; for they sow not, neither do they reap, nor gather into barns; yet your heavenly Father feedeth them. . . . Consider the lilies of the field, how they grow; they toil not, neither do they spin; and yet I say unto you, that even Solomon in all his glory was not arrayed like one of these. . . . Are not two sparrows sold for a farthing? And one of them shall not fall on the ground without your Father.'* This means that the solicitude of which the saints are the object on the part of God is of the same kind as that which surrounds the birds and the lilies. The laws of nature regulate the manner in which the sap rises in plants and blossoms out into flowers, in which the birds find their food; and they are arranged in such a way as to result in beauty. The laws of nature are also providentially arranged in such a way that, in the case of human creatures, the determination to seek first the heavenly Father's kingdom and his justice does not automatically entail death.

One can also say, if one likes, that God watches over each bird, each flower and each saint; it comes to the same thing. The relation of the whole to the parts is natural to the human intelligence. On the plane of events as such, whether one considers the universe as a whole, or as any one of its parts, carved out as seems suitable in space, in time and under whatever classification; or as another part, or yet another, or a collection of parts: in short, making use of the notions of whole and part as seems to one to be suitable, conformity to the will of God remains invariable. There is as much conformity to the will of God in a leaf which falls unnoticed as in the Flood. On the plane of events, the notion of conformity to the will of God is identical with the notion of reality.

On the plane of good and evil, there may or may not be conformity to the will of God, depending upon the relationship to good and evil. Faith in Providence consists in being certain that the universe in its totality is in conformity to the will of God not only in the first sense, but also in the second; that is to say, that in this universe good outweighs evil. Here

* Quotation: Matt. vi, 26, 28, 29 and x, 29. [Translator.]

it can only be a question of the universe in its totality, for in its individual aspects there is, unfortunately, no room for doubting that evil is present. Thus the object of this certitude is an eternal and universal dispensation constituting the foundation of an invariable order in the world. Divine Providence is never represented in any other form, unless I am mistaken, either in the sacred texts of the Chinese, the Indians and the Greeks, or in the Gospels.

But when the Christian religion was officially adopted by the Roman Empire, the impersonal aspect of God and of divine Providence was thrust into the background. God was turned into a counterpart of the Emperor. The operation was rendered easy by the Judaic element in Christianity, of which the latter, owing to its historical origin, had been unable to purge itself. In the texts dating from before the exile, Jehovah's juridical relationship to the Hebrews is that of a master to his slaves. They had been Pharaoh's slaves; Jehovah, having taken them out of Pharaoh's hands, has succeeded to Pharaoh's rights. They are his property, and he rules them just like any ordinary man rules his slaves, except that he disposes of a wider range of rewards and punishments. He orders them indifferently to do good or evil, but far more often evil, and in either case they have to obey. It matters little that they should be made to obey from the basest motives, provided the orders are duly executed.

Such a conception as this was exactly on a par with the feelings and intelligence of the Romans. With them slavery had undermined and degraded all human relations. They disfigured the most beautiful things. They dishonoured suppliants by forcing them to tell lies. They dishonoured gratitude by regarding it as an attenuated form of slavery: according to them, by accepting a favour, one alienated in exchange a portion of one's liberty. If it was a great favour, the prevailing custom made it necessary to say to one's benefactor that one was his slave. They dishonoured love: to be in love with anybody, for them, meant either acquiring the beloved as one's property, or else, if that were not possible, submitting oneself to her slavishly in order to be able to satisfy the lusts of the flesh, even if it meant sharing her with ten or twelve others. They dishonoured patriotism, by conceiving patriotism as the will to reduce all men to slavery who were not their compatriots. But it would be shorter to enumerate what they didn't dishonour. We should probably not find anything.

Amongst other things, they dishonoured sovereignty. The ancient conception of legitimate sovereignty, as far as one is able to conjecture, seems to have been extremely beautiful. One can only form a conjecture, for it didn't exist among the Greeks. But very likely it is this conception which survived in Spain until the seventeenth century, and has survived to a much feebler extent in England up to the present time.

The Cid, after being brutally and unjustly exiled, and after having conquered with his own right arm much vaster territories than those of the kingdom where he was born, was granted the favour of an interview with the king; and so soon as he caught sight of the latter in the distance, he leapt from his horse, threw himself on his hands and knees, and kissed the ground. In Lope de Vega's *Estrella de Sevilla*, the king wishes to prevent an assassin from being condemned to death, because the murder had been secretly ordered by himself. He sends for each of the three judges separately to inform him personally of his royal will. Each of them, on bended knee, assures the king of his absolute allegiance. After which, having come together again as a tribunal, they pass the death sentence unanimously. When the king demands an explanation of their conduct, they reply: 'As subjects we accept your authority in all things; but as judges we only obey our conscience.'

This conception is that of an unconditional allegiance, but an allegiance paid solely to an hereditary authority, without the slightest regard either for power or possibilities of prosperity or adversity, reward or punishment. It is precisely the same conception as that of obedience to the superior in the monastic orders. A king obeyed in this fashion really was a representative of God in the eyes of his subjects, like the superior of a monastery in the eyes of his monks; not through any illusion which would have made him appear divine, but solely as the result of a convention which was considered to be divinely ordained. It was a religious respect absolutely free from all idolatry. The same conception of hereditary authority was applied, below the person of the king, from top to bottom of the social scale. The whole of public life was thus permeated by the religious virtue of obedience, like the life of a Benedictine monastery of the best period.

Coming to our own era, this conception is still found among the Arabs, where it was observed by T. E. Lawrence; it existed in Spain up to the time when that unfortunate country became burdened with the grandson of Louis XIV and thus lost its own soul; it existed in the lands to the south of the Loire until their conquest by France, and even later, for its spirit is still discernible in Théophile de Viau.* The French monarchy hesitated for a long time between this conception and the Roman one; but it chose the Roman conception, and that is the reason why any restoration of the monarchy in France is out of the question. We should be only too thankful if any possibility existed of our being able to have a really hereditary form of royalty.

There are a certain number of indications which suggest that the Spanish conception of hereditary royalty was the same as that of the Oriental monarchies of antiquity. But the latter too often suffered damage. The Assyrians did it a lot of harm. So did Alexander—that product of Aristotle's pedagogical art, and who was never disowned by his mentor. The Hebrews, those escaped slaves, never knew it. Nor, in all probability, did the Romans either—that handful of adventurers brought together by necessity.

What replaced it in Rome was the relationship between master and slave. Already Cicero admitted with shame that he regarded himself as being half the slave of Caesar. From the time of Augustus, the Emperor was looked upon as the master

* *Théophile de Viau:* see note p. 171. [Translator.]

of all the inhabitants of the Roman Empire in the sense of an owner of slaves.

Men cannot imagine themselves being the victims of wrongs which they find it quite natural to inflict upon others. But when that, in fact, happens, to their own horror, they find it to be quite natural; in their hearts they can find nothing to produce the necessary indignation and resistance against a form of treatment which they themselves have never been reluctant to inflict. It is so at least when circumstances are such that, even for the imagination, there is nothing that can any longer serve as outward support, when the only possible resource left lies in the depths of the heart. If past crimes have destroyed that resource, total enfeeblement is the result, and one accepts no matter what degree of shame. It is on this mechanism of the human heart that the law of reciprocity is founded, expressed in the Apocalypse in the following terms: 'He that leadeth into captivity shall go into captivity'.*

Thus it is that a number of Frenchmen, having found it perfectly natural to talk about collaboration to the oppressed natives of the French colonies, went on making use of this word without any trouble in talking with their German masters.

In the same way, because the Romans regarded slavery as the basic institution of society, there was nothing that might prompt their hearts to say no to a man who claimed to have an owner's rights over them, and had victoriously upheld that claim by force of arms; nothing either which might say no to his heirs, whose property they became by right of inheritance. Hence all the cowardly acts whose enumeration sickened the heart of Tacitus, all the more so since he had taken his share in them. They used to commit suicide as soon as they received the order to do so, not otherwise; a slave cannot commit suicide, that would be robbing the master. Caligula used to have standing behind him, as he ate his meals, a row of senators wearing tunics, which was in Rome the characteristic mark of

* Quotation: Revelation xiii, 10. [Translator.]

degradation for slaves. At banquets, he would absent himself for a quarter of an hour to take a noblewoman into his private apartments, and then would bring her back flushed and dishevelled to rejoin the other guests, amongst whom was her husband. But these people had always found it perfectly natural to treat not only their slaves in this fashion, but also the colonial peoples of the provinces.

And so in the cult of the Emperor, what was made divine was the institution of slavery. Millions of slaves made an idolatrous cult of their owner.

It is that which determined the Roman attitude in religious matters. It has been said that they were tolerant. They certainly tolerated all religious practices devoid of any spiritual content.

No doubt Hitler, if the fancy took him, would be able to tolerate Theosophy without danger. The Romans were able to tolerate without the least difficulty the cult of Mithras, a faked Orientalism fit for snobs and idle women.

There were two exceptions to their tolerance. To begin with, they could naturally not endure that anybody, whoever it might be, should lay claim to property rights over their slaves. Hence their hostility to Jehovah. The Jews were their property and could not have another owner, human or divine. It simply amounted to a dispute between rival slave-owners. Finally, the Romans, out of regard for their prestige and to demonstrate experimentally that they were the masters, practically killed off all the human cattle the ownership of which was in dispute.

The second exception was in relation to spiritual life. The Romans could not tolerate anything rich in spiritual content. Love of God is a dangerous fire whose contact could prove fatal to their wretched deification of slavery. So they ruthlessly destroyed spiritual life under all its forms. They very cruelly persecuted the Pythagoreans and all philosophers associated with any authentic traditions. Let it be remarked, by the way, how extremely mysterious it is that a clear patch should once have made it possible for a genuine Stoic, drawing inspiration from Greece and not from Rome, to mount the throne; and the mystery is redoubled by the fact that he ill-treated the Christians. They wiped out all the Druids in Gaul; destroyed the Egyptian religious cults; drowned in blood and brought into disrepute by ingenious calumnies the worship of Dionysus. We know what they did to the Christians at the beginning.

Yet they felt ill at ease in their all too vulgar idolatry. Like Hitler, they knew the value of a deceptive exterior of spirituality. They would have liked to take the outer coverings of an authentic religious tradition to act as a cloak for their all too visible atheism. Hitler, too, would be pleased enough to find or found a religion.

Augustus attempted to enlist the sympathies of the clergy of Eleusis. The institution of the mysteries of Eleusis had already become almost completely degraded, it is not clear exactly why, in the time of the successors of Alexander. The massacres under Sulla, which filled the streets of Athens with blood like water from a burst dam, cannot have done them any good. It is very doubtful whether in the time of the Empire there still remained any trace of the genuine tradition. Nevertheless, the men of Eleusis refused to lend themselves to the transaction.

The Christians consented when they were too worn out with being massacred, too disheartened at not seeing the arrival of the triumphant end of the world. It is thus that the Father of Christ, accommodated to the Roman fashion, became a master and owner of slaves. Jehovah furnished the necessary means of transition. There was no longer the least difficulty about welcoming him. There was no longer any dispute over property between the Roman Emperor and him, since the destruction of Jerusalem.

The Gospels, it is true, are full of comparisons drawn from slavery. But in Christ's mouth this word is an artifice of love. The 'slaves' are men who have wanted with all their heart to give themselves to God as slaves. And although that means a gift made on the instant and once and for all, subsequently these slaves never cease for one second begging God to allow them to remain in slavery.

That is incompatible with the Roman conception. If we were God's property, how should we be able to give ourselves to him as slaves? He has emancipated us in view of the fact that he has created us. We are outside his kingdom. Our consent alone can, with time, bring about an inverse operation and convert us into something inert, something analogous to nothingness, where God is absolute master.

The truly Christian inspiration has fortunately been preserved by mysticism. But apart from pure mysticism, Roman idolatry has defiled everything—yes, idolatry; for it is the mode of worship, not the name attributed to the object, which separates idolatry from religion. If a Christian worships God with a heart disposed like that of a pagan of Rome in the homage rendered to the Emperor, that Christian is an idolater also.

The Roman conception of God still exists today, even in such minds as that of Maritain. He has written: 'The notion of right is even deeper than that of moral obligation, for God has a sovereign right over his creatures and he has no moral obligation towards them (though he owes it to himself to give them what is required by their nature)'.

Neither the notion of obligation nor that of right is compatible with God, but infinitely less so that of right. For the notion of right is infinitely farther removed from pure good. It is mixed up with good and evil; for the possession of a right implies the possibility of making either a good or a bad use of it. While, on the other hand, the performance of an obligation is always, unconditionally, a good from every point of view. That is why the men of 1789 made such a disastrous mistake when they chose the notion of right as their chief source of inspiration.

A sovereign right is the right of property according to the Roman idea, or any other idea essentially similar to it. To ascribe to God sovereign rights without obligations is to turn him into the infinite equivalent of a Roman slave-holder. This can only allow for a servile devotion. The devotion of a slave for the man who looks upon him as his property is a base affair. The love which drives a free man to bring himself body and soul into servitude to what constitutes perfect good, that is the opposite of a servile love.

In the mystic traditions of the Catholic Church, one of the main objects of the purifications through which the soul has to pass is the total abolition of the Roman conception of God. So long as a trace of it remains, union through love is impossible.

But the spiritual influence of the Mystics was powerless to destroy this conception in the Church as it was destroyed in their own hearts, because the Church needed it as the Empire before had needed it. It was necessary for the Church's temporal dominion. Consequently, the division of power into spiritual and temporal, to which reference is so often made in connexion with the Middle Ages, is a more complicated affair than one imagines. Obedience to the king according to the classic Spanish conception is something infinitely more religious and purer than obedience to a Church armed with an Inquisition, and representing a slave-holding conception of God, as was very largely the case in the thirteenth century. It is, therefore, quite possible that in thirteenth-century Aragon, for instance, it was the king who possessed a really spiritual authority, and the Church which possessed a really temporal authority. Be that as it may, the Roman spirit of imperialism and domination has never loosened its hold over the Church sufficiently for the latter to be able to abolish the Roman conception of God.

As a consequence, the conception of Providence has become unrecognizable. Its absurdity is so blatant as to numb the faculties. The true mysteries of the Faith are themselves absurd, but their absurdity is such as to illuminate the mind and cause it to produce in abundance truths which are clear to the intelligence. The other absurdities are maybe diabolical mysteries. Both the former and the latter are found mixed up together in current Christian thought like tares with the wheat.

The Growing of Roots

The conception of Providence which corresponds to God after the Roman style is that of a personal intervention in the world on the part of God in order to adjust certain means in view of certain particular ends. It is admitted that the order of the world, if left to itself, and without God's special intervention at a particular moment, for a particular end, could produce effects contrary to the will of God. It is admitted that God should practise such special interventions. But it is further admitted that these interventions, for the purpose of correcting the play of causality, are themselves subject to causality. God violates the natural order of the world so as to bring about therein, not what he wishes to produce, but causes which will produce what he wishes to produce by way of a result.

If one reflects on the subject, these suppositions correspond exactly to Man's situation in regard to matter. Man has particular ends which oblige him to make particular interventions that are subject to the law of causality. Let us imagine some great Roman magnate owning vast estates and numbers of slaves, and then multiply this to bring it up to the dimensions of the universe itself. Such is the conception of God which, in fact, rules over a portion of Christianity, and which has perhaps more or less infected the whole of Christianity, with the exception of the Mystics.

Let us imagine such an estate-owner living alone, without ever meeting his equals, without any contacts save with his slaves; one wonders how any particular end could take shape in his mind. All his individual wants are satisfied. Is he likely to consider the good of his slaves? In that case, he would involve himself in a lot of trouble, for, in fact, his slaves are a prey to crime and affliction. If attempts are made to inspire them with good feelings by enumerating all the happy sides there are to their lot—as doubtless pro-slavery preachers used formerly to do in America—it only serves to show up more clearly just how very limited that side is, what a disproportion there is between the power in the hands of the master and the respective shares in good things and bad. Since this is impossible to conceal, the slaves will be told that if they are wretched, it is because of their own fault. But even if this assertion is accepted, it doesn't throw any light on the problem of knowing what is likely to be the will of the estate-owner. It is impossible to imagine it otherwise than composed of a series of caprices, some of which are benevolent. In fact, that is exactly how one does imagine it to be.

All attempts to discover in the structure of the universe evidence of the benevolent intentions of the owner of it are without any exception on the same level as that remark of Bernardin de Saint-Pierre's on the subject of melons and meals *en famille*.* There is in all these attempts the same basic absurdity which we find in historical considerations concerning the effects of the Incarnation. The good which it is given to Man to observe in the universe is finite, limited. To endeavour to discern therein evidence of divine action is to turn God himself into a finite, a limited good. It is a blasphemy.

Similar attempts in the analysis of history can be illustrated by an ingenious idea expressed in a Catholic review published in New York at the time of the last anniversary of the discovery of America. It said that God had sent Christopher Columbus to America in order that a few centuries later there should be a nation capable of defeating Hitler. This is far worse even than what Bernardin de Saint-Pierre perpetrated; it is just appalling. God, apparently, also despises coloured races: the wholesale extermination of native American peoples in the sixteenth century seemed to him a small price to pay if it meant the salvation of Europeans in the twentieth; and he wasn't able to bring them salvation by less sanguinary means. One would have thought that instead of sending Christopher Columbus to America more than four centuries in advance, it

* . . . *meals 'en famille'* : Bernardin de Saint-Pierre was so convinced of the essential harmony in Nature, that he thought he saw a divine significance in the fact that melons indicate from the outside their division into slices, which was an unmistakable sign that they were meant to be eaten *en famille*. [Translator.]

would have been simpler to send some one to assassinate Hitler round about the year 1923.

It would be a mistake to imagine that to represent an exceptional degree of stupidity. All providential interpretations of history are unavoidably situated on exactly the same level. It is the case with Bossuet's conception of history. It is at the same time appalling and stupid, equally revolting for the intelligence as for the heart. One has to be more than ordinarily sensitive to the resonance of words to be able to regard this courtier-prelate as a great mind.

When the notion of Providence is made to enter private life, the result is no less comical. If lightning falls within an inch of somebody without touching him, he often thinks it is Providence which has preserved him. Those who happen to be a mile away from that spot have no idea that they owe their lives to an intervention on the part of God. Apparently, when the mechanism of the universe is on the point of causing the death of any human being, God asks himself whether it pleases him or not to save the creature's life, and if he decides it does he exerts an imperceptible pressure on the mechanism. He can well change the course of the lightning by an inch in order to save a life, but not by a mile, still less prevent it from falling purely and simply. Evidently people must reason in this fashion; otherwise they would say to themselves that Providence intervenes in order to prevent us from being killed by lightning at every moment of our lives, to the same extent as at the moment when it falls an inch away from us. The only time when it doesn't intervene to prevent the lightning killing such-and-such a human being is the very instant when the lightning kills him, if that indeed occurs. Everything which doesn't happen is prevented from happening by God to the same extent. Everything which happens is permitted to happen by God to the same extent.

The ridiculous conception of Providence as being a personal and particular intervention on the part of God for certain particular ends is incompatible with true faith. But it is not a manifest incompatibility. It is incompatible with the scientific conception of the world; and in this case the incompatibility is manifest. Christians who, under the influence of education and surroundings, carry within them this conception of Providence, also carry within them the scientific conception of the world, and that divides their minds into two water-tight compartments: one for the scientific conception of the world, the other for the conception of the world as being a field in which God's personal Providence is exercised. This makes it impossible for them really to think either the one or the other. The second one, moreover, will not bear serious scrutiny. Unbelievers, not being inhibited by any motives of reverence, detect easily enough the ridiculous aspect of this personal and particular form of Providence, and religious faith itself is, on account of it, made to seem ridiculous in their eyes.

The particular designs that are attributed to God are cuttings made by us from out of the more than infinite complexity of causal connexions. We make them by connecting across time certain events with certain results produced by these events, chosen from amongst thousands of other possible ones. We are right when we declare these cuttings to be in conformity with the will of God. But the same would be just as true, and without any exception, of all the cuttings which could possibly be made by every sort of human or non-human intelligence, on no matter what scale of magnitude, throughout space and time, amid the complexity of the universe.

One cannot cut out from the continuity of space and time an event as it were like an atom; but the inadequacy of human language obliges one to talk as though one could.

All the events which go to make up the universe in the total stream of time, each one of these events, each possible assemblage of several events, each connexion between two or more events, between two or more assemblages of events, between one event and an assemblage of events—all that, to the same degree, has been permitted by the will of God. All that represents the particular intentions of God. The sum of the particular intentions of God is the universe itself. Only that which is evil is excluded, and even that must not be wholly excluded, from every single aspect, but solely in so far as it is evil. From every other aspect, it is in conformity to the will of God.

A soldier suffering from a very painful wound, and thereby prevented from taking part in a battle in which his entire regiment is wiped out, may think that God has wished, not to make him suffer pain, but to save his life. That represents an extreme naïvety and a snare for self-esteem. God has wished to make him suffer pain, to save his life and to produce all the results which, in fact, have been produced; but not one of them any more than any other.

There is only one case in which it is legitimate to talk about particular volition on the part of God: that is when a particular impulsion arises in a man's soul which bears the unmistakable impress of God's commandments. But it is then a question of God considered as a source of inspiration.

The present conception of Providence reminds one of that school exercise called *explication française*,* when it is carried out by a bad schoolmaster in connexion with a piece of poetry of the first order. The schoolmaster will say: 'The poet used such-and-such a word to obtain such-and-such an effect'. That could only be true of poetry of the second, tenth or fiftieth order. In a poetic fragment of the first order, all the effects, all the resonances, all the evocatory qualities capable of being summoned together by the presence of such-and-such a word in such-and-such a place correspond in an equal degree, that is to say, perfectly, to the poet's inspiration. It is the same with all the arts. It is in this way that the poet imitates God. Poetic inspiration at its highest point of perfection is one of the human things which can by analogy furnish a conception of the will of God. The poet is a person; yet in moments when he

---

* *'explication française'*: a practical educational exercise in French schools, and which consists in analysing a given text from every point of view: language, meaning, derivation, relationship to other texts, etc. [Translator.]

reaches poetic perfection, he is shot through by an impersonal inspiration. It is in his mediocre moments that his inspiration is a personal one; and it is then not really inspiration at all. In using poetic inspiration as an image for representing to oneself by analogy the will of God, one mustn't take the mediocre form but the perfect form.

Divine Providence is not a disturbing influence, an anomaly in the ordering of the world; it is itself the order of the world; or rather it is the regulating principle of this universe. It is eternal Wisdom, unique, spread across the whole universe in a sovereign network of relations.

It is thus that it was conceived throughout pre-Roman antiquity. All the parts of the Old Testament in which the universal inspiration of antiquity has penetrated spread this conception before us clothed in language of incomparable splendour. But we are blind. We read without understanding.

Brute force is not sovereign in this world. It is by nature blind and indeterminate. What is sovereign in this world is determinateness, limit. Eternal Wisdom imprisons this universe in a network, a web of determinations. The universe accepts passively. The brute force of matter, which appears to us sovereign, is nothing else in reality but perfect obedience.

That is the guarantee accorded to Man, the Ark of the Covenant, the Covenant, the visible and palpable promise here below, the sure basis of hope. That is the truth which bites at our hearts every time we are penetrated by the beauty of the world. That is the truth which bursts forth in matchless accents of joy in the beautiful and pure parts of the Old Testament, in Greece among the Pythagoreans and all the sages, in China with Lao-Tse, in the Hindu scriptures, in Egyptian remains. It lies perhaps hidden in innumerable myths and tales. It will appear to us, before our very eyes, clothed in our own knowledge, if one day God opens our eyes, as He did Hagar's.

We perceive it even through the very words in which Hitler affirms the contrary fallacy: '. . . in a world in which planets and suns follow circular trajectories, moons revolve round planets, and force reigns everywhere and supreme over weakness, which it either compels to serve it docilely or else crushes out of existence. . . '. How should blind force be able to produce circles? It is not weakness which is the docile servant of force. It is force which is docile to eternal Wisdom.

Hitler and his fanatical young followers have never felt that as they looked up at the stars at night. But did anybody ever try to point it out to them? This civilization we are so proud of has done everything it could to conceal the fact, and so long as there remains any corner in our hearts which is capable of being proud of it, we cannot be guiltless of a single one of Hitler's crimes.

In India, they have a word whose original meaning is 'balance', which stands at the same time for the order of the world and justice. Here is a sacred text on this subject, which, in symbolical form, refers at once to the creation of the world and human society:

'God, in truth, existed in the beginning, absolutely alone. Being alone, he did not manifest himself. He created a superior form, sovereignty. . . . That is why there is nothing above sovereignty. That is why on ceremonial occasions the priest is seated above the sovereign. . . .

'Still, God did not manifest himself. He created the peasant, artisan and merchant class.

'Still he did not manifest himself. He created the servant class.

'Still he did not manifest himself. He created a superior form, Justice. Justice is the sovereignty of sovereignties. That is why there is nothing above Justice. Whoever is without power can be equal to him who has great power by means of Justice, as though by means of some royal authority.

'What is Justice, the same is also Truth. That is why when some one speaks Truth, we say: "He is just". And when some one speaks Justice, we say: "He is true". It is really because Justice and Truth are the same thing.'

A very ancient Hindu stanza runs:

> 'That from whence the sun rises,
> That wherein the sun sets,
> That, the gods have made Justice,
> The same today, the same tomorrow.'

Anaximander has written: 'It is out of indeterminateness that things take their birth; and destruction is a return to indeterminateness, which is accomplished by virtue of necessity. For things are subject to chastisement and expiation at one another's hands, because of their injustice, according to the ordering of time'.

That is the truth, and not the monstrous conception deduced by Hitler from the vulgarization of modern science. Every visible and palpable force is subject to an invisible limit which it shall never cross. In the sea, a wave mounts higher and higher; but at a certain point, where there is nevertheless only space, it is arrested and forced to redescend. In the same way, the German flood was arrested, without anybody knowing why, on the shores of the Channel.

The Pythagoreans used to say that the universe is constructed out of indeterminateness and the principle that determines, limits, arrests. It is the latter which is always dominant.

The tradition concerning the rainbow—surely borrowed by Moses from the Egyptians—expresses in the most touching way the trust which the order of the world should inspire in Man: 'And God said: . . . It shall come to pass, when I bring a cloud over the earth, that the bow shall be seen in the cloud; and I will remember my covenant, which is between me and you and every living creature of all flesh; and the waters shall no more become a flood to destroy all flesh'.*

The rainbow's beautiful semicircle is the testimony that the phenomena of this world, however terrifying they may be, are all subject to a limit. The magnificent poetry of this text is designed to remind God to exercise his function as a limiting principle. 'Thou hast set a bound that they may not pass over; that they turn not again to cover the earth' (Psalm civ).

* Quotation: Genesis ix, 14-15. [Translator.]

274

And like the oscillations of the waves, the whole succession of events here below, made up, as they are, of variations in balance mutually compensated—births and destructions, waxings and wanings—render one keenly alive to the invisible presence of a plexus of limits without substance and yet harder than any diamond. That is why things are beautiful in their vicissitudes, although they allow one to perceive a pitiless necessity. Pitiless, yes; but which is not force, which is sovereign ruler over all force.

But the thought which really enraptured the ancients was this: what makes the blind forces of matter obedient is not another, stronger force; it is love. They believed that matter was obedient to eternal Wisdom by virtue of the love which causes it to consent to this obedience.

Plato, in his *Timeus*, says that divine Providence dominates necessity by exercising a wise form of persuasion over it. In a Stoic poem of the third century B.C., but whose inspiration has been proved to be much more ancient, God is addressed thus :

'Thee this whole world that revolves around the earth
 Obeys, whither thou mayest lead it, and accepts thy
    dominion.
 Such is the virtue of the servitor thou holdest under thine
    invincible hands,
 Two-edged, flaming, eternally living, the lightning.'

Lightning, the vertical shaft of fire that darts from heaven to earth, is the flash of love passing between God and his creation, which is why 'hurler of thunderbolts' is the name above all others applied to Zeus.

It is from there that the Stoic conception of *amor fati*, love of the order of the world, regarded by them as the supreme virtue, is derived. The order of the world is to be loved because it is pure obedience to God. Whatever this universe accords us or inflicts on us, it does so exclusively out of obedience. When a friend, long absent and eagerly awaited, grips our hand, it makes no difference whether the pressure exerted be in itself agreeable or painful; if he grips too hard and hurts us, we don't even notice it. When he speaks, we don't ask ourselves whether the sound of his voice is in itself agreeable. The pressure of the hand, the voice, all is for us just the outward sign of a presence, and in virtue of that fact, infinitely precious. In the same way all that happens to us throughout the course of our life, having been brought about by the total obedience of this universe to God, places us in contact with the absolute good formed by the divine will; in virtue of this, everything, without any exception, joys and sorrows alike, ought to be welcomed with the same inward attitude of love and thankfulness.

Those men who disregard the true good disobey God in the sense that they don't obey him as a thinking creature ought to do, with the consent of the mind. But their bodies and souls are entirely subject to the laws of the mechanisms which rule in sovereign fashion over physical and psychical matter. The physical and psychical matter in them obeys perfectly; they are perfectly obedient in so far as they are matter, and they are not anything else, if they do not possess nor have any desire for the supernatural light which alone raises Man above matter. That is why the evil they cause us should be accepted in the same spirit as the evil which inert matter causes us. Apart from the compassion one ought to show for a human mind that has gone astray and suffers, they should be loved in the same way as inert matter should be loved, as forming part of the perfect beauty of the order of the universe.

Naturally, when the Romans felt obliged to dishonour Stoicism by adopting it, they substituted in place of love an insensibility based on pride. Hence the presumption, still common today, that Stoicism and Christianity are opposed to each other, whereas they are really two twin conceptions. The very names of the persons of the Trinity, Logos, Pneuma, are borrowed from the Stoic vocabulary. Knowledge of certain Stoic theories throws a vivid light on several enigmatic passages in the New Testament. A mutual exchange took place between the two conceptions because of their affinities. At the core of each we find humility, obedience and love.

The Growing of Roots

But several texts indicate that the Stoic conception was also that of the entire ancient world, right up to the Far East. The whole of humanity once lived inspired by the dazzling conception that the universe in which we find ourselves is nothing else than perfect obedience.

The Greeks were thrilled to find in science a startling confirmation of this, and that was the cause of their enthusiasm for it.

The operation of the intellect in scientific study makes sovereign necessity over matter appear to the mind as a network of relations which are immaterial and without force. Necessity can only be perfectly conceived so long as such relations appear as absolutely immaterial. They are then only present to the understanding as a result of a pure and lofty concentration emanating from a part of the mind not subjected to force. The part of the human mind that is subjected to force is that part which finds itself under the sway of needs. One has to forget entirely all about needs in order to conceive the relations in their immaterial purity. If one manages to do this, one realizes the play of forces in accordance with which the satisfaction of needs is granted or refused.

Forces in this world are supremely determined by necessity; necessity is made up of relations which are thoughts; consequently, the force which is supreme in the world is under the supreme domination of thought. Man is a thinking being; he is therefore on the same side as that which dominates force. He is certainly not lord and master of creation, and Hitler was right in saying that in believing himself to be so he is mistaken; but he is the master's son, the child of the house. Science is the proof of this. A little child belonging to a wealthy home is in many respects under the control of the servants; but when he is sitting on his father's knees and identifies himself with him through love, he has a share in the father's authority.

So long as Man submits to having his soul taken up with his own thoughts, his personal thoughts, he remains entirely subjected, even in his most secret thoughts, to the compulsion exercised by needs and to the mechanical play of forces. If he thinks otherwise, he is mistaken. But everything changes as soon as, by virtue of a positive act of concentration, he empties his soul so as to allow the conceptions of eternal Wisdom to enter into it. He then carries within himself the very conceptions to which force is subjected.

The nature of the relation and the type of indispensable concentration required to conceive it, was in the eyes of the Greeks a proof that necessity is in actual fact obedience to God. They also had another proof. It consisted in the symbols attached to the relations themselves, as the signature of the painter is affixed to a picture.

Greek symbolism accounts for the fact that Pythagoras offered up a sacrifice in his joy at having discovered the possibility of drawing a right-angled triangle inside a semicircle.

The circle, in the eyes of the Greeks, was the image of God. For a circle which turns upon itself is a movement leading to no change and one completely self-contained. The symbol of the circular movement expressed for them the same truth that is expressed in Christian dogma by the conception of the eternal act on which is based the relationship between the Persons of the Trinity.

The mean proportional was in their eyes the image of the divine mediation between God and his creatures. The mathematical researches of the Pythagoreans were concerned with finding out mean proportionals between numbers which don't form part of the same geometrical progression; for instance, between 1 and a non-quadrated number. The right-angled triangle supplied them with the solution. The right-angled triangle is the source of all mean proportionals. But since it can be drawn inside a semicircle, the complete circle can be substituted for this purpose. Thus the circle, the geometrical image of God, is the source of the geometrical image of divine mediation. Such a marvellous discovery was worth a sacrifice.

Geometry thus becomes a double language, which at the same time provides information concerning the forces that are in action in matter, and talks about the supernatural relations between God and his creatures. It is like those ciphered letters which appear equally coherent before as after deciphering.

Concern for the symbol has completely disappeared from our science. And yet, if one were to give oneself the trouble, one could easily find, in certain parts at least of contemporary mathematics, such as the theory of aggregates or the integral calculus, symbols as clear, as beautiful and as full of spiritual meaning as that of the circle and mediation.

From modern thought to ancient wisdom the path would be short and direct, if one cared to take it.

In contemporary philosophy, analyses likely to lead to a complete theory of sense perception have appeared all over the place under different forms. The fundamental truth which such a theory would reveal is that the reality of objects perceived by the senses does not reside in sensible impressions as such, but solely in the exigencies of which the impressions constitute the signs.

This sensible universe in which we find ourselves has no other reality than that of necessity; and necessity is a combination of relations which fade away as soon as they are not sustained by a pure and lofty concentration on the part of the mind. This universe around us is made up of mind materially present in our flesh.

Science, in its different branches, apprehends through all phenomena mathematical relations or what correspond to mathematical relations. Eternal mathematics, that language with a double end in view, that is the stuff of which the order of the world is woven.

Every phenomenon is a modification of the distribution of energy, and consequently is determined by the laws of energy. But there are many forms of energy, and they are disposed in a graduated order. Mechanical force, gravity or gravitation in the Newtonian sense, whose compulsion we are continually made to feel, is not the highest form. Light, impalpable and weightless, is a form of energy that, in spite of gravity, makes the trees and the blades of corn shoot upwards. We consume it in corn and in fruit, and its presence inside us gives us the necessary force to stand upright and go about our work.

Something infinitely small, under certain conditions, operates in a decisive manner. There is no mass so heavy but that a given point is equal to it; for a mass will not fall if a single point in it is upheld, provided this point be the centre of gravity. Certain chemical transformations are conditioned by the operation of almost invisible bacteria. Catalysts are imperceptible fragments of matter whose presence is indispensable for bringing about other chemical transformations. Other minute fragments, of almost identical composition, exercise by their presence no less decisive a power of inhibition; on this mechanism has been founded the most potent of medicaments recently discovered.

And so it is not only mathematics but the whole of science which, without our thinking of noticing it, is a symbolical mirror of supernatural truths.

Modern psychology is trying to turn the study of the soul into a science. With a little extra precision this could be brought about. It should be founded on the notion of psychic matter, linked with Lavoisier's axiom, which is valid for all forms of matter, 'nothing is lost, nothing is created'; or in other words, changes are either modifications of form, beneath which there is something which persists, or else they are displacements; but never simply appearances and disappearances. The notion of limit should be introduced, and the principle established that, as concerns the terrestrial part of the soul, everything is finite, limited, subject to becoming exhausted. Finally, the notion of energy should be introduced by postulating that psychical phenomena, like physical phenomena, are modifications in the distribution and quality of energy, and are determined by the laws of energetics.

Contemporary attempts to create a social science would also lead to a successful issue as the result of a little more precision. It should be founded upon the Platonic notion of the enormous animal, or the apocalyptic notion of the Beast. Social science is the study of the enormous animal and should undertake a minute description of its anatomy, physiology, natural and conditional reflexes, capacity for being broken in.

The science of the soul and social science are alike impossible, if the idea of the supernatural is not rigorously defined and introduced into science on the basis of a scientific conception, so as to be handled with the utmost precision in all matters relating to science.

If the sciences which have to do with Man were founded in this way, according to methods of mathematical precision, and at the same time maintained in close relationship with religious faith; if in the natural and mathematical sciences symbolical interpretation were to occupy once again the place it occupied formerly—the unity of the established order in this universe would appear in all its sovereign clarity.

The order of the world is the same as the beauty of the world. All that differs is the type of concentration demanded, according to whether one tries to conceive the necessary relations which go to make it up or to contemplate its splendour.

It is one and the same thing, which with respect to God is eternal Wisdom; with respect to the universe, perfect obedience; with respect to our love, beauty; with respect to our intelligence, balance of necessary relations; with respect to our flesh, brute force.

Today, science, history, politics, the organization of labour, religion even, in so far as it is marked by the Roman defilement, offer nothing to men's minds except brute force. Such is our civilization. It is a tree which bears the fruit it deserves.

A return to truth would make manifest, amongst other things, the truth of physical labour.

Physical labour willingly consented to is, after death willingly consented to, the most perfect form of obedience.

The penal character of labour, suggested by the account in Genesis, has been misunderstood for want of a just notion regarding punishment. It is a mistake to read into this text the slightest hint of a disdain for labour. It is more likely that it was handed down by some very ancient civilization in which physical labour was honoured above every other activity.

There are numerous signs indicating that such a civilization did exist, that long ago physical labour was pre-eminently a religious activity and consequently something sacred. The Mysteries—a religion which embraced the whole of pre-Roman antiquity—were entirely founded upon symbolical expressions concerning the salvation of the soul, drawn from agriculture. The same symbolism is found again in the New Testament parables. The rôle of Hephaistos in the *Prometheus* of Aeschylus seems to recall a religion of blacksmiths. Prometheus himself is precisely the non-temporal projection of Christ, a crucified and redemptive God who came down to cast fire upon the Earth; in Greek symbolism as in the New Testament, fire is the image of the Holy Ghost. Aeschylus, who never says anything at random, asserts that the fire given by Prometheus to mankind was the personal property of Hephaistos, which seems to indicate that Hephaistos is its personification. Hephaistos is a god in the form of a blacksmith. One can imagine a blacksmith's religion seeing in fire which renders iron ductile the image of the operation of the Holy Ghost upon human nature.

There may perhaps have been a time when an identical truth was translated into different sets of symbols, and when each set was adapted to a certain type of physical labour in such a way as to turn the latter into the direct expression of religious faith.

At all events, all the religious traditions of antiquity, including the Old Testament, make the various trades originate in the receipt of direct instructions from God. The majority affirm that God became incarnate in order to carry out this pedagogic mission. The Egyptians, for instance, believed that the incarnation of Osiris had had the double object of such practical instruction together with redemption through his Passion.

Whatever the truth may be which is hidden in these

extremely mysterious accounts, the belief in direct instruction in the various trades by God implies the memory of a time when the exercise of these trades was above all a sacred activity.

No trace of it remains in Homer, nor in Hesiod, nor in classical Greece, nor in the other civilizations of antiquity, so far as our scanty knowledge about them goes. In Greece, labour was held to be servile. We cannot know whether this was already so before the invasion of the Hellenes, in the time of the Pelasgi; nor whether the Mysteries preserved explicitly in their secret doctrines the memory of a time when it had been held in honour. Right at the very beginning of Greek classical times, we perceive the end of a form of civilization in which, save for physical labour, all human activities were looked upon as sacred; in which art, poetry, philosophy, science and politics were, as it were, indistinguishable from religion. A century or two later, through a process which is obscure to us, but in which money at any rate must have played an immense rôle, all these activities had become exclusively profane and divorced from all religious inspiration. The little of religion which survived was relegated to places specially associated with worship. Plato, in his age, was a survival of an already far-distant past. The Greek Stoics were a burst of flame from a still-living spark belonging to that same past.

The Romans, an atheistic and materialistic nation, destroyed systematically whatever remained of spiritual life in the countries occupied by them; they adopted Christianity only after emptying it of its spiritual content. Under their rule, every human activity without exception became something servile; and they ended up by taking away all reality from the institution of slavery, which thus prepared for its disappearance, by reducing all human beings indiscriminately to the condition of slaves.

The so-called Barbarians, of whom many, doubtless, originally came from Thrace and had imbibed the spiritual influence of the Mysteries, took Christianity seriously; with the result that we very nearly had a Christian civilization. We can discern the dawn of it in the eleventh and twelfth centuries. The countries to the south of the Loire, which formed the principal radiating centre for it, were impregnated at the same time both with Christian spirituality and ancient spirituality; at any rate, if it is true that the Albigenses were Manichaeans, and consequently inspired not only by Persian thought, but also by Gnostic, Stoic, Pythagorean and Egyptian thought. The civilization which was then in embryo would have been free from all taint of slavery. The different trades would have occupied the place of honour.

The picture that Machiavelli draws of Florence in the twelfth century is a model of what in modern jargon would be called a syndicalist democracy. At Toulouse, knights and workmen fought side by side against Simon de Montfort to defend the spiritual treasures common to both. The corporations established in the course of this period of gestation were religious institutions. All we need to do is to look at a Romanesque church, listen to a Gregorian melody, read one of the perfect poems of the troubadours, or better still, the liturgical texts, in order to recognize that art and religious faith were as indistinguishable from one another as they were in ancient Greece at its highest point.

But a Christian civilization in which the light of Christianity would have illuminated the whole of life, would only have been possible if the Roman conception of enslaving people's minds adopted by the Church had been cast aside. The relentless and victorious struggle waged by St. Bernard against Abelard shows how very far this was from happening. At the beginning of the thirteenth century, this civilization still in process of formation was destroyed by the ruin of its principal centre, that is to say, the lands to the south of the Loire, the setting up of the Inquisition and the stifling of religious thought under the sign of orthodoxy.

The conception of orthodoxy, by rigorously separating the domain relating to the welfare of souls, which is that of an unconditional subjection of the mind to external authority, from the domain relating to so-called profane matters, in which the intelligence remains free, makes impossible that mutual penetration of the religious and the profane which would be the essence of a Christian civilization. It is in vain that every day, at Mass, a little water is mixed with the wine.

The thirteenth and fourteenth centuries and the early part of the fifteenth are the period of medieval decadence. They show the progressive degradation and final eclipse of a civilization which was stillborn, the progressive desiccation of a single germ-cell.

About the fifteenth century came the first Renaissance, which was like a feeble foretaste of the resurrection of pre-Roman civilization and of the spirit of the twelfth century. The Greece of classical times, Pythagoras, Plato, then became the objects of a religious veneration that went in perfect harmony with the Christian faith. But this attitude of mind was of very brief duration.

Shortly afterwards came the second Renaissance with quite the opposite tendency. It is the latter which has produced what we call our modern civilization.

We are very proud of it, but we also know that it is sick. And everybody is agreed about the diagnosis of the sickness. It is sick because it doesn't know exactly what place to give to physical labour and to those engaged in physical labour.

Many intelligent minds exhaust themselves over this problem, groping about in the dark. No one knows where to begin, what basis to go on, what method to follow; and so all these efforts come to nothing.

The best thing to do seems to be to ponder over the old account in Genesis, situating it in its own proper atmosphere, that of ancient conceptions.

When a human being has, by committing a crime, placed himself outside the current of the Good, his true punishment consists in his reintegration into the plenitude of that current by means of suffering. There is nothing so marvellous as a punishment.

Man placed himself outside the current of Obedience. God chose as his punishments labour and death. Consequently, labour and death, if Man undergoes them in a spirit of willingness, constitute a transference back into the current of supreme Good, which is obedience to God.

This takes on a luminous clarity if, as in antiquity, one looks upon the passivity of inert matter as the perfection of obedience to God, and upon the beauty of the world as the radiance of this perfect Obedience.

Whatever, in heaven, may be the mysterious significance of death, on earth it is the transformation of a being composed of palpitating flesh and of mind, of a being who loves and hates, hopes and fears, wants and doesn't want, into a little pile of inert matter.

Man's consent to such a transformation represents his supreme act of total obedience. That is why St. Paul says of Christ himself, in connexion with the Passion: '. . . yet learned he obedience by the things which he suffered, and was made perfect.'*

But consent to suffer death can only be fully real when death is actually at hand. It can only come near to plenitude when death itself is near. When the prospect of death is abstract and distant, it is abstract too.

Physical labour is a daily death.

To labour is to place one's own being, body and soul, in the circuit of inert matter, turn it into an intermediary between one state and another of a fragment of matter, make of it an instrument. The labourer turns his body and soul into an appendix of the tool which he handles. The movements of the body and the concentration of the mind are a function of the requirements of the tool, which itself is adapted to the matter being worked upon.

Death and labour are things of necessity and not of choice. The world only gives itself to Man in the form of food and warmth if Man gives himself to the world in the form of

* Quotation: Hebrews v, 8 and 9. [Translator.]

labour. But death and labour can be submitted to either in an attitude of revolt or in one of consent. They can be submitted to either in their naked truth or else wrapped around with lies.

Labour does violence to human nature. At times there is a superabundance of youthful energy eager to spend itself and not finding a suitable outlet; at other times there is exhaustion and the will has ceaselessly to supplement, at the expense of a very great strain on itself, the lack of physical energy; there are a thousand and one preoccupations, worries, anxieties, a thousand and one desires, interests which take the mind else-where; monotony brings with it disgust, and time hangs with an almost intolerable heaviness.

The human mind dominates time and ceaselessly and rapidly surveys the past and the future, leaping over any sort of interval; but he who labours is subject to time in the same way as inert matter that can only move slowly from one moment to the next. It is in this way, above all, that labour does violence to human nature. Which is why those who labour signify the suffering labour causes them by the expression 'finding the hours drag'.

Consent to suffer death, when death is there and seen in all its nakedness, constitutes a final, sudden wrenching away from what each one calls 'I'. Consent to perform labour is of a less violent nature. But where it is absolute, it is renewed each morning throughout the entire length of a human existence, day after day, and each day it lasts until the evening, and it starts again on the following day, and this goes on often until death. Each morning the labourer consents to perform his labour for that day, and for the rest of his life. He consents to perform it whether he feels sad or happy, worried or ready for amusement, tired or bursting with energy.

Immediately next in order after consent to suffer death, consent to the law which makes work indispensable for con-serving life represents the most perfect act of obedience which it is given to Man to accomplish.

It follows that all other human activities, command over

men, technical planning, art, science, philosophy and so on, are all inferior to physical labour in spiritual significance.

It is not difficult to define the place that physical labour should occupy in a well-ordered social life. It should be its spiritual core.

light lunch

Published in 2007 by Murdoch Books Pty Limited.
www.murdochbooks.com.au

Murdoch Books Australia
Pier 8/9, 23 Hickson Road
Millers Point NSW 2000
Phone: + 61 (0) 2 8220 2000
Fax: + 61 (0) 2 8220 2558

Murdoch Books UK Limited
Erico House, 6th Floor
93-99 Upper Richmond Road
Putney, London SW15 2TG
Phone: + 44 (0) 20 8785 5995
Fax: + 44 (0) 20 8785 5985

Chief Executive: Juliet Rogers
Publishing Director: Kay Scarlett

Design Manager: Vivien Valk
Concept & Art Direction: Sarah Odgers
Design: Jacqueline Duncan
Project Manager: Rhiain Hull
Editor: Gordana Trifunovic
Production: ,Monika Paratore
Photographer: Jared Fowler
Stylist: Cherise Koch
Food preparation: Alan Wilson
Introduction text: Leanne Kitchen
Recipes developed by the Murdoch Books Test Kitchen

ISBN 978 1 74196 126 3
Printed by 1010 Printing International Ltd. in 2008. PRINTED IN CHINA.

IMPORTANT: Those who might be at risk from the effects of salmonella poisoning (the elderly, pregnant women, young children and those suffering from immune deficiency diseases) should consult their doctor with any concerns about eating raw eggs.

CONVERSION GUIDE: You may find cooking times vary depending on the oven you are using. For fan-forced ovens, as a general rule, set the oven temperature to 20°C (35°F) lower than indicated in the recipe. We have used 20 ml (4 teaspoon) tablespoon measures. If you are using a 15 ml (3 teaspoon) tablespoon, for most recipes the difference will not be noticeable. However, for recipes using baking powder, gelatine, bicarbonate of soda (baking soda), small amounts of flour, add an extra teaspoon for each tablespoon specified.

light lunch

THE ALFRESCO RECIPES YOU MUST HAVE

SERIES EDITOR **JANE PRICE**

MURDOCH BOOKS

CONTENTS

AL FRESCO FEAST

Some anonymous observer once claimed that 'good friends, good food, good wine and good weather doth a good picnic make'. Whoever they were, they were bang-on the mark. A fine day that's disturbed only by soft, balmy breezes, and an open, grassy space dotted with gracious, shady trees is, where dining outdoors is concerned, about as inviting as it gets. There's something relaxing and (especially in this giddy-paced age) almost escapist about throwing down a rug, opening up a groaning picnic hamper then sprawling in the sun and casually picking through its contents. Practically everything tastes better consumed outdoors, from sausage rolls, raised pork pie and quiche to 'smarter' fare like smoked trout puffs, papaya and prawn salad and almond friands. The stereotypical picnic, which generally involves the packing up and transporting of suitably sturdy food to some location (a park, the beach or a pretty field for instance), with all the attendant gadgets and gear (such as thermoses, plastic cutlery and plates, and folding chairs), is always a treat but it doesn't have to offer the only opportunity for dining outdoors. Many occasions, from christening parties to cocktail bashes to Christmas lunches, and all the anniversaries, birthdays and no-reason-at-all revelries in between, can be celebrated al fresco.

Food that is best suited to out-of-doors consumption is that which can be easily picked up and eaten out of hand, or served without fanfare from bowls or platters. It shouldn't be tricksy, fragile or require complex presentation in order to look good — the secret of dining outdoors is in choosing dishes that can be cooked and assembled ahead of time. Whether you're a picnic traditionalist or a cook who loves to host outdoor gatherings of a casual, contemporary sort, there's everything you'll ever need in the specially chosen recipes of *Light Lunch*.

FINGER FOOD

SWEET AND SALTY NUTS

250 g (9 oz/1²/₃ cups) blanched almonds
250 g (9 oz/2¹/₂ cups) pecans
55 g (2 oz/¹/₄ cup) sugar
1 teaspoon ground cinnamon
pinch ground cloves
¹/₂ teaspoon curry powder
¹/₄ teaspoon ground cumin

SERVES 6–8

Preheat the oven to 180°C (350°F/Gas 4). Spread the almonds and pecans on a large baking tray and bake for 5–10 minutes, or until they are crisp and lightly coloured. Remove and allow to cool.

Combine the sugar, spices, 1 teaspoon salt and ¹/₂ teaspoon ground pepper in a small bowl and mix well.

Heat a large non-stick frying pan over medium heat and add the almonds and pecans. Sprinkle the spice mixture over the nuts and stir for 5 minutes, or until the nuts turn golden. The sugar will melt and coat the nuts. Gently shake the frying pan often to ensure even cooking. If the nuts stick together, separate them with a wooden spoon. When the nuts are cooked, remove from the heat and spread them on a lightly oiled baking tray to cool.

PREPARATION TIME: 20 MINUTES   COOKING TIME: 15 MINUTES

NOTES: If you use a small frying pan, cook the nuts in batches. Cashew nuts, macadamia nuts or peanuts can be used or, if you prefer, just one variety.

Transfer the cooled nuts to tightly sealed jars or containers. They will keep for a few weeks.

CHILLI AND LEMON OLIVES

500 g (1 lb 2 oz) cured black olives (olives with wrinkled skin)
2 teaspoons finely grated lemon zest
2 teaspoons chopped oregano
3 teaspoons dried chilli flakes
olive oil

MAKES 500 G (1 LB 2 OZ)

Combine the olives with the lemon zest, oregano and chilli flakes. Transfer to a 750 ml (26 fl oz/3-cup) sterilized jar. Pour in enough olive oil to cover the olives completely. Seal and marinate in the refrigerator for at least 2 days. Serve at room temperature.

PREPARATION TIME: 10 MINUTES +   COOKING TIME: NIL

DILL, GARLIC AND ORANGE OLIVES

500 g (1 lb 2 oz) kalamata olives
3 tablespoons roughly chopped dill
1 garlic clove, bruised
4 thin slices of orange, each cut into eighths
2 bay leaves, torn
olive oil

MAKES 500 G (1 LB 2 OZ)

Combine the olives with the dill, garlic, orange slices and bay leaves. Spoon into a 1 litre (35 fl oz/4-cup) sterilized jar. Pour in enough olive oil to cover the olives completely. Seal and marinate in the refrigerator for at least 2 days. Serve at room temperature.

PREPARATION TIME: 10 MINUTES +   COOKING TIME: NIL

BABA GHANOUSH

2 large eggplants (aubergines)
3 garlic cloves, crushed
1/2 teaspoon ground cumin
80 ml (2 1/2 fl oz/1/3 cup) lemon juice
2 tablespoons tahini
pinch cayenne pepper
1 1/2 tablespoons olive oil
1 tablespoon chopped flat-leaf (Italian) parsley
black olives, to garnish

MAKES 440 G (15 1/2 OZ/1 3/4 CUPS)

Preheat the oven to 200°C (400°F/Gas 6). Prick the eggplants several times with a fork, then cook over an open flame for about 5 minutes, or until the skin is black and blistered. Transfer to a baking tin and bake for 40–45 minutes, or until the eggplants are very soft and wrinkled. Put in a colander and leave to stand over a bowl for 30 minutes to drain off any bitter juices.

Carefully peel the skin from the eggplants and chop the flesh. Put in a food processor with the garlic, cumin, lemon juice, tahini, cayenne pepper and olive oil. Process until smooth and creamy. Season with salt and stir in the parsley. Spread in a flat bowl or on a plate and garnish with the olives. Serve with toasted crusty bread or pitta bread for dipping.

PREPARATION TIME: 20 MINUTES +   COOKING TIME: 50 MINUTES

TARAMASALATA

5 slices white bread, crusts removed
80 ml (2½ fl oz/⅓ cup) milk
100 g (3½ oz) tinned tarama (grey mullet roe)
1 egg yolk
½ small onion, grated
1 garlic clove, crushed
2 tablespoons lemon juice
80 ml (2½ fl oz/⅓ cup) olive oil
pinch ground white pepper

MAKES 375 G (13 OZ/1½ CUPS)

Soak the bread in the milk for 10 minutes. Press in a strainer to extract the excess milk, then mix in a food processor with the tarama, egg yolk, onion and garlic for 30 seconds, or until smooth. Mix in 1 tablespoon of the lemon juice.

With the motor running, slowly pour in the olive oil. The mixture should be smooth. Add the remaining lemon juice and white pepper. If the dip tastes too salty, blend in another slice of bread. Serve with crackers or pitta bread for dipping

PREPARATION TIME: 10 MINUTES +   COOKING TIME: NIL

NOTE: Grey mullet roe is traditional but smoked cod's roe also gives a lovely flavour.

TZATZIKI

2 Lebanese (short) cucumbers
400 g (14 oz) Greek-style yoghurt
4 garlic cloves, crushed
3 tablespoons finely chopped mint
1 tablespoon lemon juice
chopped mint, to garnish

MAKES 500 G (1 LB 2 OZ/2 CUPS)

Cut the cucumbers in half lengthways, scoop out the seeds with a teaspoon and discard. Leave the skin on and coarsely grate the cucumber into a small colander. Sprinkle with a little salt and leave to stand over a large bowl for 15 minutes to drain off any bitter juices.

Meanwhile, combine the yoghurt, garlic, mint and lemon juice in a bowl.

Rinse the cucumber under cold water. Taking small handfuls, squeeze out any excess moisture. Combine the cucumber with the yoghurt mixture and season to taste. Serve immediately or refrigerate until ready to serve. Garnish with mint. Serve with pitta bread for dipping, or as a sauce for seafood and meat.

PREPARATION TIME: 10 MINUTES +   COOKING TIME: NIL

Taramasalata

CRISPBREAD

250 ml (9 fl oz/1 cup) lukewarm milk
1 tablespoon dried yeast
1/4 teaspoon dried fennel seeds
250 g (9 oz) stoneground flour
200 g (7 oz) coarse rye meal

MAKES 24

Line two baking trays with baking paper. Put the milk in a bowl, add the yeast and stir until dissolved. Leave in a warm place for 10 minutes, or until bubbles appear on the surface. The mixture should be frothy and slightly increased in volume. If your yeast doesn't foam, it is dead and you will have to discard it and start again.

Mix the fennel, flour, rye meal and 1 teaspoon salt in a bowl. Make a well in the centre and add the yeast mixture. Gather together and knead on a floured surface for 5 minutes, adding a little water if necessary. Divide into four portions.

Divide each portion into six pieces and shape each into a ball. Cover and leave in a warm place for 20 minutes, or until doubled in size.

Preheat the oven to 180°C (350°F/Gas 4). Roll out each ball of dough to make a circle about 13 cm (5 inches) in diameter. Cut out the centre of each circle with a round 2 cm (3/4 inch) cutter. Discard the centre, then prick each crispbread with a fork and put on a baking tray. Bake the crispbread, in batches, for 10 minutes, or until firm and dry and slightly coloured. When completely cool, store in an airtight container.

PREPARATION TIME: 20 MINUTES +   COOKING TIME: 30 MINUTES

TWO-SEED CRACKERS

250 g (9 oz/2 cups) plain (all-purpose)
flour
1 teaspoon baking powder
2 tablespoons poppy seeds
2 tablespoons sesame seeds
60 g (2$\frac{1}{4}$ oz) butter, chilled and chopped
125 ml (4 fl oz/$\frac{1}{2}$ cup) iced water

MAKES 30

Preheat the oven to 180°C (350°F/Gas 4). Line two baking trays with baking paper.

Sift the flour, baking powder and $\frac{1}{2}$ teaspoon salt into a bowl. Stir in the seeds and some pepper. Rub the butter into the flour using your fingertips until the mixture resembles fine breadcrumbs.

Make a well in the centre and add the iced water. Mix together with a flat-bladed knife using a cutting action, adding a little extra water if necessary, until the mixture comes together in soft beads. Gather together into a rough ball. Handle the dough gently and do not knead it at any stage. Divide the dough into two portions. Put one portion between two sheets of baking paper and roll out to 2 mm ($\frac{1}{8}$ inch) thick. Cover the other portion with plastic wrap.

Using a 6 cm (2$\frac{1}{2}$ inch) round cutter, cut rounds from the dough. Prick all over with a fork and transfer to the trays. Repeat with the remaining dough. Pile any dough trimmings together (do not knead) and gently re-roll. Cut out more rounds. Bake for 20–25 minutes, or until golden. Allow to cool on a wire rack.

PREPARATION TIME: 20 MINUTES   COOKING TIME: 25 MINUTES

WATER CRACKERS

250 g (9 oz/2 cups) self-raising flour
50 g (1$\frac{3}{4}$ oz) unsalted butter, chopped

MAKES 50

Preheat the oven to 220°C (425°F/Gas 7). Line two baking trays with baking paper. Sift the flour and $\frac{1}{2}$ teaspoon salt into a bowl. Cut the butter into the flour with a knife, then rub in using your fingertips. Knead in enough water (about 185 ml/6 fl oz/$\frac{3}{4}$ cup) to make a fairly stiff dough. Lightly knead the dough for a few minutes until smooth.

On a large floured board, roll the dough out until it is as thin as a wafer. Cut into rounds (you can cut a small hole in the centre of each for decoration) and bake in batches for 8–10 minutes, or until the biscuits bubble and brown. Transfer to a wire rack to cool.

PREPARATION TIME: 15 MINUTES   COOKING TIME: 20 MINUTES +

Two-seed crackers

HERB PEPPER CRISPS WITH BLUE CHEESE DIP

4 sheets lavash or other unleavened bread
90 g (3¼ oz) butter, melted
herb pepper seasoning, to sprinkle
1 tablespoon finely snipped chives

BLUE CHEESE DIP
250 g (9 oz) blue vein cheese, chopped
60 g (2¼ oz) butter, softened
1 tablespoon sweet white wine
2 teaspoons chopped mint
1 teaspoon chopped rosemary
2 teaspoons chopped oregano
90 g (3¼ oz/⅓ cup) crème fraîche or sour cream
chives, to garnish

SERVES 10

Preheat the oven to 180°C (350°F/Gas 4). Brush each sheet of lavash bread with the butter. Sprinkle with the herb pepper seasoning and chives.

Cut each lavash sheet into 20 squares. Cut each piece in half to make triangles. Place the triangles on baking trays. Bake in batches for 5 minutes, or until crisp. Remove and allow to cool. Serve with the blue cheese dip.

To make the blue cheese dip, beat the cheese and butter in a small bowl using electric beaters until smooth and creamy. Add the wine, mint, rosemary and oregano. Mix well. Fold through the crème fraîche or sour cream. Season to taste. Spoon the mixture into serving dishes to serve.

PREPARATION TIME: 30 MINUTES   COOKING TIME: 10 MINUTES

NOTES: The crisps may be stored in an airtight container for up to 2 weeks.

For a variation, combine 2 crushed garlic cloves with the melted butter before brushing over the lavash bread. Sprinkle with grated parmesan cheese and chives, cut into squares, then triangles and bake.

SUN-DRIED TOMATO PLAITS

1 sheet frozen puff pastry, thawed
1 egg, beaten
40 g (1¹/₂ oz) semi-dried (sun-blushed) tomatoes, sliced

MAKES 8

Preheat the oven to 210°C (415°F/Gas 6–7). Lightly grease a baking tray.

Lay the sheet of puff pastry on a work surface and brush lightly with the egg. Cut into 1 cm (¹/₂ inch) strips. Join three strips together at the top, by pressing. Plait them together, inserting slices of semi-dried tomato at intervals in the plait.

Place the plaits on the baking tray and bake for 10–15 minutes, or until puffed and golden. When completely cool, store in an airtight container.

PREPARATION TIME: 10 MINUTES   COOKING TIME: 15 MINUTES

SESAME SEED TWISTS

1 sheet frozen puff pastry, thawed
1 egg, beaten
1 tablespoon sesame seeds or poppy seeds

MAKES 16

Preheat the oven to 210°C (415°F/Gas 6–7). Lightly grease a baking tray.

Lay the sheet of puff pastry on a work surface and brush lightly with the egg. Sprinkle with the sesame or poppy seeds and gently press onto the pastry. Cut the pastry into 1.5 cm (⁵/₈ inch) strips. Holding both ends, twist the strip in opposite directions twice.

Place the twists on the baking tray and bake for 10 minutes, or until puffed and golden. When completely cool, store in an airtight container.

PREPARATION TIME: 10 MINUTES   COOKING TIME: 10 MINUTES

HERBED CHEESE TARTLETS

PASTRY

500 g (1 lb 2 oz/4 cups) plain (all-purpose)
flour
1 teaspoon paprika
250 g (9 oz) butter, chopped
80 ml (2^1/2 fl oz/^{1}/3 cup) lemon juice
160–200 ml (5^1/4–7 fl oz) iced water

FILLING

500 g (1 lb 2 oz) cottage cheese
2 tablespoons chopped chervil, plus
extra, to garnish
2 tablespoons chopped tarragon
2 teaspoons snipped chives
125 ml (4 fl oz/^{1}/2 cup) thick
(double/heavy) cream
24 black olives, pitted and sliced

MAKES 48

To make the pastry, sift the flour, paprika and a pinch of salt into a large bowl. Add the butter and rub into the flour using your fingertips, until the mixture resembles fine breadcrumbs. Make a well in the centre and stir in the lemon juice and the iced water. Mix with a flat-bladed knife until the mixture comes together in beads. Gently gather together and lift out onto a lightly floured surface. Flatten into a disc, wrap in plastic wrap and refrigerate for 15 minutes.

Preheat the oven to 200°C (400°F/Gas 6). Grease two 12-hole round-based patty pans or mini muffin tins. Roll the dough out on a lightly floured surface to 3 mm (^{1}/8 inch) thick and, using an 8 cm (3 inch) cutter, cut 24 rounds from the pastry and line the patty pans. Bake for 8–10 minutes, or until golden brown. Repeat with the remaining pastry.

To make the filling, beat together the cottage cheese, herbs and cream until smooth. Stir in the olives with some salt and black pepper. Spoon into the cases and garnish with chervil and black pepper.

PREPARATION TIME: 30 MINUTES +   COOKING TIME: 10 MINUTES

SMOKED TROUT PUFFS

1 sheet frozen puff pastry, thawed
1 egg, beaten
sesame seeds, for sprinkling
250 g (9 oz/1 cup) light cream cheese
2 tablespoons capers, rinsed, drained and finely chopped
2 spring onions (scallions), finely chopped
2 tablespoons chopped dill
320 g (11¼ oz) whole smoked trout, skinned, bones removed and flaked

MAKES 36

Preheat the oven to 220°C (425°F/Gas 7). Lightly grease two baking trays. Cut 36 small squares from the sheet of puff pastry. Brush the tops lightly with the beaten egg and sprinkle with the sesame seeds.

Place on the baking trays and bake for about 8 minutes, or until puffed and well browned. Allow to cool, then gently split in half horizontally.

Soften the cream cheese and blend with the capers, spring onion and dill. Spread on the bases of the squares, top with some smoked trout, then replace the pastry tops at a slight angle.

PREPARATION TIME: 25 MINUTES   COOKING TIME: 10 MINUTES

SPICY WON TON STRIPS

6 fresh won ton wrappers
oil, for frying
1 teaspoon Chinese five-spice
1 tablespoon sea salt, lightly crushed

MAKES 35

Cut the won ton wrappers into 1 cm (½ inch) strips with scissors.

Fill a deep heavy-based wok or frying pan one-third full of oil and heat to 180°C (350°F), or until a cube of bread dropped into the oil turns golden brown in 15 seconds. Deep-fry the won ton strips briefly in batches until golden brown, remove with a slotted spoon and drain on crumpled paper towels. While hot, sprinkle with a mixture of Chinese five-spice and sea salt. Allow to cool, then store in an airtight container.

PREPARATION TIME: 5 MINUTES   COOKING TIME: 10 MINUTES

MEXICAN LAYERED DIP

GUACAMOLE

3 ripe avocados

1 small tomato

1–2 red chillies, finely chopped

1 small red onion, finely chopped

1 tablespoon chopped coriander (cilantro) leaves

1 tablespoon lime or lemon juice

2 tablespoons sour cream

1–2 drops habañero or Tabasco sauce

450 g (1 lb) tinned refried beans

35 g (1¼ oz) packet taco seasoning mix

300 g (10½ oz) sour cream

200 g (7 oz) ready-made salsa sauce

60 g (2¼ oz) cheddar cheese, grated

2 tablespoons chopped pitted black olives

200 g (7 oz) corn chips

chopped coriander (cilantro) leaves, to garnish

SERVES 12

To make the guacamole, roughly chop the avocado flesh. Put in a bowl and mash lightly with a fork. Cut the tomato in half horizontally and scoop out the seeds. Finely dice the flesh and add to the avocado. Stir in the chilli, onion, coriander, lime or lemon juice, sour cream and sauce. Season to taste. Cover and refrigerate until required.

Combine the refried beans and taco seasoning in a small bowl.

To assemble, spread the beans in the centre of a large platter or dish, leaving a border for the corn chips. Spoon the sour cream on top, leaving a small border of bean mixture showing. Repeat with the guacamole and salsa sauce so that you can see each layer. Sprinkle the top with cheese and olives.

Arrange some of the corn chips around the edge just before serving and garnish with the coriander. Serve with the remaining corn chips.

PREPARATION TIME: 1 HOUR   COOKING TIME: NIL

NOTES: Tabasco and habañero sauces are both made from fiery hot chillies, so taste before adding too much.
   This dip can be made 2 hours ahead, and refrigerated, covered.

THAI BEEF SALAD IN CUCUMBER CUPS

MARINADE
80 ml (2½ fl oz/⅓ cup) kecap manis
80 ml (2½ fl oz/⅓ cup) lime juice
1 red chilli, thinly sliced
1 tablespoon sesame oil

250 g (9 oz) beef eye fillet
7 Lebanese (short) cucumbers

SALAD
½ lemon grass stem, white part only, finely chopped
60 ml (2 fl oz/¼ cup) lime juice
1–2 red chillies, thinly sliced
20 g (¾ oz) mint, finely chopped
20 g (¾ oz) coriander (cilantro) leaves, finely chopped
1 tablespoon fish sauce

MAKES 30

Combine the marinade ingredients in a bowl. Put the beef eye fillet in a non-metallic bowl, pour in the marinade and refrigerate for 2 hours, or overnight. Allow the meat to return to room temperature before cooking.

Heat a barbecue grill plate or chargrill pan and cook the beef. Cook for 7 minutes for medium, or until done to your liking. Allow to cool, then slice into thin strips. Combine the salad ingredients in a bowl and add the beef strips.

Cut off the ends of the cucumber and cut into 3 cm (1¼ inch) thick slices. Using a melon baller, scoop out the flesh from each slice to make a 'cup' about 1 cm (½ inch) thick. Fill each cup with the Thai beef salad.

PREPARATION TIME: 25 MINUTES +   COOKING TIME: 10 MINUTES

NOTE: Prepare the salad and scooped out cucumber slices separately and refrigerate, then fill just before serving.

STUFFED ZUCCHINI

4 large zucchini (courgettes)
125 g (4½ oz) minced (ground) pork
60 g (2¼ oz) raw prawns (shrimp), chopped
2 garlic cloves, crushed
2 tablespoons chopped coriander (cilantro) leaves
½ teaspoon sugar
2 makrut (kaffir lime) leaves, chopped
2 red Asian shallots, finely chopped
60 ml (2 fl oz/¼ cup) coconut cream
2 teaspoons fish sauce
1 tablespoon unsalted peanuts, chopped

MAKES ABOUT 24

Cut the zucchini into 4 cm (1½ inch) thick slices. Scoop out the centre with a melon baller, leaving 5 mm (¼ inch) of flesh around the inside of the skin as well as on the bottom of each slice.

Combine the pork, prawn, garlic, coriander, sugar, makrut leaves, shallots, 2 tablespoons of the coconut cream and the fish sauce in a bowl. Spoon into the zucchini shells. Cover and refrigerate until close to serving time.

Put the zucchini shells in a bamboo or metal steamer over a saucepan of boiling water. Cover and steam for 10 minutes, or until the filling is cooked and zucchini tender. Serve dotted with coconut cream and sprinkled with the peanuts.

PREPARATION TIME: 30 MINUTES   COOKING TIME: 10 MINUTES

Thai beef salad in cucumber cups

OLIVE AND ALMOND PALMIERS

75 g (2¹/₂ oz) black olives, pitted and chopped
95 g (3¹/₄ oz/1 cup) ground almonds
25 g (1 oz) parmesan cheese, grated
2 tablespoons chopped basil
60 ml (2 fl oz/¹/₄ cup) olive oil
2 teaspoons wholegrain mustard
2 sheets frozen puff pastry, thawed
60 ml (2 fl oz/¹/₄ cup) milk

MAKES ABOUT 24

Preheat the oven to 200°C (400°F/Gas 6). Line two baking trays with baking paper. In a food processor, process the olives, almonds, parmesan, basil, oil, mustard, ¹/₄ teaspoon salt and ¹/₂ teaspoon cracked black pepper until they form a paste.

Lay out one sheet of pastry and cover evenly with half the olive-almond paste. Fold two opposite ends into the centre to meet.

Fold the same way again. Brush the pastry with the milk. Repeat the process with the remaining pastry and filling. Cut into 1.5 cm (⁵/₈ inch) thick slices. Shape the slices into a V-shape, with the two sides curving out slightly. Place on the trays, leaving room for spreading. Bake for 15–20 minutes, or until puffed and golden. Allow to cool on a wire rack. Serve at room temperature.

PREPARATION TIME: 30 MINUTES   COOKING TIME: 20 MINUTES

NOTES: Palmiers can be cooked up to 6 hours ahead and stored in an airtight container.

You can also use ready-made olive paste.

CORN AND RED CAPSICUM TARTLETS

3 sheets frozen puff pastry, thawed
310 g (11 oz) tinned corn kernels, drained
150 g (5½ oz) red leicester cheese, grated
1 small red capsicum (pepper), finely chopped
2 eggs, lightly beaten
60 ml (2 fl oz/¼ cup) buttermilk
170 ml (5½ fl oz/⅔ cup) thick (double/heavy) cream
1 teaspoon dijon mustard
dash Tabasco sauce
snipped chives, to garnish

MAKES ABOUT 36

Preheat the oven to 200°C (400°F/Gas 6). Lightly grease three 12-hole round-based patty pans or mini muffin tins. Using a 6 cm (2½ inch) round pastry cutter, cut circles from the pastry sheets. Press the circles into the prepared tins and prick the bases all over with a fork.

Combine the corn, cheese and capsicum in a bowl and season. Whisk the eggs, buttermilk, cream, mustard and Tabasco sauce in a measuring cup with a pouring lip. Spoon some of the vegetable mixture into the pastry cases, then pour the egg mixture over the top until the cases are almost full. Bake for 20–25 minutes, or until well risen and set. Serve cold. Garnish with snipped chives.

PREPARATION TIME: 20 MINUTES   COOKING TIME: 25 MINUTES

NOTE: The tarts can be made up to a day ahead and refrigerated, covered, in an airtight container, or frozen for up to 2 months.

SMOKED SALMON AND ROCKET ROLLS

200 g (7 oz) ricotta cheese
60 g (2¼ oz/¼ cup) crème fraîche or sour cream
2 teaspoons wasabi paste
1 tablespoon lime juice
12 slices brown bread, crusts removed
300 g (10½ oz) smoked salmon
100 g (3½ oz) baby rocket (arugula), trimmed
rocket (arugula) leaves, extra, to garnish

MAKES 36

Combine the ricotta, crème fraîche or sour cream, wasabi and lime juice in a bowl.

Roll the slices of bread out with a rolling pin to flatten.

Spread the ricotta over the bread, then top with the salmon and rocket, leaving a border. Roll up lengthways, wrap tightly in plastic wrap to hold the shape, then refrigerate for 30 minutes.

Unwrap, trim the ends and cut into 2 cm (¾ inch) slices. Garnish with rocket leaves.

PREPARATION TIME: 20 MINUTES +   COOKING TIME: NIL

VIETNAMESE LETTUCE-WRAPPED SPRING ROLLS

50 g (1³/4 oz) dried mung bean vermicelli
2 tablespoons black fungus
20 rice paper wrappers
500 g (1 lb 2 oz) prawns (shrimp), peeled, deveined and finely chopped
150 g (5¹/2 oz) minced (ground) pork
4 spring onions (scallions), chopped
45 g (1¹/2 oz/¹/2 cup) bean sprouts, trimmed, roughly chopped
1 teaspoon sugar
1 egg, beaten
oil, for deep-frying
20 lettuce leaves
90 g (3¹/4 oz/1 cup) bean sprouts, extra, trimmed
1 large handful mint

VIETNAMESE DIPPING SAUCE
2 tablespoons fish sauce
2 tablespoons chopped coriander (cilantro) leaves
1 teaspoon chopped red chilli
1 teaspoon soft brown sugar

MAKES 20

Put the vermicelli and fungus in separate heatproof bowls. Cover with hot water and soak for 10 minutes, or until soft. Drain both, and chop the fungus roughly.

Using a pastry brush, brush both sides of each rice paper wrapper liberally with water. Allow to stand for 2 minutes, or until they become soft and pliable. Stack the wrappers on a plate. Sprinkle over a little extra water and cover the plate with plastic wrap to keep the wrappers moist until needed.

Combine the vermicelli, fungus, prawn meat, pork, spring onion, bean sprouts, sugar and salt and pepper in a bowl.

Put 1 tablespoon of the filling along the base of a wrapper. Fold in the sides, roll the wrapper up tightly, and brush the seam with the egg. Repeat with the remaining wrappers and filling.

Press the rolls with paper towels to remove any excess water. Heat 4–5 cm (1¹/2–2 inches) oil in a wok or deep frying pan to 180°C (350°F), or until a cube of bread browns in 15 seconds. Add the spring rolls in batches and cook for 2–3 minutes, or until dark golden brown. Drain on paper towels.

Put a spring roll in each lettuce leaf, top with 1 tablespoon bean sprouts and two mint leaves, and roll up to form a neat parcel. Serve with the dipping sauce.

To make the Vietnamese dipping sauce, combine all the ingredients in a bowl and add 2 tablespoons cold water. Mix well.

PREPARATION TIME: 50 MINUTES + COOKING TIME: 20 MINUTES

SCALLOP FRITTERS

250 g (9 oz) scallops
6 eggs
25 g (1 oz) parmesan cheese, grated
3 garlic cloves, crushed
125 g (4$\frac{1}{2}$ oz/1 cup) plain (all-purpose) flour
2 tablespoons chopped thyme
2 tablespoons chopped oregano
oil, for pan-frying
whole-egg mayonnaise, to serve

MAKES 40

Clean and roughly chop the scallops. Lightly beat the eggs and combine with the parmesan, garlic, flour and herbs. Stir in the scallops.

Heat 3 cm (1$\frac{1}{4}$ inches) oil in a deep frying pan to 180°C (350°F), or until a cube of bread dropped into the oil turns golden brown in 15 seconds. Cook the fritters in batches. Using 1 tablespoon of batter for each fritter, pour into the oil and cook for 4–5 minutes, until golden brown. Drain on crumpled paper towels and sprinkle lightly with salt. Serve with mayonnaise for dipping.

PREPARATION TIME: 20 MINUTES   COOKING TIME: 20 MINUTES +

CHEESE FRITTERS

175 g (6 oz) block firm feta cheese
125 g (4$\frac{1}{2}$ oz) mozzarella cheese
40 g (1$\frac{1}{2}$ oz/$\frac{1}{3}$ cup) plain (all-purpose) flour
1 egg, beaten
50 g (1$\frac{3}{4}$ oz/$\frac{1}{2}$ cup) dry breadcrumbs
oil, for pan-frying

MAKES ABOUT 35–40

Cut the feta and mozzarella into 2 cm ($\frac{3}{4}$ inch) cubes. Combine the flour and $\frac{1}{4}$ teaspoon black pepper on a sheet of baking paper. Toss the cheese lightly in the seasoned flour and shake off the excess.

Dip the cheese into the egg a few pieces at a time. Coat with the breadcrumbs and shake off the excess. Repeat the process with the remaining cheese and crumbs. Arrange on a foil-lined baking tray and refrigerate, covered, for 25 minutes.

Heat 3 cm (1$\frac{1}{4}$ inches) oil in a deep frying pan to 180°C (350°F), or until a cube of bread dropped into the oil turns golden brown in 15 seconds in 15 seconds. Cook a few pieces of cheese at a time over medium heat, for 2–3 minutes each batch, or until golden and crisp. Drain on crumpled paper towels.

PREPARATION TIME: 15 MINUTES +   COOKING TIME: 30 MINUTES +

NOTE: Serve with sweet chilli, plum or cranberry sauce.

SESAME SHAPES

185 g (6½ oz/1½ cups) self-raising flour
50 g (1¾ oz/⅓ cup) sesame seeds,
toasted
2 teaspoons finely grated orange zest
2 eggs
2 teaspoons sesame oil
250 ml (9 fl oz/1 cup) milk
80 ml (2½ fl oz/⅓ cup) orange juice
butter or oil, for greasing
125 g (4½ oz) sun-dried tomatoes, finely
chopped

FILLING
200 g (7 oz) cream cheese
2 tablespoons chopped coriander
(cilantro) leaves

MAKES ABOUT 30

Sift the flour and a pinch of salt into a bowl, stir in the sesame seeds and orange zest and make a well in the centre. With a fork, gradually whisk in the combined egg, sesame oil, milk and orange juice to make a smooth lump-free batter. Set aside for 15 minutes.

Heat a frying pan and brush lightly with melted butter or oil. Pour 80 ml (2½ fl oz/⅓ cup) batter into the pan and cook over medium heat for 3–4 minutes, or until bubbles appear on the surface. Turn over and cook the other side. Transfer to a plate and cover with a tea towel (dish towel) while cooking the remaining batter.

Use biscuit (cookie) cutters to cut out various shapes (you will be sandwiching three of each shape together so make sure you have the right number of each).

To make the filling, mix the cream cheese and coriander and use to sandwich together three shapes. Decorate with sun-dried tomato.

PREPARATION TIME: 35 MINUTES +   COOKING TIME: 20 MINUTES

NOTE: These can be joined and cut into shapes a day ahead. Store in an airtight container in the refrigerator.

TURKEY AND BRIE TRIANGLES

8 slices white bread
100 g (3¹/₂ oz) cranberry sauce
120 g (4 oz) sliced turkey breast
120 g (4 oz) brie, sliced
4 butter lettuce leaves

MAKES 16

Trim the crusts from the bread. Spread the slices with cranberry sauce. Add the turkey breast, brie and lettuce leaves and make into sandwiches. Cut into four triangles to serve.

PREPARATION TIME: 10 MINUTES   COOKING TIME: NIL

CHICKEN, ROCKET AND WALNUT SANDWICHES

2 tablespoons oil
250 g (9 oz) boneless, skinless chicken breast
500 g (1 lb 2 oz) boneless, skinless chicken thigh
250 g (9 oz/1 cup) whole-egg mayonnaise
100 g (3¹/₂ oz) celery, finely chopped
90 g (3¹/₄ oz/³/₄ cup) chopped walnuts
20 slices bread
1 large handful rocket (arugula)

MAKES 30

Heat the oil in a frying pan over medium heat and cook the chicken breast and thigh until lightly browned. Allow to cool, then chop finely.

Combine the chicken with the mayonnaise, celery and walnuts. Season to taste.

Make sandwiches using the chicken mixture and add the rocket to each. Remove the crusts and cut each sandwich into three fingers.

PREPARATION TIME: 15 MINUTES +   COOKING TIME: 15 MINUTES

Turkey and brie triangles

MINI QUICHE LORRAINES

3 sheets frozen shortcrust (pie) pastry,
thawed
60 g (2¹/₄ oz) gruyère cheese, grated
30 g (1 oz) butter
2 bacon slices, finely chopped
1 onion, finely chopped
2 eggs
185 ml (6 fl oz/³/₄ cup) pouring
(whipping) cream
¹/₂ teaspoon freshly grated nutmeg
chives, cut into short strips

MAKES 24

Preheat the oven to 190°C (375°F/Gas 5). Lightly grease two 12-hole round-based patty pans or mini muffin tins. Using a plain 8 cm (3 inch) cutter, cut rounds of pastry and fit in the tins. Divide the cheese evenly among the pastry bases. Cover and refrigerate while making the filling.

Heat the butter in a small frying pan and cook the bacon and onion for 2–3 minutes, or until tender. Drain on paper towels. When cool, divide the mixture evenly among the bases. Whisk the eggs in a bowl with the cream, nutmeg and a little freshly ground black pepper. Pour or spoon carefully over the bacon mixture.

Put a few strips of chive on top of each quiche to decorate. Bake for 20 minutes, or until lightly browned and set. Serve at room temperature.

PREPARATION TIME: 20 MINUTES +   COOKING TIME: 25 MINUTES

NOTE: These quiches can be cooked up to 2 days ahead and stored in an airtight container in the refrigerator. They can be frozen in single layers for up to 2 months. Reheat in a 180°C (350°F/Gas 4) oven.

PAN BAGNAT

4 crusty bread rolls, or 1 baguette, sliced into 4 chunks

1 garlic clove

60 ml (2 fl oz/¼ cup) olive oil

1 tablespoon red wine vinegar

3 tablespoons torn basil

2 tomatoes, sliced

2 hard-boiled eggs, sliced

75 g (2½ oz) tinned tuna

8 anchovy fillets

1 Lebanese (short) cucumber, sliced

½ green capsicum (pepper), thinly sliced

1 French shallot, thinly sliced

SERVES 4

Slice the bread rolls or baguette chunks in half and remove some of the soft centre from the tops. Cut the garlic clove in half and rub the insides of the bread with the cut sides. Sprinkle both sides of the bread with olive oil, vinegar, and salt and pepper.

Put the remaining ingredients on the base of the rolls, cover with the other half and wrap each sandwich in foil. Press firmly with a light weight and stand in a cool place for 1 hour before serving.

PREPARATION TIME: 15 MINUTES +   COOKING TIME: NIL

BACON AND MUSHROOM CREAM BITES

1 egg yolk, lightly beaten

2 sheets frozen shortcrust (pie) pastry, thawed

2 tablespoons oil

375 g (12 oz) mushrooms, finely chopped

4 bacon slices, finely chopped

4 spring onions (scallions), finely chopped

15 g (½ oz) flat-leaf (Italian) parsley, finely chopped

250 g (9 oz) cream cheese, softened

4 eggs

MAKES 18

Preheat the oven to 210°C (415°F/Gas 6-7). Lightly grease a shallow 23 cm (9 inch) square cake tin. Brush egg yolk over one sheet of pastry. Put the other sheet over the top and gently press together. Trim the edges to fit the tin. Prick the pastry evenly with a fork and bake for 15 minutes, or until golden brown. Reduce the oven to 180°C (350°F/Gas 4).

Heat the oil in a heavy-based frying pan. Add the mushrooms and stir over medium heat for 5 minutes, or until well browned. Remove from the heat and stir in the bacon, spring onion and parsley. Season to taste. Allow to cool.

Beat the cream cheese and eggs in a small bowl using electric beaters for 5 minutes. Add the cooled mushroom mixture and stir to combine. Pour the mixture onto the cooked pastry base. Bake for 25 minutes, or until firm and lightly browned. Allow to cool in the tin. Cut into triangles to serve.

PREPARATION TIME: 15 MINUTES +   COOKING TIME: 45 MINUTES

MINI SCONES WITH HAM, LEEK AND PORT FIGS

250 g (9 oz/2 cups) plain (all-purpose) flour
3 teaspoons baking powder
110 g (3¾ oz) butter
100 g (3½ oz) stilton cheese
2 tablespoons snipped chives
185 ml (6 fl oz/¾ cup) milk

FILLING
250 ml (9 fl oz/1 cup) port
6 large dried figs, stems removed
1 teaspoon sugar
1 large leek
1 teaspoon dijon mustard
2 teaspoons red wine vinegar
1 tablespoon olive oil
150 g (5½ oz) shaved ham

MAKES ABOUT 40

Sift the flour, baking powder and ¾ teaspoon salt into a large bowl. Coarsely grate the butter and cheese into the flour and rub in using your fingertips until the pieces are the size of coarse breadcrumbs. Stir in the chives. Pour in the milk and combine with a fork until large clumps form. Turn onto a floured surface and press into a ball.

Preheat the oven to 220°C (425°F/Gas 7). Roll the dough out on a floured surface into a 15 x 25 cm (6 x 10 inch) rectangle. With the long edge of the dough facing you, fold in both ends so they meet in the centre, then fold the dough in half widthways. Roll again into a 15 x 25 cm (6 x 10 inch) rectangle, about 1 cm (½ inch) thick. Cut rounds close together with a 3 cm (1¼ inch) cutter. Push the scraps together and roll and cut as before. Place 2.5 cm (1 inch) apart on a baking tray and refrigerate for 20 minutes. Bake for 10-12 minutes, or until lightly browned.

In a small saucepan, heat the port, figs and sugar. Bring to the boil, reduce the heat and simmer for 15 minutes. Remove the figs and, when cooled, roughly chop. Simmer the liquid for about 3 minutes, until reduced and syrupy. Put the figs back in and stir to combine. Set aside.

Discard any tough leaves from the leek, then rinse the leek. Trim off the dark green tops. Slit the leek lengthways, almost to the bottom, roll a quarter, turn and slit again. Wash well, drain and steam for about 10 minutes, or until very soft. Roughly chop, then combine with the mustard, vinegar and oil. Season.

Cut the scones in half. Put a folded piece of ham on each bottom half, top with a teaspoon each of leek and fig mixture, then replace the tops.

PREPARATION TIME: 40 MINUTES +   COOKING TIME: 45 MINUTES

BOREK

400 g (14 oz) feta cheese
2 eggs, beaten
2 large handfuls flat-leaf
(Italian) parsley, chopped
375 g (13 oz) filo pastry
80 ml (2½ fl oz/⅓ cup) olive oil

MAKES 24

Preheat the oven to 180°C (350°F/Gas 4). Lightly grease a baking tray. Crumble the feta into a large bowl using your fingers. Mix in the eggs and parsley and season with freshly ground black pepper.

Cover the filo pastry with a damp tea towel (dish towel) so it doesn't dry out. Remove one sheet at a time. Brushing each sheet lightly with olive oil, layer four sheets on top of one another. Cut the pastry into four 7 cm (2¾ inch) strips.

Put 2 rounded teaspoons of the feta mixture in one corner of each strip and fold diagonally, creating a triangle pillow. Put on the baking tray, seam side down, and brush with olive oil. Repeat with the remaining pastry and filling to make 24 parcels. Bake for 20 minutes, or until golden.

PREPARATION TIME: 1 HOUR   COOKING TIME: 20 MINUTES

MINI LENTIL BURGERS WITH TOMATO RELISH

185 g (6½ oz/1 cup) brown lentils
1 bay leaf
1 onion, roughly chopped
1 garlic clove, crushed
1 small leek, thinly sliced
1 small carrot, finely grated
80 g (2¾ oz/1 cup) fresh breadcrumbs
2 egg yolks
2 tablespoons chopped coriander
(cilantro) leaves
2 tablespoons oil
8 slices bread, cut into 4 cm
(1½ inch) squares
ready-made tomato relish, to serve

MAKES 32

Place the lentils and bay leaf in a saucepan and cover with plenty of water. Bring to the boil and simmer for 20–30 minutes, or until tender. Drain well and discard the bay leaf.

Combine half the cooked lentils with the onion and garlic in a food processor until the mixture forms a smooth paste. Transfer to a bowl and mix with the remaining lentils, leek, carrot, breadcrumbs, egg yolks and coriander. Season. Form level tablespoons of the mixture into mini patties.

Heat some of the oil in a non-stick frying pan and cook the mini patties in batches until browned on both sides, adding more oil as necessary. Drain on paper towels and serve warm, on the bread squares, with a dollop of tomato relish on top.

PREPARATION TIME: 40 MINUTES   COOKING TIME: 55 MINUTES

TAMALE BEEF AND BEAN PIES

1 tablespoon oil
1 small onion, finely chopped
250 g (9 oz) minced (ground) beef
1 garlic clove, crushed
1/4 teaspoon chilli powder
200 g (7 oz) tinned crushed tomatoes
375 ml (13 fl oz/1 1/2 cups) beef stock
300 g (10 1/2 oz) tinned red kidney beans, drained
360 g (12 3/4 oz/2 1/2 cups) masa harina
1 teaspoon baking powder
125 g (4 1/2 oz) butter, chilled and chopped
125 g (4 1/2 oz) cheddar cheese, grated
sour cream, to serve

MAKES 30

To make the filling, heat the oil in a frying pan over medium heat. Add the onion and cook over low heat for 3-4 minutes, or until soft. Increase the heat, add the beef and cook until browned all over. Add the garlic, chilli, tomato and 125 ml (4 fl oz/1/2 cup) of the stock. Bring to the boil, then reduce the heat and simmer for 35 minutes, or until the liquid has evaporated to a thick sauce. Stir in the beans and cool.

Lightly grease 30 holes in deep mini muffin tins. Sift the masa harina, baking powder and 1/2 teaspoon salt into a bowl. Rub the butter into the flour with your fingertips until it resembles fine breadcrumbs. Make a well in the centre and, with a flat-bladed knife, mix in the remaining stock, then use your hands to bring the mixture together into a ball. Divide into thirds and roll two-thirds between two sheets of baking paper. Cut out rounds with a 7 cm (2 3/4 inch) cutter and line the muffin holes. Trim the edges and reserve any leftover pastry.

Preheat the oven to 200°C (400°F/Gas 6). Spoon the filling into the pastry cases and sprinkle with the cheddar. Roll out the remaining pastry and reserved pastry as above. Cut into 4 cm (1 1/2 inch) rounds to cover the tops of the pies. Brush the edges with water and place over the filling. Trim the edges and press the pastry together to seal. Bake for 20-25 minutes, or until the pastry is crisp and lightly browned. Serve with sour cream.

PREPARATION TIME: 1 HOUR   COOKING TIME: 1 HOUR 5 MINUTES

NOTE: Masa harina is a type of white flour made from maize.

SAUSAGE ROLLS

3 sheets frozen puff pastry, thawed
2 eggs, beaten
750 g (1 lb 10 oz) minced (ground) sausage meat
1 onion, finely chopped
1 garlic clove, crushed
80 g (2¾ oz/1 cup) fresh breadcrumbs
3 tablespoons chopped flat-leaf (Italian) parsley
3 tablespoons chopped thyme
½ teaspoon ground sage
½ teaspoon freshly grated nutmeg
½ teaspoon ground cloves

MAKES 36

Preheat the oven to 200°C (400°F/Gas 6). Lightly grease two baking trays. Cut the pastry sheets in half and lightly brush the edges with some of the beaten egg.

Mix half the remaining egg with the remaining ingredients in a large bowl, then divide into six even portions. Pipe or spoon the filling down the centre of each piece of pastry, then brush the edges with some of the egg. Fold the pastry over the filling, overlapping the edges and placing the join underneath. Brush the rolls with more egg, then cut each into six short pieces.

Cut two small slashes on top of each roll and put on the baking trays. Bake for 15 minutes, then reduce the oven temperature to 180°C (350°F/Gas 4) and bake for a further 15 minutes, or until puffed and golden.

PREPARATION TIME: 30 MINUTES   COOKING TIME: 30 MINUTES

SPICY SAUSAGE ROLL-UPS

2 sheets shortcrust (pie) pastry
2 tablespoons dijon mustard
5 sticks cabanossi
1 egg yolk, beaten

MAKES ABOUT 25

Preheat the oven to 200°C (400°F/Gas 6). Cut each pastry sheet in half. Cut triangles with bases of 6 cm (2½ inches). Put a small dob of mustard at the base of each pastry piece. Cut the cabanossi into 7 cm (2¾ inch) lengths and place across the mustard on the pastry triangles.

Dampen the tips of the triangles with a little water. Working from the base, roll each pastry triangle around the pieces of cabanossi. Press lightly to secure the tip to the rest of the pastry.

Put the roll-ups on a lightly greased baking tray and brush with a mixture of egg yolk and 2 teaspoons cold water. Bake for 15–20 minutes, or until golden brown.

PREPARATION TIME: 20 MINUTES   COOKING TIME: 20 MINUTES

NOTE: These can be made up to 2 days ahead, refrigerated, then gently reheated in the oven when required.

SAVOURY POTATO EMPANADAS

60 ml (2 fl oz/¼ cup) olive oil
1 small onion, finely diced
2 spring onions (scallions), thinly sliced
1 garlic clove, crushed
100 g (3½ oz) minced (ground) beef
1 teaspoon ground cumin
1 teaspoon dried oregano
125 g (4½ oz) all-purpose potatoes, cubed
4 sheets frozen puff pastry, thawed
50 g (1¾ oz) black olives, pitted and quartered
1 hard-boiled egg, finely chopped
1 egg, separated
pinch paprika
pinch sugar

MAKES 32

In a heavy-based frying pan, heat 1 tablespoon of the oil, add the onion and spring onion and stir for 5 minutes. Stir in the garlic and cook for 3 minutes. Remove from the pan and set aside.

Heat another tablespoon of oil in the pan, add the beef and stir over medium heat until browned, breaking up any lumps with a fork. Add the onion mixture and stir well.

Add the cumin, oregano, and ½ teaspoon each of salt and black pepper, and stir for a further 2 minutes. Transfer to a bowl and cool. Wipe out the pan with paper towel.

Heat another tablespoon of oil in the pan, add the potato and stir over high heat for 1 minute. Reduce the heat to low and stir for 5 minutes, or until tender. Cool slightly and then gently mix into the beef mixture.

Preheat the oven to 200°C (400°F/Gas 6). Cut rounds from the pastry with an 8 cm (3 inch) cutter. Lightly grease two baking trays.

Spoon heaped teaspoons of the beef mixture onto one side of each pastry round, leaving a border wide enough for the pastry to be folded over. Put a few olive quarters and some chopped egg on top of the beef mixture. Brush the border with egg white. Carefully fold the pastry over to make a half moon shape, pressing firmly to seal. Press the edges with a floured fork, to decorate, and then gently transfer to the baking trays. Stir the egg yolk, paprika and sugar together and brush over the empanadas. Bake for 15 minutes, or until golden brown and puffed.

PREPARATION TIME: 1 HOUR   COOKING TIME: 40 MINUTES

NOTE: The puffs can be made 2 days ahead or frozen for 2 months.

SPICY KOFTAS

500 g (1 lb 2 oz) minced (ground) lamb
1 small onion, finely chopped
1 garlic clove, crushed
1 teaspoon ground coriander
1 teaspoon ground cumin
1/4 teaspoon ground cinnamon
1/2 teaspoon finely chopped red chilli
1 teaspoon tomato paste (concentrated purée)
1 tablespoon chopped mint
1 tablespoon chopped coriander (cilantro) leaves
oil, for frying

YOGHURT DIP
1 tomato, peeled, seeded and chopped
1/2 Lebanese (short) cucumber, chopped
1 garlic clove, crushed
1 tablespoon chopped mint
125 g (41/2 oz/1/2 cup) plain yoghurt

MAKES 45

Combine the lamb, onion, garlic, coriander, cumin, cinnamon, chilli, tomato paste and mint and coriander leaves in a large bowl and mix well using your hands. Season well, then roll into small balls (about 11/2 teaspoons each).

Heat a little oil in a large heavy-based frying pan over high heat. Cook the koftas in batches until well browned all over and cooked through. Drain on crumpled paper towels.

Combine the dip ingredients in a small bowl and mix well.

Skewer each kofta with a cocktail stick and serve with the dip.

PREPARATION TIME: 25 MINUTES   COOKING TIME: 25 MINUTES

NOTES: You can freeze the cooked koftas. When required, thaw, cover with foil and reheat in an ovenproof dish in a 180°C (350°F/Gas 4) oven for 5–10 minutes.
The dip can be made several hours ahead.

CHILLI BEEF QUESADILLAS

11/2 tablespoons oil
1 onion, chopped
2 garlic cloves, crushed
400 g (14 oz) minced (ground) beef
325 g (11 oz) ready-made Mexican black bean salsa
6 flour tortillas
125 g (41/2 oz) grated cheddar cheese

MAKES ABOUT 36

Heat 1 tablespoon of the oil in a frying pan and cook the onion and garlic for 2–3 minutes. Add the beef and cook for 5–7 minutes, or until brown, breaking up any lumps. Stir in the salsa. Bring to the boil, reduce the heat and simmer for 3–4 minutes, or until the mixture reduces and thickens. Season.

Put three of the tortillas on a work surface and sprinkle with the cheddar. Spoon the beef evenly over the cheese, then top with another three tortillas. Heat the remaining oil in a 25 cm (10 inch) frying pan and cook the stacks for 3–4 minutes each side, or until golden brown. Remove from the pan, trim off the sides and cut into 5 cm (2 inch) squares.

PREPARATION TIME: 15 MINUTES   COOKING TIME: 25 MINUTES

SPINACH PIE DIAMONDS

250 g (9 oz/2 cups) plain (all-purpose)
flour
30 g (1 oz) butter, chopped
60 ml (2 fl oz/¼ cup) olive oil
125 ml (4 fl oz/½ cup) warm water
olive oil, extra, for brushing

FILLING
420 g (15 oz) English spinach
1 leek, white part only, halved lengthways
and thinly sliced
¼ teaspoon freshly grated nutmeg
2 teaspoons chopped dill
200 g (7 oz) feta cheese, crumbled
1 tablespoon dry breadcrumbs
3 eggs, lightly beaten
2 tablespoons olive oil

MAKES ABOUT 15

Lightly grease a 3 cm (1¼ inch) deep baking tin with a base measuring 17 x 26 cm (6½ x 10½ inches).

Sift the flour and ½ teaspoon salt into a bowl. Rub the butter into the flour until it resembles fine breadcrumbs. Pour in the oil and rub it in by lifting the flour mixture onto one hand and lightly rubbing the other hand over the top. The mixture should clump together. Make a well in the centre and, while mixing by hand, add enough water to form a firm supple dough. Knead gently to bring the dough together — it may not be completely smooth. Cover with plastic wrap and chill for 1 hour.

Trim away the bottom quarter from the spinach stalks. Wash and shred the remaining leaves and stalks. Pile the spinach onto a tea towel (dish towel), twist tightly and squeeze out as much moisture as possible. Put into a bowl with the leek, nutmeg, dill, feta, breadcrumbs and ½ teaspoon cracked black pepper.

Preheat the oven to 220°C (425°F/Gas 7). Roll out just over half the dough on a lightly floured surface until large enough to line the base and sides of the tin. Lift the dough into the tin, pressing evenly over the base and sides.

Add the eggs and oil to the spinach mixture. Mix with your hand, but do not overmix. Spoon into the pastry-lined tin.

Roll out the remaining pastry on a lightly floured surface until large enough to cover the tin. Lift onto the tin and press the two pastry edges firmly together to seal. Trim the excess pastry with a sharp knife from the outer edge of the tin, then brush the top with a little extra olive oil. Using a sharp knife, mark into three strips lengthways and then diagonally into diamonds. Make two or three small slits through the top layer of pastry to allow the steam to escape during cooking.

Bake the pie on the centre shelf for 45–50 minutes, or until well browned. Cover with foil if the pastry is overbrowning. The pie is cooked if it slides when you gently shake the tin. Turn out onto a wire rack to cool for 10 minutes, then transfer to a cutting board or back into the tin to cut into diamonds.

PREPARATION TIME: 50 MINUTES +   COOKING TIME: 50 MINUTES

MINI CROISSANTS

40 g (1½ oz) butter
3 onions, finely chopped
12 pitted black olives, thinly sliced
2 tablespoons chopped flat-leaf (Italian) parsley
3 sheets frozen puff pastry, thawed
1 egg, beaten

MAKES 30

Melt the butter in a frying pan and cook the onion over medium–low heat for 20 minutes, or until golden. Remove from the heat and stir in the olives, parsley, and salt and cracked black pepper. Allow to cool. Lightly grease a baking tray.

Cut each sheet of pastry in half, then each half into five triangles with a base (shortest side) of 8 cm (3 inches). You will have a couple of odd shapes left at each end. Put a little onion mixture at the base of each triangle and roll up towards the point, enclosing the filling. Curl the ends around to form a croissant shape.

Put the croissants on the baking tray and refrigerate for 30 minutes. Preheat the oven to 200°C (400°F/Gas 6). Brush each croissant with beaten egg. Bake for 20 minutes, or until puffed and golden.

PREPARATION TIME: 30 MINUTES +   COOKING TIME: 40 MINUTES

CORN MINI MUFFINS WITH PRAWNS AND DILL MAYO

250 g (9 oz/2 cups) plain (all-purpose) flour, sifted
110 g (3½ oz/¾ cup) cornmeal
1 tablespoon baking powder
55 g (2 oz/¼ cup) sugar
2 eggs, beaten
125 g (4½ oz) butter, melted
250 ml (9 fl oz/1 cup) milk
3 tablespoons finely chopped dill
1 tablespoon lemon juice
1 teaspoon horseradish cream
375 g (12 oz/1½ cups) whole-egg mayonnaise
300 g (10½ oz) small cooked prawns (shrimp)

MAKES ABOUT 50

Preheat the oven to 200°C (400°F/Gas 6). Lightly grease two 12-hole mini muffin tins. Sift the flour into a large bowl and mix with the cornmeal, baking powder, sugar and ½ teaspoon salt. Add the eggs, butter and milk. Stir until just combined. Spoon small amounts into the muffin tins, filling the holes three-quarters full. Cook for 15–20 minutes, or until lightly browned. Turn onto a wire rack to cool. Repeat until you have used all the mixture.

Mix the dill, lemon juice and horseradish cream into the mayonnaise and add plenty of salt and black pepper.

When the muffins are cool, scoop out a small piece from the top, as you would with a butterfly cake, and spoon a little dill mayonnaise into the cavity. Top with a prawn and some freshly ground black pepper.

PREPARATION TIME: 15 MINUTES   COOKING TIME: 40 MINUTES

Mini croissants

DOLMADES

200 g (7 oz) vine leaves in brine
250 g (9 oz/1 cup) medium-grain white rice
1 small onion, finely chopped
1 tablespoon olive oil
60 g (2¼ oz) pine nuts, toasted
2 tablespoons currants
2 tablespoons chopped dill
1 tablespoon finely chopped mint
1 tablespoon finely chopped flat-leaf (Italian) parsley
80 ml (2½ fl oz/⅓ cup) olive oil, extra
2 tablespoons lemon juice
500 ml (17 fl oz/2 cups) chicken stock

EGG AND LEMON SAUCE
375 ml (12 fl oz/1½ cups) chicken stock
1 tablespoon cornflour (cornstarch)
3 eggs
2–3 tablespoons lemon juice

MAKES 24

Soak the vine leaves in cold water for 15 minutes, then remove and pat dry. Cut off any stems. Reserve some leaves to line the saucepan and discard any that have holes or look poor. Meanwhile, soak the rice in boiling water for 10 minutes to soften, then drain.

To make the filling, put the rice, onion, olive oil, pine nuts, currants, herbs and salt and pepper, to taste, in a large bowl and mix well.

Lay some leaves, vein side down, on a flat surface. Put 1 tablespoon of filling in the centre of each, fold the stalk end over the filling, then the left and right sides into the centre, and finally roll firmly towards the tip. The dolmades should resemble a small cigar. Repeat with the remaining filling and leaves.

Use the reserved vine leaves to line the base of a large, heavy-based saucepan. Drizzle with 1 tablespoon of the extra olive oil. Add the dolmades, packing them tightly in one layer, then pour the remaining oil and the lemon juice over them.

Pour the stock over the dolmades and cover with an inverted plate to stop the dolmades moving around while cooking. Bring to the boil, then reduce the heat and simmer, covered, for 45 minutes. Remove with a slotted spoon. Serve warm or cold. These can be served with lemon wedges.

Meanwhile, to make the sauce, bring the chicken stock to the boil in a saucepan. Mix the cornflour with enough cold water to make a paste. Add to the stock and stir until the mixture thickens. Simmer for 2–3 minutes, then remove from the heat and cool slightly. Separate the eggs and beat the whites in a large bowl until stiff peaks form. Add the yolks and beat until light and fluffy. Mix in the lemon juice. Gradually pour in the thickened stock, beating constantly. Return the sauce to the pan and cook over low heat, stirring constantly for 1–2 minutes. Season, to taste, remove from the heat and stir for 1 minute. Serve with the dolmades.

PREPARATION TIME: 40 MINUTES +   COOKING TIME: 45 MINUTES

NOTE: Unused vine leaves can be stored in brine in an airtight container in the fridge for up to 1 week.

GOAT'S CHEESE TARTLETS

250 g (9 oz/2 cups) plain (all-purpose) flour
150 g (5¹/₂ oz) butter, chilled and chopped
2 tablespoons milk

FILLING
12 sun-dried tomatoes, sliced
200 g (7 oz) goat's cheese, chopped
2 tablespoons chopped basil
20–30 black olives, pitted and sliced
2 tablespoons chopped spring onion (scallion) tops
4 eggs, beaten
250 ml (9 fl oz/1 cup) pouring (whipping) cream

MAKES 30

Sift the flour and a pinch of salt into a bowl. Add the butter and rub it in until the mixture resembles fine breadcrumbs. Make a well and add enough milk to mix to a soft dough, using a knife. Lift onto a floured surface and gather into a ball. Chill in plastic wrap for 30 minutes.

Preheat the oven to 180°C (350°F/Gas 4). Lightly grease two 12-hole round-based patty pans or mini muffin tins. Roll out the pastry to 2 mm (¹/₈ inch) and cut 30 rounds with an 8 cm (3 inch) cutter. Line the bases and prick the pastry lightly. Bake for 7 minutes, or until cooked but not coloured.

Arrange the sun-dried tomatoes in the bases and cover with the cheese, basil, olives and spring onion. Combine the eggs and cream in a small bowl and season. Spoon the mixture over the filling and bake, for 15 minutes, or until the filling is just set. Repeat with the remaining pastry and filling. Serve at room temperature.

PREPARATION TIME: 40 MINUTES + COOKING TIME: 25 MINUTES

SMOKED TROUT TARTLETS

1 loaf sliced white bread, crusts removed
60 g (2¹/₄ oz) butter, melted
1 smoked trout (about 300 g/10¹/₂ oz), skinned, bones removed and flaked
1 tablespoon snipped chives
60 g (2¹/₄ oz/¹/₄ cup) whole-egg mayonnaise
2 spring onions (scallions), finely chopped
1 teaspoon horseradish cream
1 teaspoon wholegrain mustard
black olives, pitted and cut into strips, to garnish

MAKES 34

Preheat the oven to 120°C (250°F/Gas ¹/₂). Flatten the bread slices with a rolling pin. Cut 8 cm (3 inch) rounds with a cutter, then brush both sides with butter. Press into two 12-hole round-based patty pans or mini muffin tins. Bake for 10 minutes, or until crisp. Cool. Repeat to use all the bread.

Put the trout in a bowl and add the chives, mayonnaise, spring onion, horseradish cream and mustard. Season and mix well.

Spoon the filling into the tartlet cases, then garnish with strips of olives.

PREPARATION TIME: 40 MINUTES + COOKING TIME: 20 MINUTES

NOTE: The bread cases can be made 2 days ahead and stored in an airtight container.

Goat's cheese tartlets

PORK SAN CHOY BAU

1 tablespoon oil
400 g (14 oz) minced (ground) pork
230 g (8¹/₂ oz) tinned water chestnuts, drained and finely chopped
125 g (4¹/₂ oz) tinned bamboo shoots, drained and finely chopped
6 spring onions (scallions), finely chopped
2 tablespoons dry sherry
1 tablespoon soy sauce
2 teaspoons sesame oil
2 teaspoons oyster sauce
tiny lettuce leaves, such as cos (romaine), iceberg or witlof (chicory/Belgian endive)
chopped mint, to serve

SAUCE
2 tablespoons plum sauce
1 tablepoon hoisin sauce
1 teaspoon soy sauce

MAKES 25

Heat the oil in a frying pan or wok, add the pork and cook, stirring, over high heat until brown all over. Break up any lumps of pork with the back of a fork. Add the water chestnuts, bamboo shoots and spring onion. Toss well and cook for 1 minute.

Combine the sherry, soy sauce, sesame oil and oyster sauce. Add to the wok, toss well and cook for 2 minutes. Remove from the heat.

To make the dipping sauce, combine all the ingredients in a bowl with 2 tablespoons water.

To serve, put about 1 tablespoon of warm pork mixture on each lettuce leaf. Sprinkle with the chopped mint. Drizzle the sauce over the top.

PREPARATION TIME: 25 MINUTES   COOKING TIME: 10 MINUTES

NOTE: The pork can be prepared early in the day and refrigerated. Reheat to serve. The dipping sauce can be mixed the day before and refrigerated.

BABY SQUASH WITH RICE STUFFING

24 baby (pattypan) yellow squash
1 tablespoon oil
2 teaspoons Thai red curry paste
1 spring onion (scallion), finely chopped
1 small red capsicum (pepper), finely chopped
185 g (6^1/$_2$ oz/1 cup) cooked jasmine rice
1 tablespoon finely chopped coriander (cilantro) leaves
2 makrut (kaffir lime) leaves, finely shredded
coriander (cilantro) leaves, to garnish

MAKES 24

Blanch or steam the squash for 5 minutes, or until just tender.

Cut a thin slice off the base of each squash to allow it to stand upright, then slice a thin piece off the top to make a lid. Using a melon baller, scoop out the flesh from the squash, leaving a thin shell. Discard the flesh.

Heat the oil in a wok, then add the curry paste, spring onion and red capsicum and stir-fry for 2–3 minutes. Add the rice and stir-fry for a further 2–3 minutes. Add the chopped coriander and makrut leaves and toss to combine.

Remove from the heat and spoon 1 teaspoon of rice into each of the yellow squash. Garnish each with a coriander leaf and gently arrange the lids on top. Arrange on a platter and serve.

PREPARATION TIME: 20 MINUTES   COOKING TIME: 15 MINUTES

NOTES: For 185 g (6^1/$_2$ oz/1 cup) jasmine rice, you will need to cook 65 g (2^1/$_4$ oz/^{1}/$_3$ cup) of rice in boiling water for about 10 minutes.
  The filling and squash can be prepared a day ahead. Cover and store separately in the refrigerator.

STUFFED CHERRY TOMATOES

16 cherry tomatoes
50 g (1^3/$_4$ oz) goat's cheese
50 g (1^3/$_4$ oz) ricotta cheese
2 prosciutto slices, finely chopped

MAKES 16

Slice the tops from the tomatoes, hollow out and discard the seeds. Turn them upside-down on paper towel and drain for a few minutes.

Beat together the goat's cheese and ricotta until smooth. Mix in the prosciutto, then season. Spoon into the tomatoes and refrigerate until needed.

PREPARATION TIME: 15 MINUTES +   COOKING TIME: NIL

Baby squash with rice stuffing

FORK FOOD

MARINATED RED CAPSICUM

3 red capsicums (peppers)
3 thyme sprigs
1 garlic clove, thinly sliced
2 teaspoons roughly chopped flat-leaf (Italian) parsley
1 bay leaf
1 spring onion (scallion), sliced
1 teaspoon paprika
60 ml (2 fl oz/1/4 cup) extra virgin olive oil
2 tablespoons red wine vinegar

SERVES 6

Preheat the grill (broiler). Cut the capsicums into quarters and grill, skin side up, until the skin is black and blistered. Cool in a plastic bag, then peel. Slice thinly, then put in a bowl with the thyme, garlic, parsley, bay leaf and spring onion. Mix well.

Whisk together the paprika, oil, vinegar and some salt and pepper. Pour over the capsicum mixture and toss to combine. Cover and refrigerate for at least 3 hours, or preferably overnight. Remove from the refrigerator about 30 minutes before serving.

PREPARATION TIME: 20 MINUTES +   COOKING TIME: 5 MINUTES

NOTE: The capsicum can be refrigerated for up to 3 days.

MARINATED FETA CHEESE

350 g (12 oz) feta cheese
1 tablespoon dried oregano
1 teaspoon coriander seeds
125 g (4 1/2 oz) sun-dried tomatoes in oil
4 small red chillies
3–4 rosemary sprigs
olive oil

SERVES 6–8

Pat the feta cheese dry with paper towels and cut into 2 cm (3/4 inch) cubes. Transfer to a bowl and sprinkle the oregano, coriander seeds and 1 tablespoon cracked black pepper all over the feta cheese.

Drain the sun-dried tomatoes over a bowl so that you retain all of the oil. Arrange the feta, chillies, rosemary and sun-dried tomatoes in a sterilized 750 ml (26 fl oz/3-cup) wide-necked jar with a clip-top lid. Cover with the reserved sun-dried tomato oil (you should have about 60 ml/2 fl oz/1/4 cup) and top up with olive oil. Seal and refrigerate for 1 week before using. Serve at room temperature.

PREPARATION TIME: 10 MINUTES +   COOKING TIME: NIL

NOTES: To sterilize a storage jar, rinse with boiling water, then put in a very slow oven until completely dry.
　　　The oil in the bottle will partly solidify when refrigerated, but will liquify when returned to room temperature.
　　　The marinated feta will keep in the refrigerator for 1–2 months. Use the oil to make salad dressings or to flavour pasta.

ARTICHOKES IN AROMATIC VINAIGRETTE

2 tablespoons lemon juice
4 large globe artichokes
2 garlic cloves, crushed
1 teaspoon finely chopped oregano
$1/2$ teaspoon ground cumin
$1/2$ teaspoon ground coriander
pinch dried chilli flakes
3 teaspoons sherry vinegar
60 ml (2 fl oz/$1/4$ cup) olive oil

SERVES 4

Add the lemon juice to a large bowl of cold water. Trim the artichokes, cutting off the stalks to within 5 cm (2 inches) of the base of each artichoke and removing the tough outer leaves. Cut off the top quarter of the leaves from each. Slice each artichoke in half from top to base, or into quarters if large. Remove each small, furry choke with a teaspoon, then put each artichoke in the bowl of acidulated water to prevent it from discolouring while you prepare the rest.

Bring a large non-reactive saucepan of water to the boil, add the artichokes and a teaspoon of salt and simmer for 20 minutes, or until tender. The cooking time will depend on the artichoke size. Test by pressing a skewer into the base. If cooked, the artichoke should be soft and give little resistance. Strain, then put the artichokes on their cut side to drain while cooling.

To make the vinaigrette, combine the garlic, oregano, cumin, coriander and chilli flakes in a small bowl. Season and blend in the vinegar. Beating constantly, slowly pour in the olive oil to form an emulsion.

Arrange the artichokes in rows on a serving platter. Pour the vinaigrette over the top and allow to cool completely.

PREPARATION TIME: 20 MINUTES +   COOKING TIME: 20 MINUTES

MARINATED YOGHURT CHEESE BALLS

500 g (1 lb 2 oz/2 cups) Greek-style yoghurt
2 teaspoons sea salt
1 tablespoon dried oregano
2 teaspoons dried thyme
350 ml (12 fl oz/1⅓ cups) olive oil
1 bay leaf

MAKES 12

Fold a 30 x 60 cm (12 x 24 inch) piece of muslin (cheesecloth) in half to make a 30 cm (12 inch) square.

Combine the yoghurt, salt and 1 teaspoon black pepper in a bowl. Line a bowl with the muslin and spoon the mixture into the centre. Bring the corners together and, using a piece of kitchen string, tie as closely as possible to the yoghurt, leaving a loop at the end. Thread the loop through the handle of a wooden spoon and hang over a bowl to drain in the fridge for 3 days.

Combine the oregano and thyme in a shallow bowl. Pour half the oil into a 500 ml (17 fl oz/2-cup) jar and add the bay leaf.

Roll level tablespoons of the yoghurt into balls. Toss in the combined herbs and put into the jar of oil. Pour in the remaining oil to cover the balls completely. Seal and refrigerate for at least 1 day. Serve at room temperature, with chunky bread.

PREPARATION TIME: 20 MINUTES +   COOKING TIME: NIL

MARINATED MUSHROOMS

250 ml (9 fl oz/1 cup) apple cider vinegar
125 ml (4 fl oz/½ cup) orange juice
1 tablespoon coriander seeds
4 rosemary sprigs
2 bay leaves
500 g (1 lb 2 oz) button mushrooms
80 ml (2½ fl oz/⅓ cup) olive oil

SERVES 4

Put the apple cider vinegar, orange juice, coriander seeds, two rosemary sprigs and one bay leaf in a saucepan and bring to boil. Add the button mushrooms and simmer for 3 minutes. Remove and spoon into a sterilized jar. Boil the liquid until reduced by half. Discard the rosemary sprigs and bay leaf and replace with fresh ones.

Stir in the olive oil. Pour the liquid over the mushrooms and seal with a layer of olive oil. Will keep, refrigerated, for 1 month.

PREPARATION TIME: 10 MINUTES   COOKING TIME: 15 MINUTES

Marinated yoghurt cheese balls

TABOULEH

130 g (4$\frac{1}{2}$ oz/$\frac{3}{4}$ cup) burghul (bulgur)
3 ripe tomatoes
1 telegraph (long) cucumber
4 spring onions (scallions), sliced
120 g (4 oz) flat-leaf (Italian) parsley, chopped
2 large handfuls mint, chopped

DRESSING
80 ml (2$\frac{1}{2}$ fl oz/$\frac{1}{3}$ cup) lemon juice
60 ml (2 fl oz/$\frac{1}{4}$ cup) olive oil
1 tablespoon extra virgin olive oil

SERVES 6

Put the burghul in a bowl, cover with 500 ml (17 fl oz/2 cups) water and leave for 1$\frac{1}{2}$ hours.

Cut the tomatoes in half, squeeze to remove any excess seeds and cut into 1 cm ($\frac{1}{2}$ inch) cubes. Cut the cucumber in half lengthways, remove the seeds with a teaspoon and cut the flesh into 1 cm ($\frac{1}{2}$ inch) cubes.

To make the dressing, put the lemon juice and 1$\frac{1}{2}$ teaspoons salt in a bowl and whisk until well combined. Season well with freshly ground black pepper and slowly whisk in the olive oil and extra virgin olive oil.

Drain the burghul and squeeze out any excess water. Spread the burghul out on a tea towel (dish towel) or paper towels and leave to dry for about 30 minutes. Put the burghul in a large salad bowl, add the tomato, cucumber, spring onion, parsley and mint, and toss well to combine. Pour the dressing over the salad and toss until evenly coated.

PREPARATION TIME: 20 MINUTES +   COOKING TIME: NIL

ANTIPASTO SALAD

200 g (7 oz) sun-dried tomatoes
200 g (7 oz) marinated black olives
200 g (7 oz) marinated eggplant
(aubergine), chopped
200 g (7 oz) marinated artichokes
200 g (7 oz) sun-dried capsicum (pepper)
3 tablespoons chopped basil
balsamic vinegar, for drizzling

SERVES 4–6

Combine the sun-dried tomatoes, olives, eggplant, artichoke and capsicum. Toss through the basil. Drizzle with a little balsamic vinegar.

PREPARATION TIME: 10 MINUTES COOKING TIME: NIL

SESAME COLESLAW

1/4 red cabbage
1/4 green cabbage
100 g (3 1/2 oz) snow peas (mangetout)
2 celery stalks
2 carrots
1 red capsicum (pepper)
whole-egg mayonnaise, to serve
1 small handful mint, finely
shredded, to serve
toasted sesame seeds, to serve

SERVES 4

Finely shred the red cabbage and green cabbage. Cut the snow peas, celery stalks, carrots and capsicum into strips.

Combine the cabbage and other vegetables in a large bowl and toss through enough whole-egg mayonnaise to lightly dress the salad. Top with finely shredded mint leaves and toasted sesame seeds.

PREPARATION TIME: 15 MINUTES COOKING TIME: NIL

Antipasto salad

HERBED POTATO SALAD

650 g (1 lb 7 oz) red-skinned potatoes
1 red onion, thinly sliced
1 tablespoon chopped mint
1 tablespoon chopped flat-leaf (Italian)
parsley
1 tablespoon snipped chives
90 g (3¼ oz/⅓ cup) whole-egg
mayonnaise
90 g (3¼ oz/⅓ cup) plain yoghurt

SERVES 4

Scrub the potatoes and cut into cubes. Cook in a large saucepan of boiling water until just tender, then drain and allow to cool completely.

Put the potatoes, onion and herbs in a large bowl. Combine the mayonnaise and yoghurt, then gently mix through to coat the potato, taking care not to break it up too much. Serve at room temperature.

PREPARATION TIME: 15 MINUTES   COOKING TIME: 15 MINUTES

AVOCADO AND BLACK BEAN SALAD

250 g (9 oz) dried black beans
1 red onion, chopped
4 roma (plum) tomatoes, chopped
1 red capsicum (pepper), chopped
375 g (13 oz) tinned corn kernels, drained
90 g (3¼ oz) coriander (cilantro) leaves, chopped
2 avocados, chopped
1 mango, peeled and chopped
150 g (5½ oz) rocket (arugula)

DRESSING
1 garlic clove, crushed
1 small red chilli, finely chopped
2 tablespoons lime juice
60 ml (2 fl oz/¼ cup) olive oil

SERVES 4

Soak the beans in cold water overnight. Rinse, then drain. Put the beans into a large heavy-based saucepan, cover with water and bring to the boil. Reduce the heat and simmer for 1½ hours, or until tender. Drain and cool slightly.

Put the beans, onion, tomatoes, capsicum, corn, coriander, avocado, mango and rocket into a large bowl and toss to combine.

To make the dressing, combine all the ingredients in a bowl and whisk. Pour over the salad and toss.

PREPARATION TIME: 15 MINUTES +   COOKING TIME: 1 HOUR 30 MINUTES

SPICY POTATO SALAD

500 g (1 lb 2 oz) baby new potatoes, halved
250 g (9 oz) green beans, trimmed, tailed and halved diagonally

DRESSING
60 ml (2 fl oz/¼ cup) olive oil
2 red chillies, seeded and sliced
1 garlic clove, crushed
1 large handful coriander (cilantro) leaves, chopped
1 tablespoon red wine vinegar
½ teaspoon caraway seeds

SERVES 6

Cook the potatoes in a large saucepan of gently simmering water for 20 minutes, or until tender but still firm. Drain and set aside.

Blanch the beans in boiling water for 2 minutes, or until bright green and just tender. Drain the beans and set aside.

To make the dressing, whisk all the ingredients in a small bowl until well combined. Pour the dressing over the combined beans and potatoes and serve immediately.

PREPARATION TIME: 15 MINUTES   COOKING TIME: 15 MINUTES

Avocado and black bean salad

CANNELLINI BEAN SALAD

425 g (15 oz) tinned cannellini beans
1 tomato, finely chopped
3 anchovy fillets, sliced
1 tablespoon finely chopped red onion
2 teaspoons finely chopped basil
2 teaspoons extra virgin olive oil
1 teaspoon balsamic vinegar
crusty bread, cut into slices, to serve
olive oil, for brushing
1 garlic clove, bruised

SERVES 6–8

Rinse and drain the cannellini beans.

Combine the cannellini beans, tomato, anchovies, onion, basil, olive oil and balsamic vinegar.

Lightly brush the slices of bread with the oil, then toast and rub with the garlic. Spoon the salad onto the bread slices to serve.

PREPARATION TIME: 20 MINUTES   COOKING TIME: 5 MINUTES

NOTE: The salad can be prepared up to a day ahead, covered and refrigerated.

FAST MELON SALAD

1 large honeydew melon
60 g (2¼ oz/2 cups) watercress sprigs, trimmed
2 avocados, sliced
1 large red capsicum (pepper), thinly sliced
220 g (7¾ oz) marinated feta cheese, crumbled into large chunks
90 g (3¼ oz) marinated niçoise olives

DRESSING
60 ml (2 fl oz/¼ cup) olive oil
2 tablespoons white wine vinegar
1 teaspoon dijon mustard

SERVES 4–6

Cut the honeydew melon into slices and arrange on a large platter. Scatter the watercress sprigs over the top. Arrange on top the avocado, capsicum, feta cheese and niçoise olives.

To make the dressing, put the olive oil, white wine vinegar and dijon mustard in a screw-top jar and shake until well combined. Drizzle over the salad.

PREPARATION TIME: 15 MINUTES   COOKING TIME: NIL

PEACH SALSA SALAD

6 large peaches, cut into wedges
1 red onion, thinly sliced
6 roma (plum) tomatoes, quartered
200 g (7 oz/1 cup) corn kernels
1 green capsicum (pepper), sliced
1 large handful coriander (cilantro) leaves

DRESSING
1 garlic clove, crushed
1 teaspoon ground cumin
1 red chilli, finely chopped
2 tablespoons freshly squeezed lime juice
60 ml (2 fl oz/¼ cup) oil

SERVES 4–6

Put the peaches, onion, tomatoes, corn kernels and capsicum in a bowl.

To make the dressing, mix together the garlic, cumin, chilli, lime juice and oil. Pour over the salad and toss to combine. Fold through the coriander leaves just before serving.

PREPARATION TIME: 15 MINUTES   COOKING TIME: NIL

RUSSIAN SALAD

MAYONNAISE
2 egg yolks
1 teaspoon dijon mustard
125 ml (4 fl oz/½ cup) extra virgin
olive oil
2 tablespoons lemon juice
2 small garlic cloves, crushed

3 tinned globe artichoke hearts
3 waxy potatoes, such as desiree,
unpeeled
100 g (3½ oz) baby green beans, trimmed
and cut into 1 cm (½ inch) lengths
1 large carrot, cut into 1 cm (½ inch)
cubes
125 g (4½ oz) fresh peas
30 g (1 oz) cornichons, chopped
2 tablespoons baby capers, rinsed and
drained
10 black olives, cut into 3 slices
4 anchovy fillets, finely chopped
black olives, to garnish

SERVES 4–6

To make the mayonnaise, beat the egg yolks with the mustard and
¼ teaspoon salt using electric beaters until creamy. Gradually add the
oil in a fine stream, beating constantly until all the oil has been added.
Add the lemon juice, garlic and 1 teaspoon boiling water and beat for
1 minute until well combined. Season, to taste.

Cut each artichoke into quarters. Rinse the potatoes, cover with cold
salted water and bring to a gentle simmer. Cook for 15–20 minutes, or
until tender when pierced with a knife. Drain and allow to cool slightly.
Peel and set aside. When the potatoes are completely cool, cut into
1 cm (½ inch) cubes.

Blanch the beans in boiling salted water until tender but still firm to
the bite. Refresh in cold water, then drain thoroughly. Repeat with the
carrot and peas.

Set aside a small quantity of each vegetable, including the cornichons,
for the garnish and season, to taste. Put the remainder in a bowl with the
capers, anchovies and sliced olives. Add the mayonnaise, toss to
combine and season to taste. Arrange on a serving dish and garnish with
the reserved vegetables and the whole olives.

PREPARATION TIME: 40 MINUTES +   COOKING TIME: 40 MINUTES

NOTE: This salad can be prepared up to 2 days in advance and
stored in the refrigerator but should be served at room temperature.

PRAWN AND PAPAYA SALAD WITH LIME DRESSING

750 g (1 lb 10 oz) cooked prawns (shrimp)
1 large papaya, chopped
1 small red onion, thinly sliced
2 celery stalks, thinly sliced
2 tablespoons shredded mint

LIME DRESSING
125 ml (4 fl oz/$\frac{1}{2}$ cup) oil
60 ml (2 fl oz/$\frac{1}{4}$ cup) lime juice
2 teaspoons finely grated fresh ginger
1 teaspoon caster (superfine) sugar

Peel the prawns, leaving the tails intact. Gently pull out the dark vein from each prawn back, starting from the head end. Put the prawns in a bowl.

To make the lime dressing, put the oil, lime juice, ginger and sugar in a small bowl and whisk to combine. Season.

Add the lime dressing to the prawns and gently toss to coat the prawns. Add the papaya, onion, celery and mint and gently toss to combine. Serve the salad at room temperature, or cover and refrigerate for up to 3 hours before serving.

SERVES 4   PREPARATION TIME: 25 MINUTES   COOKING TIME: NIL

MARINATED MUSHROOM SALAD

500 g (1 lb 2 oz) button mushrooms, halved
4 spring onions (scallions), thinly sliced
1 red capsicum (pepper), finely diced
2 tablespoons chopped flat-leaf (Italian) parsley

DRESSING
3 garlic cloves, crushed
60 ml (2 fl oz/$\frac{1}{4}$ cup) white wine vinegar
2 teaspoons dijon mustard
80 ml (2$\frac{1}{2}$ fl oz/$\frac{1}{3}$ cup) olive oil

SERVES 4–6

Combine the mushrooms, spring onion, capsicum and parsley in a large bowl.

To make the dressing, combine the garlic, white wine vinegar, dijon mustard and olive oil. Pour the dressing over the mushrooms and toss to coat. Cover and refrigerate for 3 hours before serving.

PREPARATION TIME: 10 MINUTES +   COOKING TIME: NIL

Prawn and papaya salad with lime dressing

CHICKEN AND VEGETABLE SALAD

400 g (14 oz) boneless, skinless chicken breast

3 slices fresh ginger

2 lemon grass stems (white part only), roughly chopped

2 tablespoons fish sauce

250 g (9 oz) broccoli, cut into florets

150 g (5½ oz) baby corn

100 g (3½ oz) snow peas (mangetout), trimmed

1 red capsicum (pepper), cut into strips

3 spring onions (scallions), cut into strips

125 ml (4 fl oz/½ cup) sweet chilli sauce

2 tablespoons honey

2 tablespoons lime juice

2 teaspoons grated lime zest

1 handful coriander (cilantro) leaves

SERVES 4–6

Slice the chicken into short, thin strips.

Put the ginger, lemon grass, fish sauce and 250 ml (9 fl oz/1 cup) water in a frying pan. Bring the mixture to the boil, reduce the heat slightly and simmer for 5 minutes.

Add the chicken to the pan and cook in the hot liquid for 5 minutes, stirring occasionally. Drain and allow to cool. Discard the liquid.

Bring a large saucepan of water to the boil and cook the broccoli, corn, snow peas, capsicum and spring onion for 2 minutes. Drain and plunge into iced water, then drain again.

Combine the sweet chilli sauce, honey, lime juice and zest in a small bowl and mix well. Arrange the vegetables and chicken on a serving platter. Pour the sauce over the top and gently toss. Sprinkle with the coriander leaves.

PREPARATION TIME: 30 MINUTES   COOKING TIME: 20 MINUTES

NOTE: To trim snow peas, cut or break both ends off and then pull away any strings from along the sides.

SALATA BALADI

2 tablespoons extra virgin olive oil

2 tablespoons lemon juice

1 cos (romaine) lettuce, torn into bite-sized pieces

3 ripe tomatoes, each cut into 8 pieces

1 green capsicum (pepper), cut into bite-sized pieces

1 telegraph (long) cucumber, seeded and chopped

6 radishes, sliced

1 small red onion, thinly sliced

2 tablespoons chopped flat-leaf (Italian) parsley

2 tablespoons chopped mint

SERVES 4–6

In a bowl, whisk together the olive oil and lemon juice. Season well.

Combine the remaining ingredients in a large serving bowl and toss well. Add the dressing and toss to combine.

PREPARATION TIME: 10 MINUTES   COOKING TIME: NIL

NOTE: Salad onions are sweeter than normal onions and are readily available.

CUCUMBER SALAD WITH PEANUTS AND CHILLI

3 Lebanese (short) cucumbers

2 tablespoons white vinegar

2 teaspoons sugar

1–2 tablespoons chilli sauce

$\frac{1}{2}$ red onion, chopped

1 large handful coriander (cilantro) leaves

160 g (5$\frac{3}{4}$ oz/1 cup) unsalted roasted peanuts, chopped

2 tablespoons crisp fried garlic

$\frac{1}{2}$ teaspoon chopped chilli

1 tablespoon fish sauce

SERVES 4–6

Peel the cucumbers and slice in half lengthways. Remove the seeds with a teaspoon and slice thinly.

Combine the vinegar and sugar in a small bowl, and stir until the sugar dissolves. Transfer to a large bowl and toss with the cucumber, chilli sauce, onion and coriander. Allow to marinate for 45 minutes.

Just before serving, add the peanuts, garlic, chilli and fish sauce. Toss lightly to combine.

PREPARATION TIME: 25 MINUTES +   COOKING TIME: NIL

COLD VEGETABLE SALAD WITH SPICE DRESSING

300 g (10½ oz) green or snake (yard-long) beans
10 English spinach leaves
80 g (2¾ oz) snow pea (mangetout) sprouts
1 red capsicum (pepper)
1 red onion
100 g (3½ oz) bean sprouts, trimmed

SPICE DRESSING
2 tablespoons peanut oil
1 garlic clove, crushed
1 teaspoon grated fresh ginger
1 small red chilli, chopped
2 tablespoons desiccated coconut
1 tablespoon brown vinegar

SERVES 4

Top and tail the beans and cut them into 10 cm (4 inch) lengths. Remove the stems from the spinach leaves and slice the leaves thinly. Remove about 1 cm (½ inch) of the long stems from the snow pea sprouts. Cut the capsicum into thin strips. Thinly slice the onion.

Put the beans in a large saucepan of boiling water and cook for 1 minute to blanch, then drain. Combine the beans, spinach, snow pea sprouts, bean sprouts, capsicum and onion in a bowl.

To make the spice dressing, heat the oil in a small frying pan. Add the garlic, ginger, chilli and coconut, and stir-fry over medium heat for 1 minute. Add the vinegar and 80 ml (2½ fl oz/⅓ cup) water, and simmer for 1 minute. Allow to cool.

To serve, add the dressing to the vegetables, and toss until combined.

PREPARATION TIME: 15 MINUTES +   COOKING TIME: 10 MINUTES

NOTES: Snow pea sprouts are the growing tips and tendrils from the snow pea plant.

Any blanched vegetables can be used in this salad. Try to use a variety of vegetables which result in a colourful appearance.

The spice dressing can be added up to 30 minutes before serving.

TUNA, GREEN BEAN AND ONION SALAD

200 g (7 oz) green beans, trimmed and cut into short lengths
300 g (10½ oz) penne rigate
125 ml (4 fl oz/½ cup) olive oil
250 g (9 oz) tuna steak, cut into thick slices
1 red onion, thinly sliced
1 tablespoon balsamic vinegar

SERVES 4

In a large saucepan of boiling water, cook the prepared beans for 1–2 minutes, or until tender but still crisp. Remove with a slotted spoon and rinse under cold water. Drain and transfer to a serving bowl.

Cook the pasta in a saucepan of boiling salted water until *al dente*. Drain, rinse under cold water and drain again before adding to the beans.

Heat half the oil in a frying pan. Add the tuna and onion and gently sauté until the tuna is just cooked through. Stir the tuna carefully to prevent it from breaking up. Add the vinegar, increase the heat to high and briefly cook until the dressing has reduced and lightly coats the tuna. Transfer the tuna and onion to a bowl.

Toss the beans, pasta, tuna and onion together and mix with the remaining oil, and season to taste. Allow to cool before serving.

PREPARATION TIME: 20 MINUTES   COOKING TIME: 15 MINUTES

TUNA AND WHITE BEAN SALAD

750 g (1 lb 10 oz) tinned tuna in oil
400 g (14 oz) tinned cannellini beans, drained and rinsed
1 large red onion, coarsely chopped
3 hard-boiled eggs, cut into wedges
3 tomatoes, cut into wedges

DRESSING
1 garlic clove, crushed
1–2 teaspoons thyme
1–2 teaspoons finely chopped flat-leaf (Italian) parsley
60 ml (2 fl oz/¼ cup) white wine vinegar
80 ml (2½ fl oz/⅓ cup) extra virgin olive oil

SERVES 4–6

Drain the tuna and flake into chunks.

To make the dressing, combine the garlic, thyme, parsley, vinegar and olive oil in a bowl and whisk. Season.

Combine the beans and onion in a large bowl. Add the dressing and toss. Add the tuna, toss gently, then add half the egg wedges and half the tomato. Lightly combine. Pile on a platter and garnish with the remaining egg and tomato.

PREPARATION TIME: 15 MINUTES   COOKING TIME: NIL

Tuna, green bean and onion salad

FISH AND HERB SALAD

500 g (1 lb 2 oz) smoked cod
60 ml (2 fl oz/¼ cup) lime juice
30 g (1 oz/½ cup) flaked coconut
200 g (7 oz/1 cup) jasmine rice, cooked and cooled
25 g (1 oz) Vietnamese mint, chopped
3 tablespoons chopped mint
25 g (1 oz) chopped coriander (cilantro) leaves
8 makrut (kaffir lime) leaves, very finely shredded

DRESSING
1 tablespoon chopped coriander (cilantro) root
2 cm (¾ inch) piece fresh ginger, finely grated
1 red chilli, finely chopped
1 tablespoon chopped lemon grass, white part only
3 tablespoons chopped Thai basil
1 avocado, chopped
80 ml (2½ fl oz/⅓ cup) lime juice
2 tablespoons fish sauce
1 teaspoon soft brown sugar
125 ml (4 fl oz/½ cup) peanut oil

SERVES 4–6

Preheat the oven to 150°C (300°F/Gas 2). Put the cod in a large frying pan and cover with water. Add the lime juice and simmer for 15 minutes, or until the fish flakes when tested with a fork. Drain and set aside to cool slightly before breaking it into bite-sized pieces.

Meanwhile, spread the coconut onto a baking tray and toast in the oven for 10 minutes, or until golden brown, shaking the tray occasionally. Remove the coconut from the tray to prevent it burning.

Put the fish, coconut, rice, Vietnamese mint, mint, coriander and makrut leaves in a large bowl and mix to combine.

To make the dressing, put the coriander root, ginger, chilli, lemon grass and basil in a food processor and process until combined. Add the avocado, lime juice, fish sauce, sugar and peanut oil and process until creamy. Pour the dressing over the salad and toss to coat the rice and fish. Serve immediately.

PREPARATION TIME: 40 MINUTES   COOKING TIME: 15 MINUTES

LARB

1 tablespoon oil
2 lemon grass stems, white part only, thinly sliced
2 green chillies, finely chopped
500 g (1 lb 2 oz) lean minced (ground) pork or beef
60 ml (2 fl oz/^{1}/$_4$ cup) lime juice
2 teaspoons finely grated lime zest
2-6 teaspoons chilli sauce
lettuce leaves, to serve
3 tablespoons chopped coriander (cilantro) leaves
2 tablespoons chopped mint
1 small red onion, thinly sliced
50 g (1^3/$_4$ oz/^{1}/$_3$ cup) unsalted roasted peanuts, chopped
25 g (1 oz/^{1}/$_4$ cup) crisp fried garlic

SERVES 4–6

Heat the oil in a wok and stir-fry the lemon grass, chilli and pork or beef over high heat for 6 minutes, or until the meat is cooked, breaking up any lumps. Transfer to a bowl and allow to cool.

Add the lime juice, zest and chilli sauce to the pork or beef mixture. Arrange the lettuce leaves on a serving plate. Stir most of the coriander, mint, onion, peanuts and fried garlic through the mixture, spoon over the lettuce and sprinkle the rest of the coriander, mint, onion, peanuts and garlic over the top.

PREPARATION TIME: 20 MINUTES +   COOKING TIME: 10 MINUTES

MIXED VEGETABLE SALAD

300 g (10^1/$_2$ oz) pineapple, chopped
1 telegraph (long) cucumber, chopped
250 g (9 oz) cherry tomatoes, halved
155 g (5^1/$_2$ oz) green beans, thinly sliced
155 g (5^1/$_2$ oz) bean sprouts, trimmed
80 ml (2^1/$_2$ fl oz/^{1}/$_3$ cup) rice vinegar
2 tablespoons lime juice
2 red chillies, seeded and very finely chopped
2 teaspoons sugar
30 g (1 oz) dried shrimp, to garnish
small mint leaves, to garnish

SERVES 4–6

Toss together the pineapple, cucumber, tomatoes, beans and sprouts in a bowl. Cover and refrigerate until chilled. Combine the vinegar, lime juice, chilli and sugar in a small bowl and stir until the sugar dissolves.

Dry-fry the shrimp in a frying pan, shaking the pan constantly until the shrimp are light orange and fragrant. Process the shrimp in a food processor until finely chopped.

Arrange the chilled salad on a serving platter, drizzle the dressing over the top and garnish with the chopped shrimp and mint leaves. Serve immediately.

PREPARATION TIME: 40 MINUTES   COOKING TIME: 5 MINUTES

WATERCRESS AND DUCK SALAD WITH LYCHEES

2 large duck breasts, skin on
1 tablespoon soy sauce
1/2 each red, green and yellow capsicum (pepper)
250 g (9 oz) watercress
12 fresh or canned lychees
2 tablespoons pickled shredded ginger
1-2 tablespoons green peppercorns (optional)
1 tablespoon white vinegar
2 teaspoons soft brown sugar
1-2 teaspoons chopped red chilli
1 large handful coriander (cilantro) leaves

SERVES 4

Preheat the oven to 210°C (415°F/Gas 6-7). Brush the duck breasts with the soy sauce and put on a rack in a baking tin. Bake for 30 minutes. Remove from the oven and allow to cool.

Slice the capsicums into thin strips. Discard any tough woody stems from the watercress. Peel the fresh lychees and remove the seeds. If you are using canned lychees, drain them thoroughly.

Arrange the capsicum strips, watercress, lychees and ginger on a large serving platter. Slice the duck into thin pieces and toss gently through the salad.

In a small bowl, combine the peppercorns, if using, vinegar, sugar, chilli and coriander. Serve this on the side for spooning over the salad.

PREPARATION TIME: 25 MINUTES +   COOKING TIME: 30 MINUTES

EGGPLANT SALAD

1 kg (2 lb 4 oz) large eggplants (aubergines)
125 ml (4 fl oz/½ cup) olive oil
1 onion, finely chopped
½ teaspoon ground cinnamon
4 garlic cloves, crushed
800 g (1 lb 12 oz) tinned crushed tomatoes
2 tablespoons chopped coriander (cilantro) leaves
3 tablespoons chopped flat-leaf (Italian) parsley
1 tablespoon lemon juice
2 tablespoons chopped mint
150 g (5½ oz) Greek-style yoghurt
25 g (1 oz) pine nuts, toasted

SERVES 6

Cut the eggplants into 2 cm (³/₄ inch) cubes. Put in a colander and leave to stand over a bowl and sprinkle generously with salt. Leave for 30 minutes, rinse under cold water, then pat dry with a tea towel (dish towel).

Heat 2 tablespoons of the oil in a large frying pan and fry batches of eggplant until golden, adding more oil if necessary. Drain on paper towels.

Heat another 2 tablespoons of the oil in the pan and fry the onion for 1 minute. Add the cinnamon and half the garlic, cook for 1 minute, then add the tomato. Add the eggplant and simmer, uncovered, for 1 hour, or until the mixture is quite dry. Add half of each of the coriander and parsley. Stir and leave to cool.

Mix 2 tablespoons of oil with the lemon juice and add the remaining crushed garlic and the mint. Stir into the yoghurt.

Toss the pine nuts through the salad and garnish with the remaining fresh herbs. Serve at room temperature with the garlic yoghurt dressing.

PREPARATION TIME: 20 MINUTES +   COOKING TIME: 1 HOUR 35 MINUTES

BACON, LETTUCE AND TOMATO SALAD

4 bacon slices
1 cos (romaine) lettuce
200 g (7 oz) cherry tomatoes, halved
1 avocado, chopped

DRESSING
125 g (4½ oz/½ cup) plain yoghurt
1 tablespoon wholegrain mustard
1 tablespoon lemon juice
1 teaspoon honey

SERVES 4

Fry the bacon in a frying pan over medium heat until crisp. Allow to cool on paper towels before roughly chopping.

Put the bacon in a bowl together with the lettuce, tomatoes and avocado. Toss gently to combine.

To make the dressing, mix together the yoghurt, mustard, lemon juice and honey. Drizzle over the salad and toss to combine.

PREPARATION TIME: 10 MINUTES   COOKING TIME: 10 MINUTES

Eggplant salad

GADO GADO

6 new potatoes
2 carrots, cut into batons
250 g (9 oz) snake (yard-long) beans, trimmed and cut into 10 cm (4 inch) lengths
2 tablespoons peanut oil
250 g (9 oz) firm tofu, cubed
100 g (3½ oz) baby English spinach leaves
2 Lebanese (short) cucumbers, cut into thick strips
1 large red capsicum (pepper), cut into thick strips
100 g (3½ oz) bean sprouts, trimmed
5 hard-boiled eggs, cut in half

PEANUT SAUCE
1 tablespoon peanut oil
1 onion, finely chopped
160 g (5¾ oz/⅔ cup) peanut butter
60 ml (2 fl oz/¼ cup) kecap manis
2 tablespoons ground coriander
2 teaspoons chilli sauce
185 ml (6 fl oz/¾ cup) coconut cream
1 teaspoon grated palm sugar (jaggery) or soft brown sugar
1 tablespoon lemon juice

SERVES 6–8

Cook the potatoes in a saucepan of boiling water until tender. Drain, cool slightly, then cut into quarters.

Cook the carrots and beans separately until just tender. Drain, plunge into iced water, then drain thoroughly.

Heat the oil in a non-stick frying pan and cook the tofu all over in batches until crisp. Drain on crumpled paper towels.

To make the peanut sauce, heat the oil in a frying pan over low heat and cook the onion for 5 minutes, or until golden. Add the peanut butter, kecap manis, coriander, chilli sauce and coconut cream. Bring to the boil, reduce the heat and simmer for 5 minutes. Stir in the sugar and lemon juice, stirring until dissolved.

Arrange all the vegetables, tofu and eggs on a plate around the bowl of sauce.

PREPARATION TIME: 30 MINUTES   COOKING TIME: 35 MINUTES

GARDEN SALAD

1 green oak-leaf lettuce
150 g (5½ oz) rocket (arugula)
1 small radicchio lettuce
1 large green capsicum (pepper), cut into thin strips
grated zest of 1 lemon

DRESSING

2 tablespoons roughly chopped coriander (cilantro) leaves
60 ml (2 fl oz/¼ cup) lemon juice
2 teaspoons soft brown sugar
2 tablespoons olive oil
1 garlic clove, crushed (optional)

SERVES 4–6

Tear the salad greens into bite-size pieces. Combine the salad greens, capsicum and lemon zest in a large serving bowl.

To make the dressing, whisk all the ingredients in a small bowl until well combined. Pour the dressing over the salad and toss to combine.

PREPARATION TIME: 15 MINUTES   COOKING TIME: NIL

NOTES: Make the dressing and salad just before serving. Choose a selection of your favourite salad greens for this recipe.

This is delicious served in summer with a chilled frascati or a light red wine.

BEETROOT AND NECTARINE SALAD

1.3 kg (3 lb/2 bunches) trimmed baby beetroot (beets)
4 nectarines
2 tablespoons sunflower seeds, toasted
2 tablespoons chervil

DRESSING

1 tablespoon wholegrain mustard
2 tablespoons raspberry vinegar
2 tablespoons honey
90 g (3¼ oz/⅓ cup) plain yoghurt
60 ml (2 fl oz/¼ cup) oil

SERVES 4–6

Boil, steam or microwave the beetroot until tender. Drain and allow to cool before cutting into quarters. Cut the nectarines into thick wedges. Combine the beetroot, nectarines, sunflower seeds and chervil leaves.

To make the dressing, mix together the mustard, vinegar, honey, yoghurt and oil. Drizzle the dressing over the salad just before serving.

PREPARATION TIME: 15 MINUTES   COOKING TIME: 15 MINUTES

Garden salad

MOROCCAN LAMB AND ROASTED CAPSICUM WITH FUSILLI

500 g (1 lb 2 oz) lamb fillets
3 teaspoons ground cumin
1 tablespoon ground coriander
2 teaspoons ground allspice
1 teaspoon ground cinnamon
1/2 teaspoon ground cayenne pepper
4 garlic cloves, crushed
80 ml (2 1/2 fl oz/1/3 cup) olive oil
125 ml (4 fl oz/1/2 cup) lemon juice
2 red capsicums (peppers)
400 g (14 oz) fusilli
60 ml (2 fl oz/1/4 cup) olive oil, extra
2 teaspoons harissa
150 g (5 1/2 oz) rocket (arugula)

SERVES 4–6

Cut the fillets in half if they are very long. Mix the cumin, coriander, allspice, cinnamon, cayenne, garlic, olive oil and half the lemon juice in a bowl. Add the lamb, stir to coat and marinate, covered, in the refrigerator overnight.

Preheat the grill (broiler). Cut the capsicums into large pieces and grill, skin side up, until the skin is black and blistered. Cool in a plastic bag, then peel. Slice thinly.

Cook the fusilli in a large saucepan of rapidly boiling salted water until *al dente*. Drain and keep warm.

Drain the lamb, heat 1 tablespoon of the extra virgin olive oil in a large frying pan and cook the lamb over high heat until done to your liking. Remove from the pan and cover with foil.

Heat 1 teaspoon of the oil in the frying pan and cook the harissa over medium heat for a few seconds. Be careful as the mixture may spit. Remove and put in a small screw-top jar with the remaining oil and lemon juice and shake the jar until well combined. Season to taste.

Thinly slice the lamb fillets and toss with the warm pasta, capsicum and rocket. Toss the harissa dressing through the pasta. Serve warm.

PREPARATION TIME: 25 MINUTES + COOKING TIME: 25 MINUTES

CUCUMBER, FETA, MINT AND DILL SALAD

120 g (4 oz) feta cheese
4 Lebanese (short) cucumbers
1 small red onion, thinly sliced
1¹/₂ tablespoons finely chopped dill
1 tablespoon dried mint
60 ml (2 fl oz/¹/₄ cup) olive oil
1¹/₂ tablespoons lemon juice

Crumble the feta into 1 cm (¹/₂ inch) pieces and put in a large bowl. Peel and seed the cucumbers and cut into 1 cm (¹/₂ inch) cubes. Add to the bowl along with the onion and dill.

Grind the mint using a mortar and pestle, or force through a sieve, until powdered. Combine with the oil and juice, then season. Pour over the salad and toss well.

SERVES 4   PREPARATION TIME: 15 MINUTES   COOKING TIME: NIL

CHEF'S SALAD

DRESSING
125 ml (4 fl oz/¹/₂ cup) extra virgin olive oil
2 tablespoons white wine vinegar
1 teaspoon sugar

1 iceberg lettuce
2 tomatoes, cut into wedges
2 celery stalks, cut into thin batons
1 cooked boneless, skinless chicken breast, cut into thin strips
200 g (7 oz) ham, cut into thin strips
60 g (2¹/₄ oz) Swiss cheese, cut into strips
3 hard-boiled eggs, cut into wedges
6 radishes, sliced

SERVES 4

Whisk the dressing ingredients together in a bowl until well combined. Season to taste.

Roughly shred the lettuce leaves and divide among serving plates. Top with layers of the tomato, celery, chicken, ham, cheese, egg and radish. Drizzle the dressing over the salad and serve immediately.

PREPARATION TIME: 25 MINUTES   COOKING TIME: NIL

Cucumber, feta, mint and dill salad

FARFALLE SALAD WITH SUN-DRIED TOMATOES AND SPINACH

500 g (1 lb 2 oz) farfalle or spiral pasta
3 spring onions (scallions)
50 g (1³/₄ oz) sun-dried tomatoes, cut into strips
1 kg (2 lb 4 oz) English spinach, stalks trimmed and leaves shredded
50 g (1³/₄ oz/¹/₃ cup) pine nuts, toasted
1 tablespoon chopped oregano
60 ml (2 fl oz/¹/₄ cup) olive oil
1 teaspoon sliced chilli
1 garlic clove, crushed

SERVES 6

Cook the pasta in a large saucepan of rapidly boiling salted water until *al dente*. Drain, rinse under cold water and drain again. Allow to cool and transfer to a large salad bowl.

Trim the spring onions and thinly slice diagonally. Add to the pasta with the tomato, spinach, pine nuts and oregano.

To make the dressing, combine the oil, chilli, garlic and salt and pepper in a small screw-top jar and shake well. Pour the dressing over the top of the salad and toss to combine.

PREPARATION TIME: 20 MINUTES   COOKING TIME: 15 MINUTES

PASTRAMI, MUSHROOM AND CUCUMBER SALAD

200 g (7 oz) lasagnette, broken into quarters
250 g (9 oz) sliced pastrami, cut in strips
1 celery stalk, sliced
2 small tomatoes, cut into wedges
1 Lebanese (short) cucumber, thinly sliced
80 g (2³/₄ oz) button mushrooms, sliced
1 tablespoon chopped coriander (cilantro) leaves

DRESSING
60 ml (2 fl oz/¹/₄ cup) olive oil
2 tablespoons red wine vinegar
¹/₂ teaspoon dijon mustard
1 garlic clove, crushed
¹/₄ teaspoon hot chilli oil

SERVES 4

Cook the lasagnette in a large saucepan of rapidly boiling salted water until *al dente*. Drain, rinse under cold water and drain again. Allow to cool and transfer to a large salad bowl.

Add the pastrami, celery, tomato wedges, cucumber and mushrooms to the pasta.

To prepare the dressing, combine all the ingredients in a screw-top jar and shake until well blended.

Toss the dressing through the salad and refrigerate, covered, for several hours. Adjust the seasoning and sprinkle with the coriander before serving.

PREPARATION TIME: 20 MINUTES +   COOKING TIME: 10 MINUTES

TUNA AND PASTA SALAD

500 g (1 lb 2 oz) conchiglie (shell pasta)
200 g (7 oz) beans, trimmed
2 red capsicums (peppers), thinly sliced
2 spring onions (scallions), chopped
425 g (15 oz) tinned tuna, in oil
2 tablespoons olive oil
60 ml (2 fl oz/¹/₄ cup) white wine vinegar
1 tablespoon lemon juice
1 garlic clove, crushed
1 teaspoon sugar
1 Lebanese (short) cucumber, thinly sliced
6 hard-boiled eggs, quartered
4 tomatoes, cut into eighths
80 g (2³/₄ oz/¹/₂ cup) black olives
2 tablespoons chopped basil

SERVES 6

Cook the pasta in a large saucepan of rapidly boiling salted water until *al dente*. Drain, rinse under cold water and drain again.

Cut the beans into short lengths. Combine the pasta, beans, capsicum and spring onion in a large bowl and mix well. Drain the tuna, reserving the oil, and flake with a fork.

Combine the reserved tuna oil, oil, vinegar, lemon juice, garlic and sugar in a small screw-top jar. Shake vigorously for 2 minutes, or until well combined.

Spoon the pasta into the centre of a large serving platter. Arrange the cucumber, egg and tomato around the edge of the platter, and drizzle with half the dressing. Scatter the flaked tuna, olives and basil over the salad and drizzle with the remaining dressing just before serving.

PREPARATION TIME: 20 MINUTES   COOKING TIME: 15 MINUTES

Pastrami, mushroom and cucumber salad

SPICED LAMB RICE

3 lamb shanks (about 1 kg/2 lb 4 oz)
1 large onion, sliced
10 whole cloves
1 cinnamon stick
5 cardamom pods
60 ml (2 fl oz/^{1}/$_4$ cup) melted ghee or oil
1 teaspoon crushed garlic
2 onions, extra, thinly sliced,
^{1}/$_4$ teaspoon ground cinnamon
^{1}/$_4$ teaspoon ground cloves
^{1}/$_4$ teaspoon freshly grated nutmeg
600 g (1 lb 5 oz/3 cups) long-grain white rice
^{1}/$_4$ teaspoon saffron threads
currants, to garnish
shelled pistachios, to garnish

SERVES 4

Put the lamb in a large saucepan with the onion, cloves, cinnamon stick, cardamom pods, 2 litres (70 fl oz/8 cups) water and 1^1/$_2$ teaspoons salt. Bring to the boil. Simmer for 1–1^1/$_2$ hours, or until the meat is tender, occasionally skimming any scum off the surface. Remove the shanks from the cooking liquid, then cool slightly. Strain the remaining liquid into a large measuring cup — you need 1.25 litres (44 fl oz/5 cups). If necessary, add some water.

Heat the ghee or oil in a small saucepan and cook the garlic and extra onion gently until well reduced and just golden. Add the ground spices and ^{1}/$_4$ teaspoon freshly ground black pepper.

Remove the meat from the shanks and cut into cubes. Put in a bowl with the onion and spice mixture.

Wash and drain the rice. Put half of it in a large saucepan with a tight-fitting lid and cover with the onion and lamb mixture. Put the remaining rice on top.

Cook the saffron threads in a dry frying pan over a low heat until dry and crisp, stirring constantly. Allow to cool. Put the strands in a bowl and crush with the back of a spoon. Add 60 ml (2 fl oz/^{1}/$_4$ cup) water and dissolve.

Gently pour the reserved cooking liquid and dissolved saffron into the saucepan with the rice and lamb mixture and bring to the boil. Cover, reduce the heat to very low and cook for 20 minutes. Remove the lid, then lightly fluff up the rice. Serve at room temperature, garnished with currants and pistachios.

PREPARATION TIME: 30 MINUTES   COOKING TIME: 2 HOURS

GREEN PAPAYA SALAD

370 g (13 oz) green papaya, peeled and seeded
90 g (3¼ oz) snake beans, trimmed and cut into 2 cm (¾ inch) lengths
2 garlic cloves
2 small red chillies, chopped
5 teaspoons dried shrimp
8 cherry tomatoes, halved
50 g (1¾ oz) coriander (cilantro) sprigs
40 g (1½ oz/¼ cup) chopped roasted peanuts

DRESSING
60 ml (2 fl oz/¼ cup) fish sauce
2 tablespoons tamarind purée
1 tablespoon lime juice
3 tablespoons grated palm sugar (jaggery) or soft brown sugar

SERVES 6

Grate the papaya, sprinkle with salt and leave for 30 minutes. Rinse well.

Cook the beans in a saucepan of boiling water for 3 minutes, or until tender. Drain, plunge into cold water, then drain again.

To make the dressing, combine all ingredients in a small bowl. Set aside.

Pound the garlic and chilli using a large mortar and pestle until crushed. Add the dried shrimp and pound until puréed. Add the papaya and snake beans and lightly pound for 1 minute. Add the tomato and pound briefly to bruise.

Combine the coriander with the papaya mixture and spoon onto serving plates. Pour the dressing over the top. Sprinkle with the peanuts and, if desired, sliced red chilli.

PREPARATION TIME: 25 MINUTES +   COOKING TIME: 5 MINUTES

WILD RICE SALAD

95 g (3¼ oz/½ cup) wild rice
250 ml (9 fl oz/1 cup) chicken stock
20 g (¾ oz) butter
100 g (3½ oz/½ cup) basmati rice
60 g (2¼ oz/½ cup) slivered almonds
1 tablespoon olive oil
2 back bacon slices, chopped
125 g (4½ oz) currants
30 g (1 oz) chopped flat-leaf (Italian) parsley
6 spring onions (scallions), thinly sliced
grated zest and juice of 1 lemon
olive oil, to drizzle
lemon wedges, to serve

SERVES 4

Put the wild rice and stock in a saucepan. Add the butter, bring to the boil, then cook, covered, over low heat for 1 hour. Drain.

Meanwhile, put the basmati rice in a separate saucepan with cold water and bring to the boil. Cook at a simmer for 12 minutes, then drain.

Mix the rices together in a bowl and allow to cool to room temperature.

Lightly toast the almonds in a dry frying pan for a few minutes, or until lightly golden. Heat the oil in the same pan and cook the bacon for 5 minutes, or until cooked. Remove from the pan and cool.

Combine the rice with the bacon, currants, almonds, parsley, spring onion and lemon zest and juice. Season, drizzle with oil and serve with lemon.

PREPARATION TIME: 20 MINUTES +   COOKING TIME: 1 HOUR

Green papaya salad

MIXED SEAFOOD SALAD

1.25 kg (2 lb 12 oz) large cooked prawns
(shrimp)
12 cooked yabbies or crayfish
500 g (1 lb 2 oz) scallops
125 ml (4 fl oz/$\frac{1}{2}$ cup) dry white wine
pinch dried thyme
pinch dried tarragon or a bay leaf
400 g (14 oz) salmon, trout or firm white
fish fillets, such as flake, hake or ling
6 hard-boiled eggs
150 g (5$\frac{1}{2}$ oz) mixed lettuce leaves
2 tablespoons chopped flat-leaf (Italian)
parsley
2 ripe avocados, sliced
2 tablespoons lemon juice

VINAIGRETTE
125 ml (4 fl oz/$\frac{1}{2}$ cup) extra virgin
olive oil
2 tablespoons white wine vinegar
1 teaspoon sugar
2 teaspoons dijon mustard
1 tablespoon chopped dill

GREEN GODDESS DRESSING
310 g (11 oz/1$\frac{1}{4}$ cups) whole-egg
mayonnaise
4 tinned anchovy fillets, drained, and
finely chopped
1 garlic clove, crushed
60 g (2$\frac{1}{4}$ oz/$\frac{1}{4}$ cup) sour cream
3 tablespoons chopped herbs, such as
chives, parsley or dill

SERVES 8

Peel the prawns, leaving the tails intact. Gently pull out the dark vein from each prawn back, starting from the head end.

Cut down each side of the shell on the underside of each yabby with kitchen scissors, starting at the head and working towards the tail. Pull back the flap and remove the meat from each shell. Gently pull out the vein from each back and discard each shell.

Slice or pull off any vein, membrane or hard white muscle from the scallops.

Put 250 ml (9 fl oz/1 cup) water with the wine, herbs and a pinch each of salt and pepper in a saucepan. Bring to the boil, then reduce the heat and simmer for 5 minutes. Add the scallops and poach for a few minutes, or until they have just turned white, then remove with a slotted spoon and drain on a wire rack. Add the fish fillets to the gently simmering liquid. Poach until cooked and just tender, remove with a slotted spoon and drain on a wire rack. Break into large pieces.

Combine the prawns, yabbies, scallops and fish in a bowl. To make the vinaigrette, whisk together the oil, vinegar, sugar, mustard and dill, and season, to taste. Pour over the seafood, cover and refrigerate for 1 hour.

Peel and slice the eggs, reserving 2 yolks. Put half the lettuce leaves in a deep serving bowl. Arrange half the seafood over the lettuce, reserving the vinaigrette. Sprinkle with half the parsley, top with half the avocado, drizzle with half the lemon juice, then finish with half the sliced eggs, including the extra whites. Season with salt and pepper. Repeat the layers and season to taste. Drizzle with the reserved vinaigrette. Crumble the reserved egg yolks over the top. Serve with the green goddess dressing.

To make the green goddess dressing, mix all the ingredients in a bowl and season to taste.

PREPARATION TIME: 1 HOUR +   COOKING TIME: 20 MINUTES

CHICKPEA SALAD WITH CUMIN DRESSING

220 g (7³/₄ oz/1 cup) dried chickpeas
3 tablespoons finely chopped flat-leaf (Italian) parsley
1 small red onion, finely chopped
1 garlic clove, finely chopped
60 ml (2 fl oz/¹/₄ cup) lemon juice
2 tablespoons olive oil
¹/₂ teaspoon ground cumin
pinch cayenne pepper

SERVES 6

Soak the dried chickpeas in plenty of cold water for 8 hours, or overnight. Drain, put in a large saucepan, cover with water and bring to the boil over high heat. Reduce the heat to low and simmer for 1¹/₂ hours, topping up with water to keep the chickpeas covered. Drain and cool.

Combine in a large bowl with the parsley, onion, garlic clove, lemon juice, olive oil, ground cumin, cayenne pepper and ¹/₂ teaspoon each of salt and freshly ground black pepper. Toss well.

PREPARATION TIME: 20 MINUTES +   COOKING TIME: 1 HOUR 30 MINUTES

IDIYAPPAM

225 g (8 oz) rice sticks or dried rice vermicelli
80 ml (2¹/₂ fl oz/¹/₃ cup) oil
50 g (1³/₄ oz) cashew nuts
¹/₂ onion, chopped
3 eggs
150 g (5¹/₂ oz) fresh or frozen peas
10 curry leaves
2 carrots, grated
2 leeks, white part only, finely shredded
1 red capsicum (pepper), diced
2 tablespoons tomato sauce (ketchup)
1 tablespoon soy sauce

SERVES 4

Soak the rice sticks in cold water for about 30 minutes, then drain and put them in a saucepan of boiling water. Remove from the heat and leave in the pan for 3 minutes. Drain and refresh in cold water.

Heat 1 tablespoon of the oil in a frying pan and fry the cashews until golden. Remove, add the onion to the pan, fry until dark golden, then drain on paper towels.

Cook the eggs in boiling water for 10 minutes to hard-boil, then cool them immediately in cold water. When cold, peel and cut into wedges.

Cook the peas in boiling water until tender.

Heat the remaining oil in a frying pan and briefly fry the curry leaves. Add the carrot, leek and red capsicum and stir for 1 minute. Add the tomato sauce, soy sauce, 1 teaspoon salt and rice sticks and mix, stirring constantly to prevent the rice sticks from sticking to the pan. Serve on a platter and garnish with the peas, cashews, fried onion and egg wedges.

PREPARATION TIME: 10 MINUTES +   COOKING TIME: 20 MINUTES

Chickpea salad with cumin dressing

WILD RICE SALAD WITH CHINESE ROAST DUCK

200 g (7 oz/1 cup) wild rice
200 g (7 oz/1 cup) basmati or jasmine rice
16 thin asparagus spears, woody ends trimmed, sliced
8 spring onions (scallions), thinly sliced
100 g (3½ oz) pecans, roughly chopped
100 g (3½ oz) dried cranberries
zest and juice of 1 orange
1 whole Chinese roast duck

DRESSING
125 ml (4 fl oz/½ cup) soy sauce
2 tablespoons sugar
1½ tablespoons balsamic vinegar
1½ tablespoons peanut oil
2 teaspoons sesame oil
2 teaspoons grated fresh ginger
2 small red chillies, finely chopped

SERVES 4–6

Put the wild rice in a saucepan of cold salted water, bring to the boil and cook for 30 minutes. Add the basmati or jasmine rice and continue to cook for a further 10 minutes, or until both rices are just cooked. Drain and refresh under cold water, then drain again and transfer to a large bowl.

Blanch the asparagus in a saucepan of boiling water, then drain and refresh under cold water. Add to the bowl with the rice.

Add the spring onion, pecans, dried cranberries and orange zest to the rice and mix together well.

Combine all the dressing ingredients and the orange juice in a screw-top jar and shake well.

Preheat the oven to 200°C (400°F/Gas 6). Remove the skin from the duck and break it into rough pieces. Shred the duck meat and add it to the salad. Put the skin on a baking tray and bake for 5 minutes, or until crispy. Drain on paper towel, then slice.

If necessary, shake the dressing again before pouring it over the salad. Toss to combine. Serve the salad in individual bowls, topped with pieces of crispy duck skin.

PREPARATION TIME: 15 MINUTES   COOKING TIME: 50 MINUTES

LENTIL SALAD

1 small onion
2 whole cloves
300 g (10$\frac{1}{2}$ oz/1$\frac{1}{2}$ cups) puy lentils or tiny blue-green lentils (see Note)
1 strip lemon zest
2 garlic cloves, peeled
1 bay leaf
2 teaspoons ground cumin
2 tablespoons red wine vinegar
60 ml (2 fl oz/$\frac{1}{4}$ cup) olive oil
1 tablespoon lemon juice
2 tablespoons finely chopped mint
3 spring onions (scallions), thinly sliced

SERVES 4–6

Stud the onion with the cloves and put in a saucepan with the lentils, zest, garlic, bay leaf, 1 teaspoon of the cumin and 875 ml (28 fl oz/ 3$\frac{1}{2}$ cups) water. Bring to the boil and simmer gently over medium heat for 25–30 minutes, or until the lentils are tender. Drain off any excess liquid and discard the onion, zest and bay leaf. Reserve the garlic and finely chop.

Whisk together the vinegar, oil, lemon juice, garlic and remaining cumin. Stir the dressing through the lentils with the mint and spring onion. Season well, then leave for 30 minutes to allow the flavours to develop. Serve at room temperature.

PREPARATION TIME: 15 MINUTES +   COOKING TIME: 30 MINUTES

NOTE: Puy lentils are small green lentils, available from gourmet food stores.

FAST SPINACH SALAD

2 tablespoons olive oil
1 garlic clove, crushed
2 teaspoons white wine vinegar
100 g (3$\frac{1}{2}$ oz) mushrooms, thinly sliced
300 g (10$\frac{1}{2}$ oz) English spinach leaves, torn
2 hard-boiled eggs, sliced
100 g (3$\frac{1}{2}$ oz) feta cheese

SERVES 2–4

In a large bowl, mix together the olive oil, garlic, white wine vinegar and a little black pepper. Add the mushrooms and stir to coat well.

Put the spinach leaves in a salad bowl. Add mushrooms and dressing and the egg. Toss well. Crumble the feta cheese over the top.

PREPARATION TIME: 15 MINUTES   COOKING TIME: NIL

CHICKEN AND CHORIZO PAELLA

60 ml (2 fl oz/¼ cup) olive oil
1 large red capsicum (pepper), cut into
5 mm (¼ inch) strips
600 g (1 lb 5 oz) boneless, skinless
chicken thighs, cut into
3 cm (1¼ inch) cubes
200 g (7 oz) chorizo, cut into 2 cm
(¾ inch) slices
200 g (7 oz) mushrooms, thinly sliced
3 garlic cloves, crushed
1 tablespoon grated lemon zest
700 g (1 lb 9 oz) ripe tomatoes, roughly
chopped
200 g (7 oz) green beans, trimmed and
cut into 3 cm (1¼ inch) lengths
1 tablespoon chopped rosemary
2 tablespoons chopped flat-leaf (Italian)
parsley
¼ teaspoon saffron threads dissolved in
60 ml (2 fl oz/¼ cup) hot water
440 g (15½ oz/2 cups) short-grain
white rice
750 ml (26 fl oz/3 cups) hot chicken stock
6 lemon wedges, to serve

SERVES 6

Heat the olive oil in a paella pan or in a large, heavy-based, deep frying pan over medium heat. Add the red capsicum strips and cook, stirring, for about 6 minutes, or until softened, then remove from the pan.

Add the chicken to the pan and cook for 10 minutes, or until browned. Remove from the pan. Add the chorizo to the pan and cook for 5 minutes, or until golden. Remove from the pan. Add the mushrooms, garlic and lemon zest to the pan, and cook over medium heat for 5 minutes.

Stir in the tomato and capsicum, and cook for a further 5 minutes, or until the tomato is soft.

Add the beans, rosemary, parsley, saffron mixture, rice, chicken and chorizo. Stir briefly and add the stock. Do not stir at this point. Reduce the heat and simmer for 30 minutes. Remove from the heat, cover and leave to stand for 10 minutes. Serve with lemon wedges.

PREPARATION TIME: 30 MINUTES +   COOKING TIME: 1 HOUR 5 MINUTES

NOTE: Paella pans are available from specialist kitchenware shops.

PLATES AND NAPKINS

ROSETTAS

7 g (¹/₄ oz) dried yeast
1 teaspoon sugar
560 g (1 lb 4 oz/4¹/₂ cups) unbleached plain (all-purpose) flour, sifted
50 g (1³/₄ oz) butter, softened
60 ml (2 fl oz/¹/₄ cup) olive oil
55 g (2 oz/¹/₄ cup) caster (superfine) sugar
milk, to glaze
plain (all-purpose) flour, extra, to dust

MAKES 10

Lightly grease two baking trays. Put the yeast, sugar and 125 ml (4 fl oz/ ¹/₂ cup) warm water in a small bowl and stir well. Leave in a warm, draught-free place for 10 minutes, or until bubbles appear on the surface. The mixture should be frothy and slightly increased in volume. If your yeast doesn't foam it is dead, so you will have to discard it and start again.

Set aside 30 g (1 oz/¹/₄ cup) of the flour and put the rest in a large bowl with 1 teaspoon salt. Make a well in the centre. Add the yeast mixture, butter, oil, sugar and 315 ml (10³/₄ fl oz/1¹/₄ cups) warm water. Stir with a wooden spoon until the dough leaves the side of the bowl and forms a rough, sticky ball. Turn out onto a floured surface. Knead for 10 minutes, or until the dough is smooth and elastic. Add enough of the reserved flour, if necessary, to make a smooth dough. Put in a large, lightly oiled bowl and brush the surface with melted butter or oil. Cover with plastic wrap and leave in a warm place for 1 hour, or until well risen.

Punch down the dough, then knead for 1 minute. Divide into ten portions and shape each into a smooth ball. Place the balls 5 cm (2 inches) apart on the trays. Using a 3 cm (1¹/₄ inch) round cutter, press a 1 cm (¹/₂ inch) deep indent into the centre of each ball. With a sharp knife, score five evenly spaced, 1 cm (¹/₂ inch) deep cuts down the side of each roll. Cover with plastic wrap or a damp tea towel (dish towel) and leave in a warm place for 1 hour, or until well risen.

Preheat the oven to 180°C (350°F/Gas 4). Brush the rolls with milk and sift a fine layer of the extra flour over them. Bake for 25 minutes, or until golden. Rotate the trays in the oven if one tray is browning faster than the other. Allow to cool on a wire rack.

PREPARATION TIME: 40 MINUTES +   COOKING TIME: 25 MINUTES

NOTE: These are best eaten on the day of cooking, or they can be frozen for up to 1 month.

CHEESE AND SPINACH ROULADE BRUSCHETTA

1 baguette or crusty Italian loaf
2 tablespoons oil
500 g (1 lb 2 oz) English spinach
90 g (3¼ oz) cream cheese
90 g (3¼ oz) goat's cheese
3 tablespoons tinned pimiento, drained
and finely chopped

MAKES ABOUT 24

Preheat the oven to 200°C (400°F/Gas 6). Cut the bread into 1 cm (½ inch) slices, brush with olive oil and grill (broil) until golden on both sides.

Remove the stalks from the spinach and put the leaves in a bowl. Cover with boiling water and leave for a couple of minutes, or until the leaves have wilted. Drain and leave to cool. Squeeze out the excess liquid and drain on crumpled paper towel.

Lay the spinach leaves flat, overlapping, on a piece of plastic wrap, to form a 20 x 25 cm (8 x 10 inch) rectangle. Beat the cheeses together until soft and smooth. Spread the cheese mixture evenly and carefully over the spinach. Top the cheese evenly with pimiento. Using the plastic wrap as a guide, roll up the spinach to enclose the cheese. Remove the plastic wrap and cut the log into thin slices using a sharp knife. Serve on the toast.

PREPARATION TIME: 30 MINUTES   COOKING TIME: 10 MINUTES

NOTES: The bread slices can be baked several days ahead and stored in an airtight container.

The roulade can be made a day ahead and stored, wrapped in plastic wrap, in the refrigerator. Assemble just before serving time.

SMOKED SALMON AND CAPER BRUSCHETTA

1 baguette or crusty Italian loaf
250 g (9 oz) cream cheese
2 tablespoons lemon juice
15 g (½ oz) snipped chives
100 g (3½ oz) smoked salmon, sliced
2 tablespoons baby capers, rinsed
2 dill sprigs, to garnish

MAKES ABOUT 24

Cut the bread into 1 cm (½ inch) slices, brush with olive oil and grill (broil) until golden on both sides.

Mix the cream cheese with the lemon juice and chives. Spread over the toast and top with small slices of smoked salmon and a few baby capers. Garnish with sprigs of dill before serving.

PREPARATION TIME: 20 MINUTES   COOKING TIME: 5 MINUTES

Cheese and spinach roulade bruschetta

OLIVE OIL BISCUITS WITH TOMATO FETA SALSA

7 g (¼ oz) dried yeast or 15 g (½ oz) fresh yeast

1 teaspoon sugar

185 g (6½ oz/1½ cups) plain (all purpose) flour

225 g (8 oz/1½ cups) plain (all-purpose) wholemeal (whole-wheat) flour

1 teaspoon ground cinnamon

1½ tablespoons sesame seeds, toasted

125 ml (4 fl oz/½ cup) olive oil

TOMATO FETA SALSA

4 ripe tomatoes, diced

160 g (5¾ oz) feta cheese, crumbled

80 ml (2½ fl oz/⅓ cup) extra virgin olive oil

2 tablespoons red wine vinegar

1 teaspoon dried oregano

MAKES ABOUT 45

Mix the yeast, sugar, 2 tablespoons of the plain flour and 60 ml (2 fl oz/ ¼ cup) warm water in a bowl. Cover with plastic wrap and leave in a warm place for 10 minutes, or until frothy.

Sift the remaining flours and cinnamon into a large bowl, return the husks to the bowl and stir through the sesame seeds and ½ teaspoon salt. Pour in the oil and rub it in by lifting the flour mixture onto one hand and lightly rubbing the other hand over the top. Make a well in the centre and add the yeast mixture and about 60 ml (2 fl oz/¼ cup) warm water, or enough to mix to a soft but not sticky dough. Knead on a floured surface for about 2 minutes, or until smooth and elastic. Put in a lightly oiled bowl, turning the dough to coat in the oil. Cover loosely with plastic wrap and leave in a warm place for 45–60 minutes, or until doubled in bulk.

Preheat the oven to 200°C (400°F/Gas 6). Lightly grease a baking tray. Punch down the dough to expel the air, divide it into three portions and roll each on a lightly floured surface into a long sausage shape about 30 cm (12 inches) long. Put the first roll on the baking tray. Cut through almost to the base of the roll at 2 cm (¾ inch) intervals with a serrated knife (about 15 portions). Repeat with the remaining rolls.

Cover with a tea towel (dish towel) and leave in a warm place for 30 minutes, or until well risen. Bake for 30 minutes, or until browned underneath and the rolls sound hollow when tapped. Reduce the oven temperature to 120°C (250°F/ Gas ½). Cool the rolls on the tray for 5 minutes. Transfer each roll to a cutting board and cut through the markings. Place, cut side up, on two baking trays. Bake for 30 minutes, or until the tops feel dry. Turn each biscuit and bake for a further 30 minutes, or until completely dry and crisp. Allow to cool. Store in an airtight container for up to 3 weeks.

Dunk each biscuit quickly into cold water and place on a tray. Top with the combined tomato and feta. Drizzle with the combined oil and vinegar and sprinkle with oregano. Season.

PREPARATION TIME: 30 MINUTES + COOKING TIME: 1 HOUR 30 MINUTES

SPANISH TORTILLA

125 ml (4 fl oz/¹/₂ cup) olive oil
2 large all-purpose potatoes, peeled and
cut into 5 mm (¹/₄ inch) slices
2 large onions, sliced
3 eggs

MAKES 16 WEDGES

Heat the oil in a 20 cm (8 inch) diameter deep non-stick frying pan with a lid. Place alternate layers of potato and onion in the pan, cover and cook for 8 minutes over low heat. Using tongs, turn the layers in sections (it doesn't matter if they break up). Cover and cook for 8 minutes, without allowing the potato to colour.

Put a strainer over a bowl and drain the potato mixture, reserving 1 tablespoon of the oil.

Put the eggs and a little salt and pepper in a bowl and whisk to combine. Add the potato mixture, pressing down with the back of a spoon to completely cover with the egg.

Heat the reserved oil in the same frying pan over high heat. Pour in the egg mixture, pressing down to even it out. Reduce the heat to low, cover with a lid and cook for 12 minutes, or until set. Gently shake the pan to ensure the tortilla is not sticking. Leave for 5 minutes, then invert onto a plate. Cut into wedges. Serve at room temperature.

PREPARATION TIME: 20 MINUTES +   COOKING TIME: 30 MINUTES

ROCKET AND FETA BRUSCHETTA

1 baguette or crusty Italian loaf
90 g (3¹/₄ oz) rocket (arugula) leaves
200 g (7 oz) feta cheese, crumbled
2 teaspoons finely grated orange zest
2 tablespoons olive oil
6 prosciutto slices

MAKES ABOUT 30

Cut the bread into 1 cm (¹/₂ inch) slices, brush with olive oil and grill (broil) until golden on both sides.

Arrange the rocket leaves over each piece. Toss the feta with the orange zest and olive oil. Spoon 2 teaspoons of the mixture over the rocket on each bruschetta.

Grill (broil) the prosciutto until crispy, then crumble over the bruschetta.

PREPARATION TIME: 10 MINUTES . COOKING TIME: 10 MINUTES

Spanish tortilla

CROSTINI WITH CAPSICUM ROULADE

2 red capsicums (peppers)
2 yellow capsicums (peppers)
8 English spinach leaves
1 tablespoon chopped flat-leaf (Italian)
parsley
1 small baguette
2 tablespoons olive oil
shaved parmesan cheese, to garnish

MAKES ABOUT 20

Preheat the grill (broiler). Cut each capsicum in half and grill, skin side up, until the skin is black and blistered. Cool in a plastic bag, then peel.

Remove the stalks from the spinach and put the leaves in a bowl. Cover with boiling water and set aside for a couple of minutes until the leaves have wilted. Drain and cool. Squeeze out the excess water and spread the leaves out. Pat dry with paper towels.

Lay two sheets of overlapping plastic wrap on a flat surface. Flatten out the red capsicum to form a rectangle, overlapping the ends. Lay the spinach leaves over the capsicum to make a second layer. Put the flattened yellow capsicum on top to make a third layer, making sure there are no gaps, and overlapping the ends. Sprinkle with the parsley. Using the plastic wrap to assist, roll up the capsicum tightly lengthways, sealing the ends. Wrap tightly in foil, twist the ends firmly and chill for 3 hours.

Preheat the oven to 200°C (400°F/Gas 6). Cut the baguette stick into 1 cm (^{1}/2 inch) slices. Put on a baking tray, lightly brush with olive oil, sprinkle with salt and bake for 5–10 minutes, or until golden.

Remove the plastic wrap, cut the roulade into 1.5 cm (^{5}/8 inch) thick slices and place on the crostini. Drizzle with oil. Garnish with parmesan.

PREPARATION TIME: 30 MINUTES +   COOKING TIME: 10 MINUTES

NOTE: The topping and the bread can be prepared separately up to 6 hours in advance. However, don't top the bread any earlier than 30 minutes before serving as it may go soft.

CHILLI POLENTA CAKE

165 g (5¾ oz/1⅓ cups) plain (all purpose) flour
1½ teaspoons baking powder
185 g (6½ oz/1¼ cups) polenta
125 g (4½ oz/1 cup) grated cheddar cheese
250 g (9 oz/1 cup) plain yoghurt
125 ml (4 fl oz/½ cup) milk
2 eggs
80 g (2¾ oz/½ cup) chopped red capsicum (pepper)
2 teaspoons chopped chilli
60 g (2¼ oz) unsalted butter

MAKES ONE 20 CM (8 INCH) CAKE

Preheat the oven to 200°C (400°F/Gas 6). Sift the flour, baking powder and 1 teaspoon salt into a large bowl. Mix in the polenta and cheese.

In a separate bowl, whisk together the yoghurt, milk, eggs, red capsicum and chilli.

Heat a 20 cm (8 inch) ovenproof frying pan and melt the butter. Stir the butter into the yoghurt mixture. Pour all the liquid ingredients into the dry ingredients. Mix well.

Pour into the frying pan. Cook in the oven for 25–30 minutes, or until a skewer inserted in the centre comes out clean.

PREPARATION TIME: 25 MINUTES   COOKING TIME: 30 MINUTES

CHILLI AND CORIANDER FRITTATA

3 all-purpose potatoes, cut into small cubes
2 banana chillies
2 tablespoons olive oil
1 onion, finely chopped
1 small red chilli, finely chopped
1 tablespoon chopped coriander (cilantro) leaves
5 eggs, beaten

SERVES 6

Cook the potatoes in a large saucepan of boiling water until just tender. Drain well.

Remove the seeds from the banana chillies and slice the flesh. Heat half the oil in a non-stick frying pan. Cook the banana chilli over medium heat for 2 minutes, or until softened. Remove from the pan and set aside. Heat the remaining oil in the pan. Add the onion and red chilli. Cook over medium heat for 3 minutes, or until soft. Add the potato and toss to combine. Remove from the pan and set aside.

Return half the banana chilli to the pan and sprinkle with the coriander. Layer half the potato mixture, banana chilli, and remaining potato mixture.

Pour the eggs into the pan. Cook over medium–low heat for 8 minutes, or until the eggs are almost cooked through, then put under a hot grill (broiler) for 4 minutes to cook the top. Invert the frittata onto a plate. Allow to cool, then cut into wedges. Serve cold.

PREPARATION TIME: 25 MINUTES   COOKING TIME: 30 MINUTES

VEGETABLE FRITTATA WITH HUMMUS AND BLACK OLIVES

HUMMUS
425 g (15 oz) tinned chickpeas, drained
2 garlic cloves, crushed
80 ml (2^1/$_2$ fl oz/^{1}/$_3$ cup) lemon juice
2 tablespoons plain yoghurt

2 large red capsicums (peppers)
600 g (1 lb 5 oz) orange sweet potato
500 g (1 lb 2 oz) eggplant (aubergine)
80 ml (2^1/$_2$ fl oz/^{1}/$_3$ cup) olive oil
2 leeks, thinly sliced
2 garlic cloves, crushed
250 g (9 oz) zucchini (courgettes), thinly sliced
8 eggs, lightly beaten
2 tablespoons finely chopped basil
125 g (4^1/$_2$ oz) parmesan cheese, grated
60 g (2^1/$_4$ oz) black olives, pitted and halved, to serve

MAKES 30 SQUARES

To make the hummus, in a food processor, purée the chickpeas, garlic, lemon juice, yoghurt and a pinch of black pepper.

Preheat the grill (broiler). Cut the capsicums into quarters and grill, skin side up, until the skin is black and blistered. Cool in a plastic bag, then peel.

Cut the sweet potato into 1 cm (^{1}/$_2$ inch) thick slices and cook until just tender, then drain.

Cut the eggplant into 1 cm (^{1}/$_2$ inch) slices. Heat 1 tablespoon of the oil in a 23 cm (9 inch) round, deep frying pan and stir the leek and garlic over medium heat for 1 minute, or until soft. Add the zucchini and cook for another 2 minutes. Remove from the pan and set aside.

Heat the remaining oil in the same frying pan and cook the eggplant slices, in batches, for 1 minute each side, or until golden. Line the base of the pan with half the eggplant and spread the leek over the top. Cover with the roasted capsicum, remaining eggplant and sweet potato.

Combine the eggs, basil, parmesan and some black pepper in a jug, pour over the vegetables and cook over low heat for 15 minutes, or until almost cooked. Put the frying pan under a preheated grill (broiler) for 2-3 minutes, or until the frittata is golden and cooked. Cool for 10 minutes before inverting onto a cutting board. Trim the edges and cut into 30 squares. Top with hummus and olives. Serve at room temperature.

PREPARATION TIME: 30 MINUTES + COOKING TIME: 35 MINUTES

HERBED GOAT'S CHEESE

200 g (7 oz) vine leaves in brine
3 teaspoons green or pink peppercorns,
drained and chopped
1 tablespoon chopped marjoram
3 x 100 g (3½ oz) rounds soft goat's
cheese

SERVES 6–8

Place the vine leaves in a heatproof bowl and cover with hot water to rinse away the brine. Drain well and pat dry with paper towels.

Combine the peppercorns and marjoram in a shallow bowl. Toss the goat's cheese in the mixture until the sides are well coated.

Arrange a few vine leaves, shiny side down, on a work surface. Wrap each goat's cheese round in a few layers of vine leaves.

Cook the cheese on a barbecue hotplate or under a hot grill (broiler) for 3 minutes each side, or until the outside leaves are charred. Transfer to a plate and allow to cool to room temperature. (The cheese is too soft to serve when hot, but will firm as it cools.) Use scissors to cut away the vine leaves and serve the cheese with the rye bread.

PREPARATION TIME: 20 MINUTES   COOKING TIME: 10 MINUTES

NOTE: The cheese can be wrapped in the vine leaves a few hours ahead.

MINI CRAB AND LIME QUICHES

2 sheets frozen puff pastry, thawed
2 eggs
185 ml (6 fl oz/¾ cup) coconut cream
finely grated zest of 1 small lime
2 teaspoons lime juice
200 g (7 oz) tinned crabmeat, drained
1 tablespoon snipped chives
white pepper, to season

MAKES 18

Preheat the oven to 210°C (415°F/Gas 6–7). Using two 12-hole round-based patty pans or mini muffin tins, lightly grease 18 of the holes. Cut 18 rounds of pastry, using an 8 cm (3 inch) cutter.

Beat the eggs lightly in a small bowl and add the remaining ingredients. Season with salt and white pepper. Spoon about 1 tablespoon of the filling into each pastry case.

Bake for 20 minutes, or until golden. The quiches will rise during cooking, then deflate slightly. Serve at room temperature.

PREPARATION TIME: 15 MINUTES   COOKING TIME: 20 MINUTES

Herbed goat's cheese

KIBBEH

235 g (8½ oz/1⅓ cups) fine burghul
(bulgur)
150 g (5½ oz) lean lamb, chopped
1 onion, grated
2 tablespoons plain (all-purpose) flour
1 teaspoon ground allspice

FILLING
2 teaspoons olive oil
1 small onion, finely chopped
100 g (3½ oz) lean minced (ground) lamb
½ teaspoon ground allspice
½ teaspoon ground cinnamon
80 ml (2½ fl oz/⅓ cup) beef stock
2 tablespoons pine nuts
2 tablespoons chopped mint

MAKES 15

Put the burghul in a large bowl, cover with boiling water and leave for 5 minutes. Drain in a colander, pressing well to remove the water. Spread on paper towels to absorb the remaining moisture.

Process the burghul, lamb, onion, flour and allspice until a fine paste forms. Season well, then refrigerate for 1 hour.

To make the filling, heat the oil in a frying pan, add the onion and cook over low heat for 3 minutes, or until soft. Add the lamb, allspice and cinnamon, and stir over high heat for 3 minutes. Add the stock and cook, partially covered, over low heat for 6 minutes, or until the lamb is soft. Roughly chop the pine nuts and stir in with the mint. Season, then transfer to a bowl and allow to cool.

Shape 2 tablespoons of the burghul mixture into a sausage shape 6 cm (2½ inches) long. Dip your hands in cold water and, with your finger, make a long hole through the centre and gently work your finger around to make a shell. Fill with 2 teaspoons of the filling and seal, moulding it into a torpedo shape. Smooth over any cracks with your fingers. Put on a foil-lined tray and repeat with the remaining ingredients to make 15 kibbeh. Refrigerate, uncovered, for 1 hour.

Fill a deep heavy-based frying pan one-third full of oil and heat the oil to 180°C (350°F), or until a cube of bread dropped into the oil turns golden brown in 15 seconds. Deep-fry the kibbeh in batches for 2–3 minutes, or until well browned. Drain on crumpled paper towels.

PREPARATION TIME: 45 MINUTES +   COOKING TIME: 25 MINUTES

LAYERED LAMB AND BURGHUL

350 g (12 oz/2 cups) burghul (bulgur)
400 g (14 oz) minced (ground) lamb
1 large onion, finely chopped
1 tablespoon ground cumin
1 teaspoon ground allspice
olive oil, for brushing

FILLING
1 tablespoon olive oil, plus extra
for brushing
1 onion, finely chopped
1 teaspoon ground cinnamon
1 tablespoon ground cumin
500 g (1 lb 2 oz) minced (ground) lamb
80 g (2³/4 oz/¹/2 cup) raisins
100 g (3¹/2 oz) pine nuts, toasted
plain yoghurt, to serve

SERVES 4–6

Soak the burghul in cold water for 30 minutes, then drain and squeeze out excess water. Put the lamb, onion, cumin, allspice and some salt and pepper in a food processor, and process until combined. Add the burghul and process to a paste. Refrigerate until needed. Preheat the oven to 180°C (350°F/Gas 4). Lightly grease a 20 x 30 cm (8 x 12 inch) baking dish.

To make the filling, heat the oil in a large frying pan over medium heat and cook the onion for 5 minutes, or until softened. Add the cinnamon and cumin and stir for 1 minute, or until fragrant. Add the lamb, stirring to break up any lumps, and cook for 5 minutes, or until the meat is brown. Stir in the raisins and nuts and season, to taste.

Press half the burghul mixture into the base of the tin, smoothing the surface with wet hands. Spread the filling over the top, then cover with the remaining burghul, again smoothing the top.

Score a diamond pattern in the top of the mixture with a knife and brush with olive oil. Bake for 40 minutes, or until the top is brown. Cool for 10 minutes before cutting into diamond shapes. Serve with plain yoghurt.

PREPARATION TIME: 30 MINUTES +   COOKING TIME: 55 MINUTES

TROUT, FETTUCINE AND FENNEL FRITTATA

250 g (9 oz) whole smoked trout
200 g (7 oz) fettucine
250 ml (9 fl oz/1 cup) milk
125 ml (4 fl oz/¹/2 cup) pouring (whipping)
cream
4 eggs
pinch freshly grated nutmeg
40 g (1¹/2 oz) thinly sliced fennel
4 spring onions (scallions), sliced
85 g (3 oz/²/3 cup) grated cheddar
cheese

SERVES 4

Preheat the oven to 180°C (350°F/Gas 4). Lightly grease a 23 cm (9 inch) flan dish. Remove and discard the skin and bones from the trout.

Cook the fettucine in a large saucepan of rapidly boiling salted water until *al dente*. Drain.

Combine the milk, cream, eggs and nutmeg in a large bowl and whisk until smooth. Season to taste. Add the trout, fettucine, fennel and spring onion and toss to distribute evenly. Pour into the prepared dish and sprinkle with the cheese. Bake for about 1 hour, or until set.

PREPARATION TIME: 20 MINUTES   COOKING TIME: 1 HOUR 10 MINUTES

Layered lamb and burghul

BACON AND EGG PIE

2 tablespoons oil

4 bacon slices, chopped

250 g (9 oz) frozen shortcrust (pie) pastry, thawed

250 g (9 oz) block frozen ready-made puff pastry, thawed

5 eggs, beaten

60 ml (2 fl oz/¼ cup) pouring (whipping) cream

1 egg, beaten, extra

SERVES 4–6

Lightly grease a 20 cm (8 inch) loose-based pie tin. Heat the oil in a frying pan. Add the bacon and cook over medium heat for a few minutes, or until lightly browned. Drain on paper towels and allow to cool slightly.

Roll out the shortcrust pastry between two sheets of baking paper until slightly larger than the tin. Put in the tin and roll a rolling pin over the tin to trim off any excess pastry. Refrigerate for 20 minutes. Preheat the oven to 210°C (415°F/Gas 6–7).

Line the pastry shell with a piece of baking paper and pour in some baking beads or uncooked rice. Bake for 10 minutes, then remove the paper and beads and cook for a further 10 minutes, or until the pastry is dry and golden. Allow to cool.

Roll out the puff pastry between two sheets of baking paper to a circle large enough to cover the top of the pie. Arrange the bacon over the cooled pastry base and pour the combined egg and cream over the top. Cover the pie with the puff pastry and press on firmly to seal. Trim the pastry edges and decorate the top with shapes cut from the pastry scraps. Brush with the extra egg and bake for 30–35 minutes, or until the pastry is puffed and golden. Serve at room temperature.

PREPARATION TIME: 20 MINUTES +   COOKING TIME: 1 HOUR

NOTE: Bacon and egg pie can be made a day ahead and refrigerated overnight. Allow to come to room temperature before serving.

GOAT'S CHEESE GALETTE

PASTRY
125 g (4¹/₂ oz/1 cup) plain (all-purpose) flour
60 ml (2 fl oz/¹/₄ cup) olive oil

FILLING
1 tablespoon olive oil
2 onions, thinly sliced
1 teaspoon thyme
125 g (4¹/₂ oz) ricotta cheese
100 g (3¹/₂ oz) goat's cheese
2 tablespoons pitted niçoise olives
1 egg, beaten
60 ml (2 fl oz/¹/₄ cup) pouring (whipping) cream

SERVES 6

To make the pastry, sift the flour and a pinch of salt into a bowl and make a well in the centre. Add the olive oil and mix with a flat-bladed knife until crumbly. Gradually add 60–80 ml (2–2¹/₂ fl oz/¹/₄–¹/₃ cup) water until the mixture comes together. Remove and pat together to form a disc. Refrigerate for 30 minutes.

Meanwhile, to make the filling, heat the oil in a frying pan. Add the onion, cover and cook for 30 minutes. Season and stir in half the thyme. Cool.

Preheat the oven to 180°C (350°F/Gas 4). Lightly flour the workbench and roll out the pastry to a 30 cm (12 inch) circle. Then put on a heated baking tray. Evenly spread the onion over the pastry, leaving a 2 cm (³/₄ inch) border. Sprinkle the ricotta and goat's cheese evenly over the onion. Put the olives over the cheeses, then sprinkle with the remaining thyme. Fold the pastry border in to the edge of the filling, pleating as you go.

Combine the egg and cream, then pour over the filling. Bake in the lower half of the oven for 45 minutes, or until the pastry is golden.

PREPARATION TIME: 20 MINUTES +   COOKING TIME: 1 HOUR 15 MINUTES

MEDITERRANEAN SQUARES

1 red onion
3 tablespoons pitted black olives
1 red capsicum (pepper)
1 green capsicum (pepper)
2 tablespoons basil
3 teaspoons balsamic vinegar
2 garlic cloves, crushed
60 ml (2 fl oz/¹/₄ cup) oil
3 garlic cloves, crushed, extra
30 x 40 cm (12 x 16 inch) piece focaccia
90 g (3¹/₄ oz/³/₄ cup) grated cheddar cheese

MAKES ABOUT 20

Preheat the oven to 180°C (350°F/Gas 4) and line a baking tray with foil. Slice the onion and olives. Cut the capsicums in half and cut the remaining flesh into thin strips. Finely shred the basil leaves.

Combine the onion, olives, capsicums, basil, vinegar and garlic in a bowl. Mix well, then cover and set aside.

Combine the oil and extra garlic in a small bowl. Using a serrated knife, split the focaccia through the centre. Brush the focaccia halves with the combined oil and garlic. Arrange the combined olive and capsicum filling evenly over the bottom half of the focaccia. Sprinkle with the cheese and top with the remaining piece of focaccia. Put on the baking tray and bake for 15 minutes, or until the cheese melts. Cut into squares to serve.

PREPARATION TIME: 15 MINUTES   COOKING TIME: 15 MINUTES

Goat's cheese galette

RAISED PORK PIE

1.2 kg (2 lb 10 oz) minced (ground) pork
100 g (3$\frac{1}{2}$ oz/$\frac{2}{3}$ cup) pistachio nuts,
shelled and chopped
2 green apples, peeled and
finely chopped
6 sage leaves, finely chopped
500 g (1 lb 2 oz/4 cups) plain (all-purpose)
flour
150 g (5$\frac{1}{2}$ oz) lard
2 eggs, beaten
1 egg yolk
200 ml (7 fl oz) vegetable stock
200 ml (7 fl oz) unsweetened apple juice
2 teaspoons powdered gelatine

SERVES 8

Preheat the oven to 200°C (400°F/Gas 6). Combine the pork, pistachio nuts, apple and sage leaves in a bowl. Mix well and season. Cover and refrigerate until ready to use. Wrap plastic wrap around a 6 cm (2$\frac{1}{2}$ inch) high, 20 cm (8 inch) diameter round straight-sided tin, then turn the tin over, and grease the outside base and side of the tin.

Sift the flour and 1 teaspoon salt into a bowl and make a well in the centre. Put the lard in a saucepan with 210 ml (7$\frac{1}{2}$ fl oz) water, bring to the boil and add to the flour with the beaten eggs. Mix with a wooden spoon until combined, then turn out onto a work surface and bring the mixture together to form a smooth dough. Unlike any other kind of pastry, this hot water pastry must be kept warm. Cover with a cloth and leave in a warm place for 10 minutes until cool enough to handle.

When the pastry is just warm, set aside one-third — do not refrigerate. Roll the remainder into a circle large enough to just cover the outside of the tin. Lift onto a rolling pin and place over the tin, working fast before the pastry sets. Refrigerate until the pastry hardens. Carefully pull out the tin and remove the plastic wrap. Attach a paper collar made of two layers of greased baking paper around the outside of the pastry so it fits snugly. Secure with string or a paper clip at the top and bottom. Fill the pie with the pork mixture, then roll out the remaining pastry to form a lid. Attach it to the base with some water, pressing or crimping it to make it look neat. Cut a small hole in the top.

Put the pie on a baking tray. Bake for 40 minutes and check the pastry top. If it is still pale, bake for a further 10 minutes, then remove the paper. Brush with egg yolk mixed with 1 tablespoon water and bake for 15 minutes, or until the sides are brown. Remove from the oven and allow to cool completely.

Bring the stock and half the apple juice to the boil. Sprinkle the gelatine over the surface of the remaining apple juice in a measuring cup and leave to go spongy, then pour into the stock and mix until the gelatine dissolves. Put a small funnel (piping nozzles work well) in the hole of the pie and pour in a little of the gelatine mixture, leave to settle and then pour in some more until the pie is full. Fill the pie completely so there will be no gaps when the gelatine sets. Refrigerate overnight.

PREPARATION TIME: 50 MINUTES +   COOKING TIME: 1 HOUR 10 MINUTES

BROWN RICE TART WITH FRESH TOMATO FILLING

RICE CRUST
200 g (7 oz/1 cup) brown rice
60 g (2¼ oz/½ cup) grated cheddar
cheese
1 egg, lightly beaten

FRESH TOMATO FILLING
6 roma (plum) tomatoes, halved
6 garlic cloves, unpeeled
1 tablespoon olive oil
8 lemon thyme sprigs
50 g (1¾ oz) goat's cheese, crumbled
3 eggs, beaten
60 ml (2 fl oz/¼ cup) milk

SERVES 6

To make the rice crust, cook the rice in a saucepan of boiling water for 35 minutes. Drain and set aside. Preheat the oven to 200°C (400°F/Gas 6).

Put the rice, cheese and egg into a bowl and mix until well combined. Spread the mixture over the base and sides of a lightly greased 25 cm (10 inch) flan tin or quiche dish and bake for 15 minutes.

To make the fresh tomato filling, put the tomatoes, cut side up, and garlic on a non-stick baking tray. Brush with oil and sprinkle with pepper. Bake for 30 minutes. Remove from the oven. Cool slightly. Remove the skins from the garlic. Reduce the oven to 180°C (350°F/Gas 4). Arrange the tomato halves, garlic, lemon thyme and goat's cheese over the rice crust.

Put the beaten eggs and milk in a bowl and whisk to combine. Pour over the tomatoes. Bake for 1 hour, or until set.

PREPARATION TIME: 25 MINUTES   COOKING TIME: 2 HOURS 20 MINUTES

SPINACH CROQUETTES

285 g (10 oz/1½ cups) short-grain rice
250 g (9 oz) feta cheese, crumbled
25 g (1 oz/¼ cup) freshly grated parmesan
cheese
2 eggs, beaten
1 garlic clove, crushed
2 teaspoons grated lemon zest
40 g (1½ oz/⅓ cup) chopped spring
onions (scallions)
250 g (9 oz) packet frozen spinach,
thawed, squeezed of excess moisture
1 tablespoon chopped dill
200 g (7 oz/2 cups) dry breadcrumbs
2 eggs, beaten, extra
oil, for deep-frying

MAKES 18

Cook the rice in a large saucepan of boiling water until just tender. Drain, then rinse under cold water, then drain again. Combine the rice, cheeses, egg, garlic, lemon zest, spring onion, spinach and dill in a bowl. Using wet hands, divide the mixture into 18 portions. Roll each portion into even-sized sausage shapes. Put on a tray and refrigerate for 30 minutes.

Spread the breadcrumbs on a sheet of greaseproof paper. Dip the croquettes into the extra beaten egg. Coat with the breadcrumbs and shake off the excess. Refrigerate for a further 30 minutes.

Fill a deep heavy-based frying pan one-third full of oil and heat to 180°C (350°F), or until a spoonful of the batter dropped into the oil turns golden brown in 15 seconds. Lower batches of croquettes into the oil with tongs or a slotted spoon. Cook for 2–3 minutes, or until golden and cooked through. Drain on paper towel. Repeat with the remaining croquettes. Serve cold with plain yoghurt.

PREPARATION TIME: 50 MINUTES +   COOKING TIME: 25 MINUTES

Brown rice tart with fresh tomato filling

DUTCH-STYLE BEEF AND RICE CROQUETTES

BÉCHAMEL SAUCE
20 g ($^3/_4$ oz) butter
30 g (1 oz/$^1/_4$ cup) plain (all-purpose) flour
170 ml (5$^1/_2$ fl oz/$^2/_3$ cup) milk
pinch freshly grated nutmeg

10 g ($^1/_4$ oz) butter
75 g (2$^1/_2$ oz/$^1/_3$ cup) arborio rice
410 ml (14 fl oz/1$^2/_3$ cups) chicken stock
2 tablespoons olive oil
1 onion, finely chopped
2 garlic cloves, crushed
500 g (1 lb 2 oz) lean minced (ground) beef
100 ml (3$^1/_2$ fl oz) chicken stock, extra
1 tablespoon tomato paste (concentrated purée)
1 tablespoon worcestershire sauce
50 g (1$^3/_4$ oz) gingernut biscuits, crushed (see Note)
2 tablespoons chopped flat-leaf (Italian) parsley
75 g (2$^1/_2$ oz/$^3/_4$ cup) dry breadcrumbs
oil, for deep-frying

MAKES 12

To make the béchamel sauce, melt the butter in a small saucepan over medium heat. Stir in the flour and cook for 1 minute, or until foaming. Remove from the heat and gradually stir in the milk, beating well after each addition. After the last of the milk has been added, add the nutmeg and some salt and pepper. Return to the heat and stir constantly until the sauce boils and thickens. Set aside to cool.

Melt the butter in a saucepan. Add the rice and stir to coat. Gradually stir in the stock and continue stirring until it has come to the boil. Reduce the heat and simmer for about 20 minutes, or until the rice is very tender and all the stock has been absorbed.

Heat the oil in a large frying pan and cook the onion and garlic over low heat for about 5 minutes, or until softened but not browned. Add the beef and cook for 8 minutes, or until browned. Stir in the extra stock, tomato paste, worcestershire sauce, crushed gingernut biscuits and parsley. Simmer, covered, for 20 minutes. If there is still some liquid left after this time, take the lid off and cook over high heat to reduce it.

Combine the béchamel, rice and beef and season well. Cool slightly, then refrigerate for 1 hour. Divide the mixture into twelve parts and roll each into a log approximately 7 cm (2$^3/_4$ inches) long and 3 cm (1$^1/_4$ inches) in diameter. The mixture will be soft, but manageable. Roll the logs in breadcrumbs to coat all over and put on a plate in a single layer. Cover with plastic wrap and refrigerate overnight.

Fill a large saucepan one-third full of oil and heat to 180°C (350°F), or until a spoonful of the batter dropped into the oil turns golden brown in 15 seconds. Cook the croquettes, a few at a time, turning them with tongs to give an evenly golden brown surface. Drain on crumpled paper towels.

PREPARATION TIME: 30 MINUTES +   COOKING TIME: 1 HOUR 30 MINUTES

NOTE: If gingernut biscuits are unavailable, crush 50 g (1$^3/_4$ oz) wheatmeal biscuits with $^1/_2$ teaspoon ground ginger.

FRIED CIGAR PASTRIES

16 fresh asparagus spears
2 tablespoons finely grated lemon zest
2 sheets frozen puff pastry, thawed
1 egg yolk
1 tablespoon sesame seeds

MAKES 16

Preheat the oven to 200°C (400°F/Gas 6). Add the asparagus to a large saucepan of lightly salted boiling water. Simmer for about 3 minutes, then drain and refresh under cold running water. Trim to 10 cm (4 inch) lengths.

Combine ¹/₂ teaspoon each of salt and black pepper and the lemon zest in a shallow dish and roll each asparagus spear in this mixture.

Cut the puff pastry sheets into 6 x 12 cm (2¹/₂ x 5 inch) rectangles and put one asparagus spear on each piece of pastry. In a bowl, combine the egg yolk with 2 teaspoons water and brush some on the sides and ends of the pastry. Roll the pastry up like a parcel, enclosing the sides so that the asparagus is completely sealed in. Press the joins of the pastry with a fork.

Place the parcels on lightly greased baking trays. Brush with the remaining egg and sprinkle with sesame seeds. Bake for 15–20 minutes, or until golden. Served cold with tzatziki.

PREPARATION TIME: 20 MINUTES   COOKING TIME: 25 MINUTES

VEGETABLE PASTIES

1 potato
1 carrot
1 parsnip
100 g (3¹/₂ oz) pumpkin (winter squash)
2 teaspoons oil
1 onion, finely chopped
125 ml (4 fl oz/¹/₂ cup) vegetable stock
50 g (1³/₄ oz/¹/₃ cup) fresh or frozen peas
1 tablespoon finely chopped flat-leaf (Italian) parsley
3 sheets frozen puff pastry, thawed
1 egg, lightly beaten
tomato sauce (ketchup), to serve

MAKES 12

Preheat the oven to 210°C (415°F/Gas 6–7). Lightly grease a baking tray. Peel and cut the potato, carrot, parsnip and pumpkin into 1 cm (¹/₂ inch) cubes.

Heat the oil in a frying pan and cook the onion over medium heat for 2 minutes, or until soft. Add the potato, carrot, parsnip, pumpkin and stock, then bring to the boil. Reduce the heat and simmer for 10 minutes, stirring occasionally, until the vegetables are soft and the liquid has evaporated. Stir in the peas and parsley and allow to cool.

Using a plate as a guide, cut four 12 cm (5 inch) circles from each sheet of pastry. Put 1 level tablespoon of mixture onto each round, brush the edges of pastry with water and fold the pastry over so the edges meet. Crimp the edges together to seal. Brush with beaten egg and place on the tray. Bake for 25 minutes, or until puffed and golden. Serve with tomato sauce.

PREPARATION TIME: 40 MINUTES   COOKING TIME: 50 MINUTES

CHIPOLATA SAUSAGES WITH HORSERADISH CREAM

2 tablespoons virgin olive oil

2 red onions, cut into thin wedges

2 tablespoons dark brown sugar

3 teaspoons balsamic vinegar

100 g (3½ oz) cream cheese

1 tablespoon horseradish cream

12 chipolata sausages

12 par-baked mini bread rolls

100 g (3½ oz) rocket (arugula) leaves, stalks removed

MAKES 12

Preheat the oven to 220°C (425°F/Gas 7). Heat 1½ tablespoons olive oil in a small saucepan. Add the onion and 1½ tablespoons water. Cover and cook over medium heat for about 10 minutes, stirring occasionally, until the onion is soft and starting to brown. Stir in the sugar and vinegar and cook, uncovered, for 3 minutes, or until thick. Season and keep warm.

Meanwhile, combine the cream cheese and horseradish cream in a small bowl and mix until smooth.

Heat the remaining oil in a large frying pan and cook the sausages in batches over medium–low heat for 6–8 minutes, or until brown and cooked. Remove and drain on crumpled paper towels.

Meanwhile, heat the bread rolls according to the manufacturer's instructions. When hot, slice horizontally, three-quarters of the way through, and spread with the horseradish mixture. Fill the rolls with rocket and a sausage, then onion.

PREPARATION TIME: 15 MINUTES   COOKING TIME: 25 MINUTES

NOTE: If you can't get chipolatas, you can use thin sausages and twist them through the centre.

HERBED SCALLOP KEBABS

24 cleaned scallops (without roe)
6 large spring onions (scallions), green part only
2 zucchini (courgettes)
2 carrots
20 g (³/₄ oz) butter, melted
2 teaspoons lemon juice
1 tablespoon dry white wine
2 teaspoons mixed dried herbs
¹/₂ teaspoon onion powder

MAKES 24

Soak 24 wooden skewers in cold water for 30 minutes. Wash the scallops, slice or pull off any vein, membrane or hard white muscle, then pat dry with paper towels. Cut the spring onions in half lengthways, then into 8 cm (3 inch) lengths. Line a baking tray with foil.

Using a vegetable peeler, slice the zucchini and carrots lengthways into thin ribbons. Plunge the vegetable strips into a bowl of boiling water, leave for 1 minute, then drain. Plunge into a bowl of iced water and leave until cold. Drain and pat dry with paper towels.

Roll each scallop in a strip of the spring onion, carrot and zucchini and secure with a wooden skewer.

Combine the butter, lemon juice and wine in a small bowl. Brush over the scallops. Sprinkle with the combined herbs and onion powder. Put under a hot grill (broiler) for 5–10 minutes, or until the scallops are tender and cooked through.

PREPARATION TIME: 1 HOUR +   COOKING TIME: 10 MINUTES

NOTE: Scallops can be prepared several hours ahead. Refrigerate, covered, until needed.

PROSCIUTTO-WRAPPED SCALLOPS

16 cleaned scallops (without roe)
4 thin prosciutto slices

SERVES 4

Soak 24 wooden skewers in cold water for 30 minutes. Rinse the scallops and pat dry.

Cut the prosciutto into quarters, each large enough to enclose a scallop. Wrap around the scallops and thread in pairs onto small wooden skewers. Grill under a preheated grill (broiler), or on a barbecue grill plate for 5 minutes, turning a couple of times during cooking.

PREPARATION TIME: 10 MINUTES   COOKING TIME: 5 MINUTES

Herbed scallop kebabs

MARINATED SEAFOOD

500 g (1 lb 2 oz) raw prawns (shrimp)
500 g (1 lb 2 oz) mussels, scrubbed, beards removed
125 ml (4 fl oz/$\frac{1}{2}$ cup) white wine vinegar
3 bay leaves
500 g (1 lb 2 oz) small squid tubes, sliced
500 g (1 lb 2 oz) cleaned scallops (without roe)
2 garlic cloves, crushed
125 ml (4 fl oz/$\frac{1}{2}$ cup) extra virgin olive oil
60 ml (2 fl oz/$\frac{1}{4}$ cup) lemon juice
1 tablespoon white wine vinegar
1 teaspoon dijon mustard
1 tablespoon chopped flat-leaf (Italian) parsley

SERVES 8

Peel the prawns, leaving the tails intact. Gently pull out the dark vein from each prawn back, starting from the head end.

Discard any mussels that are already open. Put the vinegar, bay leaves, 750 ml (26 fl oz/3 cups) water and $\frac{1}{2}$ teaspoon salt in a large saucepan and bring to the boil. Add the squid and scallops, then reduce the heat to low and simmer for 2–3 minutes, or until the seafood has turned white. Remove the squid and scallops with a slotted spoon and put in a bowl.

Repeat the process with the prawns, cooking until just pink, then removing with a slotted spoon. Return the liquid to the boil and add the mussels. Cover, reduce the heat and simmer for 3 minutes, or until all the shells are open. Stir occasionally and discard any unopened mussels. Cool, remove the meat and add to the bowl.

Whisk the garlic and oil together with the lemon juice, vinegar, mustard and parsley. Pour over the seafood and toss well. Refrigerate for 1–2 hours before serving.

PREPARATION TIME: 40 MINUTES +   COOKING TIME: 10 MINUTES

NOTE: Seafood should never be overcooked or it will become tough.

GARLIC LAMB SKEWERS

600 g (1 lb 5 oz) trimmed lamb steaks
1 garlic bulb
1 red chilli, chopped
2 garlic cloves, crushed
60 ml (2 fl oz/¼ cup) oil

MAKES 35

Cut the lamb steaks into 2 cm (³/₄ inch) cubes and halve each garlic clove lengthways.

Thread 2 pieces of lamb and 2 slices of garlic alternately onto 35 small metal skewers.

Mix together the chilli, crushed garlic cloves and oil. Heat a chargrill pan and lightly brush with oil. Cook the skewers for 2-5 minutes, brushing occasionally with the garlic and chilli marinade.

PREPARATION TIME: 15 MINUTES   COOKING TIME: 5 MINUTES

MALAYSIAN LAMB SATAYS

500 g (1 lb 2 oz) lamb fillets
1 onion, roughly chopped
2 garlic cloves, crushed
2 cm (³/₄ inch) piece lemon grass stem, white part only
2 slices fresh galangal
1 teaspoon chopped fresh ginger
1 teaspoon ground cumin
½ teaspoon ground fennel
1 tablespoon ground coriander
1 teaspoon ground turmeric
1 tablespoon soft brown sugar
1 tablespoon lemon juice

MAKES 8

Trim any fat or silver sinew from the lamb fillets. Slice the meat across the grain into very thin strips (if you have time, leave the meat in the freezer for 30 minutes as this will make it easier to thinly slice).

In a food processor, combine the onion, garlic, lemon grass, galangal, ginger, cumin, fennel, coriander, turmeric, sugar and lemon juice and process until a smooth paste is formed. Transfer the paste to a shallow non-metallic dish and add the lamb, stirring to coat well. Cover and refrigerate overnight.

Thread the meat onto eight metal skewers and cook under a preheated grill (broiler) for 3-4 minutes each side, or until cooked. Brush regularly with the remaining marinade while cooking.

PREPARATION TIME: 30 MINUTES +   COOKING TIME: 10 MINUTES

SPICY ROAST CHICKEN

1.6 kg (3 lb 8 oz) whole chicken
3 teaspoons chopped red chilli
3 garlic cloves
2 teaspoons peppercorns, crushed
2 teaspoons soft brown sugar
2 tablespoons soy sauce
2 teaspoons ground turmeric
1 tablespoon lime juice
30 g (1 oz) butter, chopped

SERVES 4–6

Preheat the oven to 180°C (350°F/Gas 4). Using a large cleaver, cut the chicken in half by cutting down the backbone and along the breastbone. To prevent the wings from burning, tuck them underneath. Put the chicken, skin side up, on a rack in a roasting tin and roast for 30 minutes.

Meanwhile, combine the chilli, garlic, peppercorns and sugar in a food processor or mortar and pestle and process briefly, or pound, until smooth. Add the soy sauce, turmeric and lime juice, and process in short bursts, or stir if using a mortar and pestle, until combined.

Brush the spice mixture over the chicken, dot it with the butter pieces and roast for a further 25–30 minutes, or until cooked through and rich red. Serve at room temperature.

PREPARATION TIME: 20 MINUTES   COOKING TIME: 1 HOUR

TERIYAKI STEAK KEBABS

750 g (1 lb 10 oz) lean rump steak
125 ml (4 fl oz/^{1}/$_2$ cup) soy sauce
125 ml (4 fl oz/^{1}/$_2$ cup) sherry or sake
1 garlic clove, crushed
1 teaspoon ground ginger
1 teaspoon sugar
lime wedges, to serve

MAKES 24

Cut the steak into thin strips, 15 cm (6 inches) long and thread the slices onto 24 wooden skewers.

Combine the soy sauce, sherry or sake, garlic and ground ginger and sugar.

Put the steak in a shallow non-metallic dish and marinate in the soy sauce mixture for at least 1 hour in the refrigerator, then drain.

Cook the skewers on a preheated barbecue flatplate for 3–4 minutes each side. Serve with lime wedges.

PREPARATION TIME: 10 MINUTES + COOKING TIME: 10 MINUTES

CHICKEN AND LEMON GRASS SKEWERS

1 kg (2 lb 4 oz) boneless, skinless chicken thigh
6 lemon grass stems
12 spring onion (scallion) bulbs
60 ml (2 fl oz/^{1}/$_4$ cup) soy sauce
60 ml (2 fl oz/^{1}/$_4$ cup) mirin
2 tablespoons sugar
1 lemon grass stem, white part only, thinly sliced
1 red chilli, seeded and finely chopped

MAKES 24

Cut the chicken into 2 cm (^{3}/$_4$ inch) cubes. Trim the leaves off the lemon grass stems. Cut the thicker ends of the stems into 10 cm (4 inch) lengths, then into quarters lengthways. Cut the spring onion bulbs into quarters. Make a small slit in the centre of each chicken cube and through the onion pieces, to make threading easier. Thread pieces of chicken and onion onto the lemon grass stems alternately, using 2 pieces of each for each stem.

Mix together the soy sauce, mirin and sugar. Heat a chargrill or frying pan and cook the skewers for 3-5 minutes. Brush with half the soy mixture as they cook, turning frequently. Add the lemon grass and chilli to the remaining soy mixture and serve with the skewers, for dipping.

PREPARATION TIME: 10 MINUTES COOKING TIME: 5 MINUTES

CHICKEN DRUMSTICKS WITH RANCH DRESSING

32 small chicken drumsticks
1 tablespoon garlic salt
1 tablespoon onion powder
oil, for deep-frying
250 ml (9 fl oz/1 cup) tomato sauce (ketchup)
80 ml (2½ fl oz/⅓ cup) worcestershire sauce
40 g (1½ oz) butter, melted
1 tablespoon sugar
Tabasco sauce, to taste

RANCH DRESSING
250 g (9 oz/1 cup) whole-egg mayonnaise
250 g (9 oz/1 cup) sour cream
80 ml (2½ fl oz/⅓ cup) lemon juice
20 g (¾ oz/⅓ cup) snipped chives

MAKES 32

Remove the skin from the chicken and use a cleaver or large knife to cut off the knuckle. Wash the chicken thoroughly and pat dry with paper towels. Combine 1 tablespoon cracked black pepper, and the garlic salt and onion powder and rub some into each piece of chicken.

Fill a deep heavy-based frying pan one-third full of oil and heat the oil to 180°C (350°F), or when a cube of bread dropped into the oil turns golden brown in 15 seconds. Cook the chicken in batches for 2 minutes each batch, remove with tongs or a slotted spoon and drain on paper towels.

Transfer the chicken to a large non-metallic bowl or shallow dish. Combine the sauces, butter, sugar and Tabasco, pour over the chicken and stir to coat. Refrigerate, covered, for several hours or overnight. Prepare and heat the barbecue 1 hour before cooking.

Put the chicken on a lightly oiled hot barbecue grill or flatplate and cook for 20–25 minutes, or until cooked through. Turn and brush with the marinade during cooking. Serve with the ranch dressing.

To make the ranch dressing, combine the mayonnaise, sour cream, juice, chives, and season to taste.

PREPARATION TIME: 25 MINUTES + COOKING TIME: 35 MINUTES

ROSEMARY TUNA KEBABS

3 tomatoes
1 tablespoon olive oil
2–3 small red chillies, seeded and
chopped
3–4 garlic cloves, crushed
1 red onion, finely chopped
60 ml (2 fl oz/¼ cup) dry white wine
or water
600 g (1 lb 5 oz) tinned chickpeas, rinsed
and drained
3 tablespoons chopped oregano
4 tablespoons chopped flat-leaf (Italian)
parsley
lemon wedges, to serve

TUNA KEBABS
1 kg (2 lb 4 oz) tuna fillet, cut into 4 cm
(1½ inch) cubes
8 rosemary stalks, about 20 cm (8 inches)
long, with leaves
olive oil, for brushing

SERVES 4

Cut the tomatoes into halves or quarters and scoop out the seeds. Roughly chop the flesh.

Heat the oil in a large non-stick frying pan. Add the chilli, garlic and red onion and stir over medium heat for 5 minutes, or until softened. Add the chopped tomato and the white wine or water. Cook over low heat for 10 minutes, or until the mixture is soft and pulpy and most of the liquid has evaporated.

Stir in the chickpeas with the oregano and parsley. Season to taste.

Heat a grill (broiler) or barbecue plate. Thread the tuna onto the rosemary stalks, lightly brush with oil, then cook, turning, for 3 minutes. Do not overcook or the tuna will be dry and fall apart. Serve with the chickpeas and lemon wedges.

PREPARATION TIME: 20 MINUTES   COOKING TIME: 20 MINUTES

NOTE: Swordfish, striped marlin or salmon are also suitable for this recipe.

FISH AND CUMIN KEBABS

750 g (1 lb 10 oz) skinless firm white fish
fillets, such as blue-eye, snapper
or perch
2 tablespoons olive oil
1 garlic clove, crushed
3 tablespoons chopped coriander
(cilantro) leaves
2 teaspoons ground cumin

SERVES 4

Cut the fish fillets into 3 cm (1¼ inch) cubes. Thread on oiled skewers and set aside.

To make the marinade, combine the oil, garlic, coriander, cumin and 1 teaspoon ground black pepper in a small bowl. Brush the marinade over the fish, cover with plastic wrap and refrigerate for several hours, or overnight, turning occasionally. Drain, reserving the marinade. Season just before cooking.

Put the skewers on a hot, lightly oiled barbecue flatplate. Cook for 5–6 minutes, or until tender, turning once and brushing with reserved marinade several times during cooking.

PREPARATION TIME: 10 MINUTES +   COOKING TIME: 10 MINUTES

Rosemary tuna kebabs

BARBECUED QUAIL

6 quails
250 ml (9 fl oz/1 cup) dry red wine
2 celery stalks, including tops, chopped
1 carrot, chopped
1 small onion, chopped
1 bay leaf, torn into small pieces
1 teaspoon ground allspice
1 teaspoon dried thyme
2 garlic cloves, crushed
2 tablespoons olive oil
2 tablespoons lemon juice
lemon wedges, to serve

MAKES 24 PIECES

To prepare the quails, use poultry shears to cut down either side of the backbone, then discard the backbone. Remove the innards and neck, wash the insides and pat dry with paper towels. Place, breast side up, on the bench, open out flat and gently press to flatten. Using poultry shears, cut in half through the breast then cut each half in half again into the thigh and drumstick piece and breast and wing piece.

In a non-metallic bowl, combine the wine, celery, carrot, onion, bay leaf and allspice. Add the quail and stir to coat. Cover and refrigerate for 3 hours, or preferably overnight, stirring occasionally. Drain and sprinkle with thyme and salt and pepper.

Whisk together the garlic, oil and lemon juice in a small bowl.

Heat a lightly oiled barbecue plate until hot. Reduce the heat to medium and cook the quail breast pieces for 4–5 minutes each side and the drumstick pieces for 3 minutes each side, or until tender and cooked through. Brush frequently with the lemon mixture. Serve hot with lemon wedges.

PREPARATION TIME: 40 MINUTES +   COOKING TIME: 10 MINUTES

CHILLI PRAWN SKEWERS

30 large raw prawns (shrimp)
60 g (2¼ oz) butter
1 garlic clove, crushed
2 teaspoons soft brown sugar
2 tablespoons lemon or lime juice
2 tablespoons finely chopped coriander (cilantro) sprigs
2 tablespoons finely chopped basil leaves
1 tablespoon sweet chilli sauce

MAKES 30

Peel the prawns, leaving the tails intact. Gently pull out the dark vein from each prawn back, starting from the head end.

Heat the butter in a large frying pan or wok. Add the garlic, sugar, juice, coriander, basil and sweet chilli sauce. Mix thoroughly, add the prawns in batches, then cook over medium heat for 5 minutes, or until the prawns turn pink and are cooked through.

Thread each prawn onto a bamboo skewer or strong toothpick to serve.

PREPARATION TIME: 25 MINUTES   COOKING TIME: 10 MINUTES

NOTES: Prepare the prawns several hours ahead. Cook just before serving.
   Scallops or oysters can be used instead of prawns, or alternate pieces of fish with prawns.

TANDOORI PRAWNS

1 kg (2 lb 4 oz) raw king prawns (about 24)
125 g (4½ oz/½ cup) plain yoghurt
20 g (¾ oz) finely chopped coriander (cilantro) leaves
2 tablespoons finely chopped mint
1 tablespoon chopped fresh ginger
2 garlic cloves, crushed
1 teaspoon chilli powder
1 teaspoon ground turmeric
1 teaspoon ground coriander
1 teaspoon garam masala
few drops red food colouring (optional)
2 lemons, cut into wedges, to serve

MAKES 24

Peel the prawns, leaving the tails intact. Gently pull out the dark vein from each prawn back, starting from the head end. Rinse and pat dry with paper towels.

Combine the yoghurt with the fresh coriander, mint and salt, to taste. Pour over the prawns, mix well and leave for 5 minutes.

Mix the ginger, garlic, chilli powder, turmeric, coriander, garam masala and food colouring in a large bowl. Add the prawns and marinate for 10 minutes.

Thread one prawn onto a metal skewers and barbecue for about 5 minutes. Turn the skewers once, so the prawns cook evenly. They are ready when they start to curl and turn opaque. Serve on the skewers or loose with lemon wedges.

PREPARATION TIME: 20 MINUTES +   COOKING TIME: 5 MINUTES

Chilli prawn skewers

TANDOORI FISH CUTLETS

4 firm white fish cutlets, such as
blue-eye, snapper or perch
60 ml (2 fl oz/¼ cup) lemon juice
1 onion, finely chopped
2 garlic cloves, crushed
1 tablespoon grated fresh ginger
1 red chilli
1 tablespoon garam masala
1 teaspoon paprika
500 g (1 lb 2 oz/2 cups) Greek-style
yoghurt, plus extra to serve
few drops red food colouring (optional)
baby English spinach leaves, to serve
lime wedges, to serve

Pat the fish cutlets dry with paper towels and arrange in a shallow non-metallic dish. Drizzle the lemon juice over the fish and turn to coat the cutlets with the juice.

Blend the onion, garlic, ginger, chilli, garam masala, paprika and salt in a blender until smooth. Transfer to a bowl and stir in the yoghurt and the food colouring if using. Spoon the marinade over the fish and turn the fish to coat thoroughly. Cover and refrigerate overnight.

Heat a barbecue hotplate. Remove the cutlets from the marinade and allow any excess to drip off. Cook the cutlets on the barbecue, or under a grill (broiler), for 3–4 minutes each side, or until the fish flakes easily when tested with a fork. Serve with extra yoghurt, baby English spinach leaves and lime wedges.

SERVES 4   PREPARATION TIME: 15 MINUTES +   COOKING TIME: 10 MINUTES

FRIED CRISPY CHICKEN

4 chicken leg quarters or
8 drumsticks
4 garlic cloves, chopped
3 coriander (cilantro) roots, finely
chopped
2 teaspoons ground turmeric
1 teaspoon caster (superfine) sugar
2 tablespoons chilli sauce, plus extra
to serve (optional)
oil, for deep-frying

SERVES 4

Remove the skin from the chicken pieces. Put the chicken in a large saucepan with enough water to cover it. Cover and simmer for 15 minutes, or until cooked through. Drain and cool.

Put the garlic, coriander root, turmeric, 1 teaspoon pepper, 1 teaspoon salt, sugar and chilli sauce in a mortar and pestle or food processor and pound or process into a smooth paste. Brush over the chicken, cover and refrigerate for 30 minutes.

Heat the oil in a heavy-based frying pan, add the chicken in batches and cook until dark brown, turning frequently. Drain on paper towels. Serve hot or cold with chilli sauce, if desired.

PREPARATION TIME: 20 MINUTES + COOKING TIME: 30 MINUTES

TAMARIND CHICKEN

4 boneless, skinless chicken thighs
4 chicken drumsticks
80 ml (2^1/$_2$ fl oz/^{1}/$_3$ cup) tamarind
concentrate
2 teaspoons ground coriander
1 teaspoon ground turmeric
2 garlic cloves, crushed
2 tablespoons peanut oil
2 red chillies, finely chopped
6 spring onions (scallions), finely chopped
oil, for deep-frying

SERVES 4

Remove the skin from the chicken pieces. Put the chicken in a large saucepan with enough water to cover it. Cover and simmer for 15 minutes, or until cooked through. Drain and cool.

Combine the tamarind, coriander, turmeric and garlic. Add the tamarind mixture to the chicken and toss well to coat. Cover and marinate in the refrigerator for at least 2 hours, or preferably overnight.

Heat the peanut oil in a frying pan; add the chilli and spring onion, and stir-fry over low heat for 3 minutes. Set aside.

Heat the oil in a large deep frying pan. Cook the chicken in three batches over medium heat for 5 minutes, or until the chicken is golden brown and heated through. Drain the chicken on paper towels, and keep warm while frying the remaining chicken. Serve the chicken pieces with a spoonful of the chilli mixture on the side.

PREPARATION TIME: 15 MINUTES + COOKING TIME: 35 MINUTES

Fried crispy chicken

BARBECUED ASIAN-STYLE PRAWNS

500 g (1 lb 2 oz) large raw prawns
(shrimp)
lime wedges, to serve

MARINADE
2 tablespoons lemon juice
2 tablespoons sesame oil
2 garlic cloves, crushed
2 teaspoons grated fresh ginger

SERVES 4

Peel the prawns, leaving the tails intact. Gently pull out the dark vein from each prawn back, starting from the head end.

Mix the lemon juice, sesame oil, garlic and ginger in a bowl. Add the prawns and gently stir to coat the prawns. Cover and refrigerate for at least 3 hours.

Cook the prawns on a hot, lightly oiled barbecue plate for 3–5 minutes, or until pink and cooked through. Brush frequently with marinade while cooking. Serve immediately with the lime wedges.

PREPARATION TIME: 10 MINUTES +   COOKING TIME: 5 MINUTES

NOTES: Alternatively, the prawns can be threaded onto bamboo skewers. Soak the skewers in cold water for about 30 minutes, or until they sink. This will prevent the skewers burning during cooking. After marinating, thread the prawns evenly onto the skewers and cook as stated, turning and basting occasionally during cooking.

The amount of garlic can be altered, according to taste. For a stronger flavour, double the quantity of garlic and omit the ginger. For a spicy dish, substitute two finely chopped fresh chillies for the garlic.

You can also halve the quantity of prawns and add scallops.

SWEET TREATS AND DRINKS

TURKISH DELIGHT

880 g (1 lb 15 oz/4 cups) sugar
125 g (4^1/$_2$ oz/1 cup) cornflour (cornstarch)
1 teaspoon cream of tartar
2 tablespoons rosewater
red food colouring
40 g (1^1/$_2$ oz/^{1}/$_3$ cup) icing (confectioners')
sugar

MAKES 25 PIECES

Pour 625 ml (21^1/$_2$ fl oz/2^1/$_2$ cups) water into a large heavy-based saucepan and bring to the boil. Add the sugar and stir until thoroughly dissolved. Remove from the heat.

In a large bowl, blend the cornflour and cream of tartar with 250 ml (9 fl oz/1 cup) cold water. Gradually add the blended cornflour to the sugar syrup, then return the saucepan to medium heat and stir until the mixture boils.

Reduce the heat and cook very slowly for 45 minutes, stirring often. During this time, the colour will change from cloudy to clear and golden, and the mixture will thicken.

Add the rosewater and a few drops of food colouring. Pour onto a lightly oiled 20 x 30 cm (8 x 12 inch) baking tray and leave to set. When firm and cool, cut into 2 cm (^{3}/$_4$ inch) squares and toss in the icing sugar.

PREPARATION TIME: 10 MINUTES   COOKING TIME: 1 HOUR

DATE CANDIES

150 g (5^1/$_2$ oz/1^1/$_2$ cups) walnut halves
2 tablespoons sesame seeds
100 g (3^1/$_2$ oz) ghee
600 g (1 lb 5 oz) pitted dried dates,
coarsely chopped

SERVES 6–8

Preheat the oven to 180°C (350°F/Gas 4) and line the base and two opposite sides of an 18 cm (7 inch) square slice tin with baking paper. Spread the walnuts on a baking tray and bake for 5 minutes, or until lightly toasted. Chop coarsely. Bake the sesame seeds until golden.

Melt the ghee in a large heavy-based saucepan and cook the dates, covered, over low heat for about 10 minutes, stirring often, until the dates soften. Using the back of a spoon dipped in cold water, spread half in the tin. Scatter the walnuts on top and press into the dates. Spread the remaining date mixture over the walnuts. Smooth the surface with wet fingers and press down firmly. Sprinkle with the sesame seeds and press lightly into the dates. When cool, cut into small diamonds.

PREPARATION TIME: 10 MINUTES +   COOKING TIME: 20 MINUTES

NOUGAT

440 g (15¹/2 oz/2 cups) sugar
250 ml (9 fl oz/1 cup) liquid glucose
175 g (6 oz/¹/2 cup) honey
2 egg whites
1 teaspoon natural vanilla extract
125 g (4¹/2 oz) unsalted butter, softened
60 g (2¹/4 oz) almonds, unblanched and toasted
100 g (3¹/2 oz) glacé cherries

MAKES 1 KG (2 LB 4 OZ)

Grease a 18 x 28 cm (7 x 11 inch) baking dish and line with baking paper. Put the sugar, glucose, honey, 60 ml (2 fl oz/¹/4 cup) water and ¹/4 teaspoon salt in a heavy-based saucepan and stir over low heat until dissolved. Bring to the boil and cook at a rolling boil for 8 minutes, or until the mixture reaches 122°C (225°F) on a sugar thermometer. The correct temperature is very important, otherwise the mixture will not set properly.

Beat the egg whites in a bowl with electric beaters until stiff peaks form. Slowly pour one-quarter of the sugar mixture onto the egg whites in a thin stream and beat for up to 5 minutes, or until the mixture holds its shape. Put the remaining syrup over the heat and cook for 2 minutes (watch that it doesn't burn), or until a small amount forms brittle threads when dropped in cold water, or reaches 157°C (315°F) on a sugar thermometer. Pour slowly onto the meringue mixture with the beaters running and beat until the mixture is very thick.

Add the vanilla and butter and beat for a further 5 minutes. Stir in the almonds and cherries with a metal spoon. Turn the mixture into the tin and smooth the top with a palate knife. Refrigerate for at least 4 hours, or until firm. Turn out onto a large chopping board and cut into 2 x 4 cm (³/4 x 1¹/2 inch) pieces. Wrap each piece in cellophane and store in the refrigerator.

PREPARATION TIME: 30 MINUTES +   COOKING TIME: 15 MINUTES

CHOCOLATE STRAWBERRIES

250 g (9 oz) strawberries
150 g (5½ oz) dark chocolate
100 g (3½ oz) white chocolate

SERVES 8–10

Brush the strawberries with a dry pastry brush to remove any dirt. Melt the dark chocolate in a small heatproof bowl over a saucepan of steaming water, making sure the base of the bowl does not touch the water. Dip the bottom half of each strawberry in the chocolate. Put on a baking tray lined with baking paper and allow to set.

When set, melt the white chocolate in the same way as the dark. Dip the tips of the strawberries in the chocolate and allow to set on the baking tray.

PREPARATION TIME: 10 MINUTES +   COOKING TIME: 5 MINUTES

WALNUT CHOCOLATES

100 g (3½ oz) walnut pieces
60 g (2¼ oz/½ cup) icing (confectioners') sugar
2 teaspoons egg white
200 g (7 oz) dark chocolate
30 walnut halves

MAKES 30

Chop the walnut pieces in a food processor. Sift the icing sugar and process with the walnuts and egg white until a moist paste forms. Cover and refrigerate for 20 minutes.

Roll teaspoons of the walnut paste into 30 balls and flatten slightly. Put the chocolate in a heatproof bowl. Bring a saucepan of water to the boil and remove from the heat. Sit the bowl over the pan, making sure the base of the bowl does not sit in the water. Stir occasionally until the chocolate has melted.

Dip the walnut rounds in the chocolate and transfer to a piece of baking paper or foil. Press the walnut halves gently into the top of each round and leave to set.

PREPARATION TIME: 30 MINUTES +   COOKING TIME: 5 MINUTES

NOTE: These chocolates will keep for up to 4 days.

Chocolate strawberries

CHOCOLATE CARROT SLICE

125 g (4¹/₂ oz/1 cup) self-raising flour
1 teaspoon ground cinnamon
170 g (6 oz/³/₄ cup) caster (superfine)
sugar
80 g (2³/₄ oz/¹/₂ cup) finely grated carrot
185 g (6¹/₂ oz/1 cup) mixed dried fruit
90 g (3¹/₄ oz/¹/₂ cup) chocolate chips
30 g (1 oz/¹/₃ cup) desiccated coconut
2 eggs, beaten
90 g (3¹/₄ oz) unsalted butter, melted
40 g (1¹/₂ oz/¹/₃ cup) chopped walnuts

CREAM CHEESE FROSTING
125 g (4¹/₂ oz) cream cheese
30 g (1 oz) unsalted butter
185 g (6¹/₂ oz/1¹/₂ cups) icing
(confectioners') sugar, sifted

MAKES 32

Preheat the oven to 180°C (350°F/Gas 4). Lightly grease a shallow 23 cm (9 inch) square cake tin and line the base and sides with baking paper.

Sift the flour and cinnamon into a large bowl. Add the caster sugar, grated carrot, mixed fruit, chocolate chips and coconut and stir until just combined. Add the beaten eggs and butter and then stir until combined.

Spread the mixture evenly into the prepared tin and smooth the surface. Bake for 30 minutes, or until golden. Allow to cool in the tin, then turn out onto a flat surface.

To make the cream cheese frosting, using electric beaters, beat the cream cheese and butter in a small bowl until smooth. Add the icing sugar and beat for 2 minutes, or until the mixture is light and fluffy. Add 1 teaspoon water and beat until well combined.

Spread the slice with frosting using a flat-bladed knife and sprinkle with walnuts. Cut into 16 squares, then cut each square into two triangles.

PREPARATION TIME: 20 MINUTES   COOKING TIME: 30 MINUTES

NOTES: This slice can be frozen for up to 2 months.
    The topping may be sprinkled with grated chocolate, if desired.

MINI TOFFEE APPLES

2 large apples
200 g (7 oz) sugar

MAKES 6–8

Peel the apples and use a melon baller to cut out balls, or cut the apples into cubes. Push a cocktail stick into each ball or cube.

Sprinkle the sugar in an even layer over the base of a saucepan and melt over low heat, slowly tipping the pan from side to side to make sure the sugar melts evenly. Keep the sugar moving so it does not start to colour on one side before the other side has melted. When the caramel starts to colour, keep swirling until you have an even colour, then remove the pan from the heat and stop the cooking by plunging the base into cold water. Reheat the caramel gently until runny.

Dip each piece of apple in the caramel, coating completely. Leave to dry, standing upright on a piece of baking paper. Reheat the caramel when necessary.

PREPARATION TIME: 10 MINUTES   COOKING TIME: 10 MINUTES

JAM DROPS

80 g (2³/4 oz) unsalted butter, softened
80 g (2³/4 oz/¹/3 cup) caster (superfine) sugar
2 tablespoons milk
¹/2 teaspoon natural vanilla extract
125 g (4¹/2 oz/1 cup) self-raising flour
40 g (1¹/2 oz/¹/3 cup) custard powder
100 g (3¹/2 oz/¹/3 cup) raspberry jam

MAKES 32

Preheat the oven to 180°C (350°F/Gas 4). Line two baking trays with baking paper.

Cream the butter and sugar in a small bowl using electric beaters until light and fluffy. Add the milk and vanilla and beat until combined. Sift in the flour and custard powder and mix to form a soft dough. Roll heaped teaspoons of the mixture into balls and place on the trays.

Make an indentation in each ball using the end of a wooden spoon. Fill each hole with a little jam. Bake for 15 minutes, cool slightly on the trays, then transfer to a wire rack to cool.

PREPARATION TIME: 20 MINUTES   COOKING TIME: 15 MINUTES

APPLE CUSTARD STREUSEL SLICE

155 g (5¹/₂ oz/1¹/₄ cups) plain (all-purpose) flour

1 tablespoon caster (superfine) sugar

80 g (2³/₄ oz) unsalted butter, melted and cooled

1 egg yolk

APPLE CUSTARD TOPPING

3 green apples

20 g (³/₄ oz) unsalted butter

80 g (2³/₄ oz/¹/₃ cup) caster (superfine) sugar

2 eggs

185 ml (6 fl oz/³/₄ cup) pouring (whipping) cream

1 teaspoon natural vanilla extract

CRUMBLE TOPPING

60 g (2¹/₄ oz/¹/₂ cup) plain (all-purpose) flour

2 tablespoons dark brown sugar

40 g (1¹/₂ oz/¹/₃ cup) finely chopped walnuts

60 g (2¹/₄ oz) unsalted butter, cubed

MAKES 16 PIECES

Lightly grease an 18 x 28 cm (7 x 11 inch) shallow tin and line with baking paper, leaving the paper hanging over the two long sides.

Sift the flour and sugar into a bowl. Add the butter, egg yolk and 2-3 tablespoons water and mix to form a ball. Roll out the dough between two sheets of baking paper and fit in the base of the tin. Refrigerate for 20 minutes. Preheat the oven to 190°C (375°F/Gas 5).

Line the pastry with baking paper, fill with baking beads or uncooked rice and bake for 15 minutes. Remove the paper and rice, reduce the oven to 180°C (350°F/Gas 4) and bake the pastry for 5 minutes, or until golden. Allow to cool.

Peel, core and chop the apples and put in a saucepan with the butter, half the sugar and 2 tablespoons water. Cover and cook over low heat for 15 minutes, or until soft. Uncover and simmer for a further 5 minutes to reduce the liquid. Use a wooden spoon to break down the apples until they have a smooth texture. Allow to cool.

Whisk together the eggs, cream, remaining sugar and natural vanilla extract. Spread the cooled apple over the pastry, then carefully pour on the cream mixture. Bake for 20 minutes, or until the custard has half set.

To make the crumble, mix the flour, sugar and walnuts and rub in the butter until the mixture is crumbly. Sprinkle over the custard and bake for 15 minutes. Cool in the tin before slicing into 16 pieces. These will keep in the fridge for up to 1 week.

PREPARATION TIME: 30 MINUTES +   COOKING TIME: 1 HOUR 15 MINUTES

BERRY ALMOND SLICE

1 sheet frozen puff pastry, thawed
150 g (5^{1}/2 oz) unsalted butter
170 g (6 oz/^{3}/4 cup) caster (superfine) sugar
3 eggs, beaten
2 tablespoons grated lemon zest
125 g (4^{1}/2 oz/^{2}/3 cup) ground almonds
2 tablespoons plain (all-purpose) flour
150 g (5^{1}/2 oz) raspberries
150 g (5^{1}/2 oz) blackberries
icing (confectioners') sugar, for dusting

MAKES 15 PIECES

Preheat the oven to 200°C (400°F/Gas 6). Lightly grease a 23 cm (9 inch) square shallow tin and line with baking paper, leaving the paper hanging over the two opposite sides.

Put the pastry on a baking tray lined with baking paper. Prick the pastry all over with a fork and bake for 15 minutes, or until golden. Ease into the tin, trimming the edges if necessary. Reduce the oven to 180°C (350°F/Gas 4).

Cream the butter and sugar in a small bowl using electric beaters until light and fluffy. Gradually add the egg, beating after every addition, then the lemon zest. Fold in the almonds and flour, then spread the mixture over the pastry.

Scatter the fruit on top and bake for 1 hour, or until lightly golden. Cool in the tin, then lift out, using the paper as handles. Cut into pieces and dust with icing sugar to serve.

PREPARATION TIME: 25 MINUTES   COOKING TIME: 1 HOUR 15 MINUTES

TOLLHOUSE COOKIES

180 g (6^{1}/2 oz) unsalted butter, softened
140 g (5 oz/^{3}/4 cup) soft brown sugar
110 g (3^{3}/4 oz/^{1}/2 cup) sugar
2 eggs, beaten
1 teaspoon natural vanilla extract
310 g (11 oz/2^{1}/4 cups) plain (all-purpose) flour
1 teaspoon bicarbonate of soda (baking soda)
350 g (12 oz/2 cups) dark chocolate chips
100 g (3^{1}/2 oz/1 cup) pecans, roughly chopped

MAKES 40

Preheat the oven to 190°C (375°F/Gas 5). Line two baking trays with baking paper.

Cream the butter and sugars in a large bowl using electric beaters until light and fluffy. Gradually add the egg, beating well after each addition. Stir in the vanilla, then the sifted flour and bicarbonate of soda until just combined. Mix in the chocolate chips and pecans.

Drop tablespoons of mixture onto the trays, leaving room for spreading. Bake the cookies for 8–10 minutes, or until lightly golden. Cool slightly on the trays before transferring to a wire rack to cool completely. When completely cold, store in an airtight container.

PREPARATION TIME: 20 MINUTES   COOKING TIME: 20 MINUTES

NOTE: You can use any nuts such as walnuts, almonds or hazelnuts.

FAMILY-STYLE GINGERBREAD PEOPLE

125 g (4$\frac{1}{2}$ oz) unsalted butter, softened

60 g (2$\frac{1}{4}$ oz/$\frac{1}{3}$ cup) soft brown sugar

90 g (3$\frac{1}{4}$ oz/$\frac{1}{4}$ cup) golden syrup or maple syrup

1 egg, lightly beaten

250 g (9 oz/2 cups) plain (all-purpose) flour

30 g (1 oz/$\frac{1}{4}$ cup) self-raising flour

1 tablespoon ground ginger

1 teaspoon bicarbonate of soda (baking soda)

1 tablespoon currants

ICING

1 egg white

$\frac{1}{2}$ teaspoon lemon juice

155 g (5$\frac{1}{2}$ oz/1$\frac{1}{4}$ cups) icing (confectioners') sugar, sifted

assorted food colourings

MAKES 16

Preheat the oven to 180°C (350°F/Gas 4). Line two baking trays with baking paper.

Cream the butter, sugar and golden syrup in a small bowl using electric beaters until light and fluffy. Add the egg gradually, beating well after each addition. Transfer to a large bowl. Sift the dry ingredients onto the butter mixture and mix with a knife until just combined. Combine the dough with well-floured hands. Turn onto a well-floured surface and knead for 1–2 minutes, or until smooth. Roll out the dough on a chopping board, between two sheets of baking paper, to 5 mm ($\frac{1}{4}$ inch) thick. Refrigerate on the board for 15 minutes to firm.

Cut the dough into shapes with a 13 cm (5 inch) gingerbread person cutter. Press the remaining dough together and re-roll. Cut out shapes and put the biscuits on the trays. Put currants as eyes and noses. Bake for 10 minutes, or until lightly browned. Cool completely on the trays.

To make the icing, beat the egg white using electric beaters in a small, clean, dry bowl until foamy. Gradually add the lemon juice and icing sugar and beat until thick and creamy. Divide the icing among several bowls. Tint the mixture with food colourings and spoon into small paper piping (icing) bags. Seal the open ends, snip the tips off the bags and pipe on faces and clothing.

PREPARATION TIME: 40 MINUTES +   COOKING TIME: 10 MINUTES

NOTE: When the icing is completely dry, store the biscuits in an airtight container in a cool, dry place for up to 3 days.

LITTLE LEMON TARTS

250 g (9 oz/2 cups) plain (all-purpose) flour
125 g (4¹/2 oz) unsalted butter, chopped
2 teaspoons caster (superfine) sugar
1 teaspoon grated lemon zest
1 egg yolk

FILLING
125 g (4¹/2 oz) cream cheese, softened
115 g (4 oz/¹/2 cup) caster (superfine) sugar
2 egg yolks
2 tablespoons lemon juice
160 g (5³/4 oz/¹/2 cup) sweetened condensed milk
strips of candied lemon peel, to garnish

MAKES 24

Preheat the oven to 180°C (350°F/Gas 4). Brush two round-based 12-cup shallow patty pans or mini muffin tins with oil. Sift the flour and a pinch of salt into a bowl and rub in the butter. Add the sugar, zest, egg yolk and 2–3 tablespoons iced water and mix with a knife. Gently knead on a lightly floured surface until smooth. Cover in plastic wrap and chill for 10 minutes.

To make the filling, beat the combined cream cheese, sugar and egg yolks using electric beaters until smooth and thickened. Add the lemon juice and condensed milk and beat until well combined.

Roll out the dough between sheets of baking paper to 3 mm (about ¹/8 inch) thickness. Using a 7 cm (2³/4 inch) fluted round cutter, cut rounds from the pastry. Gently press into the patty tins. Lightly prick each round three times with a fork. Bake for 10 minutes, or until just starting to turn golden. Remove from the oven and spoon 2 teaspoons of filling into each case. Return to the oven for a further 5 minutes, or until the filling has set. Cool slightly before removing from the tins. Garnish with strips of candied lemon peel, if desired.

PREPARATION TIME: 40 MINUTES +   COOKING TIME: 15 MINUTES

FAST CHOCOLATE FUDGE COOKIES

90 g (3¹/4 oz/³/4 cup) plain (all-purpose) flour
60 g (2¹/4 oz/¹/2 cup) self-raising flour
125 g (4¹/2 oz/1 cup) chopped walnuts
90 g (3¹/4 oz/¹/2 cup) chocolate chips
125 g (4¹/2 oz) unsalted butter, melted
200 g (7 oz) dark chocolate, melted
2 tablespoons golden syrup or honey
2 eggs, beaten

MAKES ABOUT 30

Preheat the oven to 180°C (350°F/Gas 4). Sift the flours into a large bowl. Stir in the walnuts and chocolate chips.

Make a well in the centre of the dry ingredients. Add the butter, dark chocolate, golden syrup and eggs. Stir until combined.

Drop level tablespoonsfuls onto a lightly greased baking tray. Leave about 4 cm (1¹/2 inches) between each cookie to allow for spreading. Bake for 12 minutes, then transfer to a wire rack to cool.

PREPARATION TIME: 20 MINUTES   COOKING TIME: 15 MINUTES

PETITS FOURS

2 eggs
55 g (2 oz/¹/₄ cup) caster (superfine) sugar
85 g (3 oz/²/₃ cup) plain (all-purpose) flour
30 g (1 oz) unsalted butter, melted

TOPPING
315 g (11 oz/1 cup) apricot jam, warmed and strained
2 teaspoons liqueur
200 g (7 oz) marzipan
400 g (14 oz) ready-made soft icing, chopped
small coloured fondant flowers, to decorate (optional)

MAKES 32

Preheat the oven to 180°C (350°F/Gas 4). Lightly grease two 4.5 x 8 x 26 cm (1³/₄ x 3 x 10¹/₂ inch) loaf (bar) tins. Line the bases and sides with baking paper.

Beat the eggs and sugar in a bowl using electric beaters for 5 minutes, until very thick and pale. Fold in the sifted flour and melted butter quickly and lightly, using a metal spoon. Divide between the tins and bake for 15 minutes, or until lightly golden and springy to the touch. Leave in the tins for 3 minutes before turning out onto a wire rack to cool.

Using a 3 cm (1¹/₄ inch) round cutter, cut shapes from the cakes. Brush the top and sides of each with the combined jam and liqueur. Roll the marzipan out to a thickness of 2 mm (¹/₈ inch) and cut out rounds and strips to cover the top and sides of the cakes.

Put the icing and 2 tablespoons water in a heatproof bowl and stand the bowl over a saucepan of simmering water. Stir until the icing has melted and the mixture is smooth. Allow to cool slightly.

Put the marzipan-covered cakes on a wire rack over a tray. Spoon the icing over each cake and use a flat-bladed knife to spread evenly over the base and sides. Reheat the icing over the saucepan if it begins to thicken. Leave the cakes to set. Carefully lift from the rack and put each in a paper petit four case. Decorate with small coloured fondant flowers, if desired.

PREPARATION TIME: 45 MINUTES   COOKING TIME: 20 MINUTES

NOTES: Fondant flowers for decorating are found in some supermarkets and in speciality shops.

Petits fours will keep for up to 2 days in an airtight container in a cool, dark place. Store in a single layer.

COCONUT SEMOLINA SLICE

50 g (1³/₄ oz) sesame seeds
125 g (4¹/₂ oz/1 cup) fine semolina
230 g (8¹/₂ oz/1 cup) caster (superfine)
sugar
750 ml (26 fl oz/3 cups) coconut cream
2 tablespoons ghee or oil
2 eggs, separated
¹/₄ teaspoon ground cardamom
fresh fruit, to serve (optional)

SERVES 8–10

Preheat the oven to 160°C (315°F/Gas 2–3). Lightly grease a 18 x 28 cm (7 x 11 inch) shallow tin.

Toast the sesame seeds in a dry frying pan over medium heat for 3–4 minutes, shaking the pan gently, until the seeds are golden brown; remove from the pan at once to prevent burning.

Put the semolina, sugar and coconut cream in a large saucepan and stir over medium heat for 5 minutes, or until boiling. Add the ghee or oil and continue stirring until the mixture comes away from the sides of the pan. Set aside to cool.

Beat the egg whites until stiff peaks form. Fold the egg whites, egg yolks and cardamom into the cooled semolina mixture. Spoon the mixture into the prepared tin and sprinkle with the sesame seeds. Bake for 45 minutes, or until golden brown. Cut into diamond shapes and serve with fresh fruit, if desired.

PREPARATION TIME: 20 MINUTES   COOKING TIME: 1 HOUR

MACADAMIA BLONDIES

100 g (3¹/₂ oz) unsalted butter, chopped
100 g (3¹/₂ oz) white chocolate, chopped
115 g (4 oz/¹/₂ cup) caster (superfine)
sugar
2 eggs, beaten
1 teaspoon natural vanilla extract
125 g (4¹/₂ oz/1 cup) self-raising flour
80 g (2³/₄ oz/¹/₂ cup) macadamia nuts,
roughly chopped
melted white chocolate, to serve
(optional)

MAKES 25 PIECES

Preheat the oven to 180°C (350°F/Gas 4). Lightly grease a 20 cm (8 inch) square tin and line with baking paper, leaving the paper hanging over the two opposite sides.

Put the butter and white chocolate in a heatproof bowl. Half-fill a saucepan with water and bring to the boil. Remove from the heat. Put the bowl over the saucepan, making sure the base of the bowl does not touch the water. Stir occasionally until the butter and chocolate have melted and are smooth.

Add the caster sugar to the bowl and stir in the eggs. Add the vanilla, fold in the flour and macadamia nuts, then pour into the tin. Bake for 35–40 minutes. If the top starts to brown too quickly, cover with a sheet of foil. When cooked, cool in the tin before lifting out, using the paper as handles, and cutting into squares. Drizzle with melted white chocolate.

PREPARATION TIME: 20 MINUTES   COOKING TIME: 45 MINUTES

ALMOND FRIANDS

160 g (5³/4 oz) unsalted butter
90 g (3¹/4 oz/1 cup) flaked almonds
40 g (1¹/2 oz/¹/3 cup) plain (all-purpose)
flour
165 g (5³/4 oz/1¹/3 cups) icing
(confectioners') sugar
5 egg whites
icing (confectioners') sugar, for dusting

MAKES 10

Preheat the oven to 210°C (415°F/Gas 6–7). Lightly grease ten 125 ml (4 fl oz/¹/2 cup) friand tins.

Melt the butter in a small saucepan over medium heat. Cook for 3–4 minutes, or until the butter turns deep golden. Strain to remove any residue (the colour will deepen on standing). Remove from the heat and set aside to cool until just lukewarm.

Put the almonds in a food processor and process until finely ground. Transfer to a bowl and sift the flour and icing sugar into the same bowl.

Put the egg whites in a separate bowl and lightly whisk with a fork until just combined. Add the butter to the flour mixture along with the egg whites. Mix gently with a metal spoon until all the ingredients are well combined.

Spoon some mixture into each friand tin to fill to three-quarters. Put the tins on a baking tray and bake in the centre of the oven for 10 minutes, then reduce the heat to 180°C (350°F/Gas 4) and bake for a further 5 minutes, or until a skewer comes out clean when inserted in the centre of a friand. Remove and leave to cool in the tins for 5 minutes before turning out onto a wire rack to cool completely. Dust with icing sugar before serving.

PREPARATION TIME: 10 MINUTES   COOKING TIME: 20 MINUTES

NOTES: These friands will keep well for up to 3 days in an airtight container.

To make berry friands, make the mixture as above and put a fresh or frozen raspberry or blueberry on the top of each friand before placing in the oven.

To make lemon friands, add 2 teaspoons grated lemon zest to the flour and sugar mixture and proceed as above.

COCONUT MACAROONS

3 egg whites
310 g (11 oz) caster (superfine) sugar
1 teaspoon grated lemon zest
1/2 teaspoon coconut extract
2 tablespoons sifted cornflour
(cornstarch)
270 g (9^3/$_4$ oz/3 cups) desiccated coconut

MAKES 60

Preheat the oven to 160°C (315°F/Gas 2–3). Line two baking trays with baking paper.

Beat the egg whites in a dry bowl using electric beaters until soft peaks form. Gradually add the caster sugar, beating constantly until thick and glossy and the sugar has dissolved. Add the lemon zest and coconut extract and beat until just combined. Add the cornflour and desiccated coconut and stir gently with a metal spoon.

Drop heaped teaspoons onto the trays, about 3 cm (1^1/$_4$ inches) apart. Bake for 15–20 minutes, or until golden. Transfer to a wire rack to cool. Repeat with the remaining mixture.

PREPARATION TIME: 25 MINUTES   COOKING TIME: 40 MINUTES

CARAMEL SLICE

125 g (4^1/$_2$ oz/1 cup) self-raising flour
90 g (3^1/$_4$ oz/1 cup) desiccated coconut
115 g (4 oz/^{1}/$_2$ cup) caster (superfine) sugar
125 g (4^1/$_2$ oz) unsalted butter, melted

CARAMEL FILLING
400 g (14 oz) tinned sweetened condensed milk
20 g (3/4 oz) unsalted butter
2 tablespoons golden syrup or honey

CHOCOLATE TOPPING
150 g (5^1/$_2$ oz) dark chocolate, chopped
20 g (3/4 oz) Copha (white vegetable shortening)

MAKES 20 PIECES

Preheat the oven to 180°C (350°F/Gas 4). Lightly grease an 18 x 28 cm (7 x 11 inch) shallow tin and line with baking paper, leaving the paper hanging over on the two long sides.

Sift the flour into a bowl, then mix in the coconut and sugar. Add the melted butter to the bowl and stir through thoroughly. Press firmly into the tin and bake for 12–15 minutes, or until lightly coloured. Allow to cool.

To make the caramel filling, put all the ingredients in a saucepan over low heat. Slowly bring to the boil, stirring, then boil gently, stirring, for 4–5 minutes, or until lightly caramelized. Quickly pour over the cooled base, spreading evenly. Bake for 10 minutes, then set aside to cool in the tin.

To make the chocolate topping, put the dark chocolate and Copha in a heatproof bowl. Half-fill a saucepan with water and bring to the boil. Remove from the heat and sit the bowl over the saucepan, making sure the base of the bowl does not touch the water. Stir occasionally until melted. Spread over the caramel slice. Refrigerate for 20 minutes, or until set. Lift the slice from the tin and cut into pieces.

PREPARATION TIME: 30 MINUTES +   COOKING TIME: 35 MINUTES

MINI PAVLOVAS

3 egg whites
125 g (4¹/₂ oz/1 cup) icing (confectioners')
sugar
150 g (5¹/₂ oz) dark chocolate, melted
250 ml (9 fl oz/1 cup) thick
(double/heavy) cream
1 tablespoon icing (confectioners') sugar,
extra
1 teaspoon finely grated orange zest
assorted fresh fruit, to garnish, such as
strawberries, cut into thin wedges,
sliced pawpaw and kiwi fruit, and
passionfruit pulp

MAKES 35–40

Preheat the oven to 150°C (300°F/Gas 2). Beat the egg whites in a large bowl until stiff peaks form. Add the icing sugar to the egg whites while continuing to beat. Add it carefully or it will fly all over the place. At this stage it is best to use electric beaters as you must now beat the meringue until thick and very solid.

Using a cutter as a guide, draw about forty 4 cm (1¹/₂ inch) circles onto two sheets of baking paper, then invert these sheets onto baking trays (so the pencil won't come off on the base of the pavlovas). Spread a little of the meringue mixture over each round — this will be the base of the pavlova. Spoon the remaining meringue into a piping (icing) bag fitted with a 5 mm (¹/₄ inch) plain piping nozzle.

Pipe three small circles on top of each other on the outer edge of each base, leaving a small hole in the centre. Bake for 30 minutes, or until firm to touch. Leave to cool in the oven with the door slightly ajar.

When cold, dip the bases of the meringues into the melted chocolate to come about 2 mm (¹/₈ inch) up the sides of the meringues, then place on trays covered with baking paper and allow to set.

Combine the cream, extra icing sugar and orange zest, stirring until just thick. If necessary, beat slightly. Spoon into a piping bag fitted with a small plain nozzle and pipe into the meringues. Top with fruit and passionfruit pulp.

PREPARATION TIME: 50 MINUTES +   COOKING TIME: 30 MINUTES

NOTE: Chocolate-dipped meringues without the filling can be made up to a week ahead and stored in an airtight container. Fill them close to serving time, otherwise they will soften.

FAST LEMON SHORTBREADS

125 g (4¹/2 oz/1 cup) plain (all-purpose) flour
1 tablespoon rice flour
100 g (3¹/2 oz) unsalted butter, chilled and chopped
¹/2 teaspoon finely grated lemon zest
1 tablespoon lemon juice

MAKES ABOUT 20

Preheat the oven to 180°C (350°F/Gas 4). Put the flours, butter and lemon zest into a food processor. Add the lemon juice and process until combined.

Roll out onto a lightly floured surface to a thickness of 5 mm (¹/4 inch). Cut out the desired shapes and place on a baking tray lined with baking paper. Bake for 10–12 minutes, or until pale golden. Allow to cool on a wire rack.

PREPARATION TIME: 10 MINUTES   COOKING TIME: 15 MINUTES

SWEET TWISTS

1 egg
1¹/2 tablespoons sugar
125 ml (4 fl oz/¹/2 cup) milk
250 g (9 oz/2 cups) plain (all-purpose) flour
oil, for deep-frying
215 g (7¹/2 oz/1³/4 cups) icing (confectioners') sugar

MAKES 45

Beat the egg with the sugar in a bowl, then stir in the milk. Sift the flour with ¹/2 teaspoon salt and mix in to form a stiff dough, adding more milk if necessary.

Roll out on a lightly floured work surface. Cut into strips about 10 cm (4 inches) long and 3 cm (1¹/4 inches) wide. Make a slit along the length, like a buttonhole. Tuck one end through the slit and pull through to make a twist.

Fill a deep heavy-based frying pan one-third full of oil and heat the oil to 180°C (350°F), or when a cube of bread dropped into the oil turns golden brown in 15 seconds. Fry three of four twists at a time, until golden brown on both sides. Drain on crumpled paper towels. Sift the icing sugar over the pastry after it is fried but before it gets cold.

PREPARATION TIME: 40 MINUTES   COOKING TIME: 10 MINUTES

NOTE: These will keep for up to 2 weeks in a dry airtight container.

NUTMEG DATE CAKE

370 g (13 oz/2 cups) soft brown sugar, plus 2 tablespoons extra
250 g (9 oz/2 cups) plain (all-purpose) flour
2 teaspoons baking powder
125 g (4¹/₂ oz) unsalted butter, chilled and chopped
1 teaspoon bicarbonate soda (baking soda)
185 ml (6 fl oz/³/₄ cup) milk
2 eggs, beaten
1¹/₂ teaspoons freshly grated nutmeg
375 g (12 oz) dried dates, roughly chopped
icing (confectioners') sugar, for dusting
whipped cream, to serve

SERVES 8–10

Preheat the oven to 180°C (350°F/Gas 4). Lightly grease a 22 cm (8¹/₂ inch) spring-form cake tin and line the base with baking paper.

Process the brown sugar with the flour and baking powder in a food processor for 10 seconds. Add the butter. Process for a further 10 seconds until the mixture resembles fine crumbs. Press half the mixture into the base of the prepared tin.

Dissolve the soda in the milk. Add the eggs and nutmeg and whisk. Pour the mixture into the remaining brown sugar and flour mixture and process for a further 10 seconds. Pour into the cake tin and scatter half the dates over the top. Bake for 55 minutes. Cool in the tin for 10 minutes. Remove from the tin and cool on a wire rack.

Put the remaining dates on top of the cake, sprinkle with the extra brown sugar and put under a very hot grill (broiler) for 1 minute, or until the sugar begins to melt. Allow to cool. Dust the top with icing sugar and serve with whipped cream.

PREPARATION TIME: 25 MINUTES   COOKING TIME: 1 HOUR

FLOURLESS CHOCOLATE FRUIT AND NUT CAKE

5 egg whites
170 g (6 oz/^{3}/$_4$ cup) caster (superfine) sugar
100 g (3^1/$_2$ oz) glacé apricots, chopped
100 g (3^1/$_2$ oz) glacé figs, chopped
80 g (2^3/$_4$ oz) glacé ginger, chopped
250 g (9 oz) blanched almonds, finely chopped
250 g (9 oz) dark chocolate, chopped
60 g (2^1/$_4$ oz) dark chocolate, melted
375 ml (12 fl oz/1^1/$_2$ cups) pouring (whipping) cream
chocolate leaves, to decorate (optional)

SERVES 8–10

Preheat oven to 150°C (300°F/Gas 2). Lightly grease a deep 24 cm (9^1/$_2$ inch) round spring-form cake tin and line the base and side with baking paper.

Beat the egg whites in a bowl using electric beaters until soft peaks form. Gradually add the sugar, beating well after each addition. Beat until the sugar has dissolved and the mixture is thick and glossy.

Using a metal spoon, fold in the fruits, ginger, almonds, and both the chopped and melted chocolate. Stir until just combined. Spread in the tin and bake for 1 hour, or until a skewer comes out clean when inserted in centre. Cool in the tin for 15 minutes. Remove from the tin and cool on a wire rack.

Whip the cream in a bowl using electric beaters until stiff peaks form. Using a piping (icing) bag with a plain nozzle, pipe swirls of cream on top of the cake. Decorate with chocolate leaves, if desired.

PREPARATION TIME: 40 MINUTES +   COOKING TIME: 1 HOUR

ALMOND TORTE

450 g (1 lb) blanched whole almonds, lightly toasted
150 g (5^1/$_2$ oz) unsalted butter, softened
400 g (14 oz) caster (superfine) sugar
6 eggs
150 g (5^1/$_2$ oz) plain (all-purpose) flour
2 teaspoons lemon zest
2 tablespoons lemon juice
icing (confectioners') sugar, for dusting

SERVES 8

Preheat the oven to 170°C (325°F/Gas 3). Lightly grease a 24 cm (9^1/$_2$ inch) spring-form cake tin. Grind the almonds finely in a food processor and set aside.

Cream the butter and sugar in a bowl using electric beaters until light and fluffy. Add the eggs one at a time, beating well after each addition. Using a large metal spoon, fold in the flour, ground almonds and the lemon zest. Stir until just combined and almost smooth.

Pour the batter into the prepared tin and bake for 1 hour 20 minutes, or until a skewer inserted in the centre comes out clean. Allow to cool for 5 minutes, then brush the top with lemon juice. Remove to a wire rack and allow to cool completely. Dust with icing sugar.

PREPARATION TIME: 15 MINUTES +   COOKING TIME: 1 HOUR 20 MINUTES

Flourless chocolate fruit and nut cake

RASPBERRY SWIRL CHEESECAKE

250 g (9 oz) plain sweet biscuits (cookies)
90 g (3¼ oz) unsalted butter, melted

FILLING
2 tablespoons powdered gelatine
500 g (1 lb 2 oz) light cream cheese, softened
80 ml (2½ fl oz/⅓ cup) lemon juice
115 g (4 oz/½ cup) caster (superfine) sugar
315 ml (10¾ fl oz/1¼ cups) whipped cream
250 g (9 oz) frozen raspberries
2 tablespoons caster (superfine) sugar, extra
whipped cream, to decorate (optional)
raspberries, to decorate (optional)

SERVES 8–10

Lightly grease a 23 cm (9 inch) spring-form cake tin and line the base with baking paper.

Finely crush the biscuits in a food processor, then mix in the butter. Spoon into the tin and press firmly over the base and up the side. Refrigerate for 20 minutes, or until firm.

To make the filling, put 60 ml (2 fl oz/¼ cup) water in a small heatproof bowl, sprinkle evenly with the gelatine and leave to go spongy. Bring a large saucepan filled with about 4 cm (1½ inches) water to the boil, remove from the heat, carefully lower the gelatine bowl into the water (it should come halfway up the side of the bowl), then stir until dissolved. Allow to cool.

Beat the cream cheese using electric beaters until creamy. Add the juice and sugar and beat until smooth. Gently fold in the whipped cream and half the gelatine.

Process the raspberries and extra sugar in a food processor until smooth. Push the purée through a fine-meshed nylon sieve to remove any pips. Fold the remaining gelatine into the raspberry mixture. Put blobs of cream cheese mixture into the tin and fill the gaps with the raspberry. Swirl the two mixtures together, using a skewer or the point of a knife. Refrigerate for 4 hours, or until set. Decorate with whipped cream and raspberries, if desired.

PREPARATION TIME: 40 MINUTES +   COOKING TIME: NIL

CHERRY CHEESE STRUDEL

500 g (1 lb 2 oz) ricotta cheese
2 teaspoons grated lemon or orange zest
55 g (2 oz/¼ cup) sugar
40 g (1½ oz/½ cup) fresh white breadcrumbs
2 tablespoons ground almonds
2 eggs
425 g (15 oz) tinned pitted black cherries
2 teaspoons cornflour (cornstarch)
8 sheets filo pastry
60 g (2¼ oz) unsalted butter, melted
2 tablespoons dry white breadcrumbs
icing (confectioners') sugar, for dusting

SERVES 8–10

Preheat the oven to 180°C (350°F/Gas 4). Lightly grease a baking tray.

Combine the ricotta, zest, sugar, fresh breadcrumbs and almonds in a bowl. Add the eggs and mix well. Drain the cherries, reserving half the juice. Blend the cornflour with the reserved cherry juice in a saucepan. Stir over medium heat until the mixture boils and thickens, then cool slightly.

Layer the pastry sheets, brushing between each sheet with melted butter and sprinkling with a few dry breadcrumbs. Form a large square by placing the second sheet halfway down the first sheet. Alternate layers, brushing with melted butter and sprinkling with breadcrumbs.

Put the ricotta mixture along one long edge of the pastry. Shape into a log and top with cherries and cooled syrup. Roll the pastry around the ricotta filling, folding in the edges as you roll. Finish with a pastry edge underneath. Place on the prepared tray and bake for 35–40 minutes, or until the pastry is golden. Dust with icing sugar. Serve cold, cut into slices.

PREPARATION TIME: 25 MINUTES   COOKING TIME: 45 MINUTES

WALNUT CAKES

200 g (7 oz) unsalted butter, softened
115 g (4 oz/½ cup) caster (superfine) sugar
2 tablespoons orange flower water
250 g (9 oz/2 cups) plain (all-purpose) flour, sifted

WALNUT FILLING
50 g (1¾ oz/½ cup) walnuts, chopped
55 g (2 oz/¼ cup) caster (superfine) sugar
1 teaspoon ground cinnamon

MAKES 28

Preheat the oven to 160°C (315°F/Gas 2–3). Lightly grease two baking trays and line with baking paper.

Cream the butter and sugar in a bowl using electric beaters until light and fluffy. Fold in the orange flower water and flour until combined. Press with your hands until the mixture comes together to make a stiff dough.

To make the walnut filling, combine all the ingredients in a bowl and mix well.

Roll heaped tablespoons of dough into balls. Press a hollow in the centre with your thumb. Place 1 teaspoon of filling into each hollow. Place on the trays and flatten slightly without folding dough over the filling. Bake for 15–20 minutes, or until golden. Cool on a wire rack and serve.

PREPARATION TIME: 15 MINUTES   COOKING TIME: 20 MINUTES

RED FRUIT SALAD

250 g (9 oz) strawberries, halved
125 g (4^1/$_2$ oz) raspberries
250 g (9 oz) cherries, pitted
1 tablespoon Cointreau
1 tablespoon soft brown sugar

SERVES 4

Put the fruit in a bowl, drizzle with Cointreau, cover and set aside for 20 minutes.

Combine the sugar with 2 tablespoons water in a small saucepan over gentle heat for 3 minutes, or until dissolved. Cool, pour over the fruit and serve.

PREPARATION TIME: 10 MINUTES +   COOKING TIME: 5 MINUTES

EASTERN FRUIT PLATTER

1 lemon grass stem, white part only, chopped

2 cm (3/4 inch) piece fresh ginger, roughly chopped

1 teaspoon soft brown sugar

125 ml (4 fl oz/1/2 cup) coconut milk

2 mangoes

1 nashi pear, quartered

6 lychees or rambutans, halved and stones removed

1/2 pawpaw, seeded and cut into wedges

1/2 red papaya, seeded and cut into wedges

2 star fruit, thickly sliced

1 lime, quartered

SERVES 4–6

Simmer the lemon grass, ginger, sugar and coconut milk in a small saucepan over low heat for 5 minutes. Strain and set aside.

Cut down both sides of the mangoes close to the stones. Score a crisscross pattern into each half, without cutting through the skin. Fold the outer edges under, pushing the centre up from underneath. Arrange with the rest of the fruit on a platter. Add the lime, for squeezing on the fruit.

Serve the coconut dressing on the side as a dipping sauce or drizzle over just before serving.

PREPARATION TIME: 15 MINUTES   COOKING TIME: 5 MINUTES

SUMMER FRUIT COMPOTE

5 apricots, halved

4 nectarines, halved

4 blood plums or other plums, stoned

4 peaches, quartered

200 g (7 oz) tinned pitted cherries

250 ml (9 fl oz/1 cup) claret

80 ml (2 1/2 fl oz/1/3 cup) dry sherry

170 g (6 oz/3/4 cup) caster (superfine) sugar

whipped cream, to serve (optional)

SERVES 8

Gently plunge the fruit in small batches into boiling water for 30 seconds. Remove with a slotted spoon and put in a bowl of iced water. Peel all the fruit except the cherries.

Combine the claret, sherry, sugar and 250 ml (9 fl oz/1 cup) water in a large heavy-based saucepan. Stir over low heat without boiling until the sugar has dissolved. Bring to the boil, reduce the heat and simmer for 5 minutes.

Add the drained fruits to the syrup in small batches and simmer each batch for 5 minutes. Remove with a slotted spoon. Pile the fruit into a bowl. Bring the syrup to the boil, reduce the heat and simmer for a further 5 minutes. Remove from the heat and allow to cool slightly—it should be the consistency of a syrup. Pour over the fruit. Serve with a dollop of freshly whipped cream.

PREPARATION TIME: 40 MINUTES   COOKING TIME: 30 MINUTES

Eastern fruit platter

SANGRIA

1½ tablespoons caster (superfine) sugar
1 tablespoon lemon juice
1 tablespoon orange juice
1 bottle red wine
500 ml (17 fl oz/2 cups) lemonade
(lemon-lime flavoured soda)
2 tablespoons gin
2 tablespoons vodka
1 lemon
1 orange
1 lime
ice cubes, to serve

SERVES 10

Put the caster sugar, lemon juice and orange juice into a large pitcher or bowl and stir until the sugar has dissolved.

Add the red wine, lemonade, gin and vodka. Cut the lemon, orange and lime into halves, remove the seeds and slice all the fruit. Add the slices to the jug and fill with ice. Stir well.

PREPARATION TIME: 10 MINUTES   COOKING TIME: NIL

LEMON AND LIME BARLEY WATER

220 g (7 oz/1 cup) pearl barley
60 ml (2 fl oz/¼ cup) lemon juice
125 ml (4 fl oz/½ cup) lime juice
115 g (4 oz/½ cup) caster (superfine) sugar
ice cubes, to serve
lemon slices, to serve
lime slices, to serve

MAKES ABOUT 1 LITRE (35 FL OZ/4 CUPS)

Boil the barley and 2 litres (70 fl oz/8 cups) water in a large heavy-based saucepan for 30 minutes, or until the liquid has reduced by half. Remove from the heat and strain.

Add the citrus juices and sugar and mix well. Serve chilled with ice, and lemon and lime slices.

PREPARATION TIME: 5 MINUTES +   COOKING TIME: 30 MINUTES

MOROCCAN MINT TEA

1 tablespoon green tea leaves
30 g (1 oz) sugar
1 large handful of spearmint leaves and stalks

SERVES 1

Heat the teapot and add the green tea leaves, sugar and spearmint leaves and stalks. Fill with boiling water and brew for at least 5 minutes. Adjust the sweetness if necessary.

PREPARATION TIME: 5 MINUTES   COOKING TIME: 5 MINUTES

NOTE: In Morocco, this light sweet tea is often served before, and always after every meal, and is prepared at any hour of the day when friends or guests arrive at a Moroccan home. It is sipped in cafés. Traditionally it is served from a silver teapot into ornately painted glasses.

ICED TEA

ice, to serve
125 ml (4 fl oz/½ cup) cold black tea
1 teaspoon sugar
lemon slices, to serve
mint leaves, to serve

SERVES 1

Put ice, cold tea and sugar in a highball glass and stir with a swizzle stick. Garnish with lemon slices and mint leaves.

PREPARATION TIME: 5 MINUTES   COOKING TIME: NIL

NOTE: Iced tea may also be made with cold herbal teas.

Moroccan mint tea

GINGERED WATERMELON JUICE

500 g (1 lb 2 oz) watermelon
2 teaspoons grated fresh ginger
6 ice cubes
wedge of watermelon, to garnish

MAKES 600 ML (21 FL OZ/2^1/2 CUPS)

Remove the skin and seeds from the watermelon and roughly chop. Put in a blender or food processor with the ginger and process for 2 minutes. Add the ice cubes and process for a further 1 minute, or until the ice is crushed. Serve garnished with a thin wedge of watermelon.

PREPARATION TIME: 5 MINUTES   COOKING TIME: NIL

HOME-MADE LEMONADE

LEMON SYRUP
6 large lemons
6 whole cloves
440 g (15^1/2 oz/2 cups) sugar

ice cubes, to serve
soda water, to serve
lemon slices, to garnish
mint leaves, to garnish

MAKES ABOUT 1.25 LITRES
(44 FL OZ/5 CUPS)

To make the lemon syrup, slice the lemons and put in a large bowl with the cloves. Cover with 1.25 litres (44 fl oz/5 cups) boiling water. Leave to infuse overnight.

Strain the water into a large saucepan. Discard the lemon slices and cloves. Add the sugar and stir over low heat, without boiling, until dissolved. Bring to the boil and simmer for 10 minutes, or until reduced and slightly syrupy. Allow to cool.

To serve, put ice in a highball glass. Pour over 2 tablespoons lemon syrup and top with soda water. Garnish with lemon slices and mint leaves.

PREPARATION TIME: 10 MINUTES +   COOKING TIME: 15 MINUTES

Gingered watermelon juice

INDEX

INDEX